The Revival *of* 1857–58

Recent titles in

RELIGION IN AMERICA SERIES
Harry S. Stout, General Editor

THE FRANK S. AND ELIZABETH D. BREWER PRIZE ESSAY OF
THE AMERICAN SOCIETY OF CHURCH HISTORY

The Revival *of* 1857–58

Interpreting an American Religious Awakening

Kathryn Teresa Long

New York • Oxford

Oxford University Press

1998

Oxford University Press

Athens   Auckland   Bangkok   Bogota   Bombay
Buenos Aires   Calcutta   Cape Town   Dar es Salaam   Delhi   Florence
Hong Kong   Istanbul   Karachi   Kuala Lumpur   Madras   Madrid   Melbourne
Mexico City   Nairobi   Paris   Singapore   Taipei   Tokyo   Toronto   Warsaw

and associated companies in
Berlin   Ibadan

Copyright © 1998 by Kathryn Teresa Long

Published by Oxford University Press, Inc.
198 Madison Avenue, New York, New York 10016

Oxford is a registered trademark of Oxford University Press

Library of Congress Cataloging-in-Publication Data
Long, Kathryn, 1950–
The revival of 1857–58 : interpreting an American religious
awakening / Kathryn Teresa Long.
p.   cm.—(Religion in America series)
Includes bibliographical references and index.
ISBN 0-19-511293-8
1. Prayer Meeting Revival (1857–1858)   2. United States—Church
history—19th century.   I. Title.   II. Series: Religion in America
series (Oxford University Press)
BR525.L56   1997
277.3'081—dc21   96-48264

1 3 5 7 9 8 6 4 2

Printed in the United States of America
on acid-free paper

For my parents,
Jack and Bertanell Long

Acknowledgments

In *Revival Sketches and Manual,* nineteenth-century minister Heman Humphrey noted the "special obligations" he owed to those who had contributed to his book. I, too, have special obligations of gratitude to the many people who have provided support and encouragement in the development of this project from doctoral dissertation to its present form. My greatest academic debt is to George M. Marsden. His counsel, critical eye, and gracious spirit, as well as the model of his scholarship, have been invaluable. Russell Richey and the late George Rawlyk read early drafts of the manuscript and made helpful suggestions for improvement. Jane Tompkins and Grant Wacker challenged me to write with clarity and conviction. Mark Noll, friend and colleague in the history department at Wheaton College, not only read the manuscript but also was a source of advice and continuing affirmation as the project moved through various stages of revision. In addition, the book as a whole is stronger as a result of suggestions from an anonymous reader at Oxford University Press.

The staffs of several libraries and archives provided research assistance. Among them were Linda Purnell and the interlibrary loan department of Perkins Library, Duke University; Ted Zaragoza, the Methodist Archives and History Center, Drew University; Boyd Reese, the Presbyterian Historical Society, Philadelphia; Bill Harris, the Speer Library, Princeton Theological Seminary; the staffs of the Divinity School Library, Duke University; the American Antiquarian Society; the Burke Library, Union Theological Seminary; the New York City Public Library; and the Library of Congress. I am also indebted to Wendy M. Miller, assistant curator at the Billy Graham Center, Wheaton College, for help in preparing the illustrations; to Rosemary Turner for early proofreading assistance; and to Matthew Chin for aid in preparing the statistical tables. Mark and Lois Shaw, Ted and Meredith Gandy, Mac and Marya Pier, and Jim and Kathy Luetkemeier all provided generous hospitality along the way that enabled me to maximize my research funds.

I am grateful to Craig and Anne Noll for their work on the index; a grant from the G. W. Aldeen Memorial Fund helped to subsidize that task. In addition, the American Society of Church History supported publication of the manuscript through the 1995 Frank S. and Elizabeth D. Brewer Prize.

Portions of chapter 1 closely follow my "The Power of Interpretation: The Revival of 1857–58 and the Historiography of Revivalism in America," which appeared in *Religion and American Culture: A Journal of Interpretation* (Winter 1994): 77–105, ©, the Center for the Study of Religion and American Culture, Indiana University–Purdue University at Indianapolis, and are used with permission.

I am also pleased to thank family members and friends who provided the tangible and intangible support that sustained me emotionally as this enterprise extended over a number of years. Myron and Jan Davis, Dan and Alice Malcolm, Martha Polo, Sue Reisenweaver, and Anne Wright were generous with their prayers, laughter, and love as I engaged in the largely solitary work of research, writing, and revision. The people of Mt. Bethel Presbyterian Church, Durham, North Carolina, and later those of the First Presbyterian Church, Wheaton, Illinois, welcomed me into their midst and reminded me that there was life beyond the bounds of the academic world. Finally, I owe a special debt of gratitude and love to my parents, to whom this book is dedicated. They have encouraged my dreams in ways that have gone far beyond what any adult child might reasonably expect.

Wheaton, Illinois   K. T. L.
August 1996

Contents

The Revival *of* 1857–58

Introduction

THE REVIVAL OF 1857–58 was hailed by contemporaries as one of the most significant events of the nineteenth century, perhaps of American religious history, or even the entire span of the history of the Christian church. They described it as "The Great Revival," the "event of the century," and "our American awakening."[1] From 1858 to the present, this revival, characterized in part by mass prayer meetings that spread from New York City to major urban centers throughout much of the United States, has captured the imaginations of American evangelicals. On September 22, 1991, when evangelist Billy Graham preached to approximately 250,000 people on the "great lawn" of New York City's Central Park, local coordinators of the event noted with satisfaction that the date of Graham's visit fell within a day of the anniversary of the beginnings of revival in 1857.[2] They hoped for a similar outbreak of religious concern in a twentieth-century context. Popular books and magazines catering to evangelical interest in revival also have celebrated the fervor of 1857–58 as America's third "great awakening."[3]

In contrast, even though revivalism has long been accepted as both a topic of interest and a useful interpretive tool for the study of religion in America, the 1857–58 Revival has been eclipsed in academic circles by scholarly fascination with earlier awakenings. The various eighteenth-century expressions of the "Great Awakening" have been subjected to intense scrutiny for their influence (or lack thereof) on the religion, politics, and social life of the pre-Revolutionary era. In a similar fashion, investigations focused on the early-nineteenth-century revivalism of the "Second Great Awakening" have produced, in the words of one observer, "some of the most important recent work in American religious history."[4] Religious fervor prior to 1835 has proved much more interesting to historians than have later revivals.

In the case of the Revival of 1857–58, there are a number of reasons for this neglect. The revival's place in history has been affected in part by changing understandings of the model of cyclical awakenings as an interpretive tool. I discuss these in connection with the impact of early Calvinist historiography in chapter 1 of this study and have done so more extensively elsewhere.[5] During the early decades of the twentieth century, the rise of "scientific history" and interest in the West as the formative influence in American life contributed to a disregard for urban revivals. At present, the awakening of the late 1850s has fallen into historical limbo as an antebellum American revival that took place beyond the generally accepted parameters of the so-called Second Great Awakening. In addition, the revival has suffered from the chronological disadvantage of having occurred on the eve of the Civil War, a blind spot for religious historians who until recently have neglected the war and the years immediately surrounding it. In terms of the broader scope of American history, the war itself, with its own civil religious overtones, loomed so large that the 1857–58 Revival was lost in its shadow. The business-oriented, masculine spin given the revival by its earliest historians tended to blur into the standard interpretations of the sectional conflict. At the same time, a "businessmen's awakening" stood as an apparent anomaly in the midst of what has been described as the "feminization" of American Protestantism.[6]

When the revival has caught the attention of religious historians, it usually has been in the context of other, more expansive concerns. The awakening has become a historical event mentioned by many authors, examined in depth by only a few.[7] Since 1957, the chapter devoted to the awakening in Timothy L. Smith's *Revivalism and Social Reform* has provided the standard interpretation of the "*Annus Mirabilis*—1858."[8] Yet Smith investigated the revival primarily to buttress his case for the close connection between the perfectionist impulse of revivalism and nineteenth-century social reform movements. It also has received careful, although not comprehensive, treatment by Richard Carwardine in the context of transatlantic revivals and by Sandra Sizer [Frankiel] as background for her analysis of the later D. L. Moody evangelistic campaigns. All three interpretations are useful but limited. The only general history of the revival, written by J. Edwin Orr and published posthumously as *The Event of the Century*, provides an extensive and helpful summary of an enormous quantity of nineteenth-century newspaper reports, as well as other primary and secondary sources on the subject, but little critical analysis.[9] In his own nuanced article on the awakening, Leonard Sweet highlighted the need for a careful reevaluation of it "within the whole context of nineteenth century patterns of revivalism."[10] Without claiming such comprehensiveness, this book is, in part, a response to that need. It seeks to place the 1857–58 Revival within the historical milieu of mid-nineteenth-century America and to suggest fresh interpretations of it in light of critical issues in contemporary scholarship.

To place the Revival of 1857–58 within the broader context of Protestant revival traditions is to locate it within a complex and creative area of study. The field has been enriched in recent years by a proliferation of local and regional studies in tandem with a growing interest in comparative investigation that has extended the social and cultural terrain. The particularities as well as the common features of revivals have come increasingly into focus, at least in reference to the Anglo-American world of the eighteenth and nineteenth centuries. As a result, both a splintering and a tentative ordering of interpretive themes have occured that in a sense have mirrored current understandings of the patterns of nineteenth-century revivals themselves.[11]

On the one hand, it is no longer possible to follow Perry Miller in nominalizing the many expressions of intense religious interest during the first half of the nineteenth century as "the Revival," a monolithic concept, uniquely American and comparable in force to the earlier Covenant. As ongoing research has made clear, participants expected, experienced, and explained revivals in a variety of ways, not a single normative one.[12] The contours of revival varied between people in the North and in the South, between those in the United States, in Canada, or in Great Britain. Revivals were affected by the traditions, rituals, and theology of different denominations, as well as by social class, urban or rural settings, gender, and race. For example, Presbyterian minister and journalist Samuel Irenaeus Prime (1812–85) recalled as a young man attending a prayer meeting, sponsored by several churches still "under the influence" of a revival, where an African-American woman rose and gave an "ardent address."[13] Prime, used to the intense but highly controlled revivals informed by Princeton theology, a tradition where women did not speak in mixed religious meetings, was shocked at her behavior. He later learned that the woman was a Baptist. In terms of race, gender, class, and denomination, Prime and the anonymous woman had experienced revival in radically different ways.

At the same time, revivals did share some common features. Prime had reference points for recognizing what had influenced the Baptist woman's behavior. At the most basic level, all revivals were characterized by what was considered an unusual increase in religious concern and in conversion experiences among a group of people. Revivals typically involved elements of active lay participation, such as communal prayer, singing, and testimony, alongside preaching by the clergy. Even in elite churches the sense of a common, immediate encounter with God during a revival tended to narrow the gap between ministers and laity. In addition, the widespread pattern of revivals in continental Europe, Great Britain, and North America that accompanied the rise of modern evangelicalism suggests that different manifestations of spiritual awakening occurred as a common response among certain groups of Protestants to the changing social and political conditions of the Enlightenment era.[14] The preaching of eighteenth-century itinerants such as George Whitefield and Freeborn Garrettson enjoyed broad audience appeal that extended across national boundaries, a phenomenon repeated in the next century by Charles Finney, James Caughey, Phoebe Palmer, and numerous others. By the time of the 1857–58 Revival, transatlantic connections were well established. As Richard Carwardine has noted, it came as little surprise that the American awakening "should soon be followed by spectacular revivals in Ulster, Wales, and many parts of Britain."[15]

Historians who have focused on revivals within the United States have had to contend with similar tensions between particularities and common characteristics. Recent attempts at a nuanced synthesis of the disparate expressions of evangelicalism among white Protestants in the United States during the first half of the nineteenth century have suggested the existence of two broad groups, divided roughly along class lines. Since the vast majority of American evangelicals accepted the validity of at least some revivals, the classification serves as a helpful paradigm for understanding revival traditions. The groups have been differentiated variously as "formalists" and "antiformalists," as elites and populists, or as groups at the center in contrast to groups at the periphery of cultural power.[16]

The formalists—usually Congregationalists, Presbyterians, low-Church Episcopalians, and English-speaking Reformed churches—stressed decorum. They valued order in worship, theological precision, and an educated ministry. Most viewed revivals as a surprising and mysterious work of God that brought an unexpected response to preaching and prayer, although this essentially Calvinist perspective waned as the nineteenth century advanced. Their revivals, most often in a church setting, were characterized by an atmosphere of "profound solemnity" and by emotional restraint, except for quiet weeping.[17] The formalists also were the groups that stood at the center of propriety and cultural power during the early decades of the nineteenth century. The New Englanders among them, in particular, viewed revival as an agent for communal renewal, as an essential element in the transformation of society and the nation. These denominations and their revivals have been the subject of many studies of the Second Great Awakening that focused on what has been described as the "hard" side of evangelicalism—its emphasis on self-discipline and social control.[18]

The "populists" or "antiformalists," in contrast, represented the "soft" side of revivalist religion—its democratic, liberating, and even fragmenting impulses. The two great movements in this category were the Baptists and the Methodists. Rather than renewing already existing churches, their revivals initially helped to create new religious communities among people "suffering in various degrees from the social strains of a nation on the move into new political, economic and geographical areas."[19] Populists stressed the emotional trauma and ecstasy of the New Birth, an experience empowering and open to all regardless of intellectual or social attainments, race, or gender. Theirs was a democratic, Arminianized gospel message in which the grace for conversion (and by extension, revival) was always available, needing only to be "stirred up" or "brought down" by preaching, prayer, testimony, or song. These groups popularized camp meetings and charismatic preachers. They also, as Curtis Johnson has pointed out, "were deeply suspicious of elite attempts to Christianize society, to reform the nation, or in any other way to improve America." They believed that the impact of revivals on the broader society would be indirect, the aggregate result of individuals being changed, one by one, through conversion.[20]

The distinctions between the formalists and the populists were not hard and fast, and below the surface was a kaleidoscope of differences in each group, some of which will be explored in this book. Like all generalizations, descriptions of the two groups become caricatures if pushed too far, but they do help to explain general trends, particularly during the first four decades of the nineteenth century. By the 1840s and the 1850s these two streams had begun to converge, particularly in urban areas. The formalists had toned down the more rigid side of their Calvinism and had begun to appropriate aspects of the methodology and style of the populists. Many Methodists and Baptists, for their part, were "formalizing," embracing the more orderly religious ethos that went with middle-class respectability. Denominational identity still was alive and well, and there were growing regional divisions between northern and southern evangelicals that boded ill for the future. Even so, the trend in American evangelicalism was toward national integration, especially in the North, where religion was much more overtly "public" than in the South.[21] This trend was paralleled by similar patterns in the broader American culture, such as in politics, commerce, and the print media, realms in which many revivalistic Protestants were deeply, if sometimes indirectly, involved.[22]

The Revival of 1857–58, perhaps the closest thing to a truly national revival in American history, represented the culmination during the antebellum period of this impulse toward integration. It mirrored both the extent and limitations of national culture on the eve of the Civil War. Appropriately, the epicenter of revival activity was New York City, the nation's first city when it came to religion, commerce, and print media. The actual awakening was a diffuse and multifaceted movement, touching the lives of millions of Americans from every major Protestant denomination. However, it quickly gained a distinct national identity in the pages of mass print, both newspapers and books. As a national event, the revival in effect acted as a prism. It captured and concentrated the attention of people throughout the different denominational streams of antebellum Protestantism and united them in a shared experience of intense personal religious concern. Then it refracted that religious impulse and the practices of piety that accompanied it across an even wider spectrum of post–Civil War, late-Victorian America. This process helped to create the beginnings of a public, transdenominational religious identity among evangelicals, especially among lay men and women in the northern states. At the same time, as the prism analogy suggests, that shared identity was expressed through a broad trajectory of individual lives.

The reconfiguration of evangelicalism that took shape in the context of the 1857–58 Revival and how it happened are central concerns of this book. The changes, I am convinced, were closely tied not only to the actual experiences of revival participants but also to interpretations of the awakening that were canonized almost immediately. Issues of interpretation lie at the heart of the structure of my argument. Instead of presenting a strictly chronological narrative, I have written a history of the revival from different angles of interpretive vision. Loosely grouped in pairs, the six main chapters of the book offer a multilayered account of the awakening. They were written as a series of overlapping essays, designed to present a cumulative picture, much as anatomy textbooks once used transparent overlays to show students the different parts of the human body. An underlying theme throughout is the power of interpretation operating on many levels as a key to understanding the Revival of 1857–58.

Chapters 1 and 2 focus on the public story of the revival. They examine the canonization in popular histories and the press of a "core narrative" that became the consensus interpretation of the event. The main publicists were two groups with a national consciousness—northern Calvinist clergy and the editors of secular, mass-circulation newspapers. Chapter 1 explores the rush by clergy from the formalist wing of evangelicalism to claim the revival and to position it within the context of a "deradicalized" American revival tradition, one shaped by Calvinists and characterized by a series of providentially ordained national awakenings. Chapter 2 points to the role of the mass-circulation daily press. Religious activism coalesced as a national awakening when it became a media event. In turn, the contours of American revivals changed as newspapers discovered the commercial potential of marketing religion.

Chapters 3 and 4 analyze the social and cultural context of the revival from the perspective of the participants themselves. These perspectives amplify and in some cases challenge the canonized history. Chapter 3 draws from diaries, memoirs, and other accounts to suggest that, for many participants, the significance of the event centered on personal relationships. Revival "happened" when friends and family members experienced evangelical conversion. Chapter 4 discusses issues of gender in light of traditional interpretations of 1857–58 as a "laymen's revival." Did an awakening occur in 1858 because businessmen "found religion"? Where were the women, traditional stalwarts of nineteenth-century Protestantism?

Chapters 5 and 6 consider questions about the relationship between revivalism and social reform. Within the patterns of nineteenth-century revivalism, what did people think a revival would or should do for the culture at large? The chapters investigate the debate in 1858 between those who insisted that genuine revival would lead to a reformation of the nation and those who found true revival in communal piety and evangelistic effort. Chapter 5 explores the triumph of a more privatized revivalism as the public consensus shifted from revivals as an instrument of cultural change to revivals as an occasion for shared piety. Chapter 6 examines contemporary critiques of the social impact of the 1857–58 awakening and looks for evidence of ethical concern on the grassroots level. Chapter 7, the concluding chapter, summarizes the legacies of the 1857–58 Revival in helping to shape a transformed evangelical revival tradition that came into its own during the 1870s.

Two appendices provide material to supplement and support the contents of the chapters. Because the chapters look at the revival from different angles of interpretive vision rather than from the perspective of a straightforward, linear account, Appendix A furnishes a chronology of selected dates and events mentioned elsewhere throughout the text and notes. Appendix B contains a series of tables illustrating the approximate numerical impact of the 1857–58 Revival in the context of church growth rates during the 1850s.

Northern Protestants figure prominently in the chapters of this book. Revivals did extend to the South in 1858 and 1859, and they were particularly significant for their influence on young men who later encouraged revivalism in the Confederate army. But as a mass religious awakening, the events of 1857–58 appeared most visibly in the North, where systems of communication and commerce were more highly developed than in the South and the population more densely concentrated in cities and towns.[23] Northern church membership increased dramatically during 1858, a vivid contrast to more modest gains earlier in the decade. The effect was less sensational in the South, in part because the revival spread more gradually there. In addition, evangelical churches were already growing at a faster pace in the region. In terms of church growth, one could argue that the South needed a smaller boost. It was the North that played catch-up in 1857–58.[24]

Finally, the chief religious interpreters of the revival were northern formalist clergy, men who drew from the Yankee/Whig tradition of a Christian republic, even the New Yorkers among them who rejected the social agenda of that tradition. The revival as a public event was primarily a northern phenomenon. Its clearest legacies can be found in the middle-class "Yankee evangelicalism" of D. L. Moody and others like him.[25]

The study also is limited to the awakening in North America and does not attempt a comparison with related revivals that took place in Great Britain during 1859 and 1860. The logistical difficulties in gaining access to British materials as well as the need for a manageable project played a role in establishing the limits. The detailed sketch of the British situation presented by Carwardine in *Transatlantic Revivalism*, as well as recent attention to the Ulster revival by David Hempton, Myrtle Hill, and Janice Holmes, suggests a complex and distinct interpretive landscape that deserves investigation on its own terms before comparisons are made.[26]

Three words that appear on nearly every page of this book are "revival," "revivalism," and "awakening." For that reason, a few comments on usage may be helpful. In the nineteenth century, "revival" commonly was used in two different ways, to refer to a local phenomenon and to a broad popular movement. In both cases, as I have already indicated, it meant an unusual increase in religious concern and of professed conversions that occurred in a communal setting. Revivals sometimes were described as "extraordinary seasons of religious interest."[27] Local revivals were periods of intense religious concern in a congregation, community, or other group such as a camp meeting. But "revival" also could refer to outbreaks of religious fervor throughout a particular denomination, region, nation, or group of countries over a prolonged period of time. This study is primarily concerned with this latter phenomenon as it occurred in 1857–58. The word "awakening" usually was reserved for such a prolonged revival movement, although on occasion it, too, was employed in the more narrow sense. Throughout this book, "revival" and "awakening" are used synonymously when they refer to the 1857–58 Revival as a popular movement. In addition, on a number of occasions I attempt to distinguish between the 1857–58 Revival as a public event, with particular characteristics attributed to it, and the awakening as simply descriptive of the widespread local and regional revivals that occurred between the autumn of 1857 and the summer of the following year. The difference between the two is, and was in 1858, a matter of interpretation. I hope the context will make the distinctions clear.

I also use the word "revivalism" in its most basic descriptive sense to refer to a pattern of revivals or a condition characterized by revivals. Some authors, either explicitly or implicitly, have attempted to distinguish between "revivalism" and "revival." The former, it is argued, should refer to deliberately organized instances of religious fervor, such as the new measures revivalism of Charles Finney, the latter to apparently spontaneous outbreaks where agency was attributed solely to God.[28] In some cases, this may be a valid distinction, but it is one I find difficult to employ consistently and fairly in writing history. Nearly all revival traditions have employed novel rituals or practices that might be described as "new measures" to encourage experiential religion. These have ranged from the public "letter days" organized by the Moravians and the English Methodists to the "Log College" academies of the New Side Presbyterians to the handbills distributed in 1858 by the YMCA.[29] It is, of course, appropriate to distinguish between the range of Calvinist and Arminian theological explanations for revivals and the changes in these explanations over time, just as it is valid to note the continuing transformation of American revivals with the rise of professionalized mass evangelism during the late nineteenth century. Even though these variations are real and important, they do not always lend themselves to a sharp dichotomy between "revival" and "revivalism."

In many other choices besides those of usage, any book inevitably is shaped by the historical perspective and interpretive agenda of its author. This work, of course, is no exception. It is informed both by my commitment to the practice of critical history and by my identification with the religious community broadly described as evangelical Protestantism.[30] I first learned about the Revival of 1857–58 and about a tradition of American revivals in the context of the evangelical community. My interest in the revival as a subject for research was piqued in part by an awareness of the contrast between evangelical affection for the event and the tendency among scholars to downplay its significance, as I pointed out at the beginning of this introduction. It seemed as if something that had remained such a part of the evangelical tradition deserved another look. In addition, I suspected that some of the neglect might stem from an aversion among historians to the emphasis on individual conversions and the self-righteous earnestness often associated with the middle-class Victorians who were the most visible participants in the revival.[31] Perhaps out of a certain sympathetic identification with the Victorians, I wanted to challenge a seemingly tacit notion that the religious lives of "respectable" people were uninteresting and insignificant.

However, as I trust the following pages will make clear, this study is not advocacy history in support either of revivals or of middle-class Protestantism per se. I hope it will provide fresh insights into the 1857–58 Revival and stimulate further research. At the same time, my concern with interpretation is in itself a call for a greater critical awareness of the underlying assumptions that have shaped understandings of revivals among both scholarly investigators and religious partisans. Insofar as the book is directed toward the evangelical community, it reflects the conviction that a truly "useable" past is one written with honesty and a certain amount of self-criticism. In evangelical circles, the Revival of 1857–58 often is presented as an exemplary historical moment, an ideal of the kind of awakening believers should long to experience. At a number of points, this study implicitly questions that perspective. I hope it will encourage ongoing critical reflection about this awakening and about evangelical revival traditions.

ONE

"Prayer-Meetings . . .
in all parts of the land"

The Revival Takes Shape as History

A MONG ITS FRONT-PAGE letters to the editor on September 30, 1858, the New York *Christian Advocate and Journal* ran a note calling for a book about the Revival of 1857–58: "Is it not the duty of the M.E. [Methodist Episcopal] Church, through some of her sons, to furnish the public and posterity a standard work on this subject? We have had a prominent share of the labors and fruits of this revival; and we owe it to God, his general Church, and the world to render our tribute of history in this matter. Who will undertake it—who?"[1]

It was a clarion call, and an answer quickly arrived, but not, perhaps, as the writer had hoped. By the end of the year five books had been written about the revival, three of them destined to become the standard primary-source accounts. But all were written or edited by men who stood in the tradition of John Calvin rather than John Wesley. The three narrative works were *The Power of Prayer*, by Samuel Irenaeus Prime; *The Noon Prayer Meeting of the North Dutch Church*, by Talbot W. Chambers; and *Narratives of Remarkable Conversions and Revival Incidents*, by William C. Conant.[2] The other two books were *The Revival and Its Lessons*, a collection of tracts written during the revival by James W. Alexander, and an anthology of sermons, *The New York Pulpit in the Revival of 1858*, edited by Prime.[3]

Although a broad spectrum of Protestants, from both North and South, were caught up in the religious enthusiasm of the late 1850s, the people who wrote the histories of the revival were almost exclusively northern Calvinist clergy. They were a group divided by a variety of internal disagreements; even so, they represented a theological tradition whose members were the self-appointed nineteenth-century custodians of revivalism as an interpretive tool for understanding American history.[4] The nineteenth century may have been the "Methodist century" in terms of religious activity and numerical success, but when it came to revivals, Calvinists told the story.[5] Along with the secular press, clergy historians played a decisive role in helping to shape the images that would become a part of the collective "social memory" of the revival, a memory shared even today by anyone who has any casual knowledge of the event. For example, the ideal of the Christian layman as an active, pious businessman and the accompanying invisibility of women were, in part, factors in the way this particular revival was portrayed, as were the carefully crafted pictures of Christian unity that downplayed divisions over slavery simmering just below the surface.

Clergy Historians "Claim" the Revival

The early histories reflected the historical and theological commitments, as well as the tensions, among two groups of Calvinists particularly well-represented in New York City, the center of publicity for the nationwide awakening. The two camps can be described in broad terms as, first, a socially conservative Old School Presbyterian/Reformed Dutch coalition and, second, a loose grouping of more progressive New School Presbyterians, Congregationalists, and Baptists.[6] Although both groups were heir to the "formalist" tradition, the New School coalition had begun to move in a more populist direction. Their differences reflected conflicts over theological, ecclesiastical, and social issues that had resulted in the New School/Old School Presbyterian schism of 1837. In general, the New School adherents and their colleagues shared an optimistic view of human ability to respond to the gospel message. They were open to the use of "new measures" in revivalism, offered women a more visible role in religious activities than did the Old School, and were more vocal in their opposition to slavery.

The Old School/Dutch Reformed group traditionally had stressed divine sovereignty over human ability. Although they believed in revivals, they were leery of any "means" that smacked of human contrivance to bring them about. The Old School Presbyterians had bitterly opposed the New School preachers' attempts to incorporate populist techniques, such as Charles Finney's Methodist-inspired new measures, into revival preaching.[7] The conservatives also maintained a greater concern for church order. They feared undue emotion, maintained carefully defined roles for men and women, and were much more cautious than the New Schoolers in speaking to the issue of slavery.

By 1858, the doctrinal differences between the two groups had become a question of style rather than substance. In practice, even the conservatives had been affected by the increasingly Arminian cast of American Calvinism and had become more activist in their approach to evangelism.[8] However, they remained circumspect in the language they used to describe salvation and more concerned for general decorum in revivals than their progressive counterparts. The substantive issues that continued to distinguish the two groups concerned social reform, particularly slavery and appropriate roles for women.[9] Although not hard and fast, the division also reflected regional influences: the Old School/Dutch Reformed group represented a native "Yorker" and Middle States constituency, while the progressives had New England roots. The conservatives established themselves as the dominant initial apologists for the Revival of 1857–58. Except for Conant's *Narratives of Remarkable Conversions*, all the books mentioned above were theirs. Prime, editor of the weekly *New York Observer*, and Alexander, pastor of the Nineteenth Street Presbyterian Church in New York City, were Old School Presbyterians; Chambers was Dutch Reformed.

What was the initial picture that emerged from their books? First, there was a basic consensus about the origin of the revival. It was a supernatural movement of God that began, appropriately enough, in an "upper room," a third-floor classroom in a building that formed a part of the North Dutch Church at the corner of William and Fulton Streets in downtown New York City.[10] The key figure was not a traveling revival preacher or even a minister at all but a former businessman named Jeremiah Calvin Lanphier (b. 1809). Described in *The Power of Prayer* as "A lone Man on his Knees," Lanphier was one of the few named "heroes" of the revival. Like so many other young men of his generation, he had come from a small town to seek commercial opportunities the city had to offer. After 20 years in "mercantile pursuits," Lanphier had become a church worker, a city missionary employed by the Fulton Street congregation.[11]

The church was located in lower Manhattan, the heart of New York's business district—a short block and a half from Broadway, less than five minutes' walk from Wall Street. In light of the location, the new missionary decided to begin a weekly prayer meeting for businessmen. He scheduled the gathering at an unusual time for that era: Wednesdays, from noon to one o'clock. The idea was to encourage working men to take a break for prayer during their lunch hour. Initially, only a few responded. On September 23, 1857, Lanphier spent the first 30 minutes of the first meeting alone before six stragglers arrived.[12] A week later, 20 men attended; the next week, between 30 and 40. After three weeks, the meeting was moved to a larger room and continued daily. It became the nucleus for the spread of similar prayer meetings, initially throughout the metropolitan area, and, within six months, to "every nook and corner of the great republic."[13]

Depending on the perspectives of their authors, the early histories offered different explanations of the cause and spread of the revival. Prime's *The Power of Prayer*, by far the most widely read account, described the growing spiritual fervor through Old School lenses. Prime repeatedly stressed the revival's providential character and nationwide influence. He ignored the severe financial panic that occurred in tandem with the revival and shattered the lives of many of the men crowding the Fulton Street meetings. Although he acknowledged that certain events might have anticipated the coming revival, from Prime's perspective the only true cause was "the sovereign grace of Him who has promised to hear and answer prayer." The "spirit of the revival" permeated the entire nation and all classes of people. Prime took care to mention such southern locales as Richmond, Charleston, Savannah, Mobile, New Orleans, Vicksburg, and Memphis.[14] Unity across nation, denomination, and class in answer to prayer was his theme, with the Fulton Street prayer meeting as "Exhibit A" of this united or "union" spirit.

Both *The Power of Prayer* and *The Noon Prayer Meeting*, the other conservative account, stressed the legitimacy and respectability of the revival. Activities or groups that might carry with them any taint of irregularity, such as women praying in public or the participation of the Young Men's Christian Association (YMCA), were omitted.[15] Nor did the books note more boisterous expressions of revivalism. Such manifestations of male piety as the Methodist "Flying Artillery of Heaven," a group of lay exhorters who made the rounds of city Methodist churches to encourage revivals, went unmentioned. Apart from Lanphier, one of the few people quoted by name in both books was the evangelical Episcopal Bishop Charles P. McIlvaine. The latter, an opponent of new measures revivalism in the 1830s, had made a ringing speech in June 1858, in which he affirmed, "I have no doubt 'whence it [the revival] cometh.' . . . I rejoice in the decided conviction, that it is 'the Lord's doing.' "[16]

While Prime and Chambers represented the socially and theologically conservative stream of revivalistic Calvinism, William Conant's *Narratives of Remarkable Conversions* portrayed the awakening from a different point of view, as clear from both the format and the content of his book. It began with a brief introduction by Henry Ward Beecher, already one of the most popular preachers in New York. In addition to his fame as a minister, Beecher, a Yankee and a Congregationalist with New School Presbyterian ties, also had gained notoriety for his political activism during the 1850s. He had been energetic in efforts to keep Kansas a free state, allied in that cause with Horace Greeley, editor of the *New York Tribune*. It was no coincidence that Conant, himself a Baptist, drew most of his information on the "Great Awakening of 1857–8" from articles published in the *Tribune*.[17] This choice of sources ensured a more multifaceted picture of the revival than Prime or Chambers provided. Jeremiah Lanphier and the Fulton Street prayer meeting still received star billing, but Conant also gave credit to the New York YMCA devotional committee for sponsoring similar meetings in other churches and devising a standard format for the noontime gatherings. He mentioned the Flying Artillery and devoted sections to church revivals in various parts of the country.

For all Conant's variety, however, he saw the revival as a national event in largely northern terms, terms that reflected the antislavery sentiment of many in the New School/New England camp. He cited popular belief that "the present descent of grace is without parallel . . . in the history of the church," then noted that "nearly every city or town of importance in the *Northern* [italics mine] portion of the United States, has now its daily prayer meetings."[18] His "Survey of the United States" contained reports from 15 northern states and only one—Virginia—in the South.[19] This picture reflected the tacit conviction among some antislavery evangelicals that the South, with its "peculiar institution," had been shut off from God's grace.[20] Conant's account reflected the beliefs of northern progressives in other ways as well. He assumed a supernatural origin to the revival. At the same time, however, he stressed the role of human activity in bringing it about and had no problem viewing the financial panic as the most important catalyst. He rejoiced in the democratization of piety, describing the revival as one "in which the people are the preacher." And he viewed the nineteenth century as "an epoch decidedly characterized by revivals" that encouraged millennial hopes.[21]

Yet despite these differences between the Reformed groups, they still shared important common ground in their portrayals of the revival. All chose to emphasize the businessmen's noon prayer meetings, what Conant called "the first and most remarkable public demonstration of the national awakening."[22] The authors knew, and acknowledged, that the revival had spawned hundreds of morning and evening church prayer meetings. Even so, the businessmen's meetings, recognized at first as the *novel* aspect of the revival—its "public" expression—soon became the *defining* aspect. Second, although all stressed the interdenominational nature of the revival, participants from Reformed denominations tended to become *primer entre pares*. In *The Power of Prayer*, it was the "hand of God" that brought "one Presbyterian, one Baptist, one Congregationalist, and one Reformed Dutch" (and no Methodist) to the first Fulton Street noon meeting.[23]

Third, although it was not the dominant motif of these early accounts, most placed the Revival of 1857–58 in the broader context of an understanding of history shaped by a cyclical view of revivalism. Prime cited the comment of a Dutch Reformed minister: "We are now . . . in the fourth great revival under the gospel dispensation. The first commenced in Pentecostal times. . . . The second commenced in the time of Martin Luther. . . . The third was in the days of Edwards, and Whitefield, and the Tennants [*sic*]. The fourth is that which now pervades our country."[24] Conant was less precise, but the subtitle of *Narratives* noted that the book included "a review of revivals, from the day of Pentecost to the Great Awakening in the last century . . . [and] an account of the rise and progress of the Great Awakening of 1857–'8."[25]

By as early as the end of 1858, then, the contours of a common revival narrative had emerged to describe what had happened from the autumn months of 1857 through late spring 1858. It described an interdenominational businessmen's revival, characterized by noon meetings for prayer that began at the Fulton Street Dutch Reformed Church in New York City and spread across the nation. These meetings were the most visible expression of a broader Great Awakening that had affected all evangelical denominations to an extent not experienced in America for more than a century, since the eighteenth-century awakening. The most influential shapers of this narrative were the conservative revivalistic Calvinists—Old School Presbyterians and Dutch Reformed. The more progressive party offered alternative interpretations, particularly concerning the geographic extent of the revival and the spectrum of groups involved. Still, they followed the same basic storyline.

Additional books, a pamphlet, and a key article on the revival published during 1859 represented challenges to and refinements of this picture by other members of these same Reformed groups. Writers from Philadelphia and Boston bid for spots at the center rather than on the periphery of the action. In New York City itself there were rumblings of dissatisfaction at the attention given to the Fulton Street prayer meeting.[26] At the same time, and most important, certain Congregationalist writers used the Revival of 1857–58 as an occasion for a bold new advocacy of a cyclical view of revivals. They believed that American history was marked by definite cycles of "great" or widespread spiritual awakenings that were the result of special divine interventions, a view associated with millennial hopes and a providential understanding of history. By locating the revival within a pattern that had shaped American destiny, they increased the historical significance of the event. At the same time, the revival served its analysts by reinforcing their conviction that the Calvinist framework of periodic awakenings was indeed "*the* American revivalistic tradition."[27]

A New Awareness of Cyclical Awakenings

The concept of increasing cycles or "waves" of revivals that would mysteriously spread throughout the land was, in itself, not new. Such Calvinist apologists for revivals as Jonathan Edwards in the eighteenth century and Presbyterian William Sprague in the early nineteenth suggested the idea as a part of their historical analyses, particularly in connection with millennial thought.[28] From his vantage point in 1831, Sprague surveyed nearly a century of American history. He concluded that "there is much in prophecy to warrant the conviction that, as the millenial [sic] day draws near, these effusions of the Holy Spirit will be yet more frequent and powerful."[29] Yet Sprague's optimism existed in tension with his concern about abuses of revivalism, first during the eighteenth-century awakening, then again during the first three decades of the nineteenth century. Sprague and other like-minded Presbyterians had joined the New Divinity clergy among the Congregationalists in their opposition to the aggressive, populist revivals of Methodists, Cumberland Presbyterians, Charles Finney, and others.[30] They identified these groups with the excesses of James Davenport, who, with other enthusiasts had "blasted" the efforts of Edwards and Whitefield during the eighteenth-century awakening.[31] As a result, although the New Englanders and their Presbyterian allies had noted broad ebbs and flows as characteristic of revivalism, during the years prior to the Revival of 1857–58 they were cautious about promoting a view of history that might be seen as a blanket endorsement of revivals.[32] Davenport cast a dark shadow, and news of the nineteenth-century western revivals was not reassuring.[33]

The Revival of 1857–58 brought a shift in that attitude. Here at last was a nationwide awakening that vindicated the theology and style of the conservative formalists. In 1831 Princeton theologian Archibald Alexander had described a true or "pure" revival: "Nothing occurs with which any pious man can find fault. . . . The convictions of sin are deep and humbling. . . . [T]he love of God is shed abroad. . . . A spirit of devotion is enkindled. . . . Prayer is the exercise in which the soul seems to be in its proper element."[34]

As the conservatives experienced it, the 1857–58 Revival fit Alexander's criteria perfectly. Buoyed by the conviction that genuine revivalism had at last triumphed, Calvinists dared to present conceptions of redemptive history and, more narrowly, U.S. history, where revivalism played a central role. To strengthen this approach, they sanitized their surveys of nineteenth-century revivals, preferring to ignore rather than rebut objectionable aspects of them.[35]

Heman Humphrey, Congregational clergyman and president of Amherst College, took the long view. In Revival Sketches and Manual, he used the first half of the book to demonstrate that the entire history of the Christian church was in fact a history of revivals.[36] Humphrey shared Sprague's millennialism. Looking back from the vantage point of the 1857–58 Revival, he believed that a new "revival epoch" had dawned with the turn of the nineteenth century. This period, in contrast to the eighteenth century, brought revivals that were "quiet and orderly and free from objections."[37] To support his claim, Humphrey included numerous reports from the *Connecticut Evangelical Magazine*, mostly written by Congregational and Presbyterian ministers.[38] Very few Methodists and no mention of Charles Finney disturbed the idyllic revival epoch Humphrey described.[39]

Also in 1859, a second Massachusetts Congregationalist, A. P. Marvin, focused his concern on the role of revivals in the nation. His article, "Three Eras of Revival in the United States," was the first detailed application of a cyclical view of revivalism to American history.[40] Marvin had an instrumental understanding of religious awakenings, shaped by millennial, Puritan, and primitivist influences. He saw revival as a supernatural act of God to restore the church from a decline in "primitive purity of doctrine." Not only did successive revivals increase the purity of the church, each revival era also was supposed to "counteract a great evil and prepare the Christian community for an important work." Furthermore, revivalism was an integral part of maintaining the piety necessary for a "great Protestant and independent empire."[41] Thus, the Great Awakening of the 1740s counteracted the errors of Arminianism and prepared the church for "the terrible trials of the Revolution." The revival era of 1797 served to exalt the sovereignty of God "in the minds and hearts of a godless generation." Yet that emphasis tended to promote personal passivity, so the "great revival of 1831" restored balance to the church by stressing "the duty of immediately giving the heart to God."[42]

As with Humphrey, for Marvin "revival" meant Calvinist revivalism and New England revivals. His revival saints were Great Awakening heroes or honored New Englanders: Edwards, Whitefield, the Tennents, Bellamy, Griffin, Mills, Nettleton. Together with other writers who analyzed the past from a post–1858 perspective, Marvin described the spiritual fervor of the colonial era as the Great Awakening, a label coined earlier but popularized at this point.[43] Marvin did not include the Revival of 1857–58 as one of his "three eras," because the event was too recent for its significance to be clear.[44] With that caveat, however, he was sure that it would "be memorable in all future time as the fourth revival era of our country." He suggested that the revival occurred to counteract the evil of "worldliness." Since lay businessmen, rather than the clergy, were most infected with that sin, it was they who were chastised by financial ruin preceding the revival, then called "to consecrate themselves and their possessions, to the Redeemer of the World."[45]

By late 1859, the spate of revival books generated by the religious interest of 1857–58 had ended. Soon Protestants of all persuasions would turn their publishing energies toward meeting the religious needs of Civil War soldiers. But during 1858 and 1859 an influential core body of primary-source material had appeared. Through this literature, Reformed clergymen had managed an impressive interpretive feat, one that built on the efforts of earlier New Divinity historians. They had placed the 1857–58 awakening squarely within the context of a "deradicalized" or formalist American revival tradition, one shaped by Calvinists, characterized by a series of national awakenings and sanitized of emotional excesses. Despite the successes of Methodist itinerants and Baptist preachers during the first half of the nineteenth century, the public image of revivalism had been established as Reformed writers defined it and would stay that way, at least among historians, for another century. Davenport's enthusiasm and Finney's excesses were outmoded. Revivals had been rescued from dangerous extremes to become a respectable, mainstream phenomenon.

Paradoxically, however, as the formalist Calvinists restored what they considered the divine initiative in awakenings, they also were popularizing a mediating position on revivalism that would characterize a broad spectrum of American evangelicals. The cyclical view maintained the supernatural character of revivals and affirmed the role of Providence in superintending the future of the church and the nation, yet at the same time allowed considerable leeway for human activity. Changed understandings of the role of prayer during the 1857–58 Revival illustrated how much the Reformed apologists had absorbed their opponent's stress on human ability. When Samuel Irenaeus Prime announced to readers that "believing PRAYER is SURE to be ANSWERED [emphasis in the original]," he shifted the accent in prayer from divine response to human activity. Such convictions by Prime and others were quite similar to Charles Finney's once controversial teaching on the "prayer of faith."[46]

Regarding conversion, the evangelistic refrain of the awakening, "Come to Jesus!" sidestepped thorny theological issues in favor of a simple biblicism. Through tracts and hymns, the crowds at prayer meetings learned that a sinner's duty was to come to Jesus by calling out to him in trusting prayer; Christ, then, would surely save.[47] The many reported conversions in answer to prayer helped to foster the idea that conversion could be experienced more quickly than was traditionally the case among many formalist Calvinists.[48] Finally, to its early historians the Revival of 1857–58 indicated that, although God had chastised the worldliness of the great cities, his mantle now rested upon those centers of commerce and the businessmen who directed them. The awakening, as portrayed historically, helped to narrow the gap between commerce and piety. Revivals had become respectable, urban, primarily male-centered and integral to the well-being of the nation. The initial histories also had introduced an idealized profile of the modern Protestant layman: a man of prayer, the "soul winner" as well as the breadwinner in Victorian America.

Why Methodists Did Not Write Revival Histories

Methodists called for histories of the 1857–58 Revival, yet no books appeared from representatives of that tradition. What might account for the absence of such works?[49] Some of that silence may have resulted from ambivalent feelings toward the religious excitement. For Methodists, the good news surrounding the events of 1857–58 was that revivalism had become respectable. As long-time revival advocates, Methodists benefited by association with that respectability.[50] This was particularly gratifying to some segments of the denomination, such as churches in the New York City area, who had already been cultivating a middle-class image and moving in a more formalist direction. However, in contrast to the attitude of the Calvinists, some Methodists recognized that by embracing the Revival of 1857–58 they were in effect repudiating aspects of their heritage. For example, a letter to the *Western Christian Advocate* expressed concern over the union prayer-meeting custom of having people who were seeking salvation stand for prayer rather than come forward to an altar: "Though we do not speak against the mode of other denominations . . . we firmly believe there is a 'more excellent way.' "[51]

Other factors were at work as well. For one, antebellum Methodists had a different historical agenda than the Reformed. As relative newcomers to the American scene, they were more interested in demonstrating that Providence had established the legitimacy and prosperity of Methodism than in revivalism as an interpretive framework. This focus shaped the major history of American Methodism written in the early Victorian period, *A History of the Methodist Episcopal Church*, by Nathan Bangs. The Methodism Bangs chronicled simply wanted to pursue its "business" as prescribed in the church's *Discipline*, "to save as many souls as possible."[52] Like their Reformed counterparts, Methodists did believe in divine agency acting through history. But while Calvinists viewed periodic awakenings as evidence of a special work of God, Methodists understood their movement—Methodism itself—as providential. Where Methodism with its missionary impulse spread, revivals happened.[53]

Methodists also had their own literary traditions and communications patterns. The stylized "revival narrative" was a traditionally Calvinist genre. Instead of publishing books on the subject, Methodists were accustomed to recording their revival accounts in diaries, journals, and the "religious intelligence" columns of their periodicals.[54] In addition, Methodist theology had little place for ebbs and flows of revivalism under divine auspices. The necessary grace for revivals was always available; revivalism was a Methodist way of life. Administrative procedures reinforced this perspective: methods of record keeping and annual reporting predisposed Methodists to "find" frequent revivals of varying intensity.[55] Nor did they need to repudiate the emotionalism of the early nineteenth century. Methodists were willing to concede and even affirm physical manifestations and gripping emotions among people "under the powerful operations of the Spirit of God."[56]

Of course, the various Wesleyan groups did recognize as a practical matter that revivals seemed to come and go in particular regions or congregations. But even here, their chronology of exceptional revivals did not agree with the Reformed interpretation of cyclical revivalism in America. For Methodists the great revival began in 1775 in Virginia.[57] Other memorable revivals marked the 1780s, for the Reformed part of an era of declension. The church also experienced extraordinary growth between 1838 and 1844, a revival period sometimes acknowledged by the Reformed but not viewed as a great awakening.[58]

Methodists rejoiced in the membership gains they enjoyed as a result of the Revival of 1857–58, greater than those of any other church body, and they recognized this awakening as a widespread phenomenon that cut across ecclesiastical boundaries.[59] Still, Methodist concern for denominational exceptionalism, lack of a theological justification for divinely ordained cycles of national revival, and an awareness that the public ethos of the revival celebrated the formalism of the Reformed more than the traditionally populist spirit of Methodism discouraged Methodists from claiming the history of the Revival of 1857–58 for their own.

The Ongoing Influence of Reformed Interpretations

During the period from the end of the Civil War to the early twentieth century, the Calvinist view of revivals, particularly the cyclical framework, became a thread in what Sydney Ahlstrom called "the 'great tradition' of American Protestant historiography."[60] Paradoxically, this happened in tandem with a growing tendency to downplay the very revival that had helped to popularize this view in the first place. Initially, however, interest in the 1857–58 Revival remained high. The activities of D. L. Moody and the growth of the YMCA helped to solidify urban revivalism as a phenomenon at the heart of mainstream Victorian America, particularly in the northern United States. Typical was historian Daniel Dorchester's remark that it was "one of the most remarkable revivals of a century full of wonders of grace."[61]

In breadth and detail, Dorchester's massive *Christianity in the United States* (1887) marked the pinnacle of nineteenth-century histories of American Christianity.[62] In its treatment of revivalism, it also symbolized the dilemma of a late-century Methodist historian and the power of a continuing Calvinist interpretive consensus. Dorchester was well aware of the key role Methodists had played in making revivals a pervasive characteristic of American Protestantism. Yet, when it came time to incorporate revivalism into a celebratory view of Christianity in the United States, he concluded that the framework for doing so and the best available sources were Reformed. Consequently, for example, Dorchester used Ezra Gillett's *History of the Presbyterian Church in the United States of America* when he wrote of revivals during the first quarter of the nineteenth century because "the history of no other denomination affords such good materials."[63] Further, Dorchester noted that the Methodist Episcopal Church gained more than 130,000 communicants as a result of the Revival of 1857–58, more than one third of the total number who joined churches.[64] But despite the dramatic Methodist growth, Dorchester told the Reformed version of the revival story, based on *The Power of Prayer* and an 1858 report to the General Assembly of the Presbyterian Church.

The other major survey of American Christianity during the second half of the century was Leonard W. Bacon's *A History of American Christianity* (1897), the summary work in the American Church History Series. Bacon incorporated Protestant denominations and Catholicism into a triumphalistic history of the "hand of Providence" over the American nation. When it came to revivals, Providence worked in a distinctly Reformed fashion. Bacon included Methodist and other sources but shaped them to fit his cyclical outline of, first, "The Great Awakening," that fostered in the colonies "the consciousness of a national religious unity" and, then, the "The Second Awakening" to save the nation from infidelity.[65]

Bacon broke with A. P. Marvin and other earlier interpreters by ranking no subsequent revival periods as awakenings in line with the first two—not that he considered the Revival of 1857–58 insignificant. On the contrary, "like the Great Awakening of 1740, it was the providential preparation of the American church for an immediately impending peril [the Civil War]."[66] However, this interpretation, one that cropped up among northerners during and after the war, pointed to growing difficulties with providential understandings of the 1857–58 Revival. In 1859, Marvin had discerned God using it to wean the nation from worldliness; in light of the increasing consumerism of American society by the time of Bacon's book, that view was hardly convincing. Spiritual preparation for national conflict was an alternative, but one that contained disturbing ambivalences.

For historians like Marvin and Bacon, the first and second awakenings were clear-cut. In them God worked on behalf of the country as a whole against external threats: the British on the one hand and infidelity on the other. But, during the Revival of 1857–58, was God preparing the chosen nation for fratricide? The issue was particularly difficult because the best-selling primary account, *The Power of Prayer*, had stressed the nationwide influence of the revival. Bacon skirted the questions by giving the providential view of the 1857–58 Revival a distinctly northern cast but then downplaying the revival as a whole. He submerged his treatment of it within a chapter on the Civil War rather than making the event a landmark in his interpretive scheme. This strategy also reflected a second reason to minimize the awakening's significance in a general history of Christianity in America: for many people the Civil War had become the key providential event of the mid-nineteenth century.

The works of Dorchester and Bacon represented the status of the revival in secondary literature on the eve of the twentieth century.[67] The cyclical view of providential awakenings articulated in the wake of the 1857–58 Revival had become accepted wisdom as a part of the history of the American nation and its faith. Yet the application of the cyclical view as an interpretive framework, coupled with the looming historical significance of the Civil War, had led to a soft-pedaling of the very revival that had helped to popularize cyclical awakenings in the first place.

The postbellum interpretations of the Revival of 1857–58 were based almost entirely on the prewar published accounts. However, during the last 30 years of the century, a new source of firsthand descriptions appeared in memoirs and autobiographies of revival participants. Many such books contained at least a mention, or brief analysis, of the revival.[68] Two in particular, however, both published in 1876, were destined to become a part of the twentieth-century "canonized" body of primary-source material: *The Memoirs of Charles G. Finney* and *The Life and Letters of Mrs. Phoebe Palmer*. The release of Finney's *Memoirs* was a publishing event, and the book quickly caught the eye of historians. In contrast, *Life and Letters* was overshadowed in the popular market by Phoebe Palmer's practical works, and revival analysts did not value the papers of a Methodist woman.[69]

Finney discussed the revival in chapter 33 of the *Memoirs*, "Revivals in Boston in 1856, '57, '58." His account followed the already established story line in noting that "in the Autumn previous to the great outburst the daily prayer-meeting had been established in Fulton st., New York."[70] He also agreed that the key element in the revival was prayer. However, Finney broadened the usual versions in four key areas. First, he placed the revival in the context of spiritual interest in Boston during fall and winter 1856–57, as well as the revival period of 1857–58. During both times Finney preached in the city at the invitation of Park Street

Church. By including the winter of 1856–57, the *Memoirs* challenged the idea in some accounts that the country was in a state of complete spiritual decline before the Fulton Street meeting began. Second, Finney explicitly presented the revival as a northern phenomenon, capping his analysis with the blunt conviction that "slavery seemed to shut it out from the South."[71]

Although this North/South distinction would become a revival truism for later historians, such as L. W. Bacon, Finney's other observations would not. He described the participation of women in the revival, telling how they overflowed the Park Street vestry for daily prayer meetings led by his wife, Elizabeth. Finney praised the "energetic efforts of the laity, male and female" in promoting the revival.[72] Finally, he mentioned the opposition to his ministry, particularly his preaching on sanctification, that surfaced when he returned to Boston in autumn 1857. The criticisms apparently did not dampen the spiritual interest, but Finney's narrative hinted that the revival unity, often touted in the earlier books, was, in fact, less than universal.[73]

Editor Richard Wheatley grouped the letters that Methodist revivalist and holiness teacher Phoebe Palmer wrote during 1857 under the heading, "*Annus Mirabilis.*"[74] From July through October Palmer and her husband, Walter, found unusual spiritual openness among participants in Methodist camp meetings in Canada around Lake Ontario and up and down the St. Lawrence River. They estimated that 2,000 people were converted and "hundreds" sanctified through their efforts.[75] The highlight was a revival that began October 8 in Hamilton, a city on the western tip of Lake Ontario, when the Palmers unexpectedly were delayed in their return home.[76] Local ministers united three denominational prayer meetings and asked the Palmers to speak to the group. Within 10 days, 500 people had been converted. In describing the revival to her sister Sarah Lankford, Palmer wrote, "We have had but very little preaching. . . . [T]his revival took its rise mainly with the laity."[77] At the time, accounts of the Hamilton revival were published in the *Guide to Holiness*, a Boston-based periodical promoting Methodist views of sanctification, and in the New York *Christian Advocate and Journal.*[78]

Palmer's impressions of the revival, contained in a posthumous collection of letters and journal entries, lacked the comprehensiveness of other, more intentional accounts. However, as one of the most detailed published records of the religious fervor by a Methodist, except for articles in the denominational press, *Life and Letters* provided several fresh perspectives. Most dramatically, Palmer's letters showed a woman—herself—leading revival activities, though certainly not in the Reformed stronghold of lower Manhattan.[79] In common with Finney's *Memoirs*, the letters told of spiritual interest that preceded the drama of Fulton Street. Palmer also highlighted the concern for sanctification that accompanied many Methodist meetings. In addition, her letters offered a picture of religious activism in "peripheral" areas, towns that were not commercial power centers on a par with New York City, Philadelphia, or Boston. From that perspective she provided new insights into the revival. In contrast to Finney's writings, however, neglect of Palmer's life and writings meant that her insights would not influence the views of historians for another 75 years.

Revisionist Efforts of the Mid-Twentieth Century

Although historians paid little scholarly attention to revivals during the early decades of the twentieth century, a few books written outside the academic arena added bits and pieces of information and suggested certain shifts in emphasis regarding the Revival of 1857–58.[80] These books, best understood as extensions of nineteenth-century interpretive frameworks, included histories of revivalism; more biographies and autobiographies; and attempts by the YMCA, then at the pinnacle of its social and religious influence, to recover its past.[81] The interest in YMCA history and the biographies of D. L. Moody that appeared after his death led to a greater association of both Moody and the "Y" with the revival.[82] "To him was due the success of the historic Noon-Day Prayer Meeting of Chicago," wrote one biographer. In addition, Moody personified the way the methods and energy of the laymen's awakening spilled over into the religious work among Union soldiers sponsored by the United States Christian Commission (USCC).[83]

For the most part, however, these new layers of information lay unnoticed by the academic world, like sediment from a bygone era, only later to fuel scholars' conflicting interpretations. But at least until the mid-twentieth century, and in many cases until much more recently, those who cared to glance into the history of the revival still saw a pool of information that reflected the same basic story Prime and his colleagues told in 1858 and 1859. The first and most significant challenge to this status quo came in 1957 with a book that has been described as the "best historical study . . . ever written on nineteenth-century revivalism," Timothy L. Smith's *Revivalism and Social Reform*.[84]

In a pioneering revisionist work, Smith sought to recover the Wesleyan tradition as a formative influence in the history of American revivals and, consequently, on mainstream American culture. With its Wesleyan-inspired corollary of ethical perfection, revivalism did more than serve as a vehicle for conversions. It also was the true source of "progressive theology and humanitarian concern" among nineteenth-century Protestants. Smith used the Revival of 1857–58 to exemplify his argument that, instead of beginning to decline, revivals had "become a dominant mood in urban religious life" for all major Protestant denominations during the years 1840–1857. In making that statement, he rejected the conventional understanding of cyclical awakenings that had dominated the history of revivals since the nineteenth century.[85]

In Smith's hands the Revival of 1857–58 underwent a dramatic transformation. For its nineteenth-century apologists, the revival was an exemplar of Calvinist revivalism, the expression of a supernatural visitation of God in response to prayer. For Smith, it came instead to represent what he called "revivalism's triumph over Calvinism."[86] The phrase pointed to a key aspect of Smith's interpretation: his redefinition of revivalism as a synonym for Wesleyan Arminianism. Since all nineteenth-century revivals were by definition Arminian, revivalistic Calvinists such as the partisans of 1857–58, were little more than Wesleyans in disguise.[87] This definitional shift enabled Smith to engage in revisionist history without actually reconstructing his narrative of the revival to stress Methodist involvement.

Smith did more than any previous historian to move out from under the interpretive shadow of the original Calvinist histories of the 1857–58 Revival. He brought to the fore the more socially progressive side of the awakening and highlighted some figures ignored in the early accounts.[88] He gave the event a certain legitimacy by depicting it as an expression of social reform and provided leads for further scholarship through his voluminous documentation. Smith rescued the Revival of 1857–58 from scholarly oblivion and pointed to the depth and breadth of a movement that until his book had been described primarily in terms of the noon prayer meetings.[89] By viewing revivals as an increasingly pervasive cultural phenomenon throughout the antebellum years, Smith stood in alliance with Methodist interpretive concerns, such as those of Nathan Bangs in the nineteenth century.

Ironically, however, Smith continued to rely primarily on Reformed sources, although he minimized the Old School Presbyterian involvement and emphasized the leadership of New School clergy and progressive Congregationalists. He did incorporate the contributions of Phoebe and Walter Palmer, but fewer than 10 of his 54 heavily loaded footnotes for the chapter on the 1857–58 Revival contained references to Methodist sources.[90] Smith's blanket reshaping of the revival in the image of progressive Arminianism continued in substance to neglect Methodists; it blurred tensions among the Reformed that had social and political ramifications; and it sketched an image of reform-minded lay involvement that may have been an expression of Smith's own optimism more than the activities of 1858.[91] As influential as *Revivalism and Social Reform* became in legitimizing the popular religion of the Methodist revival tradition and its reforming impulses, the book's treatment of the 1857–58 Revival also demonstrated the staying power of the early Calvinist accounts. Smith's book illustrated both the potential and the difficulties facing historians who sought to move beyond the mainstream corpus of primary source material on American revivals.

Who Really "Won"?

It is a truism among historians that "the winners write the history." However, as sociologists have recently confirmed, the period from 1776 to 1850 was a time when the activist "upstart sects," the Methodists and Baptists, "won" the majority of adherents to Christianity in America, and they did so with more or less continuous efforts at revivalism, allowing for local and regional variations. As a result, by 1850, 34.2 percent, or approximately one of every three, of "mainline" religious adherents were Methodists. In contrast, while Presbyterians and Congregationalists together had represented 39.4 percent of religious adherents in 1776, by 1850 their share had fallen to 15.6 percent.[92] Yet despite their loss in numerical influence, these latter two groups wrote the history and provided the texts that established a powerful American revival tradition. The "losers" won a victory of their own; they used history as a way to assimilate and contain those groups whose sheer numbers challenged their religious and cultural dominance.[93]

Both the eighteenth-century Great Awakening and its corollary of divinely ordained revival cycles were part of a Calvinist interpretive tradition that linked revivals and millennialism as keys to a providential understanding of history. This framework was threatened when certain Reformed clergymen observed perceived abuses in colonial and early nineteenth-century revivals. But the religious interest of 1857–58 confirmed that revivals were back on track, and the interpretive tradition gained new popularity. Conversely, that same tradition enhanced the importance of the 1857–58 Revival by providing it with a significant historical context. Calvinists rushed to "claim" the revival because they were able to recognize it as particularly their own. As this chapter has argued, their influence was decisive in producing the immediate, firsthand histories that shaped the collective "social memory" expressed in subsequent interpretations of the 1857–58 Revival. Because of the publicity surrounding it and the revival history it evoked, the awakening of 1857–58 became the occasion for reinvigorating a consensus view of American revival history that was itself largely the product of a Calvinist historical imagination.

Unlike the First Great Awakening, when an interpretive tradition did not assume definitive shape until a century after the revivals themselves, the 1857–58 Revival was given a history literally as it was taking place. Although the participant-observers most insistent about that history were the competing groups of Calvinist clergymen featured in this chapter, their story was both reinforced and repackaged at a number of critical points by the secular press, a powerful institution in late antebellum society. The "great metropolis" of New York City was a communications center for the nation. Both the Calvinist clergy and the secular press were groups with a national consciousness: one of a Christian republic, the other of a vast marketplace for news. Although ultimately at cross-purposes, one driven by religious ideals, the other by profit, they both recognized the revival as a significant public event. While the clergy interpreted that event from the standpoint of history, mass print helped make businessmen's piety an immediate public sensation in cities and towns across the country.

TWO

"Affording public amusement . . . [and] gratifying the curiosity"

Revivalism in the News

O N SATURDAY, FEBRUARY 27, 1858, James Gordon Bennett featured the 1857–58 Revival in the pages of his *New York Herald*, the most successful daily paper in the United States. The story got a full column of coverage on page one, topped by multiple stacked headlines:

Great Revival of Religion in New York.

Progress of the Movement.

Remarkable Conversions Among the Unrighteous.

Sinners Brought to the Way of Grace.

One of the 'Forty Thieves' Repentant.

Wonderful Manifestations of Penitence and Piety.

Revivals Elsewhere.

&c., &c., &c.,

For the first time in the nineteenth century, revivalism was splashed across the front page of a secular newspaper, appearing alongside accounts of city politics, the activities of Congress and sensationalistic crimes. To Bennett, a pioneer in human interest reporting, the historical significance of the awakening mattered little. As the headlines indicated, the revival had immediate appeal to the readers of a mass-circulation daily like the *Herald* for other reasons. It promised emotional displays, large crowds, and the prospect of "open confessions" by businessmen and politicians.[1]

While Bennett took the lead in recognizing the news value of the "great revival," his competitors wasted little time in catching up. On the following Monday, Horace Greeley, a long-time rival and editor of the powerful *New York Tribune*, devoted six columns of type—the equivalent of one full page in an eight-page daily—to "The Religious Awakening" (the lead headline). Through a series of adroit moves during the next few days, he outmaneuvered Bennett and positioned the *Tribune* as a kind of national clearinghouse for revival information. Philadelphia papers also carried reports of the New York prayer meetings on Monday, and by the end of the week the *New York Times*, the *Boston Post*, and even the distant *New Orleans Picayune* had noted the religious excitement in the nation's largest city.

During March and April 1858, the revival became a media event, covered by metropolitan dailies in all parts of the country.[2] Newspapers took the lead as publicists for it and were catalysts for the spread of its most familiar aspect, the noon urban prayer meetings. The New York press, led by the *Tribune* and *Herald* but including other respected dailies such as the *Times* and the *Evening Post*, spurred the ongoing coverage. Newspapers in other cities reprinted their stories, emulated their writing styles, and followed their practice of culling anecdotes and other accounts from the many weekly religious papers. Although the Reformed clergy shaped the narrative of the 1857–58 Revival for later historians, newspapers told the story to most Americans in the spring of 1858.

Daily newspapers, of course, were not the only available sources of information. The Revival of 1857–58 took place at a time when weekly religious papers, usually identified with a particular denomination, enjoyed a substantial circulation of their own. With more than 100 weeklies serving a total of approximately 400,000 subscribers, Protestants were very much a part of what would be described in 1860 as "a newspaper-reading nation."[3] Methodist papers were most successful: the five largest of the numerous regional editions of the *Christian Advocate* had a combined circulation of more than 90,000.[4] Among the Presbyterians, the *New York Observer* had a subscription list of 17,500, while its New School rival, the *Evangelist*, listed 13,000 subscribers. The Baptist *Watchman and Reflector* had a circulation of more than 10,000.[5] Other weeklies survived with circulations as low as 600 copies, though most seemed to range between 2,000 and 6,000. Revival news from individual churches or specific towns was a staple for these papers, and many had expanded their coverage during the winter months of 1858 as the religious interest spread among the grassroots. The weeklies became a major source of information for the secular press. However, not until the metropolitan dailies picked up the story did the Revival of 1857–58 coalesce as an national event, both in their pages and in the columns of the religious press.

People expected to read about revivals in the denominational weeklies, but the appearance of such news in the secular papers created a sensation. A letter from a correspondent in the upstate village of Troy to the *New York Tribune* captured the reaction: "The elaborate accounts of the great National religious awakening, which are just now being published in The Tribune, has [sic] created a great demand for the paper in this vicinity. Hoyt's news-room is thronged with applicants of all classes and conditions for your sheet."[6]

This comment also underscored the commercial aspect of the secular press's "discovery" of revival news: it sold papers. With the advent of the "penny press" in the 1830s, metropolitan dailies had embraced the concept of news as a product for mass consumption. Although they offered subscriptions, the *Herald* and the

Tribune maintained their high circulations through "cash and carry" sales. The papers were hawked on the streets by newsboys for two cents a copy to a more middle-class audience than that for the cheaper and smaller penny papers. Their success depended on news that sold, and the editors knew from day to day what stories appealed to a mass readership. At bottom, to editors such as Bennett and Greeley, the Revival of 1857-58 was a commodity.[7]

Historians recently have pointed out that the idea of revivalism as a commodity was not new. Modern evangelicalism, Harry S. Stout has argued, emerged in tandem with the commercialization of Anglo-American culture that began in the early eighteenth century. Along with other leisure-time activities, "religion increasingly represented a product that could be marketed," with revivalist George Whitefield as its most brilliant early entrepreneur.[8] Yet both in the case of Whitefield, and of the many "peddlers" of popular Christianity who followed him in the free market ethos of early-nineteenth-century America, evangelicals themselves were the entrepreneurs, the innovators who helped to create a popular religious "marketplace," using print media and early advertising techniques to promote their causes. In general, they were proselytizers rather than profit makers.[9] Although not always successful in avoiding entanglements with commercialism, they sought to employ the techniques and even the rhetoric of the marketplace to achieve their evangelistic goals while at the same time maintaining a distance between themselves and the selfishness and greed they often saw in the actual economic order.[10]

The role of the secular press in the Revival of 1857-58 altered this dynamic. Until then evangelicals had marketed revivalism largely through their own print media. The publicists for earlier revivals were preachers—Jonathan Edwards, Whitefield, Lorenzo Dow, Jabez Swan, Charles Finney, and others. By contrast, in the spring of 1858, Bennett and Greeley, two secular editors, became the most influential image makers for popular evangelicalism in America. More than a hundred years earlier, George Whitefield had used the colonial press to further his public relations purposes.[11] In 1858, the balance of power shifted. The press would now use revivalism for its own ends, ends that clearly included a profit motive. When the *Herald*, the *Tribune*, and other papers embraced the religious awakening as news, the secular, mass-circulation print media assumed the task of marketing revivals, at least in the public arena, a role they would continue to play into the twentieth century. This change inaugurated a more openly commercial attitude toward the activities of popular Protestantism, part of the ongoing "commodification" of religion that took place as American commercial culture expanded throughout the nineteenth century.[12]

A brief glance at the history of the relationship between revival publicity and American journalism supports these claims. With the important exception of the publicity surrounding Whitefield, information about American revivals prior to 1858 was communicated primarily through letters and religious books and periodicals, not the secular press. The first evangelical magazines originated in the 1740s to convey revival news.[13] Later, people learned about such events as the 1801 Cane Ridge camp meeting, one of the more colorful western revivals, by reading the *New York Missionary Magazine*, the *Connecticut Evangelical Magazine*, the *Methodist Magazine*, and similar periodicals.[14] Even such a popular and controversial figure as Charles Finney received scarcely a mention in the daily newspapers.[15]

The situation changed dramatically in the aftermath of the 1857–58 Revival. An early signal was an article in the *New York Evening Post*, July 15, 1859, titled "Stories About Mr. Finney, the Oberlin Revivalist."[16] More important, newspapers played a major part in shaping the images of most, if not all, the well-known revivalists after 1858, including D. L. Moody, E. P. Hammond, Sam Jones, Billy Sunday, Aimee Semple McPherson, and Billy Graham. For example, newspaper coverage legitimated Moody's success in Great Britain and helped to launch his American revivalistic career. "From the moment Moody and Sankey docked in New York in August, 1875, eastern newspapers reported their activities in the minutest detail, and the two men were compared with the 'apostles of old,' who had 'turned the world upside down.' "[17] In 1915 Billy Sunday's Philadelphia crusade became such a big story that Sunday claimed in one sermon he would use the press clippings to clear himself of responsibility before God for the city's salvation. "I gave them your message, Lord, I gave it to them the best way I could," said Sunday, defending himself in an imaginary dialogue with the deity. "You go get the files of the Philadelphia papers."[18]

Because the Revival of 1857–58 did mark the first sustained coverage of revivals in the secular, mass-circulation press, and because it drew the attention of Bennett and Greeley, two men who "ushered in modern American journalism," it provides ideal terrain to explore the initial relationship between modern journalism and popular evangelicalism.[19] What triggered the intense press coverage, and how, in turn, did such coverage affect the spread of the revival itself? What was the impact of the commercialization of revivalism in the secular media marketplace? How did it affect popular religion and, in particular, public images of revivals?

Bennett's Herald *and Greeley's* Tribune *Positioned to Market Revival News*

The idea of news as product on the free market rather than a service to political or commercial elites had been at the heart of the secular "newspaper revolution" of the 1830s, and it was a concept James Gordon Bennett grasped better than anyone else.[20] From its inception in 1835, the *New York Herald* was designed to appeal to "the great masses of the community," laborers as well as the urban middle class.[21] Bennett knew how to sell news to a broad, popular audience and how to target various segments within it. By the 1850s he had a well-established reputation as one of the most powerful and irreverent voices in American journalism. He took an independent political stance, adopted a lively and often sarcastic writing style, and broadened the traditional definition of news.

Bennett was the first to turn what had been gossip into a marketable commodity by printing society news. A lifelong Jacksonian proponent of the "common man," the editor understood the fascination of ordinary people with the lives of the rich and famous. In February 1858, for example, he gave page one coverage to the "Nuptials of the Princess Royal of England."[22] He brought sports reporting to the pages of a general interest daily with stories of horse racing, yachting regattas, and prizefighting. The *Herald* became known for its detailed and impartial financial columns. Interspersed with these innovations were the vivid accounts of murder, suicide, sex, and disaster that had become standard fare for all mass-circulation dailies. Bennett offered both the respectable and the salacious, a combination readers found hard to resist. He also was fascinated by the subject of religion.[23]

Historians of journalism generally credit Bennett as the first "to begin religion news coverage in a newspaper intended for a general audience."[24] Religious subjects, especially those involving sex or scandal, found a place in the *Herald* almost immediately. During 1836, the first full year of the paper's publication, some 30 articles referred to Maria Monk and her *Awful Disclosures*. Bennett also recognized that the Mormons made good copy. He covered the westward movements of Joseph Smith and printed extensive descriptions of Mormon activities in Nauvoo, Illinois.[25] Closer to home, in 1840 Bennett brought down the ire of the Protestant establishment when he shifted his attention to the annual Anniversary Meetings of the "Benevolent Empire." The articles were relatively inoffensive, but religious leaders were infuriated to find themselves featured in a paper that flaunted its disdain for evangelical values by printing advertisements from theaters and prostitutes, opposing temperance, and by publishing a Sunday edition. Almost simultaneously, Bennett, himself a nominal Catholic, alienated the Roman church by criticizing the doctrine of transubstantiation and calling the pope "a decrepit, licentious, stupid Italian blockhead."[26] A reaction against Bennett's contempt for traditional religion was one element behind the 1840 "Moral War": a month-long campaign by rival papers, clergy, and merchants to boycott the *Herald* and drive it out of business. Predictably, the Moral War did little in the long run except add to the paper's notoriety. Throughout his career, Bennett insisted that the *Herald* simply served as the people's representative in exposing fanaticism and the hypocrisy of religious elites. It made its editor a wealthy man in the process.[27]

The *Herald* toned down its more tasteless rhetoric during the 1840s and the 1850s, although Bennett continued to treat religion as news. He discussed the religious communitarian ideas of Robert Owen and Charles Fourier, covered the church trial of Episcopal Bishop Benjamin Onderdonk, and considered the new Catholic doctrine of the Immaculate Conception of the Virgin Mary. There were occasional sensationalistic accounts of clergymen's immorality or criminal activity. Revivals were mentioned only in passing. The closest thing to a religious "media event" in the pages of the *Herald* and other papers was the coverage of the Millerite excitement in the early 1840s.[28]

Throughout these years, many northern evangelical leaders maintained their antipathy toward the newspaper, an attitude returned in kind. Bennett, an immigrant and a Catholic, capitalized on his outsider status. The editor refused to embrace the evangelical ideal of the secular press as an agent of Christian (Protestant) civilization "on the side of Virtue and Religion."[29] He focused on the news-gathering function of the press rather than its role as teacher or moral guardian of society. The *Herald* was a business. News was the commodity, and Bennett provided more of it in a more timely fashion and better tailored to popular taste than any of his competitors. He was, in the words of one historian, "the prototypical Jacksonian, an elitist entrepreneur who exploited the masses as much as he served them."[30] To northern evangelicals in the 1850s, Bennett and his paper were a "plague," corrupting the once "respectable press" as others sought to imitate the *Herald's* success.[31]

One rival newspaper, however, had pursued an alternative route to success. The *New York Tribune*, founded by Horace Greeley less than a year after the "Moral War," embodied the ideals of those, including evangelicals, who deplored the *Herald*. If James Gordon Bennett was the "prototypical Jacksonian," Horace Greeley was the quintessential Whig. Greeley, a New Englander, represented not only the political convictions of that party, but also the social values—the moral earnestness and reforming zeal—it had absorbed from northern evangelicalism.[32] From its first issue, April 10, 1841, the *Tribune* was a newspaper with a moral agenda and an interest in improving society. "The *Tribune*," Greeley announced, "will labor to advance the interests of the People, and to promote their Moral, Social, and Political well-being." Although more overtly political than the religious family weeklies, in many other ways the paper positioned itself as the secular, daily counterpart of those publications. Initially Greeley refused to print theater advertisements, police reports, and the "loathsome details" of murder trials in order to make his journal "a welcome visitant at the family fireside."[33] The *Tribune* moved beyond most religious weeklies, however, in its crusading spirit. It was "Anti-Slavery, Anti-War, Anti-Rum, Anti-Tobacco, Anti-Seduction, Anti-Grogshops, Brothels, [and] Gambling Houses."[34] The paper was known for its "-isms," particularly Greeley's advocacy of the social ideas of Fourierism and his support of abolitionism. All such efforts had one underlying goal: social redemption, or, as Greeley put it, "the elevation of the masses."[35]

However, the *Tribune* never attempted to survive by idealism alone. Like Bennett, Greeley understood the consumer orientation of mass communications. In the *Tribune*, as his critics delighted in pointing out, Greeley began to make quiet accommodations to popular taste in order to balance ethics with profit. Within a few years of the paper's founding, it had begun to feature extensive crime reporting, and Greeley had relented on the prohibition against theater advertising. Even so, the editor recognized that the *Tribune's* controversial social and political stances would never give it a dominant share of New York City readership. Before the daily *Tribune* was a year old, Greeley had begun a weekly edition, promoted through special bulk rates and premium offers. The *Weekly Tribune* became widely popular in New England and among the transplanted Yankees of the northwestern states. It also gave Greeley a national forum.

Although its religion reporting has received little scholarly notice, the *Tribune*, alongside the *Herald*, printed religion news during the two decades prior to the Civil War. However, as Daniel Walker Howe has pointed out, religion seemed not to be a "driving force" in Greeley's life. He himself was a Universalist and appeared to share neither the evangelical impulse to promote Christianity nor Bennett's need to debunk organized religion. Greeley showed most interest in reporting on religion when it attracted broad public interest, supported his reform efforts, or reflected some sort of "novelty." On March 2, 1842, for example, the *Tribune* issued an "extra" devoted to an explanation of biblical prophecies that refuted William Miller's predictions of Christ's imminent return.[36] During the 1850s the paper covered Henry Ward Beecher's efforts to send Bibles and rifles in equal numbers to beleaguered Kansas, and it supported George B. Cheever's scathing pulpit denunciation of the Dred Scott decision.[37] In the realm of novelty, the *Tribune* reflected Greeley's passing interest in spiritualism.[38] Once again, revivals were not a subject of particular interest. Northern evangelicals recognized the *Tribune* as a secular paper, "without any fixed religious convictions," but respected it nonetheless as having "an honest purpose to promote the best interests of society."[39] On a popular level, by the mid-1850s the *Weekly Tribune* had become an "oracle" to thousands of readers throughout the northern states, many of them evangelicals.[40]

By late February 1858, Bennett's *Herald* and Greeley's *Tribune* were well positioned to market news of the 1857-58 Revival. The *Herald*, claiming a daily distribution of 62,000 copies, was "the most widely circulated daily in the United States." Because of Bennett's proslavery stance and regular coverage of the South, the paper enjoyed particular influence in that region.[41] The *Tribune*, on the other hand, dominated the North through its weekly edition. Along with other businesses, both newspapers had suffered from the financial slump following the October 1857 panic, although Greeley was the harder hit. During February and March 1858 advertisements were still down. With eight pages in their daily and weekly editions, twice those of most mass-circulation journals, the papers had space to fill.[42] The two journals operated from a city that regularly captured the attention of the nation and served as a "communications relay center" for it. News during the antebellum era "was a Northern product exported to other regions," and Greeley and Bennett were major exporters.[43]

Yet these circumstances do not fully explain why Bennett chose the last week in February to feature the revival story, or why Greeley responded with intense coverage during the next five weeks. The religious excitement in New York City and elsewhere had begun in October and had been intensifying since January. As early as January 5, 1858, Jeremiah Lanphier had visited some of the daily papers to alert editors to the noon prayer meetings.[44] Why did James Gordon Bennett decide to feature the revival as a news item at the particular point in time that he did?

"Turning . . . piety into hard cash": Coverage in the Mass-Circulation Press

There was no indication of a single, precipitating cause, but clues could be found in the *Herald's* initial week of revival coverage, both the stories on Sunday, February 21, and the flamboyant front-page splash six days later. They pointed to the importance of controversy, timing, and accessibility in enhancing the market value of revivalism as a news commodity. First was the element of controversy, long a foundation of Bennett's marketing strategy. The revival provided a new opportunity for the editor to fulfill his ongoing, self-appointed role as thorn in the side of New York City's Protestant establishment. The New York City Sabbath Committee, founded a year earlier, had designated this particular Sunday as a day of united concern for the "obligations of the Christian Sabbath" and had asked Protestant ministers in the metropolis to preach on the subject. Those worried about Sunday desecration laid much of the responsibility at the feet of the secular press for printing Sunday papers and filling the streets with the "Sunday news-crying nuisance" of newsboys.[45]

A major offender, Bennett displayed his unrepentant attitude not only by printing a Sunday paper but also by devoting a part of that issue to religious news and creating the ironic effect of putting the Protestants themselves in the Sunday *Herald*. Although Bennett did not comment directly on the February 21 observance, he did juxtapose two editorials to make a statement on the subject. In "A Religious Revolution," an editorial on the revival, he presented a tongue-in-cheek description of "merchants, bankers, politicians, financiers" as repentant sinners, making "oral confession that they have done those things which they ought not to have done, and left undone those things which they ought to have done." One column over, in a separate editorial, Bennett made clear what Protestants really should confess: their attempts "to drive the working classes to church on their only day of rest." Sunday was "the poor man's day for exercise, enjoyment and fresh air." Bennett used the revival to underscore class divisions in the city and to reinforce his campaign to keep Sunday safe for newspaper sales.[46]

February 21 was also the first Sunday in Lent. This meant nothing to most revivalistic Protestants, who ignored such "popish" observations. But to Bennett, Lent signaled a season particularly suited to publishing articles on religion. For one thing, Catholics and Episcopalians had scheduled daily services throughout the period, so "the revival may be said to embrace all churches, although the forms are somewhat different." Such a statement put the editor in a position to cover the revival without alienating his Catholic readers. The 40 days of Lent also provided a limit for coverage. "The revival will probably continue during the lent, and may be over some time about Easter," the paper noted, in a statement as much of intent as of prophecy.[47] From a press standpoint, Bennett's prediction turned out to be fairly accurate. Horace Greeley would culminate his revival reporting with a special "Extra" edition of the *Tribune*, Saturday, April 3, the day before Easter. Regional papers, especially in the North, followed the New York lead. As a result, the revival as a "media event" reached its climax during March, although momentum continued well beyond that month. Bennett and his *Herald* had ensured that the rhythms of the Catholic church year would help shape the contours of a very Protestant revival.

In addition to the role of controversy and timing in increasing the news value of the revival, by late February evangelicals in New York City had accelerated their public relations efforts, making the spreading spiritual excitement a hard story to ignore. Thousands of cards had been distributed on the streets of New York City to advertise the Fulton Street prayer meeting. On February 20, the city YMCA sent a circular letter—in effect, a press release, publicizing additional businessmen's prayer meetings—to secular papers throughout the country.[48] New York City was home to half a dozen of the most influential religious weeklies in the nation, and their pages contained a growing number of reports and anecdotes about various local revivals. In his editorial, Bennett mentioned several stories, evidence he had been scanning the religious papers. As part of its later feature coverage, the *Herald* printed reports of revivals in Connecticut, Massachusetts, New York, Ohio, and Illinois taken from the *Evangelist* and the *Observer* to establish the event as worthy of national as well as of local importance. All this demonstrated that news was plentiful and that the religious excitement was generating broad public interest. Bennett could get much the same message if he simply looked out a window. The *Herald* building sat on the corner of Fulton and Nassau Streets, only a two- or three-minute walk from the Fulton Street prayer meeting. The revival began, as Bennett later noted, "almost under the shadow of the *Herald* office."[49]

Bennett's editorial voice in these initial articles was self-satisfied. The revival was a story he could cover thoroughly, but with characteristic satire, as a bit of a joke. The skeptical outsider, Bennett poked fun at what he considered evangelical illusions of transforming "this city which our rural friends are fond of comparing to London, Gomorrah, Babylon, and other disreputable places."[50] He lauded piety that stayed out of politics: "We are returning to first principles. Already we see the decadence of the political and the fighting parsons. Beecher preaches Sharp's rifles no more."[51]

Yet Bennett did not have the field to himself for long. The week the *Herald* broke the revival story, Greeley was busy with politics. He published a special *Tribune* "Extra" denouncing the proslavery Lecompton constitution in Kansas the day Bennett put revivalism on the front page. Two days later, however, the *Tribune* made up for its loss in timeliness by the comprehensive attention it gave the revival. Greeley recognized that his newspaper, already with some base among northern evangelicals, could further appeal to that market. He took a sympathetic, "insider" stance toward the religious excitement, and, although Greeley never said so, the rumor among evangelicals was that he had hired a minister to help with reporting.[52] From its initial, extensive coverage on March 1 up to the "Extra" five weeks later, the *Tribune* provided the most complete record of the revival to appear in any single newspaper, secular or religious.[53] Selections from the material were eventually reprinted as the final 100 pages of William Conant's book, *Remarkable Conversions*.

Greeley's interest in the revival was more than simply economic. The editor of the *Tribune* was fascinated by new trends, and this was a revival with a novelty: the noon prayer meetings, "held in the center of the business circles of the city, and sustained largely by the most prominent business men." The revival's respectability also appealed to the Whig temperament. It was an orderly awakening, with a high "moral tone . . . great sobriety, and a commendable freedom from undue excess."[54] Most important, Greeley initially had hopes that the spiritual fervor would enlighten people in support of his political agenda. In two early editorials, he and Bennett exchanged barbs over the potential political significance of the event. Greeley disputed Bennett's suggestion that the revival had arrived because churches had decided to mind their own business and leave politics alone.[55] The *Tribune* editor argued the opposite: "Simultaneously with the deep interest felt and expressed by the great body of the religious men of the North in the attempt to save Kansas from the evils and horrors of Slavery, . . . we see a revival breaking out and extending over the country quite unprecedented in its character."[56] Greeley expressed his hope that the revival would bring "a great increase" to the Republican party and "infuse into it . . . additional zeal, earnestness and sincerity."[57]

Such rhetoric, however, soon disappeared in favor of human interest stories as both editors recognized the largely apolitical nature of the awakening. Greeley would not write another editorial analyzing the revival until he penned a few chastened comments a month later.[58] If the editor maintained a political agenda, it merged with his sales strategy. He had lost readers due to the financial panic and the shrillness of his attack on slavery during the previous year. By tapping into the evangelical public's fascination with revivals and by capitalizing on the good will the *Tribune* coverage generated, he could restore the paper's financial stability, build readership, and enhance his own future influence. Greeley sought these ends through a careful marketing strategy. Most revival news in the *Tribune* was "sold" to various readers at least three times: in the daily edition, in the *Weekly Tribune*, and in the heavily advertised revival "Extra."[59] During the five weeks prior to Easter, in addition to imitating the religious weeklies with seemingly endless lists of revival statistics and church involvement, the *Tribune* employed the techniques of popular journalism to highlight the human side of the awakening. There were stories of prizefighters converted, of the excitement people felt at taking over a theater for prayer, and of eccentric but harmless characters—a Methodist woman dubbed "Screeching Harry" and a ne'er-do-well, "boorish" Tommy Lloyd.[60]

The revival stimulated the sales of religious literature. Even before the height of the excitement, some observers had commented that the religious press had withstood the financial panic better than the secular book or periodical trade.[61] Most people seemed to agree with S. I. Prime's comment that "never has God so honored the instrumentality of tracts and news papers [*sic*]."[62] One report noted that "the Tract House is thronged daily with ladies and gentlemen soliciting and purchasing tracts and books."[63]

In his efforts to capitalize on this demand, Greeley sometimes appeared to be trying to turn the *Tribune* itself into a tract. There were a number of anecdotes—some published in the paper itself—about people claiming that the *Tribune* had been a factor in their Christian conversion.[64] The paper even featured a popular poem, "What's the News?" that expressed the excitement among religious people over the revival as news:

> Whene're we meet you always say,
>   What's the news? What's the news?
> Pray what's the order of the day?
>   What's the news? What's the news?
> My Savior has done all things well,
> And triumph'd over death and hell—
>   That's the news! That's the news!
>   . . . .
> His work's reviving all around—
>   That's the news! That's the news!

And many have redemption found—
    That's the news! That's the news![65]

Such content, along with the journal's role in publicizing the noon prayer meetings, did increase the *Tribune's* popularity among evangelicals. Charles Finney later commented that the "paper was instrumental in doing very much to extend the work. All honour to Mr Greeley for the honourable course he pursued."[66] Detractors scoffed at the *Tribune's* turn toward religion as little more than Greeley's "knack of turning . . . piety into hard cash."[67]

"The Great Revival" as a National Event

The evidence did seem to indicate that this was a businessmen's revival in more ways than one, yet there was accuracy in Finney's statement as well. Publicity in the *Tribune* and in competing New York and Philadelphia papers, including the *Herald*, helped to further the revival in two ways. First, it brought an image of cohesiveness to the widespread religious interest. Prior to the secular press coverage, the different religious weeklies had reported extensive local and regional revivals, often from their own denominations, but these had no common identity as "*The* Religious Awakening" or "*The* Great Revival" (italics mine) until the dailies named the revival during the first week in March.[68] A survey of the religious papers after that point, however, shows that their editorials subsequently reinforced the image of the revival as a national event.[69]

Second, the secular press emphasized noon prayer meetings in urban business centers as the unique characteristic of the 1857–58 Revival, and publicity in the dailies promoted the spread of those meetings. Although revivals occurred in many places in the United States and some in Canada during autumn and winter 1857–58, the noon businessmen's prayer meeting at the Fulton Street Church in lower Manhattan was an unusual expression of the revivalistic fervor.[70] Until the secular press coverage began, only four such noon prayer meetings had been established in the nation: the Fulton Street meeting; two other Manhattan meetings begun in mid-February by the YMCA, including one at the John Street Methodist Church; and a YMCA-sponsored prayer group in the anteroom of Jayne's Hall in Philadelphia.[71]

The growth of the Jayne's Hall meeting illustrated the potential impact of newspaper publicity. The meeting had been moved to the hall from a church on February 3, and during the month of February, attendance increased gradually—from 20 people initially to about 60 at the end of the month. On March 1, the *Pennsylvania Inquirer* and *Philadelphia Evening Journal* both reported the religious excitement in New York City. On Saturday, March 6, the *Philadelphia Press* gave the revival front-page coverage. Although they made no mention of any press influence, the Philadelphia YMCA noted in a later account that on Monday, March 8, "almost as in an instant, the whole aspect of affairs underwent a most surprising change."[72] That day, 300 people arrived to pray, a crowd that would swell to more than 4,000 by the following Friday.

Urban businessmen's meetings were organized in Boston, March 8; in Louisville, March 15; in Chicago, March 22; and in New Orleans, March 24. Places such as Cincinnati, Cleveland, and Indianapolis, as well as many smaller towns, followed suit during the same time period.[73] The South picked up the trend more slowly than the North, in part because news flow was less direct to those cities, in part, perhaps, because of widespread antipathy toward Greeley's *Tribune* and other northern papers.[74] The *Charleston Daily Courier* insisted that the South and West had been experiencing an "unusual awakening" for several months prior to the New York City excitement. It credited the focus on New York, Philadelphia, and Boston to press attention: "The appearance and decided development of the revival in New York first . . . received the notice of the secular press, and many readers are therefore disposed to overlook other and previous demonstrations."[75] Even so, by April the *Louisville Courier* noted that "large daily union meetings are now held in St. Louis, Nashville, Mobile, New Orleans and Charleston."[76]

The relationship between publicity in the popular press and the spread of the urban prayer meetings, while important, was not one of simple cause and effect. Other factors were involved, chief among them the efforts of the YMCA in many urban areas. Association members often took responsibility for organizing and promoting the gatherings.[77] In addition, after the secular papers directed public attention to the revival, it quickly became a full-fledged media event, involving most means of communication available in the mid-nineteenth century: the mass-circulation dailies, the religious press, religious advertising on city streets, the telegraph, and personal letters. There was the kind of excitement and "contagious diffusion" of news that extended beyond commercial communications channels.[78] Yet, even in light of these parallel developments, the involvement of secular newspapers, reinforced by the religious press, was a major factor in helping participants feel part of a widespread, simultaneous religious event, the closest thing to a truly national revival in American history.

An account of the Louisville prayer meeting illustrated the press influence. One thousand people filled the hall of the Masonic Temple at 8 AM, Friday, March 26. The first speaker used an anecdote from the noon meeting in Philadelphia to challenge the audience to seek salvation. He was followed by a minister who prefaced his remarks with a reference to "reading an account of the glorious work now going on in New York." In addition, the reporter writing the story assured readers that Louisville was not "the only place in which the work of religion is . . . going on. Our exchanges bring us the news of the same thing from different parts of the state." The newspaper story concluded with excerpts from the *Lebanon (Tenn.) Republican Banner*, the *Chicago Journal*, the *Philadelphia Bulletin*, and the *New York Express*.[79]

Sometimes the connection between the flow of news and the increased religious activity was even more direct. H. J. Eddy, a Baptist minister from Bloomington, Illinois, wrote the *New York Tribune*: "Your accounts of the revival . . . have aroused some of the ministers and churches in our little city, and as a consequence there are four churches opened for meetings every day and night, the most of them being thronged to their utmost capacity. Your faithful reports are read in the churches, commented on, and sent from house to house to be read."[80] Yet, overall, instead of clear patterns of news flow, it seemed more as if the initial coverage from the *Tribune* and the *Herald* had opened the floodgates, causing a torrent of print from all sides. These reports, printed and reprinted many times, helped to create an atmosphere of religious excitement.

As the publicity spread, James Gordon Bennett became increasingly petulant, although the *Herald* continued its news coverage. He groused about Horace Greeley "hard at work trying to turn a penny by issuing 'Revival Tribunes' full of pious information and godly news."[81] Bennett stuck with his skepticism and used satire to trivialize the religious interest. He printed tables showing a total daily attendance at city prayer meetings of more than 6,000, then published other tabulations showing that on the same days more than 14,000 New Yorkers went to the theater, noting "it would seem that Satan still has the majority."[82] The editor also appropriated the rhetoric of revival to comment on politics and commerce, celebrating in one headline the "Revival of Spring Business—The Weather, Opera and the Balls."[83] A few others echoed Bennett's refrain. A correspondent to the *Boston Evening Transcript* wrote from New York, "Nature has revived. . . . Fashion has also revived. . . . [M]usic has revived. . . . [R]uffianism has revived. . . . But what are all these revivals compared with that of Religion and of Business."[84] Although not widespread, such comments anticipated the commercialization of the rhetoric of conversion that became popular in American advertising and other arenas of public persuasion during the final decades of the nineteenth century.[85]

For most evangelicals, however, the *Herald* and its compatriots were isolated hecklers in the midst of a press showing encouraging signs of sanctification. "Never before this year has such a significant and encouraging modification been seen in the tone of the secular presses on religious affairs," editorialized the Baptist *Examiner*. Religious weeklies gossiped in their columns that "in the editorial corps of our principal papers are a considerable number of pious and truly evangelical Christians."[86] Evangelicals pointed to the secular press coverage as evidence of the supernatural origin of the revival. Samuel Irenaeus Prime wrote, "With scarcely an exception the daily and other papers make mention of the work in terms which indicate their good wishes for its continuance. Such a state of things is altogether unprecedented and we regard it as an evidence of the all pervading power of the Holy Spirit."[87]

This eagerness to view the revival coverage as the sign of a dawning millennial day for American journalism forestalled any critical analysis among evangelicals of the secular press's role in the revival. Throughout the antebellum period Protestants had become increasingly convinced that the medium of mass print would be a key instrument for inaugurating the millennium.[88] As a result, the efforts of the dailies were celebrated, not criticized. They even inspired two ultimately unsuccessful attempts to establish "Christian" daily papers in New York City.[89] Evangelicals had known for more than a century that revivals were news; now the popular papers had reached the same conclusion. The day when the press would lend its "incalculable influence" to "the cause of Christ's kingdom" seemed close at hand; revival was spreading; God was working.[90] Such an exciting scenario had no place for the possibility that the secular press reports might have unanticipated long-term consequences for popular Protestantism. On the contrary, it encouraged what R. Laurence Moore has described as an increasing tendency for nineteenth-century Protestants to foster the commercialization of religion: "Religious leaders delightedly seized upon market logic . . . because it brought their mightiest dreams for doing God's work into the realm of possibility."[91]

One or two religious weeklies did acknowledge the influence of the marketplace on the mass-circulation dailies. The *Western Recorder* noted that "some of the daily journals of N. York devote several columns to revival intelligence, for which they find themselves amply remunerated by an increase of circulation."[92] Yet no one discussed how this profit motive might affect the actual coverage of the revival. The words of caution that were issued originated among the secular dailies themselves. The *New York Evening Post*, a Republican paper edited by William Cullen Bryant, for years had survived on a modest circulation and had resisted the tactics of the popular dailies.[93] In an editorial on March 11, the paper defended its low-key approach to the revival: "The devotional exercises and the religious experiences and opinions of a people . . . are invested with a character of privacy that ought not to be violated for the purpose of affording public amusement or gratifying the curiosity of the skeptic."[94]

The *Post*'s criticisms honed in on a key element of the revival coverage in the mass-circulation dailies: their tendency to sensationalize the awakening. The popular press, led by Bennett and Greeley, realized that there was a limit to public interest in the standard summaries of revival meetings and conversion statistics as they traditionally had been reported in religious weeklies. Mass audiences wanted glimpses of private dramas of salvation; they wanted to eavesdrop on the prayer meetings; they were curious about the involvement of the famous. One popular anecdote, "Jessie's Gold Ring," concerned Jessie Frémont, wife of explorer and presidential candidate John C. Frémont. According to the story, Mrs. Frémont had attended a Sunday service at Plymouth Congregational Church during the revival. A collection was taken for the poor in the congregation. Having no money with her, Jessie Frémont removed an engraved gold ring and gave it as an offering. Although it was a private gesture, what someone like Frémont dropped into the collection plate had become news.[95]

This was a "soft" sensationalism, compared to the stories of "Dissipation, Degradation and Death," that were the staple of the genre.[96] Even so, it signaled a new trend in the way modern, mass journalism would treat American Protestantism. Religion had been sensationalized by Bennett and perhaps a few others since the days of Maria Monk. However, such reports were relatively few, and they focused on religious figures or groups considered to be on the fringes of society: Mormons, Millerites, communitarians, or early spiritualists. Editors, except for Bennett's occasional jab, had treated Protestant Christianity with a measure of deference. When they published Protestant news at all, it was limited to brief notices of services or meetings and the activities of elites, usually ministers. Such "serious" coverage continued, but the attention to revivalism in 1858 marked the popularization of middle-class Protestantism in the secular press.[97] Sensational or human interest reporting about Protestants became an accepted practice. From a commercial perspective, sensationalism meant that the press marketed revivalism in 1858 primarily as entertainment rather than information. Part of the dynamics and some consequences of this new emphasis were evident in the secular press coverage of one man during the revival, a boxer and petty criminal named Orville Gardner.

Orville Gardner "Joins the Ranks": The Press Creates a "Celebrity Convert"

Today little more than a footnote in American sports history, in 1858 Gardner was a well-known bare-knuckle fighter in the New York City metropolitan area. A native of Maine, the fighter was born in the late 1820s and made a name for himself in the boxing ring from about 1845 to 1855. During that period, according to the *New York Times*, he was considered one of the "pluckiest fighters" alive.[98] Bare-knuckle prizefighting, Gardner's sport, had come to the United States through English and especially Irish immigrants after the War of 1812.[99] Its increasing popularity during the second third of the nineteenth century alarmed northern evangelicals who viewed the gambling and violence that often accompanied prize-fights as sin. In addition, the brutality of the boxing ring contradicted the ideals of a virtuous republic and the millennial dreams of moral progress that were so much a part of Victorian Protestantism. Earnest middle-class evangelicals were appalled by a sport where a human being, the "image of God," was battered by his opponent into a "loathsome ruin."[100] In part due to the opposition of clergy from these groups, bare-knuckle prizefighting was against the law in most states prior to the Civil War.

Nonetheless, the sport flourished as a clandestine activity among working-class, immigrant communities; it was part of a violent urban underworld of bars, gambling, and street gangs. There were also indications that despite official condemnation from pastors and legislators, many middle-class Victorian men were fascinated by the sport. In a society where hard work, responsibility, and self-control were the ideals, men were drawn to boxing's competitive aggressiveness and physical masculinity. Successful daily newspapers formally condemned prize-fighting on their editorial pages, yet catered to their male, middle-class readers by printing blow-by-blow accounts of the most important fights. A series of widely publicized championship contests "made boxing America's single most important spectator sport from the late 1840s through the Civil War."[101] In addition to being the spiritual epicenter of the Revival of 1857–58, New York City also was the capital of American prizefighting at that time.

Orville Gardner was a part of this milieu. He established his reputation with a victory over an opponent named Allen McFee in 1847, fighting 33 rounds in 1 hour, 19 minutes for a purse of $800.[102] In subsequent contests, Gardner earned the nickname "Awful" Gardner, a designation he lived up to outside of the ring as well as in it. In 1853, Gardner made the front page of the *New York Times* after he bit off part of another boxer's ear in a hotel brawl. Two years later, he was sentenced to six months at Sing-Sing Penitentiary for starting a fight and breaking the jaw of a business traveler in New York City.[103] By the spring of 1858, when the New York newspapers focused their attention on the religious revival, Gardner had retired from the ring and was working as a trainer.

On March 4, 1858, only a few days after Bennett and Greeley had launched their all-out revival coverage, the first hint surfaced that Gardner's fortunes and the press interest in revivalism would intersect. That day, the *New York Sun*, a penny paper, ran a small note informing readers of rumors that "a well known pugilist, a clever fellow, but heretofore a hard case, had evinced a deep interest in the salvation of his soul, and was likely to become a Christian."[104] But it remained for Horace Greeley and the *Tribune* to identify Gardner by name and to make him one of the first "celebrity converts" in American history, certainly the first Christian sports celebrity.[105] Greeley did so just one day later, announcing as the lead news item on the revival that "the celebrated Orville Gardner, ... prize-fighter and trainer of pugilists, has been recently brought under the influence of the general revival." Gardner, the story continued, was in a small town outside New York where for several days he had been attending inquiry-meetings at a Methodist church. Observers were convinced of the boxer's "earnestness and seriousness," and reports were that he had "become hopefully converted."[106]

From then on, *Tribune* readers were treated to regular updates on Gardner's unfolding religious pilgrimage. "More About Orville Gardner" announced a headline, Monday morning, March 8, 1858. The article that followed offered details of the fighter's conversion as they had been recounted in a Sunday evening prayer meeting. Fortunately for reporters, Gardner had experienced what evangelicals commonly described as a "remarkable conversion." It was a dramatic story, full of the sensationalistic details that made great newspaper copy. The article told of Gardner's week-long struggle toward faith. At one point, under deep emotional distress, Gardner reportedly was praying so loudly in a private home that curious neighbors gathered outside. "What is that?" they asked, according to the article. "It's Gardner praying for mercy," came the reply. Only a few days later, while riding horseback to another town, Gardner startled his companion by suddenly shouting "Hallelujah!" He apparently had been struck by a sense of God's presence, an experience that carried overtones of the Apostle Paul on the road to Damascus. Soon the transformed fighter was proclaiming to his ruffian friends, "I have got religion." The newspaper article closed with the promise that within two weeks Gardner himself would appear at a New York City Methodist church to give a firsthand account of his conversion.[107] Subsequent articles noted that four brothers of Gardner were so moved by what had happened that they, too, professed conversion. In a separate incident, the previously belligerent "Awful" Gardner informed police officers who sought him on an old charge of assault and battery that he "had become a reformed man, and should offer no resistance to their authority."[108]

Gardner's conversion quickly became one of the publicity sensations and most often reprinted newspaper stories of the revival. "A pugilist of great celebrity ... [has] become a converted man," proclaimed the *Richmond (Virginia) Whig*. Tongue-in-cheek, a correspondent to the *Boston Post* wrote, "Only three weeks ago it was easier to believe that Jonah had swallowed the whale than that 'Awful' Gardner would have become a saint. Yet such he is at the present moment."[109] The *Louisville Journal*, the *Charleston Courier*, and the *Chicago Tribune* were other prominent daily newspapers that carried the story. A number of religious weekly papers followed the lead of the secular press, including the *Examiner*, the

New York Observer, and several regional *Christian Advocates*.[110] The press coverage stirred up such interest that Wall Street lawyer George Templeton Strong noted in his diary a couplet that formed part of a popular jingle: "Ye Saints rejoice, give cheerful thanks/For Awful Gardner's joined your ranks."[111]

While the "saints" may have rejoiced that such a notorious sinner had experienced a dramatic change of heart, the kind of coverage Gardner received represented a new commercialism with ongoing implications for popular Protestantism in the United States. First, the secular press had shifted the focus in revivalism from the changed lives of ordinary people to the conversion of the notorious or the well-known. A new category, that of "famous converts," became a feature of American evangelicalism. Second, the merchandising of revival news as entertainment contributed to an ongoing disassociation of revivalism from its theological and ecclesiastical roots, a by-product of commercialization that reflected changing patterns in the relationship of revivals to popular culture. Third, through their fascination with personalities such as Gardner and with the unusual, newspaper reports solidified the image of the religious awakening as a predominantly male-oriented event. They helped to popularize an early version of masculine Christianity that would be reinforced by the militant piety of the Civil War and that anticipated the "manly Christianity" of the late nineteenth century.

Broadening the Category of Religious "Celebrity"

When a young Boston woman visited New York City in January 1858, she wrote to her cousin from the metropolis: "I went . . . to Dr. Cheever's [church] two Sundays since and heard a very good sermon. I expect I shall float about while in town . . . to hear the celebrities."[112] As her comments indicated, the idea of religious "celebrities" was not a concept created by the 1857–58 Revival. But the usual subjects of such fame were clergymen: in New York, Congregationalists George Cheever or Henry Ward Beecher, Unitarian Edwin Chapin, and even the young minister Methodists were calling their own American "Spurgeon," W. P. Corbit, a preacher who could draw a crowd of 3,000 people on a Sunday evening.[113] George Whitefield, of course, was the prototype for all this, the first minister recognized as a celebrity in America. Fame was associated with the pulpit or platform, not with one's conversion during a revival.

This did not mean that revivalistic Protestants had lost interest in the conversion stories that had been a standard feature of revival literature since the eighteenth century. The dramatic narratives of laymen and laywomen had maintained their place in religious newspapers and tracts during the first half of the nineteenth century. However, for the most part, the subjects of these narratives remained anonymous, a convention that the religious press still followed during the 1857–58 Revival. For Protestants, deleting specific names from conversion accounts increased the didactic value of these stories by making them parables containing universal lessons for the unconverted. It also preserved what many people considered the "essentially solemn and sacred" character of the conversion experience and protected the privacy of the new convert.[114]

To the secular press, these often formulaic narratives of "remarkable conversions" were not remarkable enough. What for evangelicals had once been a "new religious history," one that elevated the significance of ordinary people and their actions, held little novelty for the mass-circulation dailies.[115] In their coverage of Orville Gardner, newspapers linked the traditional conversion story with the identity of a well-known, even notorious, layperson to create the new category of celebrity convert. It was a designation—and a narrative form—that caught on both in secular and in religious circles during the second half of the nineteenth century. By 1910, evangelist Wilbur Chapman would comment that he knew "all the famous converts in America."[116] These stars of the sawdust trail, including converted alcoholics such as former newspaper editor Henry F. Milans, often accompanied Chapman and other revivalists in their citywide crusades. Nearly a century after the 1857–58 Revival, much of the publicity surrounding the 1949 Los Angeles crusade that brought evangelist Billy Graham his first national attention was due to the news value of several professed converts with celebrity potential: Los Angeles television personality Stuart Hamblen; Olympic track star and World War II hero Louis Zamperini; and a former seminary student with alleged ties to organized crime, James Arthur Vaus.[117]

The emphasis on revivalism as entertainment also meant that the techniques of sensationalism were applied to religion reporting. Published accounts of Orville Gardner's conversion epitomized many of the hallmarks of the sensationalistic style, particularly a certain voyeurism that came with the blurring of the public and the private realms of religious experience. For example, the stories made public to a general readership the private details of Gardner's search for faith: his initial complacency, his agonizing pleas for mercy, his dramatic experience of grace complete with the awareness of a blinding white light. They titillated the imagination with the idea of a notorious sinner, a "hard case," a man who had lived by his wits and his fists, humbled into a docile reformation. Reporters also quoted verbatim Gardner's own colloquial language. He spoke of lying awake at night under conviction of sin: "I could not sleep, my sins looked so bad. . . . I wiggled and waggled around on the bed all night; the Lord was striving with me."[118]

Of course, out of a desire to proselytize, evangelicals themselves had for years employed variations of some of the same techniques the press used. Some used sensationalism as a tactic to capture reader interest in moralistic tracts or books, such as the graphic scenes in T. S. Arthur's temperance novel, *Ten Nights in a Barroom* (1854).[119] Revivals, even the most sedate, incorporated an element of entertainment. The ebullient fervor of camp meetings and traveling preachers has been described as "arguably the first, large-scale, popular entertainments in the United States."[120] However theologically questionable they might have been, these practices were developed as strategies designed to attract audiences and to foster the values of popular religion. The skeptical and the curious, for example, could find plenty of amusement on the fringes of the revival service or camp meeting. A group of Orville Gardner's boxing cronies reportedly filled the balcony of the Methodist church while the pugilist knelt at the altar below.[121] Evangelicals tolerated this behavior because such audiences necessarily were exposed to the Christian message and the church community in the process.

When revivals became newspaper entertainment, the values of an emerging commercial culture, especially a concern for profit, began to overshadow religious motivations in the marketing of revivalism. The press coverage of Orville Gardner certainly affirmed Protestant commitments to religious conversion and moral transformation. But just as certainly, the newspapers appropriated such values "and placed them on a cash basis."[122] Cash, whether creating newspaper profits or covering an evangelist's expenses, would play an increasingly important role in urban revivals after 1858. In addition, while the secular press coverage of the 1857–58 Revival did provide publicity that attracted people to church services or prayer meetings, it allowed many others to satisfy their curiosity without ever coming near the actual revival settings. Both the preeminence of the profit motive and the disassociation of the revival-as-entertainment from actual revivals can be seen as secularizing tendencies, that is, as a distancing of revivalism from its original religious context.[123] This does not mean that popular religion was "secularized" in 1858. However, the awakening was appropriated and reshaped by mass-circulation dailies that represented the vanguard of a new consumer culture. During the final decades of the nineteenth century these same forces of consumerism would absorb and transform the religious values that had given meaning to much of antebellum America.[124]

Finally, the Orville Gardner story reflected a third trend associated with the sensationalism of the secular press coverage: newspaper fascination with the conversion and piety of men. Paradoxically, it was also the press, through its more objective statistical reports on the revival, that provided the information to document the presence of thousands of women at prayer meetings and other activities. Women were very much a part of this businessmen's revival. Nonetheless, during an era when pious women seemed to be the norm of a "feminized" Christianity, the human interest angle of this revival clearly lay in the stories of men professing faith in Christ or taking time in the midst of the workweek to pray.

On the surface, much of the initial attraction of Gardner's conversion narrative lay in the contrast between the "wickedness" of his former life and his enthusiastic embrace of Christianity rather than with his reputation as an athlete. A man whose life had been punctuated by arrests for assault and battery was now shouting "Hallelujah" in classic Methodist style and affirming that he "expected to die shouting hallelujah."[125] Even so, some published reports carried hints that Gardner was admired for more than his decision to leave a life of sin. One account, first published in a religious weekly but reprinted by the secular press, described the scene at a prayer meeting where the boxer was speaking: "He is a well built man, evidently possessing great muscular strength and activity, and has a voice which was distinctly heard in all parts of the house."[126] That characterization, coupled with the enormous popularity of the Gardner story, suggests that there was some attraction to the former prizefighter for his rugged masculinity as well as for his new-found piety.

In March 1858, almost simultaneous with Gardner's conversion, the *Atlantic Monthly* published an article deploring the physical weakness of most Americans, particularly American clergy. The author even took the daring step of advocating boxing lessons as a healthful form of exercise that included the additional benefit of training in self-defense. "Not long since," the article noted, "a New York clergyman saved his life in Broadway by the judicious administration of a 'cross-counter' [punch]."[127] The article went on to inform Americans of the "muscular Christianity" that already was becoming popular in Great Britain.[128] Other images publicized during the 1857–58 Revival anticipated the more overtly masculine Christianity that became a common feature of post–Civil War American Protestantism. There were the businessmen's prayer meetings; special meetings for the police and for firefighters; the visibility in New York City of a Methodist all-male revival team called the "Flying Artillery"; and the popularity of the hymn "Stand Up, Stand Up for Jesus" with its militant imagery and its line "Ye that are men now serve him."[129] Although the secular press did not create this more masculine piety, it did publicize such images.

Press sensationalism spilled over into anecdotes about the revival as well. A number of papers dared to print revival "jokes" or popular doggerel. Even the usually staid *Evening Post* added a few notes of humor to its columns, including the story of "A Charitable Sister":

> A young lady, fond of the pomps and vanities of this world, had a beautiful set of jewelry. She became "converted." In relating her experience, she said, "When I had found the Lord, I was convinced that if I continued to wear the jewelry I should go to Hell, and so I took it all off, and gave it to my sister."[130]

The *Charleston Courier* published a facetious hymn directed toward the bulls and bears of Wall Street:

> That sink of sin, the Broker's board,
>   Visit in mercy, gracious Lord;
> Break, thou, their horns and draw their claws,
>   That they may turn and fear thy laws.[131]

This type of informality signaled that there would be no reverent distance between secular reporters and popular religion after 1858. An occasional editor or correspondent would still profess horror at the idea of "Religion . . . being made the subject of 'reports,' anecdotes, jokes and 'profitable matter,' " but most were more than happy to profit from the new style of religious news.[132]

THREE

The Influence of Family, Church, and Association

Personal Perspectives on the Revival

T HE PRESS REPORTS and popular histories provided the narratives and promoted the images that gave the Revival of 1857–58 its public and historical
identity. As with other events and ideas in a culture profoundly shaped by the
printed page, the awakening gained significance when it appeared in print. Yet
the standard story of businessmen at prayer was, as noted earlier, a selective
account and also surprisingly impersonal. With the exception of Jeremiah Lanphier, Orville Gardner, and, later, D. L. Moody, specific individuals rarely were
associated with the revival. Published reports seldom identified the people featured in the many stories of answered prayer or of conversion. In part, this reflected the anonymity of mass urban revivals. Apart from the celebrity and
human interest stories, the news of this awakening centered around the magnitude of its collective appeal, particularly to men: around the reports of
thousands crowding downtown halls and churches to pray. In addition, to
clergy historians anonymity validated the revival's genuineness and supernatural
character. "No name, except the name that is above every name," they insisted.
Jesus Christ alone was to be exalted.[1]

What, then, can we know about the real people caught up in the religious
excitement that affected various regions of North America from autumn 1857
into the summer of 1858? What insights and new perspectives do a broader spectrum of voices bring to the traditional story? Some glimpses from diaries, memoirs,
and other accounts suggest that, although the revival may have been a mass movement in terms of the total number of people involved and the communications
strategies employed, it was far from impersonal. For many participants, the awakening occurred in the context of a web of relationships involving family, church,
and a new kind of voluntary association.

The "Family and Friends" Awakening

Despite her declining health, 58-year-old Methodist itinerant preacher Hannah Reeves participated alongside her husband, William, during the winter of 1857–58 in a "glorious revival of religion" in East Liverpool, Ohio. From East Liverpool, the Reeveses traveled to Cincinnati for a series of meetings in the Sixth Street Methodist Protestant Church. On the Sunday they arrived, William preached and administered the Lord's Supper. But only when Hannah spoke to the Sunday School were "the hearts of many . . . melted like wax before the fire. . . . It was the beginning of the gracious revival that followed."[2]

Hannah preached at a different church that afternoon and filled the next day with conversation and visiting. On Monday evening, exhausted, she arrived once again at Sixth Street, slipped into a pew, and fell asleep. According to her biographer, "Just as she was beginning to enjoy the luxury of a brief doze, her husband tapped her on the shoulder, saying, 'It is time to commence service.' " Hannah awoke to pray and exhort once again. Two days later she spoke a final time and left Cincinnati so weak that the 1857–58 Revival effectively ended her preaching career.[3]

If the revival marked the "crowning labor" toward the conclusion of Hannah Reeves's life, it signaled the beginning of more than half a century in the ministry for a shy young lawyer in New York City. One May morning in 1858 at his wife's urging, Lyman Abbott overcame his reticence and asked participants in the Plymouth Church prayer meeting to pray for his younger brother, Edward. A week later, a letter arrived from Edward, recounting a newfound commitment to God. Lyman Abbott was deeply impressed with this answer to prayer. Although he did not undergo a traditional conversion experience himself, Abbott pointed to the "ministry of Henry Ward Beecher and the revival of 1857–58" as the key influences in his decision to leave law for the ministry.[4] It was the beginning of a path that would lead Abbott to prominence as an influential voice for Protestant liberalism in the late nineteenth and early twentieth centuries.

The revival also foreshadowed the future for a Philadelphia woman, a self-styled skeptic of Quaker parentage. In an attempt to deal with grief over the death of her five-year-old daughter, Hannah Whitall Smith began to attend a Bible class in early 1858. She initially dismissed Philadelphia's noon prayer meetings as "only another effort of a dying-out superstition to bolster up its cause."[5] The excitement sparked her curiosity, however, and Smith attended one of the gatherings. She experienced there what she described as a kind of spiritual illumination and became convinced of the reality of God. A few months later, in late August or early September, she was converted.[6] To Smith, the year 1858 represented one of a series of pivotal epochs in a spiritual journey she later used in books and lectures to promote the principles of Keswick holiness in Britain and the United States.

The future was not as bright for other young people. Twenty-year-old James E. McClellan became "interested in religion" in Worcester, Massachusetts, in 1858, shortly before leaving to attend Pierce Academy in Middleborough. There McClellan attended student prayer meetings and "identified himself at once with the cause of religion."[7] About the same time, he joined the First Baptist Church in his hometown of Grafton, near Worcester. For the next few years, McClellen continued his education and taught school. On September 15, 1862, he joined a company that became a part of the Fifty-First Regiment Massachusetts Volunteers. The regiment spent the first six months of 1863 in coastal North Carolina. McClellen participated in evening "devotional exercises" in camp and established a Sunday school for freed slaves in Beaufort. He had expressed interest in reenlisting and joining an "African brigade," but drowned when a late-night misstep plunged him into the Chesapeake Canal near Baltimore, as the regiment marched home to Massachusetts.[8]

The stories of Reeves, Abbott, Smith, and McClellen provide a glimpse of the varied personal impact of a revival that produced a net increase among evangelical churches of nearly half a million people during a three-year span, about twice as many as during the previous three years.[9] There may have been many others who professed conversion but did not join an evangelical church, a group difficult to measure numerically. Nor can membership statistics measure changes in the lives of people already on the church rolls.

Although the public image of the event was that of businessmen at prayer, references to the revival in diaries, memoirs, and letters indicate its importance to a broad cross section of emerging middle-class America. Ministers, members of frontier churches, urban women, college students—the experience belonged to them as much as it did to the businessmen. Leaders of late-nineteenth-century Protestantism whose early adulthood was influenced by the revival ranged from Lyman Abbott and Hannah Whitall Smith to Moody, missions leader A. T. Pierson, controversial higher critic Charles Augustus Briggs, pioneer missionary Lottie Moon, Confederate apologist J. William Jones, and Mennonite Bishop John Fretz Funk.[10] With little fanfare, professional evangelists such as Charles Finney and Baptists Jacob Knapp and A. B. Earle rallied during the fervor of 1858 to meet the popular demand for preaching and counsel. So, too, did pastors, educators, and theologians, including Francis Wayland in Rhode Island, Horace Bushnell in Connecticut, and John A. Broadus in Virginia.[11] Although apparently to a lesser extent, the awakening also touched people belonging to groups outside the mainstream of Protestant America, including certain ethnic denominations and blacks.[12]

Such a widespread expression of religious interest challenges the narrative instincts of historians, who want a story with a distinct beginning, an ending, and a clear cast of main characters. As a popular movement, the Revival of 1857–58 had numerous beginnings, numerous endings, and hundreds of thousands of participants. In addition to the publicized, urban phase of the revival, many other events were happening at the same time, in roughly parallel fashion. Some began months before the intense publicity; others extended months beyond it.

Despite difficulties in ascertaining accurate numbers, church growth statistics from the 1850s can indicate approximately the numerical contours of this varied religious movement. As noted earlier, the net increase in church membership among major Protestant denominations between 1856 and 1859 was more than 474,000 people, about twice that of the period between 1853 and 1856. Not surprisingly, because of their overall strength, Methodists and Baptists gained the most church members. In 1856, together they represented 76 percent of the total membership of the five denominational groups analyzed in appendix B; during the next three years they accounted for 79 percent of the net total of new church members, more than 370,000 people. Presbyterians made up about 12 percent of Protestants in 1856, and their share of the net increase in church membership by 1859 was 11 percent, nearly 53,000 people.[13]

Yet these and other statistics mask numerous variations between regions and denominations. Gains across the board were most dramatic in the North and most intense there during 1858. Northern Methodists posted increases for that year of 16.6 percent, northern Baptists of 12.8 percent, and Old School Presbyterians of 7.9 percent. Except for the southern Presbyterian churches, which peaked in 1859, gains in the South were solid but less dramatic. Southern Methodists grew by 6.7 percent in 1858 and 3.1 percent in 1859. Even so, the denomination's long-term growth rate during the 1850s was about the same as that of its northern counterpart. Baptists in the lower South reported increases of 5.4 percent in 1858 and 7.3 percent in 1859. Taken together, these rates match the one-year peak in the northern Baptist growth rate during 1858, but southern Baptists fall behind if growth rates in the two regions are compared between 1856 and 1859.[14]

There were other stories within denominations as well. Although the New School Presbyterian growth rate for 1858 was a relatively modest 3.09 percent, it was a dramatic (if short-lived) reversal of the stalled growth and even losses that had plagued the denomination during the decade of the 1850s. Part of the interdenominational character of the revival was signaled by the fact that, for a few, intense years, denominational groups such as Presbyterians and Congregationalists shared in receiving new church members in numbers almost proportionate to their denominational size, in contrast to their long-term antebellum pattern of falling behind the more aggressive Methodists and Baptists.[15]

In its many regional and denominational expressions, the revival, of course, involved much more than numbers. Sampling the experiences of participants "from the bottom up," as this chapter does, provides one way to recreate the personal impact of what happened. What one finds through such an approach is the deeply relational character of the movement. An event described as the laymen's or businessmen's revival might, from the grassroots, just as accurately be named the "family and friends" awakening. On the local level, people professed conversion and were caught up in the spiritual fervor through the influence of mutually reinforcing webs of relationships centered around the institutions of family, church, and the newly formed Young Men's Christian Association.[16] Evangelicalism had long depended on such relational networks in fostering conversion, but the 1857–58 Revival demonstrated their continuing effectiveness and adaptability in undergirding what was characterized as a mass urban movement.[17]

The October 1857 experience of Phoebe and Walter Palmer in Hamilton, Ontario, one of the earliest recognized expressions of the revival, illustrated the importance of social ties to spiritual fervor. During her first evening speaking engagement in the town, Phoebe Palmer emphasized the need for members of the three local Methodist churches to seek the conversion of others. She told people assembled at a joint prayer meeting that if they would "go to work on the morrow to invite their unconverted friends and neighbors to Christ, gracious results might be seen the ensuing evening." Thirty people promised to bring at least one new person to the next meeting and "to invite as many as possible." New recruits, in turn, pledged "to unite . . . in bringing their unsaved friends to Jesus."[18] By the end of a week, revival meetings were crowded, and more than 100 people had professed conversion. The Palmers spent about two weeks in Hamilton and the ranks of the "saved" swelled to 500.

Just like a growing body of scholarship during the past decade, the example of the Ontario revival emphasizes the inadequacy of the traditional identification of revivalistic Protestants and American individualism that has been fostered by images of solitary Methodist circuit riders and accounts of individual conversions.[19] The anonymous conversion narratives published during the 1857–58 Revival, carrying such titles as "Conversion in a Rail Road Car," "Met Christ at the Wheel," "Found Christ in the Parlour," and "The Man that Found Christ at the Lamp Post," reinforced the individual focus, although a closer examination reveals that nearly all of these and other stories happened in the context of personal relationships.[20] The stress on conversion, coupled with a deep-rooted commitment to communal piety, had created a pattern of religious expression among revivalistic Protestants that was both individualistic and relational.[21]

Focusing on the social character of the revival also will provide a fresh approach to understanding the catalysts that intensified religious fervor. Not every town or city enjoyed the presence of a revivalist such as Palmer, although many had ministers willing to devote their energies to revivalism when conditions seemed ripe. In many parts of the United States during the winter and spring of 1858, a constellation of external factors created conditions favorable to intense religious activity on the part of church, family, and YMCA members. Increasing publicity in religious newspapers during February and by the secular press in March upped expectations and helped the revival to coalesce as an unusually intense public expression of conversionist piety. The remainder of this chapter presents a number of the external catalysts that provided the background for the family and friends awakening and then explores the relational dimensions of the revival itself.

External Catalysts: Panic, Politics, and Providence

Richard Carwardine has pointed out the difficulties in attempting to explain revivals "as a product of a particular set of political or socio-economic conditions."[22] No such simple cause/effect relationship has been demonstrated in the case of antebellum religious fervor, in part because each of the various revival traditions in North America maintained an internal rhythm shaped by its own characteristic religious rituals. Even into the 1850s, for example, Scots-Irish Presbyterians, particularly in the South and West, still centered their revivals around festive "sacramental seasons," drawing people from a number of churches to celebrate communion and to hear preaching during the summer months.[23] Methodists transformed some aspects of this Presbyterian practice into camp meetings as a favored vehicle of spiritual awakening. However, revivals also followed other rhythms of Methodist church life, accompanying quarterly meetings and watchnight services on such holidays as Christmas and New Year's Day.[24] Baptists adopted "protracted meetings," days, or even weeks, of preaching and prayer in local church settings.[25] At the same time, these familiar patterns could intensify or adapt in response to external influences, particularly crisis situations, in a society still accustomed to viewing such occasions as evidence of the chastening hand of Providence.[26] Most contemporary observers who did not see prayer as the sole agency pointed to the financial Panic of 1857 as one of the major "preparatory processes" that precipitated the 1857–58 Revival. Yet other elements were at work as well, including the political situation, social pressures, and, even more prosaically, the weather, to create a "window of opportunity" favorable to a large-scale, interdenominational awakening.[27]

They were the "melancholy days," wrote Walt Whitman to describe the financial collapse that took place in the autumn of 1857.[28] Other observers captured the tension and uncertainty in more graphic terms. Wall Street lawyer George Templeton Strong recorded his impressions of the run on banks in New York City on October 13, the day before payment in hard currency was suspended. Businessmen jammed the sidewalks outside the principal banks of Wall Street. "It was a most 'respectable' mob, good-natured and cheerful in its outward aspects but quivering and tingling with excitement. They laughed nervously, and I saw more than one *crying*" (italics in original).[29]

A financial crisis had been brewing throughout the boom years of the 1850s, a period when Americans had indulged in a "national predilection for speculations of all sorts," including get-rich-quick schemes involving commodities, securities, mortgages, and, above all, land speculation.[30] The land boom was driven in part by large-scale railroad expansion. In the decade following 1850, railroad mileage grew from 8,589 miles to 30,793. The federal government was generous with land grants, giving railroad companies 24 million acres between 1850 and 1857. In turn, the railroads financed their operations by selling the land to speculators who gambled that the commercial access and new towns alongside the tracks would increase land values. Not only businessmen were tempted. Thousands of small farmers in the Old Northwest mortgaged their farms to invest in railroad stock or lands.[31] In addition to land dealings, an expanding economy and steady inflation meant that speculators of all sorts were inclined to keep or trade bank notes over long periods of time instead of redeeming them short term. As a result, the value of paper notes outran the metal reserves that backed them.

The first sign of serious trouble came with the failure of the New York branch of the respected Ohio Life Insurance and Trust Company on August 24. New York financial institutions held most of the company's $5 million in liabilities, and they tipped the first in a long line of financial dominoes by calling in other outstanding loans. Money became tighter, distrust spread, financial uncertainty grew throughout September, and rural banks and city businesses began to fail. On September 25, depositors stormed Philadelphia banks, which suspended payment the next day. The stock market fell, and by mid-October New York City banks closed as well; Chicago institutions already had collapsed. Boston followed New York so that by October 14, the collapse was complete.[32]

"These are trying times for merchants and for all classes in the community," wrote the elderly merchant and abolitionist Lewis Tappan. "May God sanctify losses and trials to individuals and to the nation."[33] As the commercial center of the country, New York City was hard hit by the panic with "clerks, mechanics, factory employees, domestics, and day laborers . . . turned out on the streets as employers retrenched or shut down their businesses."[34] Estimates of unemployment in the city ranged from 30,000 to 100,000. Some 40,000 were said to be out of work in Philadelphia and 20,000 in Chicago. In light of these conditions, it was not surprising that attendance at the Fulton Street noon prayer meeting grew in tandem with the financial strain. Businessmen had both the time and the motivation to pray. Even the *Journal of Commerce*, a financial paper, urged its readers to "steal awhile away from Wall Street and every worldly care, and spend an hour about mid-day in humble, hopeful prayer."[35]

As the high unemployment figures suggested, financial distress from the panic extended well beyond the business community. Banks resumed specie payment in mid-December, and the appearance of normalcy began to be restored. But shock waves continued to reverberate throughout the country. Economic stagnation, scarce money, and unemployment extended well into 1858, and throughout the year in many regions. Although the American economy had experienced depressions before, none had matched the widespread severity of the Panic of 1857. It had "the dubious distinction of being the first modern crisis in America history from the point of view of the [economic] suffering it entailed."[36]

As noted previously, businessmen described the scene in cataclysmic terms. "A nightmare broods over society," were the words of Peter Lesley, an employee of the American Iron Association, to writer Lydia Maria Child.[37] Those a step or two removed from the business community were more laconic, yet they, too, communicated a certain desperation. "A gloomy time in business circles," noted Benjamin Adams, pastor of the Duane Street Methodist Church in New York City. "Bought butter, coal, etc—my mind rather gloomy & depressed."[38] Peter Woods, a construction worker and Methodist lay preacher, had even more reason for concern. A chronic eye condition had worsened, Woods was going blind, work was scarce, and he had a wife and two daughters to support. "I was very anxious to get a place for Maria [his elder daughter] with some Christian family, but I did not succeed," he recalled. Woods later recorded his gratitude to God when a minister in the neighborhood, perhaps sensing the family's plight, offered the girl a position helping his wife.[39]

Indications were that the suffering and uncertainty many Americans experienced turned their thoughts toward religion. The Midwest was another area that reeled from the panic. Widespread local revivals began to appear there in late 1857 and in January 1858, a period when the impact of the panic had penetrated into rural areas, yet a time before the noon prayer meetings in New York and Philadelphia had been publicized.[40] A Minnesota pastor made the connection explicit. In describing 1858 as "the first spiritual harvest year of our history," he noted, "[w]e owe not a little to the 'hard times,' so called, for our religious prosperity. A wild spirit of speculation was rife everywhere, and men in the Church and the world were 'in haste to be rich.' That delusion is somewhat arrested by the present stringency, and men begin to seek the 'true riches.' Some of the best revivals are now in progress in this territory that I ever witnessed."[41]

The panic not only highlighted the folly of speculation, it also accentuated rising social stresses in American life. Among them were increasing lawlessness, including violence and corruption, and a vast influx of immigrants, mostly German and Irish. Because they settled in urban enclaves and maintained their predominant allegiance to Catholicism, these newcomers seemed unassimilable to many American Protestants.[42] In addition, lawlessness and immigration often appeared in tandem. The police report for one Chicago district from March 1857 to March 1858 indicated that more than 80 percent of those arrested were of German or Irish descent; only 11 percent were identified as native-born Americans.[43]

As young men in New York City, both Charles Augustus Briggs and Lyman Abbott associated social disorder with the new immigrants. Disgusted with the Democratic sweep of the city in the 1856 elections, Briggs complained that his uncle had lost because of corrupt voting practices: "[Uncle John] had 200 more votes in his ward than he had the last election but the Democrats naturalise[d] 1500 foreigners in the course of a few weeks . . . [T]he foreign vote is enough in this city to defeat the Americans. We dont know what the country is coming to.— So many foreigners overrunning the country anybody that lives in the City sees the necessity of an American party."[44]

Abbott described New York City's 1857 Fourth of July riots in a letter to his fiancée. On the evening of the Fourth he had followed crowds into Manhattan's "Bloody Sixth" Ward, a predominantly Irish tenement area north of city hall that encompassed the notorious "Five Points" with its slums and saloons.[45] From the balcony of a cheap hotel, Abbott watched two gangs, the Irish "Dead Rabbits" and their archrivals, the "Bowery Boys," fight in the street below. They began by hurling rocks and bricks at one another and quickly advanced to pistols and muskets. Soon leaders in the vanguard of both groups—a young Italian from the Bowery Boys and a "great strapping Irishman" from the Dead Rabbits—had been killed. A crowd of nearly a thousand people jammed adjacent streets to get a glimpse of the action. Abbott's own excitement waned when a stray bullet reached the balcony, barely missing his head. "It was the first time I ever saw a riot," he wrote, "and I think it was the most horrible sight I ever saw."[46]

Disorder in the wake of the financial panic further confirmed the association of immigrants and lawlessness. Crowds of unemployed immigrant workers staged a series of demonstrations from November 5–19, 1857, in New York City. On November 10, one mob marched on city hall, and Mayor Fernando Wood called out the police to clear the building of demonstrators. A day later, the militia was mobilized to protect the lower part of the city. Though less threatening than the crowds in New York, jobless workers also demonstrated in Philadelphia, Harrisburg, Chicago, Newark, Trenton, St. Louis, and Louisville.[47] A precise relationship between the labor riots and the revival is difficult to establish. Nonetheless, the demonstrations contributed to a general sense of social instability. In addition, later revival literature repeatedly offered examples of Roman Catholics converted—as explicit demonstrations of the power of God's grace and implicit affirmations of conversion as a sure pathway to Americanization. And the most widely publicized revival convert, "Awful" Gardner, was a bare-knuckle fighter and Bowery thug.[48]

Although the connection between immigrants and lawlessness was often explicitly made, the panic demonstrated that easy money could be the downfall even of respected native-born businessmen. One of the most disturbing aspects of the Ohio Life Insurance and Trust Company's failure was the discovery that Edwin C. Ludlow, the New York manager, not only had made poor lending decisions but had embezzled huge sums from the company's assets.[49] Shortly after the revelation of Ludlow's misdeed, evangelicals were dismayed to learn that Frederick W. Porter, long-time corresponding secretary of the American Sunday School Union, had engaged in similar activities, supposedly bilking the union of more than $88,000.[50] Such news served almost as an aftershock, reinforcing the initial sense of disaster and disarray that accompanied the actual financial and employment losses. Sermons and lectures on such topics as "Dishonesty in Business" proliferated in urban areas. Other preachers simply reemphasized time-honored calls to repentance and conversion.[51]

Not only did the panic bring social problems and the need for spiritual renewal into stark relief, the financial downturn also provided a lull during the winter months of 1857-58, a kind of "liminal time" when out-of-work or financially strapped Americans could reassess their lives and make new plans. "In this transition state," wrote one Missourian, "the word of life has gained access to many ears once closed to Gospel truths."[52] Other factors, including an unusually mild winter, contributed to the sense of a suspension in the normal rhythm of life. On January 12, 1858, "pansies were blooming in the fields" near Boston. A few weeks later an Illinois resident marveled that "winter, out here, has been more like the month of April than December and January." Mild weather extended across the northern states, a welcome change from temperatures the year before, when severe cold had led to a coal shortage in Cincinnati and suffering in many sections of the country.[53] The moderate temperatures favored extended religious gatherings and large turnouts.

Given the increasingly bitter debates throughout the 1850s, a relatively calm political climate also prevailed across the nation during the winter of 1857-58 and into the following spring. Tight money and the absence of national contests during the fall of 1857 kept a lid on political enthusiasms during the final months of that year, except for continued congressional debates over the controversial Lecompton constitution. The most significant political moment came on December 9, when Senator Stephen A. Douglas publicly opposed President James Buchanan on the floor of the Senate over the latter's proslavery Kansas policy. Douglas's speech marked open division along sectional lines within the national Democratic party. Divided, the Democrats would be prey to a growing Republican challenge in the North. Nonetheless, there was a fairly quiet transitional period during the first half of 1858 as politicians worked out the implications of Douglas's stand and continued to hope for a peaceful solution to the Kansas statehood question. Not until the northern Republicans triumphed in the autumn congressional elections of 1858 would the ramifications of Democratic disintegration become obvious and intense.

In much of antebellum America, politics and religion were the primary social diversions and "principal institutional competitors" for people's leisure time. Political campaigns and religious revivals in common functioned as social events, as entertainment, and as moral or spiritual crusades.[54] While certainly not impossible, sustaining the intensity of both at the same time, especially as nationwide public events, could be difficult.[55] A dramatic flattening of evangelical church growth, particularly in the North, during 1856 may have been related to the distraction and "'almost continual uproar'" surrounding that year's presidential election.[56] In the case of the 1857–58 Revival, the absence both of sensationalist politics and Wall Street excitement during the peak revival months from February to April 1858 made press coverage of the urban prayer meetings more attractive than it otherwise might have been to circulation-hungry editors such as James Gordon Bennett and Horace Greeley. If political events in 1857 moved the nation to the brink of sectional crisis, as historian Kenneth Stampp has argued, then the early months of 1858—even through the summer of that year—marked a pause, a time-out, before the countdown toward Armageddon resumed.[57]

The Family Role in the Awakening

For many serious Protestants, the pause occasioned by the political and economic slowdowns of 1857–58, plus an unusual sense of the presence of God in church or midday prayer meetings, represented a special opportunity to seek salvation for themselves or a loved one.[58] It was a chance they did not intend to miss. Some agonized over their own lives. After a Sunday full of religious observance, John F. Funk, a young Chicago clerk, arrived home to record in his diary, "Felt sad and weary. My heart is still unsatisfied. I am forever longing and grasping after something I have not got."[59] Yet more striking was the outpouring of concern expressed for family and friends by people who were themselves already converted. Requests on behalf of relatives flooded the prayer meetings: "a sister in Massachusetts desires prayers for a brother seventy years of age," "a brother for a sister in Pennsylvania," "a mother . . . for a large family," "a minister for four brothers."[60] At a Philadelphia meeting attended by 500 people, the leader made no pretense of even trying to read the requests that had piled up on the table in front of him. He was, however, sure of their contents: "Doubtless we all feel just in the same way for our unconverted friends and relatives."[61]

Such concern was hardly unusual in a society that referred to children as "little immortals" and considered heaven and hell literal realities. But its depth and the family focus do suggest that the revival reflected something much deeper than simply businessmen lamenting their losses. Below its publicized surface, the religious interest of 1857–58 showed Victorian Protestants grappling with the pressures of a mobile society, with a growing preoccupation about death, and with religious changes that had made family members feel increasingly responsible for one another's salvation.

A number of studies have documented Victorian concern for death. Often-noted corollaries have been the rise of a friendlier, more anthropomorphic view of heaven and the coexistent downplaying of hell.[62] However, the widespread sentimentalization of the afterlife so often identified with the Victorians did not peak until the post–Civil War years.[63] During the decade of the 1850s, attitudes still were very much in a state of transition. Particularly among evangelical Protestants, anticipation of heaven was tempered by the knowledge that a conversion experience was the essential prerequisite for getting there. Sacred songs popular in the 1857-58 Revival, including "Homeward-Bound," "The Eden Above," and "The Shining Shore," celebrated heaven as a celestial home. But cautionary hymns, such as "Awaked by Sinai's Awful Sound" and "Sinners, Turn, Why Will Ye Die," persisted.[64]

Well-known novelist and writer Harriet Beecher Stowe exemplified the ambivalence of the period. In *Uncle Tom's Cabin* (1851-52), Stowe portrayed her pious child heroine, Little Eva, as an angel on earth, representing the nearness of heaven. For Eva, the "new Jerusalem" was almost in sight, just beyond the clouds, and heavenly "spirits bright" visited the child in her sleep.[65] Yet on July 9, 1857, five years after *Uncle Tom* was published, Stowe's oldest son, Henry, died. He was 19 and had never had a conversion experience. For all Stowe's romanticized visions of the afterlife, she was haunted by fears of Henry's damnation. She agonized over the goodness of a God who had cut short her best efforts to encourage Henry's profession of faith and "had hurried him into eternity without a moment's warning, without preparation."[66]

As revival interest spread throughout the nation, Stowe was working through her grief and doubt by writing her most autobiographical novel, *The Minister's Wooing*. A first installment appeared in the *Atlantic Monthly* in December 1858. Although the book reflected the development of Stowe's theological thought in a "Christocentric liberal" direction, evangelical convictions died hard.[67] In late spring 1858, as the revival peaked in her brother's Brooklyn church, Stowe spent several weeks assisting Henry Ward Beecher. Quietly, inside the Plymouth Church, she exercised the ministerial role she had long expressed through informal relationships and her writing.[68] Stowe counseled inquirers after the daily morning prayer meeting and paid special attention to young people.

An observer noted that "for several Saturday mornings [Stowe] gathered together, in a smaller room, as many of the young people as were able and willing to join her at the close of the prayer-meeting, for the purpose of instruction, preparatory to their union with the church."[69] The eternal fate of her own eldest might be in doubt, but Stowe was doing everything in her power to assure that other people's children were safely in the fold. In this context, it was not surprising that three "Beecher grandsons"—Stowe's second son, Fred; Henry Ward's oldest son, Henry B.; and George B. Beecher, the son of Harriet and Henry Ward's deceased brother, George—joined Plymouth Church during the revival.[70]

If Henry Stowe's death represented the worst fears of evangelical families, the widely publicized death of Dudley Tyng in the midst of the revival, while also tragic, epitomized the evangelical ideal of dying well. Tyng, 34, was an evangelical Episcopalian, child of a clergyman, and himself rector of the controversial Church of the Covenant in Philadelphia.[71] He was a popular YMCA speaker and had shared in the leadership of the Philadelphia union prayer meetings during March 1858. On April 13, Tyng was involved in a farm accident, severely injuring his arm, which was amputated a few days later. His condition deteriorated. When death appeared inevitable, Tyng accepted the verdict "with the utmost calmness and delight." He reportedly affirmed, "I dearly love you all, but I had rather be with Jesus than with my dearest ones on earth." Tyng bid his wife and two sons farewell, made a final attempt to proselytize his physician, and exhorted his friends to "stand up for Jesus." Then, after asking family members to sing "Rock of Ages, cleft for me," he died.[72] One account of his final hours, written for the Boston *Watchman and Reflector*, closed with the notice of several other sudden deaths. The writer concluded, "Thus God is speaking in His providence, 'Be ye also ready.' "[73]

As the Stowe example illustrated, Victorian society invested mothers with a special moral responsibility to help their children (and often their husbands) prepare for conversion and thus "be ready" to meet their Maker at any time.[74] Though their participation was downplayed in revival accounts, women flocked to prayer meetings in pursuit of that goal; gratitude to "praying mothers" or "praying wives" was an almost formulaic aspect of many conversion testimonies.[75] An anecdote mentioned in a New York City prayer meeting by a man from Kalamazoo, Michigan, summarized the prevailing perception of feminine influence:

> At our very first [union prayer] meeting some one put in such a request as this: 'A praying wife requests the prayers of this meeting for her unconverted husband, that he may be converted and made a humble disciple of the Lord Jesus.' . . . A stout burly man arose and said, 'I am that man, I have a pious praying wife. . . . ' In the midst of sobs and tears, another man arose and said, 'I am that man, I have a praying wife. . . . I want you to pray for me.' Three, four or five more arose and said, 'we want you to pray for us too.' . . . Thus the revival began.[76]

Every man in the revival, it seemed, had a praying wife, every child a praying mother.

Yet, great as the feminine influence over personal relationships and piety, in the intense atmosphere of revivalism *all* converted family members sought to influence their unregenerate loved ones. Within the family context, the lines of religious effort were drawn not on the basis of gender but between the converted and those who had not experienced salvation. In the glow of his new-found faith, college student Charles A. Briggs wrote his sister, urging her to become a Christian, sounding the familiar refrains of relationships and eternal destiny:

> All your friends would be rejoiced to see you a Christian. You yourself would be full of joy. Your life will be happier in this world & in the world to come you will have life everlasting. Do you want to be separated from your brother & sister when they shall be with Jesus? Are you willing to be with the devil in torment?
>
> You might be the means of your father's conversion. O then we would be a happy family united in the Lord.[77]

Far removed from Briggs's privileged world at an elite Virginia university, a struggling Minnesota farmer harbored his own family concerns. Levi Countryman, 26, an ex-New Yorker, found himself unsuited to life on the Northwest frontier, but with a wife and infant son his options seemed limited. In addition to dismay over his own temper and the burden of financial debt, Countryman worried that his wife did not share his Christian faith. He and Alte loved one another, she was a good housekeeper, but she had "no religion at heart . . . and lacks but that to make her a complete wife." The revival came late to Dakota County, but in November 1858, the Countryman family made "a new start for the kingdom of Heaven." On December 8, Alte went forward during a protracted church meeting and Levi could write, "Bless the Lord Oh my soul."[78]

Back on the East Coast, 17-year-old William David Stuart followed in the footsteps of his businessman father, George H. Stuart, by involving himself in the Philadelphia revival prayer meetings and by organizing a mission Sunday school for poor black children. Yet throughout the revival months, he, too, fretted in his diary and through letters over the unconverted state of his fiancée, Mary Ella Johnson. "I fear," he wrote her, "that you are not of the fold of Christ . . . that while God is pouring out His Holy Spirit in refreshing showers . . . you remain untouched."[79] With the intensity expected of an evangelical youth in frail health, and perhaps a touch of brotherly superiority, Stuart also wished that his sisters "had more serious thoughts."[80] By May 1858, Johnson had professed faith in Christ and, on May 28, joined the First Reformed Presbyterian Church.

Part of Stuart's concern over his fiancée stemmed from Mary Ella's plans to leave during the summer of 1858 for two years in Europe. From Stuart's perspective, for her to make such a journey, while she was unconverted, would tempt Providence.[81] For most Americans in 1858 a junket to Europe was an unlikely prospect, but many would have identified with Stuart's fears for the well-being of a loved one separated from the protective influences of family and church. During the middle third of the nineteenth century, people by the droves—especially New Englanders—left familiar surroundings to settle the Midwest, to try their luck in California gold fields, or to seek their fortunes in growing urban areas.[82] These emigrants faced the physical dangers of the journey and of the new surroundings. They also jeopardized their souls by venturing into areas where religion did not yet exercise the influence it enjoyed in the settled villages of the Eastern seaboard.

This situation increased the religious anxieties and the activism of evangelical families.[83] Revivals were the occasions when people would experience conversion and join a church. But families provided much of the prayer, example, personal conversation, and psychological pressure to prepare them for those moments. The prayers and letters of family members followed children or other relatives as they went West or headed for the city. And, as these examples have demonstrated, families were a powerful impetus in the spread of revivalistic fervor.

Local Churches and an Activist Clergy

Families, however, were not the only important social context. Although the home increasingly became a locus of spirituality for Victorian Protestants, local revivals still were centered in churches, and church membership remained an important confirmation of spiritual rebirth. In the conversionist dynamic of the 1857–58 Revival, church and family efforts reinforced one another. Religious interest began in the fall and early winter 1857–58 through widespread church-based revivals.

The efforts of a New Hampshire Baptist minister were typical of many clergymen. In a letter to the *Watchman and Reflector*, signed "J. K. C.," the minister explained how he had begun to visit families and organize prayer meetings in one village: "In going from house to house the writer soon found several persons serious. This feeling increased till about the first of September, when all at once God appeared in a prayer-meeting, at the close of which a number became . . . deeply convicted. . . . The work progressed till some twenty-five have been hopefully converted. The revival influence has remained in the parish till now."[84]

As revivals spread, some churches of different denominations began to cooperate in "union" meetings to meet seemingly overwhelming community interest in religion. While such united efforts were much celebrated during the 1857–58 Revival, there were precedents among antebellum Protestants for this type of interdenominational response, particularly during periods of religious awakening. It was easier to set aside doctrinal differences or local jealousies when ministers felt swamped by inquirers' demands, and when there obviously were plenty of converts for everyone. In addition, their prevalence in 1857–58 also reflected the growing respectability of the populist Methodist and Baptist denominations, as well as increasing evangelical desire to present a united front against perceived Catholic encroachment.[85]

Although the lay leadership in the urban prayer meetings repeatedly was cited by contemporaries as a novel characteristic of the awakening, that observation should not overshadow the active clerical role both in supporting many noon meetings and in sustaining revivals in their churches. Many ministers were like Henry Ward Beecher, who, in the words of one biographer, "resolved to postpone his other activities and devote full time to spreading the new revival."[86] Minister and educator Francis Wayland, pastor of the First Baptist Church in Providence, Rhode Island, was another such clergyman, often frequenting the Providence businessmen's prayer meetings. True to his own commitments to Baptist piety and common sense philosophy, he exhorted the men to act on the basis of accepted beliefs: "You believe that there is a God; that you have a soul which must live forever. Is it not the plainest dictate of prudence now to secure its eternal happiness? Is it not the greatest madness to neglect it?"[87]

Although there was plenty of preaching, ministers, too, understood the role of personal relationships in fostering revival. Wayland, 63, drove himself to exhaustion cultivating the spiritual interest within his own congregation. He preached, led church prayer groups, walked the streets of the city visiting inquirers, counseled girls from a "Young Ladies' School" who attended the church, and sat in on Sabbath School and young people's meetings.

Other "exhausted-minister" narratives, cutting across denominations, belied the notion that the ministers sat back and let the laypeople run the revival. For example, religious excitement in New York City's Twenty-Seventh Street Methodist Episcopal Church seemed to last about as long as did the energy of pastor Thomas Osborn. Osborn, according to later reports, conducted nightly meetings for six months straight. As a result, the church "shared largely in the great revival that swept over the land, more than six hundred souls being converted at its altar."

A person converted during that period remembered how "with marvelous skill [Osborn] marshaled the forces of the church, laboring night after night, and spending the day going from house to house."[88]

At the Bridge-Street Presbyterian Church in Georgetown, outside Washington, D.C., John H. Bocock "labored, prayed, visited and preached for ninety days without intermission," breaking his health in the process. As with Osborn, Bocock's efforts centered on his own church. In addition to nightly preaching and Sunday services, he "visited from house to house and held separate daily inquiry meetings for men and women." Bocock's biographer highlighted 1858 as "the year of revivals," a time when "one of the most powerful works of grace vouchsafed to the [Bridge-Street] church took place."[89] Even Horace Bushnell, who in 1836 had criticized the "artificial firework" of revivalism, found himself drawn into the religious concerns of his parishioners and of businessmen in Hartford, Connecticut.[90] Following the set ministerial pattern, Bushnell entered into the frenetic pace of revival activities, yet it was the intense emotion of the meetings that drained him most. "He realized that in these services, and especially in the prayer-meetings, he 'had been strung up to the highest point of tension.' "[91] After receiving new members at the communion table and preaching on the first Sunday in May, he left for an extended rest.

In summary, during autumn 1857, scattered local revivals appeared, encouraged by the social context of church and family, especially in the wake of the financial panic. There was little indication, however, that these were unusually widespread or part of a broader trend until late December and early January.[92] By January, denominational periodicals were beginning to include extensive "revival summaries" in their news columns.[93] Starting in mid-March, news of businessmen's and union prayer meetings in urban areas increasingly overshadowed the local church efforts. As chapter 2 indicated, the urban gatherings became a national phenomenon, almost a fad, as news of the success of such activities in New York City and Philadelphia spread. Imitators of those meetings seemed to spring up everywhere, at all hours.[94] Even while they did, however, denominational efforts continued, with the union work as an overlay of activity. If they wanted, people could spend their days going from meeting to meeting. Motivated variously by spiritual concerns, curiosity, or a search for entertainment, some did. During the business slowdown, a pious Philadelphia man attended "an early morning prayer-meeting, a noon business man's prayer-meeting, an afternoon union prayer-meeting at three o'clock, a lecture or prayer-meeting in the evening, and an inquiry-meeting after that."[95]

Ministers clearly shared the popular evangelical desire to see men and women converted, and the revival's stress on interdenominational unity helped to prepare the way for post–Civil War Protestant ecumenism. But despite the many clerical affirmations of lay leadership and of the new spirit of cooperation, there were other, competing forces that pulled the ministers' focus back, if not to their denominations, certainly to local congregations and to the ministerial role. One of the most basic was money. Particularly in urban areas, the rapidly shifting population created a "revolving door" effect in many congregations where membership additions often were offset by people who transferred their membership elsewhere.[96] This situation made it difficult for churches to sustain a stable financial base. Church-centered revivals not only improved piety, they usually loosened purse-strings as well.

New York City's Eighty-Sixth Street Methodist Episcopal Church was a case in point. Located in Yorkville, a village a few miles from downtown Manhattan, the church in the 1850s was described as "a way station for migrating Methodists."[97] Those who remained became discouraged, debt mounted, and the church building fell into disrepair. In the fall of 1856, there was talk of abandoning the location. A year later, however, under A. G. Osbon, a new pastor, a protracted meeting caught the flame of revivalism. The meeting "continued through the winter, and one hundred joined the church on probation, of whom all but four were admitted into full membership." By the end of 1858, church membership numbered 185 and a new building, dedicated January 30, 1859, was underway.[98]

The revival also brought 350 new members and added prosperity to Henry Ward Beecher's Plymouth Church. "In January, 1858, before the revival began, the church raised $16,300 in pew rents at the annual auction of seats. In the following year this sum jumped to $26,052, an increase of about 60 percent."[99] Participation in union meetings was fine, but for most ministers, the "bottom line" of revivalism depended on membership growth in local congregations.

This concern for local church life lay behind some clergymen's uneasiness toward the independent, lay focus of many urban prayer meetings. Ministers recognized, though usually in a muted fashion, that a prayer-meeting revival undermined the role of the church by downplaying the place of preaching and the sacraments in spiritual renewal. Dutch Reformed minister Talbot Chambers found it necessary to refute a layman who suggested that "the great power of the Church for the conversion of souls now consisted in the union prayer meeting and the union Sunday school."[100] The idea that the locus of revival centered in such independent, voluntary associations also contributed to clerical ambivalence toward the third in the triad of social systems that undergirded the 1857–58 Revival: the YMCA.

The YMCA: Revivalism and New Social Groupings

The YMCA, a Protestant voluntary society imported from England in 1851, came into its own in the United States during the 1857–58 Revival.[101] Its prominence in the awakening reflected, once again, the tendency for revivalism to flow along the channels of personal relationships. While the "benevolent societies" that had flourished during the first half of the nineteenth century were controlled largely by clergy and oriented toward offering physical or spiritual aid to the "less fortunate," the YMCA was a peer-oriented affinity group. It provided mutual support and religious encouragement, as well as an organizational base, for young Protestant men congregated in cities or on college campuses. It represented an adaptation of the participatory, voluntary impulse of antebellum Protestantism to the social realities of urban America, particularly the increasing differentiation along the lines of class and gender. This differentiation had created enclaves of middle-class men isolated from the traditional influences of church and family.[102]

The YMCA filled this religious vacuum during the revival with an exuberance that alternately encouraged and worried local ministers. They were excited over the sense of increased religious activism among lay men, that is, over the idea that the Revival of 1857–58 was a particularly "male" awakening. On the other hand, ministerial concern centered around whether this new manifestation of voluntary piety ultimately would complement or compete with local congregations. In the heat of youthful zeal, occasional "Y" members lent support to such concerns by claiming "that our Associations were called to enter upon the whole work of preaching the gospel and of evangelizing the world, for which the church and the ministry had proven unequal."[103]

More commonly, however, the YMCA sought to allay ecclesiastical fears by stressing the association's function as a surrogate family. A circular sent to newspapers throughout the country by the New York City "Y" devotional committee took this approach. The letter, dated February 20, 1858, mentioned the successful results of the businessmen's prayer meetings at Fulton Street and the John Street Methodist Church and then appealed to concerned family and friends:

> We would take this opportunity of impressing upon the parents or friends of all
> . . . young men, (who may be one of the one hundred and fifty thousand, be-
> tween the age of sixteen and thirty-five, we have in our city,) that a line, with
> the address, business or residence, directed to "E," Box 3,841, will ensure them
> a personal invitation to attend these meetings, and similar ones held especially
> for young men.[104]

Through efforts such as this, the YMCA, too, sought to participate in the fluid, mutually supportive web of relationships directed toward conversion that church and family enjoyed in nineteenth-century evangelical Protestantism. Two college campuses where the first student associations were organized as a result of the 1858 religious fervor illustrated the complementary roles that church, family, and the "Y" could play.[105]

Both schools—the University of Virginia and the University of Michigan—were state universities, places influenced by religion but proud of their nonsectarian status.[106] Students at the Virginia school apparently were isolated from the effects of the financial panic, but in the winter of 1858 religious "seriousness" was intensified by a different sort of tragedy. A typhoid epidemic broke out among the students; by April more than 20 had died. "It was a year of sorrow," an alumnus later wrote. "We thought more about God and more of God, and of the opportunities we had lost, of doing good to those who were now gone from us."[107] At about the same time, John A. Broadus, pastor of the Charlottesville Baptist Church, held a series of revival meetings. Broadus had taught at the university during the early 1850s, had served for a year as chaplain, and was a favorite preacher among the students.[108] In response to his meetings a revival began in the town and at the university. In April a community YMCA was formed in Charlottesville. Shortly afterward Dabney Carr Harrison, a young Presbyterian minister then serving as the university chaplain, suggested forming a similar organization on campus.[109]

Despite an early summer recess because of the typhoid danger, religious interest remained high when students returned to campus in October 1858. Within days an organizational meeting was held for the YMCA, and on October 12, a constitution was adopted. The association attracted nearly equal numbers of Episcopal, Baptist, and Presbyterian students and served as a central agency to coordinate their various activities.[110] Most popular were prayer groups organized in the student boarding houses near the campus. Students saw themselves as developing "that talent [for prayer] . . . so often sadly wanting in churches and families."[111] During the 1858–59 school year, an estimated 200 men participated in some weekly meeting for prayer, about one third of the student body. Fifty students volunteered as Sunday school teachers in Charlottesville or in outlying "mission" schools.

Although the YMCA positioned itself on campus as an interdenominational voluntary society, it also framed its purpose in family imagery, describing the students as "orphans" due to their separation from home and family: "Those coming here as orphans, in some sense, deprived by the very . . . nature of their relations at the University, of the advantages and supports of a life at home, may still enjoy 'the luxury of doing good' and give evidence of their adoption into that 'house not made with hands.' "[112]

For "Y" members, "doing good" meant encouraging conversions through prayer gatherings or in Sunday schools. As a second-year student, Charles Briggs was among those whose spiritual lives were shaped by this milieu.[113] Briggs's experience reflected the web of family, church, and the YMCA relationships. Even before he was converted, Briggs was urged to join the fledgling "Y" by his uncle, Marvin Briggs. In October the young Briggs signed on as a charter member, and by the end of November he had experienced conversion. Within a week Charles had publicly affirmed his commitment by joining the First Presbyterian Church in Charlottesville; Marvin Briggs had been a member of the church the previous year when he had lived in the community. Charles Briggs threw himself into the campus religious work, becoming a regular participant in several prayer meetings and Bible classes. In letters to Marvin, "he quoted extensive statistics of the numbers of converts and the growth of various Christian organizations in the area."[114] During this period he wrote the letter to his sister quoted earlier, urging her to seek salvation.

With the outbreak of the Civil War, many former Virginia students carried the devotional practices associated with the YMCA into army camps, blending revival fervor with the Confederate cause. Most notable among them was John William Jones, first treasurer of the campus association. Jones, the "fighting parson," served initially as a private, then as chaplain to the 13th Virginia Regiment. He later celebrated the piety of the southern soldier in his history of the war years, *Christ in the Camp*.[115] Among the troops, the YMCA influence was particularly evident in the Army of Northern Virginia during the winter of 1862–63 when makeshift chapels were sites for "circulating libraries and daily prayer meetings, Sunday-schools, literary societies, [and] Young Men's Christian Association meetings."[116]

At the University of Michigan, the idea for a Students' Christian Association (SCA) came from the mother of two of the young men involved. Adam and Edwin

Spence were among a group of undergraduates disillusioned with the tone of the existing Society of Missionary Inquiry. From their perspective, the "so-called reports on missionary subjects made once a month . . . were given in a flippant way and by persons irreligious and even immoral."[117] During the Christmas holidays, 1857-58, when the two brothers and their friends met in the Spence home in Ann Arbor for prayer, Elizabeth Spence suggested that they pattern a new organization after the YMCA, in her words, a "wide-spreading league of Christian youth."[118]

In early 1858 the association was formed, a move that coincided with a growing mood of "deep and solemn thoughtfulness" among the student body concerning religion.[119] With the support of university president Henry Philip Tappan, a minister, the SCA organized prayer meetings and a student visitation plan. On January 21, George Beck, a Michigan student, noted in his diary that "strong revivals of religion are taking place around us and in our midst."[120] The university marked the annual day of prayer for colleges by suspending classes February 24. Beck described the day's activities: "Dr. Tappan gave us a lecture, after which the students held a prayer meeting. In the afternoon a sermon was preached at the Presbyterian church and in the evening a union prayer meeting was held at the Congregational church."[121] Spiritual concern in the Ann Arbor community paralleled that on the university campus: Methodist, Presbyterian, Congregational, and Baptist churches reported substantial membership growth.[122]

The revival period established the SCA as an influential campus organization, a position it maintained throughout the nineteenth century. The group sustained a strongly conversionist emphasis at least until the 1880s and sent a steady stream of Michigan graduates into the ministry.[123] Adam Spence, prime mover behind the founding of the SCA, later joined the Michigan faculty. He became a key advocate for the establishment of YMCAs on university campuses during the late 1860s.[124]

"The Recent Revival"

By June 1858, there were clear signs that the revival excitement had crested, although waves of religious interest continued to affect some churches and communities even through the winter of 1858-59, as the situation at the University of Virginia illustrated. In the deep South, particularly Georgia and Alabama, some revivals occurred in May and over the summer months. In an account published in August, churches in Natchez, Mississippi, claimed that 600 people had professed conversion, about one-tenth of the city's population. In Columbus, Georgia, religious interest also was intense during the summer.[125] Just as the revival had begun in a scattered fashion, so, too, it waned gradually, affected by variables in local conditions, regions, and denominations.

The many individuals who had been caught up in the religious fervor, rarely acknowledging an end to or lessening of the excitement, simply shifted their activities. For frazzled ministers such as Bushnell, Wayland, and Bocock, the change was obvious. By late May or early June they felt free to leave their pulpits and take steps to restore their health. Other people resumed ordinary activities but continued to ponder their encounter with the revival. Future holiness leader Hannah Whitall Smith was among many Philadelphians who left the city to vacation at the Jersey shore. On holiday with family, Smith continued her personal religious quest, noting in her diary, "I have brought my Bible to Atlantic City this summer with a determination to find out what its plan of salvation is."[126] Aided by a tract from a helpful houseguest, Smith spent the summer deducing principles of salvation from a series of Bible verses much as one might diagram a set of sentences.[127]

In New York City, secular newspapers had begun to curtail their coverage shortly after Easter. As early as the following Wednesday, April 7, George Templeton Strong noted in his journal, "Revival less talked of."[128] No friend of revivalism, Strong was somewhat premature in the assessment. His comments did reflect an ebb in the public stir surrounding the prayer meetings, but many evangelicals remained heavily involved. For some of them, the downturn began about a month later, during the annual benevolent society Anniversary Week celebrations when the festive mood of the meetings was soured by an acrimonious split in the prestigious American Tract Society (ATS). The rupture came over the organization's long-standing policy of avoiding any reference to slavery in their publications, a stance that alienated the antislavery sympathizers among the membership. It also served as a vivid reminder that the revival and its vaunted unity represented a hiatus from, and not a solution to, the country's deepest moral conflict.[129]

However, for the majority of New York Protestants—those not embroiled in such issues—the return to a more normal religious atmosphere was largely a function of the natural rhythm of church life. In New York, as in Philadelphia and other urban areas, the onset of summer brought a change of focus to both church and family. City congregations were accustomed to curtailing their activities, sometimes closing entirely, during the scorching days of July and August when everyone who could left town for more healthful locations. The revival accommodated this practice: interest peaked in late spring, new members were received in churches on communion Sundays during May and June, and the exodus for the shore or the mountains began around July 4.[130]

Vacationers were urged to take their piety with them. A letter in the *Christian Advocate and Journal* exhorted readers to establish prayer meetings in Cape May and other resort areas: "If men have found time to leave their banks, offices, counting-rooms, store, and shops, and . . . women . . . their domestic affairs and spend an hour together in prayer and praise, surely we may expect you to spare an hour each day from your recreation to worship the Lord your God."[131] Except for those who combined vacation with camp meeting, only a few organized attempts were made to follow the writer's advice.[132]

Men whose employment kept them in Manhattan maintained the Fulton Street and John Street prayer meetings, but most church involvement in New York City fell off. By July, Nathan Bangs was writing a series of essays on "The Recent Revival," urging Methodists not to settle into indolence but to sustain their commitment to spirituality.[133] Dutch Reformed minister Thomas De Witt described the situation the following September: "We are opening our churches anew, our pastors and our members are returning; our prayer meetings in the churches and our congregations have been invaded by absence."[134] Autumn did see renewed interest in the downtown businessmen's meetings, which were fast becoming institutions as well as tourist attractions. However, there was little evidence of the recovery of revival enthusiasm among churches.

The New York experience was duplicated in other urban areas where religious interest had been evident. Attendance dwindled over the summer at the Boston businessmen's meeting,[135] as well as those in Philadelphia and Chicago. In general, with the onset of summer, spontaneous enthusiasm diminished and the urban prayer meetings became institutionalized, supported by a core of faithful in each place. Fall brought a resurgence, followed by a second leveling. This 1858–59 "rebound" kept memory of the revival alive but only palely reflected the previous year's fervor.

Several city YMCAs exhibited a continuing enthusiasm into the summer months, in part because the many young men in the associations could not afford to leave the cities and enjoyed the fulfillment and diversion of religious activity. In addition, most YMCA chapters had embraced the revival only in February or March, months after many churches had become involved.[136] So their members were less exhausted.

Some of these newly energized associations, aware that the novelty of the downtown prayer gatherings had helped to attract crowds, attempted to rejuvenate religious interest with other attention-getting means of evangelism. For example, YMCAs in Philadelphia and Cincinnati sponsored tent meetings during the summer months, evidence of efforts to bring a stylized camp meeting atmosphere to the urban gatherings. The elaborate "Union Tabernacle" tent in Philadelphia was a "muslin church" that could hold up to three thousand people.[137] As its sponsors had anticipated, thousands of people turned out for prayer meetings and preaching services during the four and a half months the tent remained in Philadelphia. The changed nature of the revival, however, was indicated by statistics suggesting that the interest manifested was more curious than religious. Out of an aggregate attendance estimated at 150,000 people, the YMCA could point only to some 200 conversions.[138]

Although enthusiasm waned during the summer and fall, popular acceptance of the religious awakening had been widespread among Protestants. Even so, not everyone, even among those in the mainstream revivalistic denominations, found the spiritual excitement appealing. Two thirds of the University of Virginia student body, for example, remained unmoved. During the winter months of 1859, 19-year-old Frances Willard avoided prayer meetings at the North Western Female College in Evanston, Illinois. In the midst of a period of religious skepticism, Willard shied away from revival enthusiasm. "I'm afraid I will never be converted," she wrote. "I think I shall never be moved by these meetings."[139] W. K. McClee, a Delaware businessman, admitted that the urban gatherings did little for him: "I have perhaps been benefitted by my attendance. Yet something more than this is required of me. I cannot bring my mind to it. I would do good, but evil's always present with me."[140] Both Willard and McClee participated in the intense religious concern of the era, but they found no relief through the revival.[141]

However, for many other people the scene at the Wesleyan Grove camp meeting grounds on Martha's Vineyard during the summer of 1858 more accurately summed up the revival's impact. As a result of the awakening, 70 new "canvas homes" were added to the bucolic tent city, each symbolizing a family newly united in a shared faith and safely within the borders of church membership.[142] On a personal level, for these Protestants, the family and friends revival had been a success.

FOUR

A "Desire . . . that the ladies would keep away"

Gender Tensions and the Masculinization of Urban Piety

The INVOLVEMENT OF church and family in the awakening at the local level reflected patterns with deep roots in American revivalism and also revealed an allegiance to evangelical values, including a commitment to revivals, throughout much of the nation in 1858. However, while traditional practices continued to prevail in many villages and towns, the face of Protestant piety in cities was changing. One of the most striking new departures, highlighted by the success of the Fulton Street prayer meeting and the spread of the YMCA, was its apparent masculinization. In an era when women often were considered innately more spiritual than men and religion fell within the female "sphere," urban men suddenly seemed to have experienced a dramatic transformation.[1] Typical was the editorial assessment of the *Christian Advocate and Journal* that the revival "prevails chiefly among a class of men who are usually the least affected by revivals—the practical business men [*sic*] of the cities."[2] Repeatedly, observers of the revival pointed to an unusual degree of male involvement as a distinguishing characteristic of the event. Although businessmen received the most notice, religious interest among other specifically male enclaves of urban America—firefighters, policemen, and, in the port cities, sailors—was highlighted as well.[3] For the most part, women were invisible.

While secular newspapers focused on dramatic male conversions, such as that of Orville Gardner, and on men's presence at the prayer meetings, the religious press celebrated something else: the initiative and leadership of Christian laymen in promoting the revival. "In all former revivals," wrote Samuel Irenaeus Prime, "the hidden, aggregated power of a thoroughly awakened laity was not known."[4] No one denied a clerical presence at the urban gatherings, but Prime and others insisted that the work "has been conducted by laymen. It began with them. . . . Clergymen share in the conduct [of the noon meetings], but no more than laymen, and as much as if they were laymen."[5] Another writer went so far as to describe the lay leadership as a novel "order of things." If not a *novus ordo seclorum*, such high-profile religiosity among middle-class, urban men promised to be at least a new order for nineteenth-century evangelicalism.[6]

As we have already seen, the idea that the Revival of 1857–58 represented a particularly male expression of revivalism, a phenomenon described as a businessmen's revival or, more broadly conceived, a laymen's revival, became the consensus interpretation. Late-nineteenth-century analysts, looking at the United States Christian Commission and the YMCA as the institutionalized expressions of the awakening, described the revival as introducing "a new era in the nation's spiritual life," one marked by the activity of laymen in contrast to the clerical leadership of earlier years.[7] Reference to a "businessmen's awakening" served as a convenient shorthand among historians to indicate both nonclerical male participation and the move of revivals from rural to urban settings.[8]

These interpretations were partly correct. Because of their involvement in the downtown prayer meetings and the intense publicity given them by the press and clergy, businessmen *were* the most visible participants in the urban revivals. This visibility, in turn, signaled an important shift in perceptions of Protestant lay piety. During much of the first half of the nineteenth century, church women and ministers were viewed as the stalwart Protestants, while nonclerical men were identified with worldly pursuits.[9] It was a division of responsibilities, some have suggested, that enabled Americans to embrace both laissez-faire capitalism and the ideals of a virtuous republic.

"Pious women would keep their husbands and sons moral; productive men would work to become successful entrepreneurs in order to provide for their wives and children; and together they would form Godly homes, the epitome of Christian progress."[10] In contrast, the revival popularized a different ideal: the Christian businessman as the modern Protestant layman, an image that would rival the powerful symbol of the praying mother as an icon of Protestant piety. Beginning in 1858 and continuing into the twentieth century, businessmen assumed an increasingly prominent profile as the mainstays of public Protestantism.[11]

The narrative of the "laymen's awakening" was not entirely accurate, however, in its implication, as one historian later put it, that "the masses of church women took a backseat in the revival."[12] Although the clergy and the press paid little attention, women flocked to city prayer meetings and seemed to experience conversion at about the same rates as men. If the revival provided patterns of piety that were later institutionalized in the predominantly male Christian Commission and the YMCA, women, too, appropriated and adapted these same strategies in the founding of the first Young Women's Christian Association (YWCA) and later in the formation of the Women's Temperance Crusade (WTC).[13] What was different about this awakening was that women were restricted to the periphery of a publicly masculinized Protestantism. A combination of factors, including social geography, theological agendas, and the press coverage contributed to their exclusion. Although in general women were denied formal church leadership, earlier revivals had often provided them with what Donald G. Mathews has described as "social and psychological space."[14] Through conversion and the intensity of the revival experience, they found both spiritual autonomy before God and a valued place in the church community. In contrast, at the most popular urban prayer meetings of 1857–58, the "space," whether literal or psychological, belonged to men. The much celebrated leadership role for evangelical laymen came at a cost as women found themselves shut out of the public world of urban revivalism. Their story alongside the men's is a part of the businessmen's revival.

Women's Place in a Masculine Millennium

Newspaper reports, church records, and scattered anecdotal evidence all indicate that women responded eagerly to the Revival of 1857–58, even in metropolitan areas. In New York City, for example, women in uptown residential areas crowded prayer meetings near their homes in numbers equal to, perhaps even surpassing, the attendance at the businessmen's meetings. Only three days after the news of 600 men at prayer in the Fulton Street church had made the front page of the *Herald*, a much smaller note on page five of the *Tribune* recorded that "a thousand ladies . . . and more than fifty gentlemen" had filled an afternoon prayer meeting at a Dutch Reformed church on the corner of Fifth Avenue and Twenty-First Street, near Madison Square.[15] Scattered reports on subsequent days mentioned other union prayer meetings that were a "full nineteen-twentieths ladies" or "principally composed of ladies."[16] At the uptown Church of the Puritans a daily prayer group specifically for women originated.[17] Women were energetic participants in the door-to-door visitation organized by various churches during the peak revival period; an exchange of letters in the *New York Evening Post* questioned the appropriateness of young women making calls as late as nine o'clock at night.[18]

Elizabeth Finney served as the catalyst behind a similar interest in prayer among women in Boston, one that predated the businessmen's prayer meeting in that city by more than three months. Shortly after her arrival in December 1857, Finney organized daily "ladies' prayer meetings" from 4:00 to 4:30 PM in the vestry of the Park Street Church, the church where her husband was preaching. Charles Finney noted that "the ladies would fill the room to its utmost capacity, and then stand about the door on the outside as far as they could hear on every side."[19] He later described the Boston revival as a women's movement, "characterized far above all precedent by the individual activity and labour of the female members of the churches. If the business men have had their daily meetings, so have the women; if the men have visited and conversed with individuals, so have the women. . . . In Boston, I have seen the vestries crowded to suffocation with ladies' prayer meetings."[20]

As the religious interest heightened, Elizabeth began an additional daily meeting for women in the Old South Chapel from 9:00–10:00 AM, immediately following the union prayer meeting. The visibility of Elizabeth Finney's leadership and the response from Boston women were recognized in later accounts of the local revival, but neither became a part of the histories written by New York City clergymen.[21] Massachusetts women not only prayed, they also voiced the same general concerns that men did. For example, the revival solidified evangelical antagonism toward popular Unitarian preacher Theodore Parker. Among his letters, Parker saved his reply to a woman, Julia Bridges, in response to her correspondence expressing concern for his soul.[22]

New York City church membership records reflect the religious response among women as well. In a sampling of five active revival churches with extant membership lists, women made up 60 percent or more of the new members or probationers received during 1858 in four of the churches. For example, of the 350 people who joined Henry Ward Beecher's Plymouth Church, 211—exactly 60 percent—were women. The one exception in the sample was the Second Street Methodist Church where half of the new names on membership lists belonged to men. A difference there may have been that a number of Second Street parishioners belonged to the men's Flying Artillery prayer team, and the church was a center for male revival activity. In contrast, two thirds of the nearly 300 people who joined the Thirteenth Street Presbyterian Church were women.[23]

Such numbers, of course, cannot be definitive for the entire revival, or even for New York City, but they support the idea that the majority of those represented in the columns of conversion and church membership statistics published to document the awakening were women. The assumption that the common phrase "heads of families" referred exclusively to men has sometimes led to confusion in interpreting the statistics.[24] Yet as the following news note referring to the Third Presbyterian Church in Newark, New Jersey, demonstrated, the phrase could indicate marital status rather than gender: "It may be interesting to mention that of this number [113 new members] fifty-two were heads of families—twenty-one being married gentlemen, and thirty-one married ladies. Of sixty-one unmarried persons, twenty-seven were young men, and thirty-four were young women."[25]

If large numbers of women were caught up in the religious fervor, why did they receive so little attention in the press and in subsequent narrative accounts? Why did men get the limelight instead? The answers have to do with understandings of urban public space in the nineteenth century, as well as with the religious dimensions of the cultural roles prescribed for men and women. The Revival of 1857–58 took place during a period when the differentiation of urban geography into commercial and domestic space was closely correlated to gender distinctions, although such social boundaries were always complex.[26] For middle- and upper-class city dwellers, the commercial areas were primarily a "public" ("male") domain, domestic space was "private" ("female").[27] This differentiation meant that men and women spent most of each workday in geographically and socially separate settings.[28] Furthermore, with a few exceptions the public spaces of the cities were not considered suitable places for respectable women. As Glenna Matthews has observed, a "public woman" was considered a harlot, while the phrase "public man" referred to an ideal citizen.[29]

Most of the publicity surrounding the 1857–58 Revival focused on prayer meetings in downtown business districts considered male turf. Although the respective percentages of women and men who engaged in religious activities seem roughly similar to those in earlier expressions of antebellum revivalism, even in cities, the men who responded in this revival were much more noticeable, concentrated as they were in enclaves separated from women. Commercial and residential patterns in New York City most clearly illustrate this situation, although the same trends existed on a smaller scale in other urban areas.

By the late 1850s, with the exception of tenement neighborhoods, lower Manhattan had become New York's "business quarter." In addition to offices and shops, the area had theaters, hotels, and boarding houses, all catering to men, while middle-class and wealthy residential areas were located in the upper wards of the city.[30] As a result, few middle-class women had occasion to be in the vicinity of the downtown prayer meetings at midday. One of the early press reports of the Fulton Street meeting acknowledged this practical reality: "There were . . . some ladies, but very few, for the simple reason that this church is in the midst of the business part of the city. The majority of the attendants [at prayer meetings], however, in the churches up town is composed of the fairer portion of the converts."[31]

The distance between the commercial and residential areas of the city also affected the contents of the press coverage. As noted earlier, some of the businessmen's prayer meetings occurred literally next door to the offices of both the religious and the secular press.[32] The Fulton Street and John Street meetings, located a short block apart, were less than a five-minute walk from the offices of the *Observer*, the *Examiner*, the *Independent*, the *Evangelist*, as well as the *Herald* and *Tribune*. A stroll over to Burton's Theater, another highly publicized venue, took only three or four minutes longer. Reporters gravitated to these nearby gatherings. In contrast, the prayer meetings in residential areas were two or three miles uptown, beyond a comfortable walking distance.

Of course, convenience was not the only, or even the most important, reason the press paid attention to businessmen at prayer. In the tradition of "man-bites-dog" journalism and in reflection of mid-century gender stereotypes, men at prayer during the lunch hour were news. Praying women were not. Part of the excitement surrounding the revival communicated by ministers and by the press came from the sense of change, even of reversals, in the usual social arrangements. These reversals were perceived on a number of levels: laymen replacing clergymen in spiritual leadership, men praying instead of women, the secular or business sector of the city coming under the influence of the sacred. To some, these shifts were the ingredients of sensationalistic journalism. Others saw them as evidence of God's Spirit at work. William C. Conant acknowledged the concern New York Protestants had felt as they watched downtown churches close in order to follow their parishioners to the new residential districts:

> They little thought how soon this sad retreat of gospel institutions, before the advance of commercial enterprise, would be followed by a descent of the Spirit which should crowd not only the churches, but stores and theatres in this same "business quarter," with multitudes daily, not weekly, seeking the Lord. The indications are, that the business part of the city will be likewise distinguished as the praying part of the city.[33]

Yet there was more to the invisibility of women in the Revival of 1857–58 than the simple explanation that women were in the wrong place at the wrong time or had been eclipsed by the novelty of male piety. In different ways, the secular and religious interpreters of the event were participants in another reversal, this one rhetorical. In a sense, they turned the ideology of separate spheres on its head to portray male religious superiority. Instead of worldly men and pious women, revival accounts conveyed the opposite impression. Although it contained a backhanded acknowledgment of female devotion, the *Tribune* article describing 1,000 women in prayer at the Fifth Avenue church sounded a condescending note:

> It had been maliciously asserted that these afternoon prayer meetings were so largely attended for the same reason that the Matinees at the Academy are, because there are so many ladies who have nothing to do and fine dresses to show; but the ladies who filled the church . . . yesterday showed by the rich simplicity of their dress that they had another object than to exhibit it. . . .
>
> In . . . prayer nearly all of the vast audience of ladies participated, by bowing so low that scarcely more than their shoulders was seen, and the pillars which support the nave of the church seemed to rise out of a flooring carpeted with sables.[34]

Businessmen were pious for their prayers; women were pious in spite of their fashions. The financial panic might have chastened male "worldliness," as some believed, but from the press perspective it had not had the same effect on women.

Women who challenged the social boundaries and came downtown to attend the noon prayer meetings were subject to even more critical scrutiny. In the Fulton Street crowd, wrote one reporter, were " 'fine ladies,' who sometimes have Christian hearts in spite of unchristian fashions."[35] During the second week of meetings at Burton's Theater, the *Herald* wondered whether the female contingent really had come to pray: "There was a very large attendance of ladies, and it was observed . . . that a short time previous to the hour of commencing the exercises . . . a number were seen to leave Stewart's store, corner of Broadway, and hasten to the theatre to secure seats."[36]

While the newspapers stressed female fashion-consciousness and materialism, clergymen pictured the revival as a kind of masculine millennium. They pointed to the exceptional quality of all-male devotion. Talbot Chambers wrote of the Fulton Street meeting that "at first the entire company was made up of men, and the swell of so many male voices singing lustily the songs of Zion was like the sound of many waters." His final phrase referred to passages in the New Testament book of Revelation where the praises of the redeemed in heaven at the final judgment are compared to the "sound of many waters." When women arrived, the worship became more mundane. "After a time ladies began to drop in . . . and the singing, with their voices intermingled, became softer and more like the praise of an ordinary worshipping assembly."[37]

Both Chambers and Samuel Irenaeus Prime emphasized the superior effectiveness of male piety. The traditional ideal of the praying mother portrayed a long-suffering woman whose prayers followed her husband and sons for years before they were answered.[38] Men, in contrast, brought the same attitude and expectations of success and efficiency to prayer that they did to commerce. As Prime made clear, "These are business-men, and they address themselves to the great business before them."[39] Chambers echoed his description: "While there is no irreverence, there is a promptness, an earnestness, a directness, which allow no dragging, and show that men have come together for a purpose, and mean, with God's blessing, to accomplish that purpose."[40] The results demonstrated that when men prayed, God paid attention. "They were answered with a promptness and celerity never surpassed in the history of the church."[41] Men who previously had "given their country its preeminence in the daring, intense, and unexampled progress of worldly enterprise" now brought that same productivity to prayer. The use of the telegraph—an invention that represented male and, in evangelical eyes, millennial technology—to link the noon prayer meetings in various cities reinforced such views.[42]

The atmosphere of a men's millennium was guaranteed by the tacit agreement among most promoters of the union meetings in New York City that women would not be allowed to speak or pray aloud in mixed groups, that is, in the majority of the prayer meetings they attended. The revival not only occurred in public space, it also involved public prayer. Women were expected to remain silent at the Fulton Street prayer meeting and at the YMCA-directed meeting in the John Street Methodist Church. They were either prohibited or strongly discouraged from public participation at most of the other union meetings, with only a few exceptions. The rationale was that women speaking or praying in public fell into the category of a "controverted point," an area of disagreement between denominations, and therefore was not to be discussed or practiced in the interdenominational meetings. In addition, those most adamant against the practice, the socially conservative Calvinists, also were most influential in controlling the format of the New York City noon meetings and in promoting those meetings as a model for the revival nationwide. None of the interpreters of the 1857–58 Revival, whether early apologists or subsequent historians, acknowledged that one reason the event was a businessmen's or laymen's revival was that the men themselves limited women's participation, particularly in the publicized urban prayer meetings.

Among evangelicals, the issue of women speaking or praying in public religious assemblies was primarily a Calvinist debate. Methodists and Baptists traditionally had allowed women to recount their religious experience, to preach or "exhort," and to pray in mixed company, though neither group accepted women as ordained ministers.[43] The question had sparked controversy among revivalistic Calvinists in 1827 when eastern and western factions had met at New Lebanon, New York, to debate Charles Finney's new measures. The conference split along regional lines over whether women could pray "in social meetings, of men and women, for religious worship." The easterners, led by Lyman Beecher, opposed the idea both because of what they viewed as biblical prohibitions and because the practice violated social order as shaped by the ideology of separate spheres. Finney and the westerners were in favor, based on alternative interpretations of the biblical texts, the demonstrated effectiveness of praying women in the Finney revivals, and the precedent already set by Baptists and Methodists.[44] The Presbyterian Church formalized its opposition in 1832 in a pastoral letter from the General Assembly to the churches. While the governing body approved "meetings of pious women by themselves for conversation and prayer," the letter cautioned that "to teach and exhort, or to lead in prayer, in public and promiscuous [mixed] assemblies, is clearly forbidden to women in the Holy Oracles."[45] That conviction bolstered the position of socially conservative Calvinists 25 years later when they were caught up in a prayer-meeting revival that found its locus in such "public and promiscuous assemblies."

Although there were awkward moments, restrictions on the participation of women did not pose a problem during the early stages of the urban revivals, when the Fulton Street meeting was little more than an unusually popular men's prayer group, unique in its format and appeal to businessmen, yet still only one among many local expressions of increased spiritual concern throughout the country. But gender tensions began to build in late February 1858, when crowds at the Fulton and John Street churches increased dramatically, and newspaper publicity presented these downtown gatherings as the focal point of "a great revival of religion in New York."[46] Women, like men, were drawn to the business district in order to be at the center of the action.

As the revival heightened in intensity, so did the confusion over whether the prayer groups, strictly speaking, were businessmen's (male) or union (interdenominational) meetings. To theologically conservative revivalists, the terms were nearly synonymous, since they assumed that those who publicly participated in both cases would be middle-class men. When Prime wrote of the union prayer meeting as "now a '*type*' " of interdenominational unity and cooperation, he held up the Fulton Street meeting, with its restrictions on women, as the prototype.[47] "Union" referred to a breaking down of denominational barriers, not to unanimity on issues of gender. However, to Methodists, particularly a Methodist woman such as Phoebe Palmer, both men and women should have been able to speak and pray at a union meeting. Palmer had been holding just such a weekly gathering in her home for years to promote holiness teaching.[48] Although there is no evidence that Palmer herself ever attended one of the downtown noon meetings, other Methodist and Baptist women did arrive, with expectations that differed from those of the men in charge.

The restrictions on women also had the ironic effect of making the downtown meetings more attractive to them, even as silent participants. A downtown church or theater filled with hundreds of merchants, clerks, or sailors who spoke of their experiences and offered prayers was much more lively than an uptown meeting with 1,000 quiet women and 50 men. In consequence, growing numbers of women began to arrive at the downtown prayer sites, increasing the overcrowding and sparking some complaints. On March 9, the *Tribune* reported about 100 women in attendance at Fulton Street: "[The women] . . . occupied the front seats, and were very cheerfully accorded their places, although a desire has been repeatedly expressed by some that the ladies would keep away from this meeting, and attend others not so specially designed for business men."[49]

An article a few days later noted that "the number of ladies who attend the John-street meeting is comparatively few, and they sit chiefly in the gallery."[50] By the end of the month, with more women present, that seating arrangement had been formalized "in order that the body of the house may be occupied by business men, for whose benefit the meeting is particularly designed.[51] The description of a union prayer meeting in Albany, New York, indicated that the same practice was followed in other cities.[52] Newspaper reports also provided evidence of a migration of women into the business districts for prayer in Philadelphia and Chicago.[53] Occasionally a man would take preemptive action to make clear the rules of the prayer meetings. At the Duane Street meeting in New York City, another lower Manhattan prayer site, a "gentleman rose, and observed that as that was a union-meeting he hoped that the females would desist from taking any active part in the proceedings."[54]

The large numbers of women who attended the downtown noon prayer meetings despite the tensions suggested that the heightened spiritual interest was sufficiently strong to motivate women to challenge the social conventions that reserved the "public space" of the business district for men. Yet in the midst of the social and religious reversals that accompanied the revival, the prohibition against women speaking and assuming any public role of religious leadership proved resistant to change. Even among women, the majority seemed content to support the revival in socially acceptable ways: by remaining silent, submitting their prayer requests in writing, and limiting their activities to religious efforts within their families or among other women.[55] Others, however, felt compelled to pursue a sometimes controversial activism. The experiences of three women who sought the more activist role—two Methodists and one Congregationalist—illustrate the difficulties such women faced and the strategies they used.

Olney, Palmer, and Roberts:
Women Activists in the Businessmen's Revival

In New York City, the opposition to the public participation of women surfaced most dramatically in the stir surrounding a female Methodist exhorter named Harriet Olney.[56] Olney, who had undergone intensely emotional experiences of conversion and sanctification during the 1840s, was a holiness advocate distressed by the trend toward gentility and order in the city's wealthy Methodist churches. She insisted that urban Methodists needed to recover the "old ways" of an emotive faith and exuberant worship. A familiar figure in local Methodist churches and area camp meetings, Olney was a dramatist at heart and enjoyed speaking or singing in religious gatherings. She had earned the nickname "Shouting Harriet" by persistently voicing her enthusiasm during sermons with exclamations of "Glory to God" and other responses.[57]

In mid-February, Olney began attending one of the first noon meetings sponsored by the YMCA, held in the Ninth Street Reformed Dutch Church, north of Washington Square. According to her account, she came in response to the invitation on a card church members distributed door to door. After attending one meeting, she asked a member of the organizing committee if women were permitted to speak: "He said he thought so, although he did not know that any of them would. A lady present remarked that if I felt it my duty to speak, I ought certainly to do so, as she did not think the speaking on the day of Pentecost was confined exclusively to the men."[58]

Olney spoke briefly the following day and was not challenged. However, when she spoke again at greater length two days later, the leader cut her off, explaining that the meeting was for prayer rather than for commentary. Undaunted, Olney fell to her knees and continued audibly in prayer. When she arrived for the next meeting, a committee member asked her not to speak, "as there were quite a number who would leave and not come again if I did." Olney complied and moved her participation to an uptown union meeting in a Methodist church, where both men and women spoke freely.[59]

At face value, the incident represented little more than initial uncertainties about the boundaries of women's participation in the YMCA-led union meetings, as well as attempts to control a confident, enthusiastically religious woman. Yet when the story surfaced in the *Tribune* a month later, its contours had changed. Olney was excoriated in a way that served notice to other women who might be tempted to speak at the prayer meetings: "At the very outset [of the prayer meetings], a woman known by the rather strange cognomen of 'Screeching Harry,' took part in the exercises, and by her terrific wailings several ladies were taken home sick. The Committee promptly told her, however, that her services must be dispensed with, and she has not made her appearance since."[60]

Olney did not miss, nor would other *Tribune* readers, the significance of the name change from Shouting Harriet to Screeching Harry. Not only did she lose her identity as a woman, the alteration contained a thinly veiled allusion to "Old Harry," a nickname for the devil.[61] Women who spoke in prayer meetings challenged the social order, and they might even be in league with Satan himself. Olney countered with a letter to the editor containing her side of the story and blaming the YMCA committee for supplying misinformation. She also attempted to further vindicate herself and take advantage of the publicity by publishing a pamphlet, "The Christian Experience of Harriet Olney," and placing an advertisement for it in the *Tribune*.[62]

Never one to avoid attention, Olney appeared on March 25, less than 10 days later, at Burton's Theater, an old playhouse that the YMCA and neighborhood businessmen rented during a three-week period for prayer meetings. American evangelicals had long viewed the theater as the devil's territory—a "school of vice" and "a haunt of obscenity."[63] Sacralizing an edifice once used for such purposes represented an apparent triumph for the Kingdom of God, but it left some people feeling nervous. A day before Olney arrived there, the *Tribune* had printed a letter from "A Looker On," questioning "the expediency of the whole Burton-operation."[64] The correspondent feared that the "sensation" produced by the use of a theater would lead to excesses and detract from the "sober, real character" of the revival. He was particularly concerned about the influence of the location on women: "People—especially women—abandon the up town quiet meetings for this new sensation. The movement loses its solemn and almost awful character and becomes a kind of clap-trap."[65]

There was some basis for the caution advocated in the letter. The "Old Theater" was a place where social boundaries between men and women were less well defined than in church buildings, where most of the union meetings were held. The women who traditionally had frequented the balconies of working theaters, especially the notorious "third tier," were prostitutes.[66] In the eyes of respectable New Yorkers, they had left all notions of social propriety behind. In addition, as the *Herald* had noted in an earlier article, the Burton's prayer meeting was particularly attractive to women because it was located right around the corner from the only public space in lower Manhattan specifically designed for them: A. T. Stewart's department store, the first such establishment in the country. Along with displays of merchandise, Stewart's had a rotunda where women could gather, as well as a public "ladies parlor" on the second floor. Whether they wished to shop or not, women who arrived early for the prayer meeting at Burton's could go into the store rather than wait on the city streets.[67]

Despite the fears that frivolous women would flood the theater and ruin the atmosphere, a member of the Burton's committee defended the prayer meeting in a letter to the *Tribune* the next morning. He denied any desire for sensationalism, arguing that Burton's was leased by neighborhood merchants "for the simple and only reason that no other public hall existed in the vicinity adapted to the purpose in view." In an unusual move among the organizers of the downtown meetings, the anonymous writer defended the presence of women. He appealed to the Pentecost of the early church when "all classes and conditions of men" gathered for worship and, in that context, concluded, "nor can I believe it best to adopt the suggestion of your correspondent in regard to 'women.' Against them our doors at least will not be closed."[68]

The message of the letter was not lost on women following the progress of the revival. By 11:30 that morning, 30 minutes after the doors were opened, Burton's Theater was filled to overflowing; women were prominent in the crowd. The *Tribune* noted that "the number of ladies was larger than upon any previous occasion."[69] Harriet Olney was among this group. During the course of the proceedings, after several men had commented on the significance of praying in a theater, Olney rose and spoke on the same theme:

> Fixing her eyes on the people [she] assured them that she had early given herself to Jesus, and was determined to act well her part on the great stage of life. True, the theaters of the world boasted of their stars, but never was there in any place such a star as that which lighted up the hearts of that assembly, and beaconed in the way to eternal joy. . . . As she retired to her chair she gradually sank down with a loud 'hallelujah,' and buried her face in her garments.[70]

The meeting continued without incident. It marked the final recorded instance of Olney's participation in the revival.

Harriet Olney was at most a minor figure in the Revival of 1857–58, but she was significant for her role as the only woman identified by name who participated publicly in the New York City union meetings. The press reports and narrative accounts of the revival in New York documented only five women, including Olney, as having spoken in the prayer meetings. Three of the five were at Burton's Theater and two at a union meeting in an uptown Methodist church.[71] A frontal assault on the religious and social conventions of the day was not a risk many women wished to take. Those who did sought gatherings likely to be sympathetic to activist women—either Burton's Theater, an interdenominational stronghold of the progressive revivalists, or meetings under Methodist auspices.

When Methodist holiness speaker and revivalist Phoebe Palmer challenged the religious restrictions on women in the revival, she chose her terrain carefully. Although Palmer was a lifelong New Yorker and shared many of the same convictions as Harriet Olney, she stayed away from the public sector of the city.[72] As an upper-middle-class Victorian, Palmer emphasized that she had no desire to modify "the social or domestic relation" allotted to women.[73] However, she was passionately convinced that the relationship between women and the church needed change; it was God's will that all Christian women participate publicly in religious gatherings.[74] She knew from the results of her work in Hamilton, Ontario, the previous autumn, that urban revivals could take place in the context of such an egalitarian piety.[75]

The peak revival period of March 1858 found Palmer responding to speaking invitations from churches in a cluster of upstate New York towns, friendly territory, an area where the revivalist and her holiness teachings were known.[76] In addition, in Owego, Binghampton (today's Binghamton), and Union boundaries between public and private space were more fluid than in metropolitan areas, and there were no powerful Calvinist establishments to confront. Even so, Palmer was astute in negotiating between customary gender restrictions and her own sense of ministry. In the three towns, she spoke before both men and women in Presbyterian and Congregational, as well as Methodist, churches, but always with the approval of the minister. There is no record of Palmer leading meetings during her visit where laypeople prayed or spoke in mixed groups.[77] Instead, Palmer herself, in her customary public role as revival preacher, was the most visible example of an active laywoman.

The revivalist did, however, address groups of women regarding their religious "duties." Of such a gathering in Owego, held in a Presbyterian church, she wrote, "It seems to be rather an outspoken belief, on the part of the ministry, that the female membership of the various churches ought to be brought out to pray, and speak, and exercise their various gifts. This extra service has been appointed in view of our . . . advising them in regard to duty on this subject."[78] Palmer's account suggested that at least some ministers in outlying areas where the pool of businessmen was smaller were more flexible in their attitudes toward female involvement in the revival than were clergymen and laymen in the big cities.[79] In her eyes, these upstate ministers rather than the organizers of businessmen's prayer meetings were the harbingers of a genuine awakening, "a revival of Christianity after the apostolic fashion."[80]

Despite such positive signs, the more general public emphasis on a male millennium contradicted Palmer's teaching on women's spiritual gifts. *The Promise of the Father*, written in the midst of the 1857–58 Revival, was her response.[81] Historians have recognized the book as an able defense of women's right to speak in religious assemblies and to share fully with men all other responsibilities of Christian lay work.[82] It had a secondary theme as well, one less noticed. In harmony with Palmer's 1857 call for "a laity for the times," *The Promise of the Father* presented an alternative, gender-inclusive vision of true revival piety.[83]

First, and most central, she built her case for women's activism. Palmer stressed the "Pentecostal argument," the view that women and men alike had been given the Holy Spirit, beginning with the Pentecost of the early Christian church. In the New Testament account of that day, Palmer suggested, both men and women took part in public preaching that resulted in the conversion of 3,000 people. She believed that such activism for Christians of both genders was normative for the church at all times.[84] Palmer was not alone in her appeal to Pentecost in justification of women's public ministry. As noted above, supporters of Harriet Olney and of women at Burton's Theater likened the 1857–58 Revival to Pentecost and used the comparison to support a public role for women. *The Promise of the Father* was, however, the first careful development of the argument and its implications by an American Protestant.[85] As such, it was a landmark apologetic for the public ministry of women in the nineteenth century, an apologetic born in part out of the gender tensions surrounding the Revival of 1857–58.

Those tensions also proved creative in furthering Palmer's thought about the "laity"—her preferred term—required for a spiritually vital church. A year earlier, in a series of letters to the *Christian Advocate and Journal*, she had challenged Methodist ministers to "expect every member, whether male or female, to do something toward saving souls from death." When such a level of lay involvement was reached, "the revival will already have come with power."[86] Now writing in the midst of a revival symbolized by exclusively male piety, she offered alternative models of gender-inclusive devotion and service. In contrast to the press and Reformed ministers' spotlight on the Fulton Street prayer meeting, *The Promise of the Father* provided a detailed description of Palmer's "Tuesday Afternoon Meeting": "Any one has perfect liberty to rise and request prayers, or relate the dealings of God with his soul, drop a word of exhortation, exposition, or consolation, or pour out his heart in prayer or praise. . . . Whether male or female, all are one in Christ Jesus."[87] The only limitation was that participants were expected to have some interest in holiness teachings; otherwise, "the utmost freedom prevails."[88]

Finally, in her book Palmer presented the idea of "Soul-saving bands," groups of men and women who pledged to meet together weekly and to spend 30 minutes each day as individuals in personal evangelistic efforts. The bands could substitute for the exclusively male Flying Artillery team so popular in New York City or even for the YMCA as a social group that used evangelism to foster revival. The first Soul-saving bands had been formed in the context of Palmer's Hamilton revival.[89] By including their story and organizational plan in the book, Palmer connected her ideals of a laity for the times, her experience in the religious fervor of 1857–58, and her apologetic for an inclusive revival piety that welcomed women.[90]

Faithful to the convictions of their Methodist heritage, Harriet Olney and Phoebe Palmer assumed roles that included direct or indirect challenges to the sanctions against women's participation in the 1857–58 Revival. Women in Calvinist denominations, on the other hand, were more likely to work within the social and religious mores that characterized the revival and to shy away from publicity. Except in the occasional context of benevolent activities, a "lady" was not supposed to allow her name to appear in a newspaper, secular or religious.[91] Harriet Beecher Stowe stood out through her editorials in the *Independent* as the only Reformed woman in evidence during the Revival of 1857–58. But even Stowe, an established public figure, soon moved from the limelight to work quietly with her brother at Plymouth Church.

Yet the revival and the religious energy surrounding it did broaden the horizons of Calvinist women. It contributed to the initial impulse that propelled the post–Civil War women's missionary movement, an effort first spearheaded by Sarah Doremus, a New York City Dutch Reformed church member.[92] In addition, a Reformed woman, Caroline D. Roberts, took advantage of the revival enthusiasm to found what became recognized as the first Young Women's Christian Association in the United States. Although information is sketchy about Roberts's life and activities, what is known points to the revival's impact among upper-class urban women.[93]

In 1847, Caroline D. Smith of Hartford, Connecticut, became the second wife of Marshall O. Roberts, a self-made New York City financier. The couple had a Fifth Avenue mansion, an extensive art collection, and a secure place among the city's social and political elite. They also worshipped at the Broadway Tabernacle, the church that had grown out of Charles Finney's revival activities in the 1830s.[94] In February 1858, Caroline Roberts began a women's union prayer meeting that met daily at an uptown Congregational church, the Church of the Puritans. The following November the Ladies' Christian Association was formed, with Roberts as the first "directress." Using a constitution patterned after that of the YMCA, the new association sought to provide practical aid to young working women and to "surround them with Christian influences."[95] By 1860, the association was holding noon religious services for women employed in the printing operations of the American Tract Society and for the five hundred employees of a hoop skirt factory. In June of the same year, they opened a boarding house for students, seamstresses, and others who could not afford the usual cost of "respectable" rooms—seven years before the first YMCA building with dormitory facilities was dedicated.

Early YWCA historians emphasized that such efforts were born out of the religious fervor of 1857–58. In describing the association's religious activities, one noted, "They [the Ladies' Christian Association] were fresh from an uplifting, regenerating, rejuvenating religious experience, which made the whole city of New York a place for which Christ had died, and although timid and hesitant over the ordeal, they found their way to the places where girls were and at a time when they were at liberty."[96] As the post–Civil War spread of YWCAs indicated, the revival helped to rechannel female evangelistic and benevolent efforts in urban centers toward young working women, many from rural areas, at a time when religious activity among the poor had become increasingly professionalized.[97]

A New Public Role for Evangelical Men

The impact of the revival on Philadelphia banker George H. Stuart (1816–1890) contrasted sharply with its effect on the women just discussed. While the circumstances surrounding the religious awakening combined to eclipse the contributions of women, they thrust men like Stuart into new public roles. Like Phoebe Palmer and Harriet Beecher Stowe, Stuart already was an active religious worker by the time the revival swept his city. At age 42, he had served nearly a quarter century as a Sunday school superintendent and was a manager of the American Sunday School Union. The Scots-Irish businessman also was an elder in the Reformed Presbyterian Church and had been the catalyst behind the formation of the Philadelphia YMCA in 1854. Even so, the events of 1858 proved to be a turning point in Stuart's life. Until then, his primary influence had been through philanthropy and behind-the-scenes efforts; in the revival, Stuart became widely known as a Christian layman and speaker. According to the editor of his auto-biography, "It was in the vast public meetings of that year that he discovered the capacity he had of reaching and holding the most varied audiences."[98]

As chairman of the downtown meeting in Philadelphia, Stuart appeared fre-quently on the platform at Jayne's Hall and also served as a kind of messenger to the New York gatherings. In the process, he revealed a flair for public relations. The *Tribune* reported his suggestion that the young men of the John Street church send greetings by telegraph to their counterparts in Philadelphia. They did so and a day later received a reply from Jayne's Hall signed by none other than Stuart himself, back in his home city. A series of telegraphed exchanges followed between New York and Philadelphia, as well as among other cities. The idea generated excitement and publicity and contributed to the sense of nationwide momentum.[99]

Stuart's rise to prominence during the revival, his leadership in the YMCA, and his business reputation all contributed to his selection in 1861 as chairman of the United States Christian Commission, the agency organized by the "Y" and other evangelicals to meet the needs of the Union troops. He held the post throughout the Civil War and considered it "the great work" of his life.[100] Stuart brought the active, public style he had cultivated during the revival to the USCC. He became an expert fund-raiser, synthesizing revivalistic and business techniques to drum up contributions and using the Associated Press to publicize the results.[101] He also delighted in periodic opportunities to work directly with the troops. On one oc-casion Stuart and six others, including Episcopal bishop Charles McIlvaine, were on horseback en route to Fredericksburg, Virginia, when they made contact with a contingent of Union soldiers who had 1,500 Confederate prisoners under guard. Riding ahead, Stuart requested permission to hold a brief religious service, and, by the time McIlvaine arrived, the troops were in formation to hear him preach. A New York merchant from Stuart's group led singing, Stuart himself offered prayer, and the bishop provided the sermon before the troops moved on. This joint venture illustrated the USCC ideal, that "clergyman and layman worked side by side, spoke at the same meetings, [and] proclaimed the same Gospel."[102]

Stuart's experiences illustrated the masculine piety popularized by the Revival of 1857–58, a style of religious activism that later commentators came to associate with a "new era" in Protestant church life. It was characterized by a synthesis of business and religion, an expanded range of public ministry opportunities for middle-class urban males, and the extension of lay religious activism into a public arena outside the boundaries of the church. Scholars in recent years have assigned many of these characteristics, particularly the linkage between business and religion, to the "masculinization" of Protestantism between 1880 and 1920. They assume that until then the ideology of separate spheres retained its entrenched supremacy and that urban revivals reflected sentimentality and the domestic ideal.[103] Certainly sentiment—the shared, carefully controlled religious feeling that characterized the mass prayer rallies—was an important factor in the awakening. Yet it was sentiment within the context of a masculine world. The publicity and ongoing impact of the 1857–58 Revival point to its significance as the most important overtly masculine expression of popular Protestant piety in the United States prior to the Men and Religion Forward Movement more than half a century later.

As the label of a businessmen's revival suggested, the awakening celebrated a new sense of the compatibility between religion and the world of commerce. Revival sympathizers interpreted it in terms of the "masculine millennium" mentioned earlier. They believed that piety would invade and sacralize commercial space and its inhabitants: "We trust that since prayer has once entered the counting-room it will never leave it; and that the ledger, . . . the blotting-book, the pen and ink, will all be consecrated by a heavenly presence."[104] Individual merchants were encouraged to exchange the "tricks of trade" for Christian principles, "to have the same religion for 'down town' which they had for 'up town'. . . the same for the counting-room as for the communion table."[105] There were scattered instances of this kind of change. Occasional anecdotes circulated in the prayer meetings about men who repaid outstanding debts or rectified dishonest dealings. In addition to the prayer meetings at Burton's and the downtown churches, a few smaller groups were established in stores and even in a print shop.[106]

Yet in most instances, influence seemed to move in the opposite direction as business methods were used to stimulate religious fervor. The revival celebrated not so much the religious transformation of business or of businessmen as the affinity between urban revivals and a nascent corporate culture. The structure, organization, and methods of the business world shaped the urban phase of the 1857–58 Revival. The noon meetings were viewed as an appointment with God. They were scheduled to fit into the rhythm of the business day and reflected the intense time consciousness of Victorian men.[107] Prayer, as we have seen, was considered a productive activity. The uniform format for the proceedings resembled an agenda as much as a guide for worship. The directions stipulated that the opening hymn, Bible reading, and leader's prayer were not to occupy more than 12 minutes; in addition, at precisely 12:30 PM, the leader was to interrupt the proceedings and allow those who desired prayer to stand for 30 seconds; and, finally, at 12:55 he should announce the closing hymn, "any one having the floor yielding immediately." The newspapers commented on the "peculiar legislative ability" needed to direct the proceedings.[108] It was a businessman's job.

Publicity posters for the prayer meetings hung alongside advertisements for consumer goods or entertainments, positioning religion as an enterprise that belonged in the business districts. The initiative of YMCA workers in New York City, Boston, and Philadelphia in distributing fliers and hanging banners reinforced the press publicity and, except for presidential campaigns, made the revival one of the nation's first mass advertising efforts. A correspondent for the *Louisville Courier* described the results in Philadelphia:

> Side by side with glowing announcements of 'Selling off at cost,' 'Last night of Dan Rice,' and 'Greatest living curiosity,' you will see in big letters ... such announcements as these: 'Go to hear Chapman preach,' 'Prayer meeting at Jayne's Hall from 12 to 1 o'clock,['] and 'Christ died to save sinners.' Immense posters are up on the street corners; banners are hung out, and cards are suspended to lamp-posts, inviting all ... to come in and pray.[109]

In Boston, Theodore Parker pointed to the advertisements as evidence that the revival was purely "a business operation."[110] Parker meant the comment as a criticism, but for many evangelicals the description had become an accolade. Charles Finney, never shy about the use of promotional methods, chided the New York clergy for not recognizing that they had gotten a businessmen's revival because they went about organizing it "like business men." With a certain satisfaction, he noted, "They took pains to give public notice of these meetings, as they would notify matters of business or politics. They used the appropriate means, and it was remarked almost immediately after, 'Now God is answering prayer.' "[111]

This businesslike approach to revival piety appealed to the evangelically oriented merchants, clerks, and aspiring entrepreneurs who populated the downtown business districts alongside their nonevangelical colleagues. Despite stereotypes perpetuated by rhetoric associated with the ideology of separate spheres, the revival demonstrated the existence of significant numbers of urban men sympathetic to evangelical piety. Although they by no means represented the majority of men in the cities, their status as members of the dominant British-American commercial community made them an influential subgroup, one that until this time had no particular religious identity.

Evangelicals traditionally had seen married men as the spiritual heads of individual households, responsible for conducting family worship. Within the home, they served as "ministers" to the "little church" that was the family.[112] Robert Burns's poem, "The Cotter's Saturday Night," widely quoted in nineteenth-century books and tracts, captured the ideal of the father presiding over religious exercises within the family circle:

> The priest-like father reads the sacred page,
>   How *Abram* was the *friend of God* on high;
> Or *Moses* bade eternal warfare wage
>   With Amalek's ungracious progeny
> ....
> Then kneeling down, to Heaven's Eternal King,
>   The *saint*, the *father*, and the *husband* prays.[113]

In addition, the popular character of eighteenth-century revivals encouraged churches to increase opportunities for laymen. The office of church elder as a kind of "deputy pastor" had grown in importance among Presbyterians by the beginning of the nineteenth century. Elders exercised church discipline, examined prospective members, and took action to encourage vital piety within local congregations. In small towns, the elders concerned themselves with the moral and religious well-being of the community as well as the church.[114] Methodists and Baptists were even more open to laymen, allowing scores of volunteers to serve as part-time local ministers and lay exhorters, although among Methodists ordained ministers retained control of church hierarchy.[115]

However, these roles for laymen in both family and church were modeled after those of a minister and presupposed the unity of a pre-industrial society where church, family, and the workplace were integrated into a common social space. Families, as patriarchal units, composed the community and supported public religion. With the growth of urban areas and the increasing identification of church and family with the private, domestic sphere—a woman's world—the religious role of laymen who made up the emerging middle class became less clear. At the same time, the openness of a democratic society, increasing professionalization, and the lure of commercial opportunities all meant that by the late 1850s, young men who eschewed manual labor had a much wider range of vocational opportunities available to them than existed a half century earlier.

Even in the colleges, traditionally nurseries for the ministry, students seeking success and influence no longer automatically looked toward the pulpit. In 1859, Heman Humphrey, minister and retired president of Amherst College, nostalgically recalled the male piety of an earlier era: "At that time [early nineteenth century], when a student was converted in college, or before . . . , it was taken for granted by everybody, that he intended to devote his life to the service of Christ in the gospel. It was so at Yale, in the revival of 1802. I cannot call to mind a single convert who did not at once ask, 'Lord, what wilt thou have me to do?' and who did not set his heart upon becoming a preacher. . . . How different, alas, from what we witness now!"[116] Vocationally, men were moving farther from the church, into a lay or "secular" world, while the dominant model of lay piety was feminine, that of the "praying mother."[117] Role models for Protestant men were still those who made a career out of Christianity: clergymen or the few missionary heroes such as David Brainerd and Adoniram Judson.[118]

As more and more Protestant men sought their fortunes in urban centers during the 1840s and 1850s, a new body of literature began to appear, mostly written by ministers, extolling the benefits of Christian character in achieving true business success.[119] The books also exhorted merchants to use their wealth wisely and suggested that Christianity and the marketplace could be linked in ways other than marriage to a pious woman. In 1855, Baptist Henry Clay Fish acknowledged "that it is now almost at the peril of his piety that a Christian young man embarks in business, especially if of a commercial or professional character." Yet Fish also assured his readers that there was "no real antagonism between business and piety." Otherwise, "why has God commanded us to be 'diligent in business,' and at the same time to 'grow in grace?' "[120] Harking back to the Calvinist idea of all work as a calling, Fish insisted that Christians could dedicate their businesses to God's service, to "the sublime end of saving men from the power and dominion of sin and death." A person pursuing such a course could be "another bright example of a *business Christian*" (italics in original).[121]

"Be diligent in business," the paraphrase of a New Testament directive, became a recurring theme among evangelicals during the 1850s. It stood both for commercial enterprise and for the need to do the "great work" of God.[122] At the founding of the Providence, Rhode Island, YMCA in 1854, Methodist Elder Robert Allyn proclaimed, "We want laymen to go out and do business for God, and thus introduce the principles and practices of christianity [sic] into every day business life."[123] Historian James Findlay has emphasized the importance of these ideas to the young D. L. Moody, coming of age as a Christian and a businessman in Chicago. Like others of his generation, Moody identified the religious activism and individual responsibility required of an "earnest" Christian with the secular values of the Victorian business culture—hard work, initiative, and practicality.[124]

The didactic literature and the establishment of the early YMCAs, along with the long-standing dependence of church leaders on Protestant businessmen to fund reform efforts, had laid the groundwork for the "Christian businessman" as an ideal concept of evangelical manhood prior to the events of 1857–58. The revival publicity popularized the image, lending it both divine sanction and social legitimacy before a national audience. The revival also demonstrated the practical effectiveness of businesslike piety and, in turn, offered men ways to make piety an extension of their careers rather than an activity isolated from them. In an editorial written during the early stages of the religious fervor, Walt Whitman commented, "Most men who profess religion keep their coats buttoned over it, so that it is only by accident, if at all, that you learn they profess to have any."[125] The revival provided men with acceptable ways to "go public" with their faith.

Although he did not have the institutional involvements George Stuart did, Chicago businessman John V. Farwell (1825–1908) also had been a professed Christian long before the spring of 1858. At the urging of his Methodist parents, Farwell had responded to a camp meeting altar call while still a child. Later, as he worked to establish a dry goods business in Chicago during the 1850s, the young merchant kept the Sabbath faithfully. His diaries expressed a deep Christian commitment and the genuine pleasure he found in attending Sunday class meeting at the Clark Street Methodist Church. On Sunday afternoons, he often visited the services of other denominations: Presbyterian, Baptist, and, occasionally, Episcopalian.[126]

Yet before the revival Farwell apparently was one of the many businessmen whose faith remained a private matter. In the midst of the religious fervor, he was invited to a home prayer meeting by some associates who intended, Farwell suspected, "to help me to be a Christian." To preempt their efforts and clear up any doubts, Farwell decided "to attend the noon prayer meeting in Metropolitan Hall, which was crowded every day, and let every one know where I stood."[127] Although he did not speak during the meeting, the merchant did rise as a public indication of his religious commitment. That simple act became a kind of second conversion experience. Throughout the rest of his life, Farwell emphasized the "necessity of confessing Christ at every opportunity before men."[128] He became a tireless religious worker, a generous supporter of the Chicago YMCA, and the principal financial backer for his good friend, Dwight Moody.

It was no coincidence that Farwell, Stuart, and others like them channeled their newly awakened Christian activism through the YMCA. The masculine millennium ministers envisioned found its fullest expression not so much through churches as through the YMCA, an overtly male voluntary association. To the extent that the 1857–58 Revival was a businessmen's revival, the YMCA was the nationwide "company" that emerged from it. The annual North American convention held at Troy, New York, in July 1859 reflected changes stemming from the increased religious interest of the preceding two years. Nearly 300 delegates from 72 YMCAs attended the convention, more delegates "than at the five preceding conventions combined." The increase represented both the popularity and growing sense of national identity the revival had given the association.[129]

The YMCA provided an institutional setting particularly suited to the businesslike piety of evangelical men. Through its requirement that all voting members be communicants in evangelical churches, the organization aligned itself with mainstream, middle-class Protestantism. At the same time, however, the association's independent status, decentralized structure, and stress on lay leadership offered a congenial atmosphere for young entrepreneurs. Although rhetoric during the revival celebrated lay leadership, in most ecclesiastical settings clerical control remained strong.[130] The YMCA offered independently minded clerks and merchants a sense of Christian identity while enabling them to sidestep the disciplinary oversight, organizational responsibilities, and theological wrangling of the institutional church. They were free instead to focus their energies on wide-ranging opportunities for evangelistic outreach.

In contrast to the settled routine of the Fulton Street prayer meeting, with its close ties to the Dutch Reformed church, YMCA members repackaged the devotional and conversionist emphasis of the revival in a variety of settings.[131] They launched prayer meetings for firemen and newsboys, pitched a revival tent on the Boston Common, and copied the Methodist Flying Artillery prayer teams.[132] Young men like Moody in Chicago and John Wanamaker in Philadelphia became innovators in urban mass evangelism. The fact that Moody was moving from a business career into full-time religious work while Wanamaker, a paid YMCA secretary during the revival, was headed toward a successful future as a merchant demonstrated the affinity of the two vocational paths. Moody could drum up customers for Christianity with the same initiative he had applied to boot and shoe sales; Wanamaker later used the mass advertising techniques he had employed to promote the prayer meetings to market men's suits.

YMCA projects provided the initial outlet for entrepreneurial religious activism, but it was through the United States Christian Commission during the Civil War that the modern male piety became an established and respected feature of northern Protestantism. The USCC gave newly awakened men a challenging task that strengthened their sense of masculine evangelical identity. In addition, it provided YMCA workers with a nationwide social network composed of men like themselves, invested male piety with prestige as the efforts of Christian businessmen were associated with the "great cause" of the Union, and furthered public interest in interdenominational mass evangelism.[133]

Almost simultaneous with Lincoln's first call for troops on April 15, 1861, local YMCA members launched religious work among the volunteers. Young men from the Washington, D.C., association distributed New Testaments and tracts to the five Pennsylvania companies who were the first to reach the capital. In New York City, Vincent Colyer, an artist and YMCA member, assessed the spiritual needs of the Sixth Massachusetts Volunteers as they passed through the city on April 17. A month later the "Army Committee" of the New York City YMCA was organized. The committee held religious services for troops stationed in and around the metropolitan area, printed and distributed 100,000 pocket hymn books, and encouraged "Union Prayer Meetings for the Soldiers" in local churches. In Chicago at about the same time, Moody and his businessman friend B. F. Jacobs began religious work at Camp Douglas, on the city's South Side.[134]

These early efforts were local initiatives and reflected much of the spontaneous style of the 1857–58 Revival. But in the aftermath of the Union defeat at Bull Run and facing the probability of a prolonged conflict, YMCA delegates from 15 northern cities met in November 1861 to establish the USCC, a national evangelism and soldier's aid agency that became, in effect, the wartime YMCA. A number of the executive committee members, including the commission's permanent chairman, George Stuart, and its first secretary and treasurer, Benjamin F. Manierre, had been activists in the Revival of 1857–58.[135] Relying in large part on existing local YMCAs, the USCC opened a central agency in Philadelphia and regional branch offices in strategic urban centers such as Baltimore, Boston, Chicago, Louisville, Cincinnati, and St. Louis. The sites became collection and distribution centers for religious literature and supplies for the troops delivered to soldiers by the USCC's volunteer "delegates"—laymen, clergymen, and a few women—who served six-week stints as religious workers in hospitals, military camps, and at the front.

After a slow start the first year, in part due to old rivalries between different city YMCAs, the commission evolved into an efficient national organization. During the final two and a half years of the war, the USCC achieved a cohesion and national identity that had eluded the YMCA throughout the previous decade. The 47 men who served for various periods on the commission itself, as well as the 5,000 delegates in the field, established relationships that would last into the postwar years. Such was Moody's experience during his four terms of service as a USCC field delegate. In addition to earning a "national reputation as an Association worker,"[136] the lay evangelist became personally acquainted with YMCA members from across the country.

These contacts would later prove invaluable to Moody's success as an urban evangelist. "William E. Dodge, George Stuart and John Farwell were the key leaders of the Christian Commission in New York City, Philadelphia, and Chicago. Ten years later each of them played important roles in organizing Moody's revivals in their respective cities."[137] Not only did they know Moody from the war years, but each of these later supporters, Dodge as well as Stuart and Farwell, had seen Moody-style evangelism prefigured in the 1857–58 Revival.

USCC involvement also gave businessmen who did not enlist a way to blend piety and patriotism in service to the Union cause. To the end of his life George Stuart cherished a handwritten note from Abraham Lincoln commending the efforts of the Christian Commission. Both Stuart and Farwell fondly recalled crisis moments during the war when each used his particular executive skills to ease hardships among the troops. For example, in July 1863, during a USCC meeting at Saratoga Springs, New York, Stuart received a telegram from a naval officer engaged in the siege of Charleston. It read, "For God's sake send us a cargo of ice, as our men are dying for want of cooling drinks." Lacking available funds, Stuart visited the dining rooms of three nearby resort hotels and appealed to the guests. By the end of the dinner hour, he had raised enough money "to have a vessel chartered for Charleston, and loaded with ice, lemons, and other materials for making cooling drinks."[138] For his part, Farwell told of buying "all the codfish in Chicago" as a remedy for the chronic intestinal complaints of soldiers fighting in Tennessee; on another occasion he purchased the city's inventory of woolen gloves. "Neither . . . was regulation army rations or clothing, but they were much appreciated by sick and freezing soldiers."[139] Just as organizational skills were required to run a union prayer meeting, only executive ability could get things done in wartime.

At the field level, the instructions made clear that USCC service was a man's job, requiring volunteers with aptitudes for *"Preaching, Business, and Working"* (italics in the original). Ministers were welcome, but "quite as indispensable. . . . [are] those who have a knowledge of the world, experience in business, and ability in affairs." It was assumed that all would share the characteristics of "piety and patriotism, good common sense and energy."[140] Because the workers over-whelmingly were men, experienced in some of the hardships of military life, and engaged in religious work specifically directed toward men, their presence among the troops strengthened the link between masculinity and evangelicalism.[141] Many of the tracts distributed in the army had military themes, and delegates tried to masculinize their evangelistic techniques through such methods as distributing packages of "Scripture cards" that could be used for games instead of the omni-present decks of ordinary playing cards.[142] These gestures, as well as the real serv-ices USCC agents rendered to lonely, wounded, and dying men, created a reservoir of goodwill toward the YMCA and businesslike Christianity that extended into the postwar years.[143]

Finally, the USCC not only strengthened the subculture of masculine evangelical piety, it also reinforced the association between such piety and the interdenomi-national mass evangelism popularized through the Revival of 1857–58. Many of the actual methods used by Christian commission delegates to proselytize soldiers were not new. Methodists, Baptists, and benevolent society colporteurs all had engaged in itinerant preaching, prayer meetings, and literature distribution throughout the first half of the nineteenth century. During the war, as in the earlier revival, standardized versions of these tactics were embraced by middle-class men and employed in an overtly nonsectarian, public context to reach a specific, target audience. These evangelists, lay and clerical, carried out their work in the midst of the largest male enclave the country had ever seen, the Union army, and they did so under the badge of the *United States* Christian Commission. The very name implied belief in a common American Christianity, not only expressed through the formal rhetoric of a national civil religion, but also in the shared middle-class evangelicalism of the USCC volunteer.[144] Soldiers and Christian Commission workers alike practiced this faith in interdenominational "chapel tents" and in YMCA "rooms" near base camps rather than in churches. Lay male piety brought religion into such public places, both in the army and in urban centers.

Toward the Manly Christianity of the Late Nineteenth Century

In her study of the Men and Religion Forward Movement of 1911–1912 as an expression of the masculinization of middle-class Protestantism, Gail Bederman has pointed to two key strategies organizers used to make religion attractive to men. The first involved efforts to "defeminize" Protestantism by aligning it "to the masculine world of business" through advertising campaigns and efficient organizational practices. The second was the attempt to find challenges within the context of Protestant Christianity great enough to capture the imaginations of ambitious men, "church work manly enough for men to do."[145] Yet the Men and Religion Forward campaign was not a new departure, but rather an attempt to recover the piety of a half century earlier. Both elements were already present in the Revival of 1857–58 and its sequel, the evangelistic outreach of the USCC during the Civil War. Coupled with newspaper publicity extolling the public piety of urban businessmen, they helped to popularize a new ideal of Christian manhood: the Christian businessman as a lay activist.

This subculture of evangelical male piety became a progenitor of the more militant manly Christianity of the late nineteenth century. During the 1860s and 1870s, it flourished in the context of the YMCA, whose massive buildings in urban business districts bore testimony to the presence of Protestant male piety in the public arena.[146] It made inroads in various denominations as well and in the renaissance of the Sunday school movement. Laymen's organizations appeared in Baptist churches as early as 1864, and by 1874 a national convention was held in Brooklyn to consider the role of laymen in the denomination.[147] Methodists, in both North and South, voted to give laymen representation in the decision-making structures of the church in the years immediately following the Civil War.[148] Businessmen "alumni" of the 1857–58 Revival also sought to make Sunday schools more efficient. Produce dealer and real estate investor B. F. Jacobs was "the first Sunday school expansionist."[149] In 1868 he began to advocate standard lessons and teacher preparation materials that would be used by schools worldwide. This led to the development of the International Uniform Lesson curriculum of the International Sunday School Conventions. John Wanamaker furthered the effort in 1871 by purchasing the *Sunday School Times*, a struggling weekly paper, and providing the financial backing that made the paper a powerful influence for standardized Sunday School work.[150]

Although not emphasized in this chapter, the Revival of 1857–58 also contributed to a corresponding upsurge of male piety within southern evangelicalism. Its symbol was the pious soldier and later the war veteran/revivalist who synthesized conversionist piety, manliness, and the "lost cause" into a particular southern religious ethos.[151] Reflecting the cultural setting of the South, this model developed roughly parallel to its northern counterpart. However, the isolation of the region after the war, together with northern industrial, political, and religious dominance, helped to make the image of the successful Christian businessman the prevailing ideal of modern evangelical piety.

The presence of an overtly masculine lay piety in evangelicalism prior to the Civil War challenges interpretations that explain the religious "gender coding" of midcentury Protestants in terms of pious women and capitalist men. Although in absolute numbers the middle-class Protestantism of the nineteenth century continued to attract more women than men, it displayed a characteristic flexibility in adapting to the values and rhetoric of home *and* marketplace.[152] On occasion, evangelicals of both genders appropriated language from the other to accomplish their purposes. YMCA chapters often spoke of their meeting rooms as providing a "substitute . . . for the domestic circle, and the family altar."[153] In contrast, Annie Wittenmyer (1827–1900), an Iowa woman whose executive abilities easily equaled those of male Christian Commission leaders, insisted that the women in charge of the special diet kitchens for wounded soldiers sponsored by the USCC be given a written "Manager's Commission," certifying their authority and duties.[154]

However, as this chapter has shown, the fact that evangelical piety did not always correspond exactly to the ideology of separate spheres did not mean that it had no gender coding or that it was not affected by the gender-based mores of the broader culture. The existence of a male subculture of businesslike Christianity probably contributed to the tendency of national voluntary societies to organize along gender lines during the post–Civil War years. This separatism was evident in temperance crusades, in the missionary movement, and in the young men's and young women's associations.[155] Anne Scott has suggested that "condescension and opposition" from Protestant men "may have been one reason so many [women] turned their energies to the WCTU and the YWCA where there were no men to hamper them."[156]

A key element of D. L. Moody's appeal to popular, middle-class audiences may have been his ability to synthesize the Victorian business culture with Victorian sentimentalism, that is, to bring together masculine and feminine evangelicalism. The synthesis reflected the personalities of Moody and his associate and song leader Ira Sankey. Both were admired for their masculinity. Moody with his beard and bulky physique was described during the 1870s as a "muscular Christian." Sankey, others wrote, "might easily be taken for a middle-aged merchant or professional man." Clean-shaven, better looking than Moody, he introduced an element of masculine sex appeal to the revival platform.[157] Yet especially in the religious context of an evangelistic campaign, each man also was comfortable with open expressions of feeling, even tears, that is, in twentieth-century terms, his feminine side.

As Sandra Sizer [Frankiel] has demonstrated, both preaching and song in the Moody/Sankey revivals used images of domesticity to create the "community of feeling" conducive to evangelical conversions.[158] Part of Moody's success was his ability to combine the order and efficiency of businesslike Christianity with the religious sentiment and human warmth of the domestic ideal. In ways that have yet to be fully explored, both the "Christian businessman" and the "praying mother" were present in the Moody campaigns. His meetings reflected an enduring evangelical attachment to feminine religious exceptionalism as well as the increasing influence of lay male piety. They also made clear that, in terms of the public character and organization of modern revivals, the businessmen had taken charge.

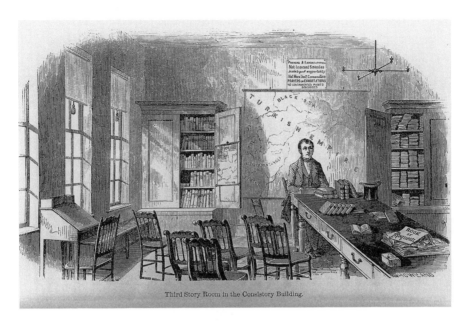

Third Story Room in the Consistory Building.

FIGURE 1. A lone man in an "upper room": Jeremiah Lanphier, businessman-turned-city missionary, waited in a third-floor meeting room for the handful of participants who attended the first noon prayer meetings in late September 1857 at the North Dutch [Reformed] Church on Fulton Street in lower Manhattan. From Talbot W. Chambers, *The Noon Prayer Meeting of the North Dutch Church.*

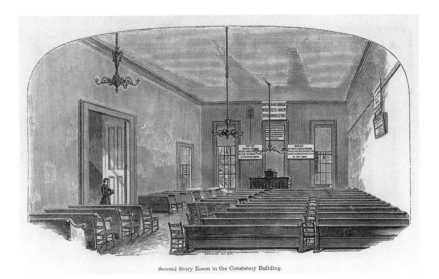

Second Story Room in the Consistory Building.

FIGURE 2. A new location: As attendance grew in early October 1857, the Fulton Street prayer meeting was moved down a floor to a second-story lecture room in the same church building. Placards at the front and sides of the room explained the procedures and rules of the meeting. During the peak revival period in March 1858, rooms on all three floors of the church were filled as an estimated 600 people crowded in each day to pray. From Chambers, *The Noon Prayer Meeting.*

FIGURE 3. As the revival fervor spread, middle- and upper-class women began to join businessmen for daily prayer from noon to one o'clock at the Fulton Street church. Although women were allowed to attend, they were asked to refrain from praying audibly and from engaging in any other form of public speaking. From Chambers, *The Noon Prayer Meeting.*

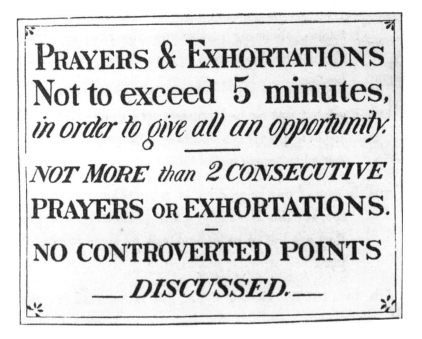

FIGURE 4. Written guidelines ensured orderly, businesslike prayer meetings, evidence of the "formalist" character of urban, middle-class revivals. During the Revival of 1857–58, "controverted" (controversial) points included comments concerning slavery and its abolition or whether women should be permitted to pray aloud in interdenominational prayer meetings. From Chambers, *The Noon Prayer Meeting.*

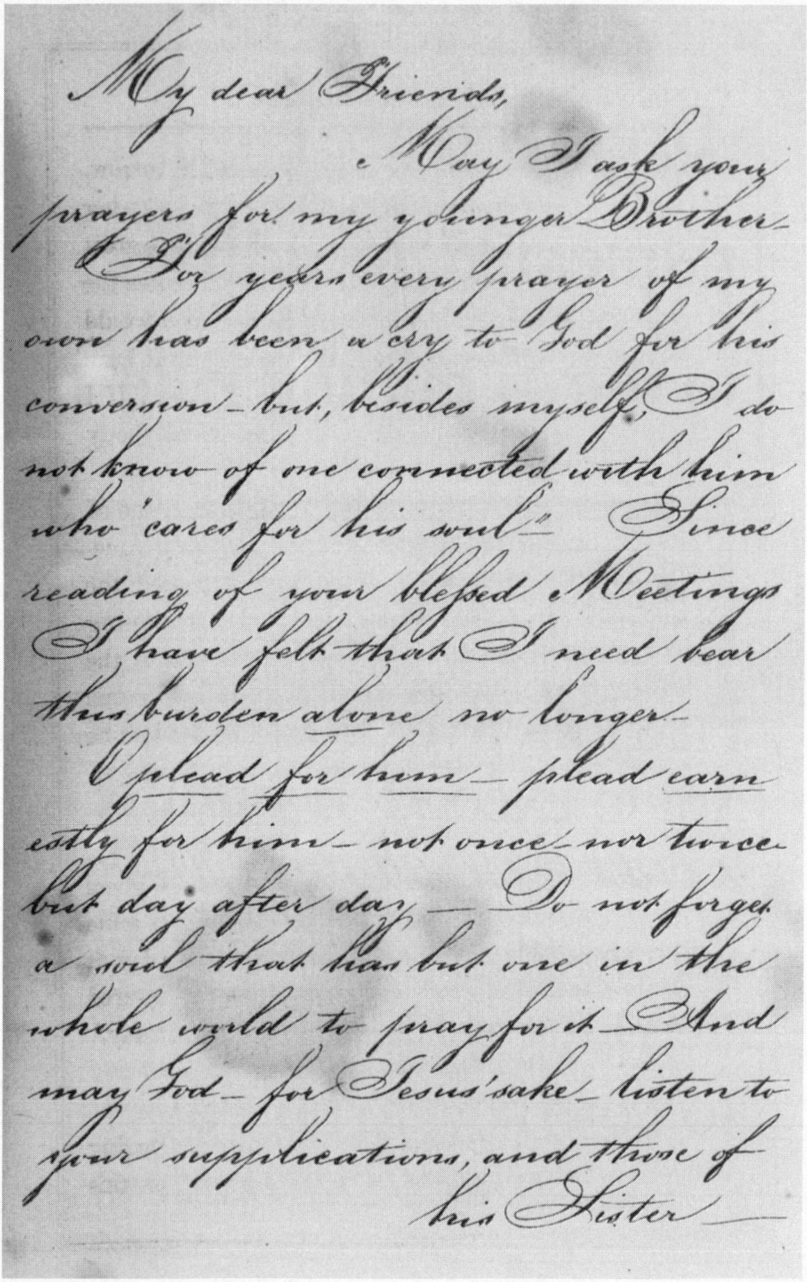

My dear Friends,

May I ask your prayers for my younger Brother — For years every prayer of my own has been a cry to God for his conversion — but, besides myself, I do not know of one connected with him who cares for his soul. Since reading of your blessed Meetings I have felt that I need bear this burden alone no longer —

O plead for him — plead earnestly for him — not once — nor twice but day after day — Do not forget a soul that has but one in the whole world to pray for it — And may God — for Jesus' sake — listen to your supplications, and those of

his Sister —

FIGURE 5. "O plead for him." Written prayer requests from family members flooded the revival meetings. In this note, a woman sought prayers for the conversion of her brother. From Chambers, *The Noon Prayer Meeting*.

FIGURE 6. The "Union Tabernacle," a tent in Philadelphia that could hold up to three thousand people for revival prayer meetings, foreshadowed the "tabernacles" or special structures built for later urban revivalists. From Edwin M. Long, *The Union Tabernacle*.

FIGURE 7. Inside the Union Tabernacle: Child evangelism was one focus of the tent meetings. Here local ministers on the platform and an audience of adults appear to be acknowledging pious children. From Long, *The Union Tabernacle*.

FIGURES 8 AND 9. Evenly matched: The involvement of couples Phoebe and Walter Palmer (*top*) and Elizabeth and Charles Finney (*right*) challenged the public image of the Revival of 1857–58 as a kind of masculine millennium. Sometimes with Walter at her side, sometimes alone, Phoebe Palmer served as a revival speaker/preacher in Canada and upstate New York, while Elizabeth Finney organized women's prayer meetings in Boston in conjunction with Charles's preaching engagements. Palmer photo from *Four Years in the Old World*; Finney photo courtesy Oberlin College Archives.

FIVE

"Great Revival" or "Great Reformation"?

The Privatization of Northern Revivalism

DESPITE THE GENERAL public satisfaction over the success of the awakening, some voices questioned whether the relational piety of family and friends or the celebrated masculine millennium of the urban prayer meetings should qualify as true or genuine revival. In a front-page column of the *Independent* in early March 1858, Harriet Beecher Stowe suggested that "reformation" was the appropriate goal of religious fervor.[1] "Instead of the *great revival of* 1858," she wrote, "we should be happy to read the *great reformation of* 1858" (italics in original). From Stowe's perspective, genuine revivals would "bless society" as well as convert individuals. Moving more overtly toward the tone of a jeremiad, she insisted that evaluating a revival by its moral and social effects was fair: "A revival of religion that brings no repentance and reformation is false and spurious. . . . We believe in no raptures, in no ecstasies, in no experiences that do not bring the soul into communion with Him who declared He came to set at liberty them that are bound and bruised."[2]

Stowe's column was written just before revival began at Henry Ward Beecher's Plymouth Church, where she herself became an active participant. The Plymouth Church meetings strongly emphasized personal piety but were strangely silent about concern for the oppressed. In subsequent editorials over the next few weeks, Stowe muted her rhetoric considerably, much to the dismay of abolitionist papers such as the *Anti-Slavery Standard*.[3] Even so, the issues she had emphasized continued to surface in sermons and newspaper columns, particularly among those, such as Congregational minister George B. Cheever and Unitarian Theodore Parker, who equated genuine spiritual awakening with increased antislavery sentiment. They repeatedly argued that community moral transformation must accompany any true revival. William Goodell, a founding member of the American Abolition Society, expressed their position succinctly: "The Christianity that does not prompt to prayer and action for the oppressed, cannot be the Christianity of

Christ."[4] This view challenged the approach of the union prayer meeting organizers, who stressed conversionist piety and prohibited the mention of any controversial subjects in revival prayer meetings.

In essence, Stowe, Cheever and others were raising questions about a religious revival's impact on a local or national community. Nineteenth-century evangelicals agreed that the word "revival" described an intense period of religious interest, marked by an increased number of conversions. They disagreed, however, in their interpretations of the public significance of such intense religious concern. To what degree did revivals affect the community beyond the church? Were they exclusively conversionist or should revivalism serve as a catalyst for social reform?

Forestalling such questions, southern religionists had disconnected revivalism from the slavery controversy by establishing a consensus that removed religion—and, by extension, revivals—from the public sphere. Whether through a Baptist-inspired understanding of the separation of church and state or the Old School Presbyterian doctrine of the "spirituality of the church," southern "religion . . . was concerned with souls, not society; with personal salvation, not the body politic."[5] In actual practice, religious beliefs played a crucial role in shaping the particular moral vision of the South, and southern evangelicals rarely were "as apolitical as most of them publicly insisted." Even so, they did share a commitment to avoid direct connections between religion and politics.[6]

Northerners, split since the 1830s over their stances toward slavery, suffered more acutely from the tensions inherent in evangelicalism's "explosive potential for reform and its equally powerful tendency to limit and contain that impulse," what James H. Moorhead has called "the divided conscience of antebellum Protestantism."[7] Contributing to the strain were other, potentially contradictory values, in particular the twin commitments within northern revivalism to moral absolutes and social harmony.[8] Politically, the split often ran between those Richard Carwardine has identified as antislavery "free-soil evangelicals" and the more conservative "unionist evangelicals."[9]

Evangelicalism's divided conscience was clearly present in the contrary assessments of the 1857–58 Revival. Congregationalist Cheever charged that, through their silence about slavery, "our revivals of religion become accessory to it, . . . a fawning, cringing, whining piety."[10] In contrast, describing his opposition to "political praying," socially conservative Old School Presbyterian Samuel Irenaeus Prime came down firmly on the side of "harmony and spirituality" in his assertion that "nothing ought to be said or done in a union prayer meeting to wound the sensibilities of any of the worshippers."[11] The two represented the conflicting socially "progressive" and "conservative" camps of revivalistic Calvinists mentioned previously in the context of their interpretations of the revival.[12] Cheever's New England approach to social reform placed religious awakenings in the context of community morality and disinterested benevolence. Prime's socially conservative Princetonian piety perceived revivals primarily in devotional and conversionist terms, as a means of revitalizing and extending the influence of the church. In contrast to the southern approach, however, both men assumed that revivals had some relationship to the social order and shared a common commitment to the ideal of the American nation as a virtuous, Christian republic and to the role of religion in supporting that ideal. Prime, however, understood the connection as indirect: revivals affected the welfare of the nation through the spiritual influence of a vital church and converted, morally reformed individuals. Cheever's point of view was more radical: a revived church would take immediate public stands on reform issues.

Despite interpretations that have linked mid-nineteenth-century revivalism with social reform efforts, evidence suggests that the Revival of 1857–58 had very little direct social or ethical impact.[13] Instead, it marked a public triumph of socially conservative revivalism and consequently a narrowed focus of northern revivals along the Old School lines. It signaled a de facto rejection of the combination of revivalist piety and community moral reform that had been a part of the New England formalist tradition reinvigorated through the early Finney revivals. In its place a more circumscribed, overtly pietistic image of revivals emerged, one in which activity focused on prayer and evangelism and "community" largely became limited to experiences of shared feeling among middle-class people. The most obvious factor behind this shift was the failure of New England revivalism to resolve the divisive issue of slavery. As a result, in the 1840s and 1850s, concerned evangelicals increasingly turned from revivals to the political arena as a more effective means to advance antislavery sentiment and other elements of their moral agenda, including such issues as temperance and anti-Catholicism.[14]

Other circumstances contributed as well. Socially conservative revivalism appealed to the entrenched commercial interests of urban centers, it reflected the changing nature of community in a rapidly industrializing society, and it promised a spiritual harmony congruent with the widespread desire to preserve the national union. This initial transformation of public revivals from an instrument of cultural change to an occasion for shared piety anticipated the much discussed evangelical retreat from social and cultural reform that some scholars see beginning in certain contexts during the post–Civil War years.[15]

Although this chapter contrasts revival traditions from New England and the Middle States, once again the focus is New York City. During the 30 years before the Civil War, the city had been the object of concern for competing groups of revivalistic Protestants. Throughout the spring of 1858 it was the main arena for much of the public debate over the social role of a genuine religious revival. The New York setting offers insights into why revivals became more socially conservative and what the significance might have been for northern evangelicals on the eve of the Civil War.[16]

New York City in the 1830s and 1850s: Two Revival Traditions

On March 17, 1858, at the first noon prayer meeting in Burton's Old Theater, Dutch Reformed minister Theodore Cuyler reminded the packed crowd that this was not the first time a New York City playhouse had become "a house of prayer, and not a haunt of profanity." It had happened once before, during "the great revival of 1831," when a committee of businessmen had purchased the Chatham Street Theater as a chapel for Charles Finney's revival efforts.[17] "For three years this house [Chatham Chapel] was used for revival meetings. . . . That glorious revival of 1831 brought into the churches of this city many of our most active and faithful christians [sic], many of those who are now prominent in the benevolent movements of the day. May this present awakening be equally fruitful in enriching God's Church, and blessing a sinful world!"[18]

Cuyler's wish represented a desire on the part of some that the 1857–58 Revival rejuvenate the revival spirit spread by Finney and his progressive Yankee sponsors in New York City during the early 1830s. That dream, however, never materialized. The meetings at Burton's Theater, while widely publicized, lasted not quite three weeks.[19] Even during that brief period, they reflected how much the social conservatism of middle-class urban merchants had watered down the reform emphasis of the New England revival tradition. For example, Finney's Chatham Chapel had begun as a part of the "Free Church" movement, a reform effort designed to abolish pew rentals and open Protestant churches to the poor. In contrast, the noon meetings at Burton's Theater obviously appealed to an upper-middle-class, churched audience. A *Tribune* report described the crowd at one meeting as made up "principally of business men," plus about 200 women and 50 ministers. The same report noted that "the street in front was lined with carriages."[20]

In addition, Chatham Chapel had been at the heart of the early antislavery movement in the city: in 1833, a mob had stormed the church when abolitionists met there to form the New York City Anti-Slavery Society.[21] During the Burton's Theater prayer meetings, there were only two recorded mentions of slavery, both in the form of prayer requests from slaves.[22] The most publicized was slipped in by Henry Ward Beecher at the close of a conversionist message. When the well-known pastor read a request from Isabella White, a Methodist woman who had escaped from slavery and sought prayers for safety as she traveled to Canada, he did so not as a call to moral concern but as a metaphor for spiritual urgency. After reading the petition, Beecher challenged the audience: "Now, I want to know if there is a man in this congregation who desires to get rid of his sins as much as this poor woman did to get rid of her slavery?"[23]

Even more significant than these differences, however, Burton's Theater never came to represent the ethos of the 1857–58 Revival as the Fulton Street prayer meeting did or as Chatham Chapel did for the earlier spiritual fervor. Nevertheless, Cuyler's reference to the Chatham Street church was important. A comparison between the New York City revivalism of the early 1830s and that of the late 1850s provides insights into the different revival traditions that captured public attention during each period and the shift in attitudes toward moral reform over a 30-year span.[24]

The Free Church Movement: New England–Style Revivalism and Community Moral Reform

The Free Church movement in New York City eventually came to include 11 churches, organized in poorer districts of the downtown area between 1830 and

1840. Most were at least nominally Presbyterian and belonged to the city's Third Presbytery, a so-called "revival" presbytery because it was dominated by New School clergy who advocated the use of new measures. The most famous of these ministers was Charles Finney, pastor of the Chatham Street Chapel (Second Free Church) from 1832 to 1836 and its successor, the Broadway Tabernacle (Sixth Free Church, Congregational), during 1836 and 1837.[25]

Finney's presence and the Free Church movement as a whole represented efforts by a group of newly rich Yankee transplants in the metropolis to spread their faith and culture among the urban poor and the unchurched middle classes. Headed by silk merchants Arthur and Lewis Tappan, these businessmen chafed under the constraints of the more conservative New York social and religious establishment. The "Sons of the Pilgrims," as Lewis Tappan called them, longed for city churches whose growth and innovation would parallel the dynamism of their expanding business enterprises.[26] And they assumed an intimate connection between revivalism and community social reform.

Chatham Street Chapel represented this relationship. A barn-like structure, the chapel could accommodate 2,500 people for revival services. It "squatted in the midst of the slums" of the Five Points tenement district, an area the New Englanders viewed as ripe for moral reform.[27] Just as they were "rescuing from Satan one of his haunts" by transforming a theater into a church, the Free Church founders trusted that evangelism and benevolent effort would rescue the surrounding neighborhood.[28] In later years, Lewis Tappan stated explicitly that all the revivalistic Free churches "had been instituted to produce a reform, and it was thought that every branch of Christian benevolence . . . ought to [have] been engrafted on the Free church system."[29]

Many such benevolent enterprises were. In addition to the New York City Anti-Slavery Society at the Chatham Street Chapel, both the Female Moral Reform Society and the Young Men's Anti-Slavery Society were founded in 1834 at the Third Free Presbyterian Church. Also, workers from a number of the Free churches propelled the expanded visitation activities of the New York City Tract Society into slum and tenement areas.[30] To further reinforce the connection between revivalism and moral reform, the annual anniversary meetings for the major national societies of the "benevolent empire" met in the Chatham Street Chapel from 1832–1836.[31]

By 1834, the four Free churches established in the city in as many years were flourishing, with a combined membership of nearly 1,600 people. The *New York Evangelist*, a religious weekly established in 1830 by the same coalition of Yankee merchants, publicized the churches, along with other revival and benevolent activities. Between such publicity, the presence of Finney, the novelty of Chatham Chapel, and the benevolent energy of the Tappans and their friends, the Free churches were the most visible expression of New York City revivalism during the decade of the 1830s.

Stressing revivalistic piety and community moral transformation, the Free Church movement was the urban embodiment of a revival tradition that had roots in the community ideals and covenantal framework of seventeenth- and eighteenth-century American Puritanism.[32] Whether they favored or opposed the new measures, the nineteenth-century heirs of this New England tradition were convinced that revivals would accomplish "the complete moral renovation of the world" by "elevating the intellectual, spiritual, and social condition of men."[33] When they spoke of "moral renovation" and social elevation, they envisioned the impact of revivals on entire communities: "It is found . . . in instances almost innumerable, that a revival has renovated . . . a community; has driven away vice; has encouraged industry; has given a spring to intelligence . . . where chilling selfishness, or hateful discord, or unblushing crime, seemed to have established a perpetual reign."[34]

Eighteenth-century theologian and pastor Samuel Hopkins provided a powerful conceptual foundation for the ethical side of New England revivalism through his doctrine of "disinterested benevolence," a moralistic variation of Jonathan Edwards's explanation of the nature of true virtue. Hopkinsian disinterested benevolence has been described as "rendering selfless love to God and humanity."[35] In the hands of nineteenth-century Yankee revivalist/reformers such as Finney and the more conservative Lyman Beecher, the idea boiled down to the obligation of the truly converted "to do good for others."[36] This "good" involved more than an occasional nod to the Golden Rule. Rather, as Finney taught, it meant "being useful in the highest degree possible . . . whatever may be the sacrifice."[37] In addition, the millennialism of Finney, Beecher, and other ministers extended this ethical imperative to ever-broadening community units: local towns, the nation, and even the world.

The combination of the zeal engendered by revivals, the idea of community as a moral unit, and the compulsion of disinterested benevolence provided much of the impetus behind the formation and growth of the benevolent empire, as well as for such special projects as the Free Church movement.[38] It also made the New Englanders and their revival tradition allies with Whig politicians, as that party emerged during the second quarter of the century, in a common desire to improve people and society.[39] As a result, the New England pattern of combining revivals and reform became the most publicly influential ideal for the way revivals should affect American society. It was a pattern that assumed common social goals, and therefore social harmony, on the basis of a shared commitment to conversionist piety and unselfish service.[40] This ideal, while widely disseminated, found its most fertile soil in areas of Yankee migration, including upstate New York and the upper part of the Old Northwest, places where relatively homogeneous communities most closely replicated the Puritan village.[41]

The environment in urban centers such as New York City was much less conducive to success. Explosive population growth, the separation of middle-class business and residential districts, heterogeneity reinforced by increasing immigration, and an almost constant population flux all made the traditional stable community an illusive ideal.[42] Even Protestant churches suffered from the general instability. Fifty-one of the Presbyterian churches established in New York City during the nineteenth century were dissolved before the century was over; 17 had a life span of less than five years.[43] Equally significant for the future of evangelical social reform were the tensions that arose, on the heels of revivalism and the prosperity of the benevolent empire, over the issue of slavery.

The New York City Free Church movement became a microcosm of these pressures and their effects. For example, despite the commitment of the Chatham Street Chapel to an antislavery position, two of the key leaders, Finney and Lewis Tappan, were unable to resolve their differences over whether blacks were indeed free, as whites were, to sit wherever they liked in the church.[44] Although all the Free churches promised open seating, in fact, as Tappan recalled, "it was understood, by whites and blacks, that the colored people should sit by themselves in a certain place in one of the galleries."[45] The Chatham congregation admitted blacks to the main floor but still segregated them to designated pews on one side of the church. In a letter written several years later, Tappan expressed his disappointment: "We were never able, though Mr. Finney was the pastor, to abolish the distinction altogether, . . . and allow people to sit, in fact, as they were invited to do, wherever they chose. . . . Finding nothing could be done in a matter so dear to my heart, I left the church."[46]

From Finney's perspective, he had made his opposition to slavery clear from the pulpit, and, in contrast to most northern ministers, the revivalist barred Christian slaveholders from partaking in the sacrament of communion in the church. Still, he was seeking to maintain some modicum of respectability for a congregation whose social stance was far outside the mainstream in a city where commercial interests fostered a deep-seated fear of alienating the South.[47] In 1833, after local rowdies attacked a group of blacks as they were leaving a Chatham Chapel service, the *Courier and Enquirer* noted, "Another of those disgraceful negro outrages, etc., occurred last night at that common focus of pollution, Chatham Street Chapel."[48] Such a reputation, added to the lingering notoriety of the chapel as a former theater, threatened to divert attention and attendance and thus undermine Finney's primary commitment to revival preaching.

The divisive antislavery activities of many of the Free churches have been cited as a major factor contributing to their decline in the late 1830s, as moderates began to distance themselves from any hint of extremism.[49] But other factors were at work as well. Despite the egalitarian aims of the Free Church ideal, in reality upwardly mobile middle-class parishioners and even lower-class church members resented the identification of "Free Church" with "poor church."

Samuel D. Burchard, called in 1839 as pastor of the Third Free (Houston Street) Church, described the situation he found when he arrived:

> They were divided among themselves in reference to the practical issues of the day. They were burdened with a heavy debt. Their high standards of reform; their total abstinence and antislavery views had awakened a stormy public and popular prejudice against them.
>
> The Third Free Church was the rallying point of all reformatory movements. It was stigmatized as 'the abolition church' and its locality as "brimstone corner." . . . With its unsightly building, not withstanding the favor of God and all its previous success, [it] could never become a self supporting church. It was built for *poor people*, and the self sustaining element, even though *there* converted, would not abide[50] (italics in original).

The church already had resumed pew rentals out of financial necessity, and Burchard's solution for its survival also was conservative. He focused on preaching "the simple gospel unaffected by any popular or prevailing prejudice ... studiously avoiding the questions at issue among the people."[51]

The decision of Charles Finney to move from Chatham Chapel to the newly constructed Broadway Tabernacle in 1836 reflected a tacit recognition of a similar situation. In addition to the antislavery controversies, Chatham Chapel's location discouraged middle-class attendance. In contrast, the Tabernacle was in a completely different neighborhood: "It was the active center of New York City in the 1830s, with new business houses and recent construction round about."[52] Slowly but surely the New Englanders were finding their community in the Protestant middle class and retreating from the humanitarian ideal of the earlier revivalism. In so doing, their religious efforts became more compatible with the social conservatism of the city's Protestant establishment. Finney's departure in 1837 to live full-time in Oberlin, Ohio, and the financial panic that same year were additional circumstances that signaled the decline of the Free Church attempt to bring the New England vision of revival and community reform to the tenements of New York City. By the early 1840s, most of the Free churches had either dissolved or relocated under the traditional system of pew rental.[53]

The New England vision of revivalism and united community reform as foundations for present social stability and future millennial prosperity proved illusive, not only in New York City but throughout the North during the quarter century preceding the Civil War. Splits among the major Protestant denominations, increasing sectional identification, and agitations within the benevolent societies presented a picture of institutional fragmentation rather than social harmony. Occasional voices continued to promote revivals as instruments of reform, but socially active Protestants increasingly sought common ground in political action rather than religious effort. In fact, they often channeled the religious zeal once reserved for revivals into electoral campaigns. As Richard Carwardine has demonstrated, the Liberty, Free Soil, Know Nothing—and especially the Republican—parties represented a fusion of the revivalistic, crusading spirit of northern evangelicals and specific social/political agendas.[54] In effect, as Yankee activists attempted to impose their vision of a godly republic on the nation, revivalistic politics were taking the place of religious revivals as agents of social transformation.

The activities of Henry Ward Beecher illustrate the change. Throughout the 1850s, in his attitudes toward both temperance and slavery, Beecher began to advocate political action in contrast to his earlier commitment to moral influence associated with revivalism. In 1854 he helped to mobilize New York's "Maine Law evangelicals," those Protestants who wanted to see the state pass prohibition legislation patterned after the 1851 Maine bill. Their political clout eventually led to the nomination and election of a "dry" governor, Myron H. Clark, who signed the desired prohibition bill in 1855.

A year later, Beecher, already famous for his support of armed resistance to slavery in Kansas, sought a leave of absence from his church so that he could campaign for John C. Frémont and the new Republican party. The party's national committee paid Beecher to spend two or three days a week on the stump for their candidate. Yet despite this activism and Beecher's opposition to slavery, he later refrained from enlisting the revivalistic piety of 1858 on behalf of the issue.[55] According to one historian, Beecher's attitude confirmed that he "no longer retained the earlier generation's faith in the effectiveness of revivalism as an instrument for national reform." Instead, he viewed revivals simply as "useful devices for reaffirming men's belief in God."[56] During this same period, Beecher began to reconceptualize the New England concept of disinterested benevolence to accommodate the affluence of his Brooklyn congregation.[57] His innovations signaled the transformation of the New England revival tradition.

From the beginning of the Free Church movement, the New York City Presbyterian and Dutch Reformed establishment had resented the efforts of New Englanders to impose a Yankee religious culture on the metropolis.[58] During the 1830s and 1840s they had objected to new measures revivalism, to antislavery agitation, and to what they felt was an "invasion of their city . . . by the Congregationalists in violation of the Plan of Union."[59] The Free Church movement had been a serious challenge to the establishment, but the subsequent decline of that project and the city's entrenched conservatism regarding slavery strengthened the position of the socially conservative Reformed element. Although the Free Church revivalism clearly had reflected the New England tradition, the more recent Yankee interest in political crusades meant that New York City revivalism in 1857–58 would take on a different character, one that would contribute to a much broader shift in understandings of the public role of revivals.

New York City Revivalism in 1857–58: Social Conservatives and the Fulton Street Prayer Meeting

When, in late March 1858, a correspondent from *Harper's Weekly* decided to observe the noon prayer meetings firsthand, he stopped by the overflowing Burton's Theater, then followed "the current of the crowd" to the Fulton Street meeting. There, too, "were the same crowds and the same exercises. The sounds of prayer and exhortation and singing were all mingled, and people were constantly pouring up and down the stairs."[60] Yet the writer juxtaposed this scene of intense religious activity against the continuing daily life of the metropolis: "In the street the shops were open, the drays and wagons passing, the busy crowds streaming along the sidewalks; truckmen were swearing, boys shouting, and the envelope-man closing over all with his mighty refrain of 'F-O-U-RRR C-E-N-T-S.' "[61]

During the height of the 1857–58 Revival, perhaps as many as 20 noon prayer meetings met throughout the city and 100 more convened in churches and halls during the early morning or evening hours.[62] Even then, observers agreed that, while the revival captured public attention, the face of the city remained relatively unchanged. Prime discussed this situation in the pages of the *New York Observer* when he considered "What Fruits the Revival Should Yield":

> Though in this city alone we may number the converts by thousands, and in the country by tens of thousands, we know that the numbers are so small compared with the vast multitudes remaining unchanged, that we have no right to expect any perceptible improvement in the masses of the community. . . . Crime is not likely to be checked because here and there a criminal has be-

come an honest man. . . . Wall street will be as rife with fraud, and the Stock Board as full of gambling as it has been, and the whole world around us will move on as if the Providence and Spirit of God had not combined to arrest men in their mad career, and . . . had not turned their thoughts by force for a time heavenward.[63]

This analysis reflected Prime's staunchly conservative outlook, yet the overall tone of his article was optimistic. The "fruit" of the religious fervor would be expressed through another channel: a more united, revitalized Protestant church. "Prayer, zeal, faith, money and men" would be newly consecrated for the "salvation of a world in sin."[64]

Prime and the *Observer*, the influential Old School paper he edited for more than three decades, represented a theologically moderate Presbyterian revival tradition that built on the theology and piety of Princeton Seminary.[65] These Old Schoolers were known for their opposition to new measures revivalism, but three other emphases that affected their stance toward social reform more clearly distinguished the Presbyterian outlook from that of the New Englanders: (1) an understanding of revivalism that centered on a revitalized church rather than a transformed secular community, (2) a concern for doctrinal purity over moral reform as essential to social stability, and (3) a certain biblical literalism that led Old School Presbyterians to reject such doctrinal innovations as "disinterested benevolence."

Perhaps because, with a few exceptions, Presbyterians "did not have a tradition of establishment in America," they were more inclined to identify revivals with a revitalized church than to associate church and community automatically.[66] Themes similar to those in Prime's editorial were evident in the early 1830s in letters from Middle States Presbyterians that formed a part of the appendix to William Sprague's *Lectures on Revivals*. While Sprague, in the New England fashion, projected the impact of revivalism outward through various levels of social transformation, Princetonians Archibald Alexander and Samuel Miller concentrated their analyses on the church.[67] John McDowell, a Presbyterian minister from Elizabethtown, New Jersey, used language that reflected the same focus as he recounted a period of awakening in his church: "[The revival] . . . was general through the congregation, and in a few weeks extended into neighboring congregations, and passed from one to another, until in the course of the year, almost every congregation in what was then the Presbytery of Jersey, was visited."[68]

The Princetonians also associated conversionist piety with an increased interest in doctrinal truth rather than a heightened sense of moral obligation. Alexander wrote, "The impressions on the minds of the people in such a work [a revival] are the exact counterpart of the truth; just as the impression on the wax corresponds to the seal." The result would be "an inextinguishable desire to promote the glory of God, and to bring all men to the knowledge of the truth."[69] Such revivals, however, were not divorced from society. The extension of a revitalized church and the spread of doctrinal purity would have a salutary impact on the social order as a whole. Archibald Alexander's son, James W. Alexander, made this point during the Revival of 1857-58. "Such an increase of the church is desirable," Alexander emphasized, "because it glorifies God . . . and because it is demanded by the present state of our city and nation."[70]

From his pulpit in New York City, Alexander was more concerned about the influx of immigrants into American cities and to the western states than he was about slavery: "Unless the means of grace can be made in some degree to keep pace with the growth of our population, our rising States must be abandoned to error, infidelity, and disorder."[71] Whereas the New Englanders linked social harmony to a shared moral consensus expressed through benevolent activity, Alexander tied it to correct belief, conversion, and involvement in a Protestant church. Error and infidelity were greater threats than immorality. The Presbyterians were not oblivious to ethical concerns, but they believed that true doctrine would have a greater long-term moral influence on society than specific humanitarian efforts.[72]

Scholarly discussions reflecting the commitment of Princeton theologians such as Charles Hodge to a conservative, literal approach to biblical exegesis further reinforced the emphasis on doctrinal correctness in the moderate Presbyterian tradition. For example, the Princetonians rejected such speculative theological constructions as Hopkinsian disinterested benevolence and the "higher law" doctrine invoked by antislavery evangelicals.[73] Also, in light of the "plain sense of scripture," Hodge argued that slavery was not a sin in itself, nor was slaveholding inherently evil since the Bible clearly allowed the institution.[74]

On a popular level, this appeal to a common sense interpretation of the written biblical text among the Presbyterians was translated into a more encompassing, socially conservative constitutionalism. In a February 1858 *Observer* editorial, Prime grouped all the competing factions of the tumultuous 1850s, whether in the church or the state, into two parties, "conservatives" and "progressives," based on their attitudes toward written texts.

> The conservative party is for holding fast to the written law. The progressive party is for a wide interpretation of the rule. Adherence to the constitution in the state, in the church, in the benevolent association, is the only safe principle on which men can be held together to act harmoniously and efficiently.
>
> Conservative men follow the plain precepts of the Bible, and do not expect or desire to have them improved. . . . Radical men are always quarrelling with Scripture, disregarding it, or evading it.[75]

Social harmony was based on a shared commitment to the rules, to the dictates of the written word. A stable society depended on respect for the law, whether the law of the land or the law of God.[76] Even revivals were bound by written rules, both in their conformity to perceived biblical truths and in written guidelines for revival practices. Much of the celebrated unity of the 1857–58 Revival was built around strict adherence to detailed instructions for the conduct of prayer meetings and the behavior of participants. Leaders' guides prescribed the format of the noon meetings in precise detail.[77] Placards on the lecture room walls at the Fulton Street church or in other auditoriums spelled out specific guidelines to those in attendance: "Prayers and Exhortations not to exceed five minutes"; "Not more than two consecutive prayers or exhortations"; "No Controverted Points Discussed."[78]

This Presbyterian revival tradition, while smaller and much less visible than the New England approach, nonetheless had affinities with the social and cultural setting of the merchants and bankers who constituted the middle class of urban centers such as New York. Church-centered revivalism was a good "fit" for the fluid urban community, and conservative biblicism had parallels within the growing contractual focus of commercial trade. A theological tradition that distanced itself from direct humanitarian reform also appealed to merchants with large financial interests in the South.

By the 1850s, only a few of the evangelical businessmen in the city, most notably New Englanders Lewis and Arthur Tappan, publicly opposed slavery. The more common view was that expressed by a merchant to abolitionist Samuel J. May: "There are millions upon millions of dollars due from Southerners to the merchants and mechanics alone, the payment of which would be jeopardized by any rupture between the North and the South. We cannot afford, sir, to let you and your associates endeavor to overthrow slavery. It is not a matter of principles with us. It is a matter of business necessity."[79]

This is not to say that socially conservative New York Protestants had no interest at all in certain forms of benevolence. Prime himself served for a year as secretary of the American Bible Society; both he and J. W. Alexander wrote for the publications of the American Tract Society and the American Sunday School Union. Not coincidentally, these three groups were the national societies with the strongest Presbyterian and Middle States support, organizations that remained within the good graces of the Old School Presbyterians after the doors of the church were closed to New England–dominated groups.[80] They also were societies that associated social harmony with teaching and the distribution of literature.

In addition, throughout the 1840s and 1850s, these three societies resisted pressures from antislavery advocates to limit their activities in the South. Their rationale reflected a conservative attitude toward social change: "Each piously claimed 'nothing to do with political questions or social institutions' because of its preoccupation 'with the way of salvation for lost men.' "[81] At the same time, each society maintained a concern for social stability and the preservation of the Union. These national societies mirrored Presbyterian pride at the national scope of their denominations, reflecting the conservative commitment to "social and ecclesiastical cohesion."[82] Sunday school workers were assured that they need not "despair of this republic so long as we have an *American* Bible Society, an American Tract Society, and American Sunday-School *Union*" (italics in original).[83] If not always by churches per se, social stability could be promoted by united efforts in support of conversionist aims. But such stability came at the exclusion of direct efforts for social reform.

The Revival of 1857–58 expressed this same approach, with the Fulton Street prayer meeting as a key example. Prime considered the noon gathering in the North Dutch Church the archetype of what he viewed as a new model of Protestant piety: the union prayer meeting. Although the Fulton Street meeting was interdenominational, for Prime its origin in a Dutch Reformed church had providential significance. That denomination, he pointed out, was not "mixed up in the questions, controversies and divisions of the day." In addition, it was "distinguished for purity and soundness of doctrine, above suspicion and above re-proach."[84] In other words, it both reflected the revival tradition of Middle States Calvinists and provided a neutral setting where a variety of Protestants could gather.

Prime neglected to point out that ethnic and regional isolation had helped the Dutch Reformed to maintain their peace and purity. In a similar fashion, the touted unity and harmony of the Fulton Street meeting was achieved in part by its own brand of social and spiritual isolationism. Merchants and clerks of a variety of denominations, as well as some sailors from the nearby docks, did flock to the meeting. But the poor, blacks, and women—people whose very presence appeared to threaten social harmony—found the atmosphere less than congenial. The story of the origin and popularity of the meeting also was a story of retreat from those groups.

Jeremiah Lanphier, the lay worker credited with organizing the noon prayer meeting at Fulton Street, originally had been hired by the North Dutch Church as a missionary to canvass the neighborhoods around the church, an area popu-lated mainly by lower-class immigrant families.[85] The project was an attempt to reverse a membership decline as long-time parishioners moved further uptown. The church elders declared empty pews free to all and engaged Lanphier "in order that the 'poor may have the Gospel preached to them.' "[86]

The new missionary soon found his most receptive audience, however, among the young clerks and the business travelers who filled the boarding houses through-out the area. He hung notices in the different houses, advising guests that specific pews had been reserved for them at the church, and supplied maids with similar cards to leave in guests' rooms. Pleased church officials soon noted the results: services filled and, "contrary to what is usual in ordinary places of worship, the greater part of the congregation was composed of men." These visitors made for a transient congregation; nonetheless, "the ministers who occupied the pulpit took particular pleasure in preaching the Gospel to an audience of this character."[87] Based on this success and directed to a similar audience, Lanphier decided to begin his lunchtime prayer meeting. The focus of his work had changed from that of missionary to the poor to chaplain for businessmen.

On September 23, 1857, Lanphier first hung a placard outside the church an-nouncing, "Daily Prayer Meeting, from 12 to 1 o'clock." The first person to arrive was a woman, whom Lanphier saw as he looked out the window of an upstairs room. He rushed down and asked her to leave: "Madam, this is a workingmen's [businessmen's] meeting; it is not intended for women. If women come, men will hesitate to come in their working clothes."[88] Within a few months, as the revival fervor spread and the future of the prayer meeting was assured, the doors were opened to women. However, throughout the revival and for years afterward, they were not allowed to speak publicly during the hour-long session. The most famous casualty of this policy was Maggie Van Cott, who later would become the first woman licensed to preach in the Methodist Episcopal Church in the United States. Van Cott, who managed her invalid husband's wholesale drug business, attended the Fulton Street meeting on one occasion when she was in the downtown area. During the meeting, she stood and spoke briefly "of the power of Christ to save," as male participants had. On the way out, Van Cott was informed that the gathering was "strictly a men's meeting" and that there were "plenty of places elsewhere where women can speak."[89]

Blacks had similar troubles. In late March 1858, an unidentified black man wrote a letter to the editor of the *New York Tribune*, detailing how he and a woman, the only two African Americans at a Fulton Street meeting, had been ushered from the second-floor prayer gathering to an empty room on the third floor. "The colored people have good meetings 'up' here," they were told. The parallel with segregated balconies, the so-called "Nigger heaven" of many Protestant worship services, was too great and the pair left. The man concluded his letter: "I told her [his companion] that these things were a part of the American Religion; and while I disapproved the attempt to get up 'a colored man's prayer-meeting,' we should have to adopt some other means to enjoy the full fruition of the blessings of the outpouring of the spirit, than by having an 'interesting time' up there by ourselves."[90]

Such incidents were not mentioned in denominational newspapers or the later books about the revival. Just as no "controverted" (controversial) points were discussed in the prayer meetings themselves, clergy who edited religious papers or wrote the histories avoided divisiveness in their published accounts. Besides, to conservatives, these and other episodes reflected prevailing standards in a hierarchical society and were not cause for widespread concern. Instead, apologists for the revival emphasized the laudable characteristics of the Fulton Street gatherings: the harmonious, nonsectarian atmosphere; the emphasis on prayer; the high number of reported conversions.

The decades of the 1840s and 1850s had seen enough acrimonious strife in church and society; the apparent harmony of the prayer meetings provided a welcome contrast. In addition, the efficiency of businessmen's piety and the sense of heightened supernaturalism that accompanied the revival promised an ultimate social impact that overshadowed any immediate shortcomings. Conservatives noted a fresh "confidence in God" based on the potential influence of group prayer. Enthusiasm over what could be accomplished through prayer alone pushed the conservative Calvinists in a more devotional direction. Instead of an ethical imperative, or even the traditional concern for doctrinal purity, prayer had become a "new element of usefulness and power": the basis for Christian unity and a source of direct, divine intervention to transform the nation.[91] According to conservatives, it was the "deep and all-pervading earnest piety" of the 1857–58 Revival, rather than political activism or social reform, that would "rouse up the national conscience, to arrest the national decay."[92]

A Consensus View of Piety

As stories emerged from Fulton Street and countless similar prayer meetings of hundreds, even thousands, of people converted in answer to prayer, the hope of a revitalized church burned brightly. The devotionalistic focus of the conservatives seemed to strike a responsive chord in other cities as well. The expectation that personal piety alone would lead eventually to social transformation was a theme that echoed across a broad spectrum of northern Protestants, particularly among people in urban areas. Not only did it resonate with the Middle States Calvinists, it also was compatible with church-centered millennialism, as well as the more individualistic piety of some Baptists and Methodists.

Many associated revival piety with anticipations of a coming millennium that encompassed much more than the increased spirituality of middle-class men. Episcopal Bishop Charles P. McIlvaine, an evangelical, interpreted the revival, with its spirit of prayer, mass conversions, and stress on unity, within such a framework. He viewed the awakening as a link between the outpouring of the Holy Spirit during the "first days" of Pentecost and the Spirit's descent upon "all flesh" during the "last days" of the millennium. McIlvaine noted that, just as at Pentecost, during the Revival of 1857–58, "thousands [had been] converted, as it were in a single day." Why not, then, see it as a foretaste of "what is to be, and must be, wider and wider, more and more wonderfully, till the whole promise is fulfilled, and the Spirit indeed is poured out on all mankind?" When that happened, not only every person in the United States but "in all the earth" would experience Christian conversion. The "purity and simplicity . . . [and] the love and devotedness" of a revitalized church would characterize all humanity.[93] McIlvaine was much more preoccupied with unity and harmony than with solutions to social ills.

James W. Alexander echoed McIlvaine's hopes. Prayer, in its dependence on God, "[g]ave glory to the Divine agency" rather than to human achievement. As God was glorified, the millennial dawn at last would come. The revitalized religion of that new day was the only lasting solution to social and political fragmentation. He sketched such a vision from the pulpit: "Such a dawn of glory as this upon our churches would extend its beams to our remotest Missions. Religion would be to our national Union a cement worth more than all political ties and compromises."[94]

For other evangelicals caught up in the religious fervor, particularly Baptists and Methodists, the stress on personal piety confirmed long-standing convictions that the only true path to social change came through individual conversions.[95] In a popular essay published shortly before the revival, Baptist Henry Clay Fish expressed this more individualistic approach: "The religion of Christ converts men one by one,—sanctifying a single heart, reforming a single life, elevating a single character,—and thus operates upward and outward through the mass of humanity; just as the particle of leaven, to which it is likened, operates upon the particle lying next to itself, and it upon another, until the whole lump is leavened."[96]

Methodists, too, traditionally understood their mission more as personal salvation than as the New England Calvinists' societal redemption or the moderate Presbyterians' church renewal. God's providential design for the Methodist church, according to its *Discipline*, was "to reform the continent, and spread Scripture holiness over these lands."[97] Methodism, in other words, was God's special instrument for bringing the Christian gospel to the North American continent. By the 1840s and 1850s, Methodists had become more politically active, and some were recognizing publicly that even evangelistic efforts exercised a "politically and socially constructive influence" on society. Still, many continued to believe that influence should be indirect, "purely religious in its intent and operation."[98] This religious focus was central in several articles by Phoebe Palmer, published in early 1857, urging ministers to rally Methodist laymen and laywomen to greater involvement "in the great work they are called to do, by way of winning souls to Christ." For Palmer, personal evangelism was the primary task God had given to each Methodist, layperson or clergyperson. When every individual responded to the challenge, then "the design of God in raising her [the church] up would speedily be met, the continent would be reformed, and Scriptural holiness spread over these lands."[99]

Prominent Methodist apologists of the 1857–58 Revival—Abel Stevens, Nathan Bangs, and Phoebe Palmer—all represented middle-class or formalized New York City Methodism. Even for Methodists, the genteel atmosphere of the metropolis fostered "safe" opinions on such subjects as slavery, as well as a generally conservative social stance.[100] Bangs, the aging elder statesman of Methodism, spoke briefly at the first anniversary of the Fulton Street prayer meeting, September 23, 1858. From his perspective, a noteworthy effect of the revival was its ability to bring denominations together, to tear down "sectarian prejudices" in favor of a common piety. "I feel as though it was my duty to preach principally upon experimental and practical religion, and I am ready to give the right hand of fellowship to every man that will join me upon that theme."[101] As a series of essays he had written earlier made evident, the revival encouraged Bangs in his efforts, along with Palmer and others, to promote the Methodist emphasis on holiness. As one biographer put it, the retired Bangs "found peace in the quest for personal piety."[102]

Still at the height of his career, *Christian Advocate* editor Abel Stevens was promoting peace along other avenues. Nominally an antislavery moderate, Stevens nonetheless consistently aligned himself with church conservatives in efforts to suppress abolitionist dissent, mollify the northern Methodist border-state conferences, and promote "homogeneous opinions" on slavery that would not further threaten church or national unity.[103] He also advocated a similar homogeneity within the YMCA. A delegate to the first transatlantic "Y" conference in Paris in 1855, Stevens proposed a plan for an international YMCA confederation. Included was a clause specifying that controversial subjects should not "be permitted to interrupt . . . [the] harmony" of the Association.[104]

During his speech, Stevens expressed the hope that a united YMCA would encourage Christian unity in the United States despite abolitionist agitation. In 1858, he was quick to praise the spiritual focus and "Christian catholicity" of the revival: "It is full of hope to all men who long for a more perfect Protestant unity. It shows how easily the great Head of the Church may, . . . when his people shall devote themselves to their essential work, prostrate all walls of partition between them, and, . . . bind them forever together in the unity of the Spirit."[105]

Whether grounded in the Baptist and Methodist emphasis on individual conversions or the Presbyterian and Episcopal heritage of a revitalized church, a remarkable consensus emerged among spokespersons for all these traditions on the characteristics that stamped the awakening of 1857–58 as a genuine religious revival. Traits commonly highlighted in various publications included (1) its spontaneous, providential origin, sometimes expressed as the "work of the Holy

Spirit"; (2) the stress on Christian unity ("union"); (3) the focus on prayer; (4) lay involvement, both in prayer meetings and in the "personal work" of evangelism; (5) widespread conversions; (6) calmness and order of the meetings; and (7) general public acceptance, both among Protestants and the "secular" public.[106]

As such a list indicated, the criteria for judging the revival authentic involved expressions of external devotional activity. They were limited to observable, outward criteria rather than characteristics of the inner life. Absent was the careful theological and psychological analysis of a Jonathan Edwards, or his concern for local church and community transformation.[107] Gone, too, was the subsequent New England emphasis on moral duty and disinterested benevolence. A new public understanding of revivalism was replacing the New England tradition, one that focused on devotional and conversionist piety. Most clearly articulated in 1858 by Middle States Calvinists, it embraced the social conservatism and devotional concerns of many northern Protestants. In the conflicting tugs of the "divided conscience," the harmony and order of revivals had triumphed over moral absolutism, and the imperatives of evangelism over specific reforms. Protestant unity, fragmented since the late 1830s, was being reconstituted on a new foundation. A unified Protestantism would no longer be attempted on the basis of joint benevolence, but—as the 1870s would confirm—as an *evangelical* alliance, however shaky that venture ultimately might prove.[108]

By choosing conversionist piety while at the same time retreating from controversy, northern Protestants had shifted their understanding of revivalism in a socially conservative direction. Paradoxically, however, the move enabled them to retain an optimistic attitude toward American society. Just as they understood the apparently spontaneous spiritual fervor of 1857–58 as evidence of divine intervention, as the effect of the Holy Spirit unsullied by humanly contrived new measures, so the conservatives expected God to work in a similarly dramatic, though perhaps less rapid, way "on the social, the political, the religious character of this nation."[109] James W. Alexander summarized the common sentiment: "On omnipotence we cannot count too much. God is able to do for us exceeding abundantly above all that we ask or think."[110] When a united church prayed, and particularly when lay men and women turned to religion, God would intervene directly to resolve any problems in the social order. As a modern historian has summarized this public theology of revivalism, "political change was to emerge out of a nonpolitical revival."[111] Few elaborated the specifics, but confidence in such a scenario was widespread. The *Watchman and Reflector* affirmed that "the morality of the world is dependent on the piety of the church, and in general improves or declines in direct ratio with it."[112] Critics, however, found those sentiments dangerously shallow when they masked a continued northern Protestant unwillingness to take a strong stand against slavery.

SIX

"Where is the evidence of your revival of religion?"

Critiques of the Revival's Social Impact

A S SUGGESTED IN THE introduction to chapter 5, the most important sustained critique of the newly "spiritualized" public theology associated with the 1857–58 Revival came from two groups of disaffected New Englanders: non-evangelical abolitionists and evangelical antislavery radicals.[1] Abolitionists had long condemned as unchristian the timid attitude of many northern Protestants toward slavery, and the prohibition of prayers concerning slavery from the union meetings under the "no controversy" policy did nothing to change their opinion. The radical evangelicals were less willing to reject the revival outright, but they opposed its abdication of moral responsibility. In particular, they viewed the retrenchment of the American Tract Society after bitter debates throughout the spring of 1858 as proof that revival piety did little to transform "worldly prudence." The arguments of each group of critics, articulated most effectively by Unitarian Theodore Parker and Congregationalist George B. Cheever, reflected the moral absolutism of the New England tradition and a continuing allegiance to the goal of community moral reform.

Neither Parker's nor Cheever's critiques sparked a full-blown controversy; in the interest of harmony, revival apologists largely ignored them. Nor have historians paid much attention to such voices of dissent.[2] True, the two men represented relatively small, though vocal, constituencies in comparison to the hundreds of thousands who flocked to prayer meetings. Even so, their analyses and the incidents surrounding them illuminate the tensions that continued to trouble northern Protestants despite their consensus vision of a devotionalistic revival.

Theodore Parker attacked the revival head-on in two sermons from his lectern in Boston's Music Hall, one on Easter Sunday, April 4, 1858, the other a week later. Published as "A False and True Revival of Religion" and "The Revival of Religion Which We Need," Parker's sermons negated the positive picture that adherents of the consensus view of the revival wished to convey. Whereas adherents stressed the event's providential origin, he pointed to promotional techniques: "[T]hey . . . advertise in newspapers. . . . [T]hen they hang out their placards at the corners of the streets."³ Revivalists insisted on the necessity of faith in Christ; to Parker, any doctrinal formulation, even the abbreviated "Come to Christ," was a bigoted concern for right belief over enlightened action. People at prayer meetings sought conversions; Parker scorned the absence of ethical concern: "I do not hear any prayer for temperance, any prayer for education, any prayer for the emancipation of slaves, for the elevation of women, for honesty, for industry, for brotherly love; any prayers against envy, suspicion, bigotry, superstition, spiritual pride, malice and all uncharitableness."⁴

At bottom the difference was between evangelicals' supernatural religion and Parker's natural one. Evangelicals, committed to the need for a changed heart, were convinced that God would intervene to solve societal problems. Parker believed that as men and women developed their internal "religious faculty," they would find the strength to initiate their own millennium. The task of humanity was to "outlearn" and "outgrow" the "five great evils of mankind": "war, wicked government, slavery, selfish antagonism in society, the degradation of women."⁵

Many of Parker's criticisms of supernaturalist faith in contrast to natural religion reflected the standard polemics of his theistic Unitarianism. He had long since rejected both the supernaturalism of orthodox Christianity and the need for any historic grounding for faith, including the actual existence of Christ.⁶ What distinguished these sermons, however, was Parker's vehement distinction between piety and ethics. He was, as one historian correctly observed, enraged about the behavior of Boston evangelicals.⁷ Parker's anger had roots in the contrast he saw between the moral vacillation of socially conservative Protestants and the self-righteous certainty of their piety. As in New York City, the revival in Boston included merchants and ministers who refused to antagonize the South by speaking out against slavery. As Parker pointed out, they, too, belonged to the ATS and sanctioned its silence about the evils of the day. They supported the American Bible Society, and it "dares not give the New Testament to a single slave." Closer to home, Nehemiah Adams, prominent minister of Boston's Essex Street Congregational Church and author of the sympathetic *South-side View of Slavery* (1854), sponsored revival prayer meetings in his church. Did anyone care? "Not at all," thundered Parker, "he believes in the damnation of Unitarians, Universalists, and babies not wet with baptism; he needs no repentance."⁸

This moral blindness alone would have irritated Parker, who had been indicted in 1855 for aiding in the escape of a fugitive slave and who was a member of a secret committee supporting John Brown's proposed Virginia raid. But in an added insult, although Boston evangelicals had refused to pray about slavery, they had not hesitated to target Parker himself during the prayer meetings. Because of his clearly heterodox beliefs and his popularity as a preacher, revival participants saw Parker almost as a local manifestation of the Antichrist, leading multitudes astray. Since early 1857, there had been a growing movement to pray for his conversion. When, even in the heat of revival, Parker showed few signs of softening toward the evangelical position, a group of laymen intensified their petitions, asking that, if Parker were beyond "saving influence," God would "remove him out of the way, and let his influence die with him." Others prayed that God "would send confusion and distraction into his study" so that he could not preach. There was a suggestion that those involved in the revival unite daily at one o'clock to pray for Parker. To Parker, already ill with symptoms of tuberculosis and having endured numerous visits and letters from well-meaning Christians, such prayers were the last straw. Evangelicals, he wrote one woman, seemed to know little of "the love of God, or [of] morality."[9]

This scenario—earnest prayer warriors seeking Theodore Parker's conversion, his "confusion," or his death—should not be overemphasized. Overall, there was far more weeping for the unconverted in revival prayer meetings than petitions for vengeance. The incident was not so much a case of religious vindictiveness as it was a reflection of the evangelical view of history as a cosmic battle between the forces of good and evil.[10] Just as participants in the revival believed that God would intervene directly to resolve social ills, so they believed Parker a direct representative of the devil. He was, as Charles Finney put it, exerting an "evil influence" in Boston and should be either converted—in other words, won to God's side—or destroyed.

However, the attacks on Parker and the contrast between his and the revivalists' ethical emphases did illustrate the shift away from the New England tradition as well as the circumscribed nature of revival piety. The "five great evils" Parker condemned—war, bad government, slavery, conflict between rich and poor, and the degradation of women—were all moral issues that reflected a community-oriented social awareness. All had found at least some evangelical partisans earlier in the nineteenth century when the New England revival tradition was in its ascendancy.[11] None was a concern of the 1857-58 Revival. The ethical concerns that did surface in 1857-58 centered on individual vices that could be cured through conversion: individual drunkards and gamblers who changed their ways, prostitutes who requested prayer.[12] But as the Parker episode made clear, evangelicals found harmony most easily as they prayed for conversions and against those who obstructed such piety. A commitment to conversionist piety defined a "Bible Christian." On that point the revivalists, or at least those in the mainstream, agreed.[13]

One highly visible exception was George B. Cheever, pastor of the Congregational Church of the Puritans in New York City. Cheever, descendent of several generations of New Englanders, shared the evangelical commitment to piety and revivals.[14] As early as 1845, he had called for "a general revival of religion, North and South" as "the way, indeed, in which we hope God will remove the evil of slavery."[15] Throughout the 1850s, as he grew ever more strident in his condemnation of slavery and of those who waffled in their opposition to the institution, Cheever nonetheless refused to side with the Garrisonian abolitionists of the National Anti-Slavery Society because of their blanket condemnation of the Protestant church. Cheever's church participated in the Revival of 1857-58, and one of the pastor's sermons, "The Christian's Duty in Time of Revival," was so purely pietistic and conversionist that even his opponents among the conservative evangelicals would have found little in it to dispute.[16]

However, as a quintessential New England revivalist/reformer, he broke with social conservatives by insisting that piety must be the cornerstone of an explicit public theology. Cheever maintained that "the church is the conscience of the nation," and it was obligated to apply the Bible to national sins, even the "political sin" of slavery: "Where the Church does not apply God's Word against sin there both the conscience toward God and the spirit of liberty are debauched and wasted, and the nation ripens for destruction."[17]

By 1858, Cheever had become the foremost evangelical spokesman against slavery. Fearless and eloquent in his oratory, he had gained national prominence through a series of Sunday evening sermons during March and April 1857, when he denounced the Supreme Court's Dred Scott decision and advocated civil disobedience as a religious imperative. He also had become embroiled in controversy, in part for the boldness of his social stance, in part because he loved the prophet's mantle too well. Cheever was notoriously quick to summon divine judgment on all whose ideas differed from his, whether the president of the United States, the chief justice of the Supreme Court, or the deacons of his own church. During this period, as Robert York noted, " 'Time-serving' ministers, 'pussy-footing' editors, 'south-side' merchants, the American Tract Society, any persons or organizations which upheld slavery or straddled it, found themselves within the range of Cheever's devastating fire."[18] Socially conservative Protestants resented Cheever's "thus saith the Lord" approach to what they considered political issues. The *Observer* denounced him, and a small but wealthy group of his church members, including three deacons and a number of merchants, pressed Cheever to resign.[19]

Within this context Cheever evaluated the Revival of 1857–58. Although privately he rejoiced in "such a season of refreshing from the presence of the Lord," publicly he criticized the revival on two counts, accusing its supporters of passivity in the face of social ills.[20] First, he charged that the revival distracted evangelicals from the issue of slavery. As a result, pulpits were silent about it, and two "revivals" came to flourish simultaneously: a revival of religion and a revival of sympathy for slavery. Second, he maintained that the revival did nothing to change tacit northern acceptance of slavery. The decision of the American Tract Society to refrain from publishing any material that touched on the subject suggested to Cheever that the "fruit" of the revival had soured and claims of the "presence and power of God's Spirit" were a travesty.[21]

The catalyst for Cheever's sermon "The Two Revivals" was a movement among New York businessmen to support James Buchanan and to urge Congress to admit Kansas as a state under the proslavery Lecompton constitution. Several thousand businessmen signed a petition during the last two weeks of February 1858 endorsing Buchanan's policies, and even more people attended a mass meeting on March 4.[22] Cheever linked support of Lecompton, with its proviso forbidding any interference with slaveholding as a property right, to the Dred Scott decision and saw both as tools for the extension of slavery throughout the United States. Support of Lecompton, then, was support of the "great national crime" of slavery.

Cheever hinted that the instigators might be taking advantage of popular preoccupation with the revival: "Perhaps . . . they think that Christians . . . are too much occupied with the revivals of religion in their own congregations to pay any attention to the morals of the government or country, or to remember the claims of oppressed and enslaved humanity, or to raise any outcry from the Word of God against the perpetration of such vast political and social crimes."[23] Whatever the reason, Cheever was convinced that two revivals were "rushing on, side by side, if not hand in hand," the one a revival of religion, the other a revival of evil: "Is there no antagonism? Are these genuine and true yoke-fellows?"[24]

In his fear that Christian satisfaction with "the mere theory of conversion and of righteousness" might overshadow opposition to slavery, Cheever particularly targeted ministers.[25] He saw the revival emphasis on lay leadership as a smoke screen, enabling northern clergymen to keep a low profile and avoid their responsibilities. If the church was the nation's conscience, then the voice of conscience was the pulpit. Cheever maintained the New England tradition of ministers as guardians of "the moral and spiritual well-being of the community."[26] In effect, he longed for the old days of the 1830s when abolitionists had access to northern pulpits and drew their strength from Christian convictions: "It is a revived and true Christianity . . . that must resuscitate the early fire and power of abhorrence against this infinite abomination."[27] However, the action of the American Tract Society during the anniversary meetings in May 1858 stood as public testimony that those days were gone forever. Revivalism had come to play a much more limited role in human affairs.

"The trade argument":
Conservatives Triumph in the ATS

Conflict over the course of the tract society had escalated as the revival flourished.[28] Debates about the society shared newspaper space alongside news of the religious awakening, sounding notes of discord among stories of prayer meeting harmony and unity.[29] Christian abolitionists had criticized the society for years, charging that it published materials condemning a wide range of vices and evils yet remained silent about sins connected with slavery. The society erred, critics added, not only in acts of omission but in those of commission as well. Its publishing committee censored all references to slavery when the society reprinted religious books. Christian abolitionists, including William Jay in 1853 and Cheever in 1856, attacked the society for hypocrisy and for following policies based on expediency rather than sincere piety. The society did nothing to allay such suspicions when it elected the conservative Nehemiah Adams to the publishing committee in 1854. The committee, usually made up of five or six members, had final say on all ATS publications, and each member possessed an absolute veto.

Change seemed likely in 1856 when a surge in northern antislavery sentiment led to a modest victory for the society's reform-minded minority. A new committee was formed to investigate ATS policy toward slavery and abolition. This group, composed of both conservatives and progressives, hammered out a compromise. They recommended that the ATS avoid the "political aspects" of slavery but publish materials condemning the moral evils that could accompany the practice, such as cruelty by slave owners. The recommendation was adopted in May 1857 and shortly afterward the society approved a tract entitled the *Duties of Masters*.

Southerners immediately cried foul and accused the ATS of becoming a tool for "Northern fanatics." The South Carolina Tract Society demanded that the ATS rescind the new policy or southerners would form their own organization.[30] Inundated with such objections, the officers of the society withdrew the disputed tract in September 1857. From then until the May 12, 1858, anniversary meeting showdown, different sides within the organization traded accusations and arguments.

The contours of the debate suggested that the Revival of 1857–58 had effected little change in northern attitudes toward slavery, although the awakening's stress on unity may have strengthened the tendency of some antislavery moderates toward conciliation. The lines were not clearly drawn, but the conflict had overtones of the tensions between Yankees and the conservative "Yorkers." The tract society reformers, those who supported change, represented an attempted coalition between Yankee abolitionists and antislavery moderates, plus New School and other supporters. The coalition, however, broke down over the issue of moral absolutism. George Cheever and Lewis Tappan advocated the abolitionist stance, calling on the reformers to introduce a resolution before the ATS declaring slavery a sin and mandating it to publish "a tract on the sinfulness of American slavery." Moderates, including Leonard Bacon, Joel Hawes, Asa D. Smith, and Stephen Tyng, Sr., wanted to stand firm behind the original compromise, to reaffirm that "the American Tract Society can and ought to publish . . . upon those moral duties which grow out of the system of slavery." Echoes of the revival sounded in their desire to pursue "tranquillity [sic] and peace" as "the right course." The reformers chose Tyng as their spokesperson.[31]

They were opposed by an establishment group, the socially conservative officers of the tract society and their supporters. These included some moderates convinced that any action except a return to strict silence regarding slavery would "dismember" the ATS and exacerbate sectional tensions.[32] The morning of the annual meeting, May 12, 1858, more than 1,300 male members of the society, a majority of them New York City merchants, jammed the Dutch Reformed Collegiate Church in Lafayette Place.[33] The crowd clearly favored the ATS establishment, evinced not only by the final vote but also by the catcalls and jeers that greeted opposing resolutions. The attitude of the crowd changed from initial reserve to a tumult Cheever described as close to a "Christian mob."[34] Critics later charged that many merchants in the galleries supported the conservatives principally from economic motives, just as others had rallied two months before in favor of Lecompton. Their mood had shifted from that of 1856 when sympathy toward "bleeding Kansas" seemed the more pragmatic stand. By May 1858, businessmen were convinced that offending the South would spell disaster for commercial interests already weakened by the financial panic—an attitude they would maintain until the outbreak of the Civil War.[35]

With the conservatives in charge of the meeting, the ATS reformers were outmaneuvered from the start.[36] Both sides had chosen evangelical Episcopalians as respected and neutral spokespersons: Charles McIlvaine for the establishment and Stephen Tyng for the reformers. McIlvaine offered a resolution approving the action of the executive committee. In support, he argued that Protestant unity, both interdenominational and national, could be protected only by carefully "fencing" the field of common ground where evangelicals stood "together and in harmony." Otherwise, unity would be destroyed, Protestants would self-destruct, and the "realms of infidelity" would gain victory by default.[37] Tyng offered his alternative resolution, seeking unity on a different foundation: the affirmation that the moral aspects of slavery were part of the "vital godliness and sound morality" the ATS was constitutionally mandated to promote. Tyng's resolution was defeated, and disruptions accompanied the speeches of subsequent reformers, including Thompson, Bacon, and Cheever. In the end, the executive committee was supported by a five-to-one vote, and the assembly reelected the entire publishing committee, including Nehemiah Adams and four New York ministers who had participated in the Revival of 1857-58: William R. Williams, William Adams, Benjamin Cutler, and Thomas De Witt.[38]

Observers noted the contrast between prayer meeting harmony and the tract society debacle. At a meeting of the American Congregational Union the following night, William T. Eustis, a New Haven minister, spoke in glowing terms of the revival in Connecticut. Eustis extolled "the catholicity of spirit which the Revival had everywhere manifested, and . . . its effect in breaking down walls of partition between Christian denominations." Then he turned to the subject of the ATS:

> When, yesterday morning . . . visiting this city for the first time since the manifestation of divine grace among you, I entered a convocation where I heard reverend men on the one side pressing the argument of worldly prudence, saying, It is expedient, it is profitable; and on the other side the . . . unanswerable declaration, It is true, it is right; and then the clamorous applause that went up for the trade argument . . . I was disposed to ask, 'Where is the evidence of *your* revival of religion?' (italics in original).[39]

George Cheever spoke more harshly. He poured disdain on "an executive committee of the godliest, staid, conservative ministers and elders in the community," who saw "their whole duty" as that of maintaining "peace and union."[40] As the country had acquiesced to Buchanan on Lecompton, so the church stood silent before the ATS: "God speaks for the slave, they [the tract society] speak for the owner. What kind of piety is this? What fruit of a revival is this?"[41] Cheever and others lambasted the Society for establishing a Mason-Dixon line for sin: "South of such a line you must not speak of such and such sins."[42]

The critics failed to realize in this instance that the real Mason-Dixon line for northern evangelicals was the boundary Charles McIlvaine had mentioned. In the American Tract Society as in the Revival of 1857-58, Protestants chose unity within a limited common ground fenced off by a few essential doctrinal points and a commitment to conversionist piety.[43] There was still room inside the fence for opposition to already "unpopular sins," such as drinking, prostitution, and card playing—those personal vices most evangelicals thought were wrong and did not practice anyway. But divisive social issues remained outside the pale. Such a move once again was a step away from the earlier New England ideal of a religiously and morally harmonious "righteous republic." In this retreat from social reform, the ATS decision was more truly an "evidence" of the Revival of 1857-

58 than either William Eustis or George Cheever recognized. Protestants justified their actions, both in response to Theodore Parker and in the tract society conflict, by appealing to the twin priorities of unity and evangelism. As noted earlier, they did so from a position of postmillennial optimism. They had not yet climbed into the premillennialist lifeboat that would be captained during the Gilded Age by D. L. Moody, a protégé of this awakening.[44] But there were continuities between the cultural retreat symbolized by that craft and the limited terrain now occupied by these earlier revivalists.

Even the vaunted revival unity had more of a downside than its proponents recognized. As the ATS discovered when its Boston auxiliary withdrew shortly after the May meeting, and as the nation would find three years later, superficial unity resembled wallpaper covering cracks in a building. Eventually the structure crumbled anyway. When divisions came, the revivalistic piety that had fostered harmony could paradoxically exacerbate differences. Each side felt its position had been sanctified by the blessing of God and so defended it all the more tenaciously.[45]

Did Popular Reformist Tendencies Exist Beneath the Public Theology?

Although the rules of the union prayer meetings could prohibit such controversial topics as slavery, they could not keep Christian abolitionists from making efforts to appropriate the revival emphasis on prayer for their own cause. In 1859, the American Tract Society, Boston, the antislavery splinter group from the New York City ATS, offered $100 for "the best tract on the duty and importance of praying for the abolition of slavery and oppression." Two authors shared the prize. One of them, James Thome, in *Prayer for the Oppressed*, urged Protestants to use the "renovated instrumentality of prayer, in the hands of a revived church" as a weapon against American slavery.[46] At about the same time Thome's tract was published, George Cheever's brother Henry was on the road as secretary of the newly formed Church Anti-Slavery Society. As part of the society's push for more aggressive antislavery activities within the northern churches, Henry Cheever and other officers encouraged abolitionists to sponsor quarterly or monthly church prayer meetings for those in bondage.[47]

Such activities were samples of the way some northern Protestants did attempt to channel revival piety toward social reform in the wake of the events of 1857–58. Their efforts were on the periphery of most northern church life and received little public attention. Indeed, they were ignored by the editors of mainstream religious periodicals.[48] But these examples raise the question of whether, behind the publicized activities of the urban prayer meetings and central revival figures, the revival might have fostered a popular groundswell of ethical concern. Setting aside the issue of slavery, were there connections, for example, between the 1857–58 Revival and efforts for urban social reform? Was there a reinvigorated temperance or Sabbatarian emphasis? What was the social significance of the YMCA and the Christian Commission? In other words, even if the public image of revivalism moved in a more circumscribed direction, on the grassroots level was there a connection between revivalism and social reform activities?[49]

The answer is a mixed one. The awakening did not reflect the burst of ethical concern some historians have attempted to connect with midcentury revivalism. However, neither was it the sort of "great reversal" others have identified among evangelicals in the early twentieth century, "when all progressive social concern, whether political or private, became suspect among revivalistic evangelicals."[50] The imperatives of benevolence and duty, while most clearly tied to New England theology, had been a central part of the mindset of most antebellum evangelicals, and those ideas did not vanish in 1858. They were, however, adapted to changing conditions and directed into new channels. On the one hand, as noted in the last chapter, reform-minded Yankees turned their attention to politics. The Republican party platform of 1860 reflected evangelical social concerns in its opposition to the spread of slavery, its anti-Catholicism, and its concern for political corruption.[51] On the other hand, at the popular level as well as in the public arena, the social side of revivalism increasingly came to be identified with conversionist piety.

One reason was that the 1858 awakening simply had no substantive ethical message apart from the twin assumptions that individual regeneration would somehow help to bring about social reform and that there was power in prayer. This was one consequence of the desire to downplay potentially divisive preaching or teaching. When evangelicals sought harmony by applying a "gag rule" to the prayer meeting, they not only silenced women and forestalled abolitionists, they also muted more general ethical concerns.[52] Few ministers sounded the themes of disinterested benevolence or radical holiness that had inspired evangelicals in the 1830s and 1840s.[53] In fostering the devotional piety of prayer, singing, and testimonies, the revival did help to create a religious climate among middle-class Protestants in which both Methodist and Keswick ("victorious life") holiness emphases on selfless love and "power for service" would later flourish. But these emphases came into their own only after the late 1860s; they were not a part of the fabric of popular religious concern in 1857–58.[54]

Not only did the concept of social concern as an expression of revivalism begin to narrow, its object also became more circumscribed. Instead of targeting the oppressed, as in the case of slavery, or the destitute in the city, or social outcasts such as prostitutes, evangelicals concentrated more and more on people like themselves—groups within the middle class with special needs, such as young urban men and women, or members of the upwardly mobile, usually northern European, "working poor." For example, John Wanamaker's "institutional church," Bethany Presbyterian, a Philadelphia congregation that began as a Sunday school during the revival, offered its range of social services primarily to those "with hopes of fulfilling their aspirations to middle class status."[55]

Just as they exemplified the spirit of the Revival of 1857–58 in so many other areas, the YMCA and the United States Christian Commission also illustrated the shifting social focus. Caught up in disputes over slavery and suffering from organizational difficulties and financial uncertainty, the North American "Y" was floundering when the awakening swept the nation. "Reborn" in an atmosphere of revival, the YMCA reflected the religious fervor of the times. Enthusiastic young men promoted many of the most popular urban prayer meetings, including one in Cleveland crowded with 2,000 participants at the height of the religious fervor. A prayer service in San Francisco outgrew the association's downtown meeting rooms and had to be transferred to a church where " 'many souls [were] hopefully converted.' " The Charleston "Y" experienced similar circumstances and moved its meetings to a large hall. In Baltimore the "Y" had "five early morning meetings with four later in the day."[56]

The organization bore the pietistic and evangelistic imprint of the revival until the end of the Civil War and throughout the rest of the nineteenth century. During the immediate postrevival years, the zeal of many young YMCA members for the "general promulgation of the Gospel" threatened to overwhelm the association's original, more specific purpose of improving the condition of young urban clerks and merchants by surrounding them with evangelical influences.[57]

With the outbreak of the Civil War, this evangelistic zeal concentrated on the soldiers of the Union army. Lemuel Moss, a member of the Christian Commission and its first historian, noted that "from the beginning the army was recognized as a field for evangelical effort."[58] In 1864 the Commission's executive committee affirmed that there was no "more interesting and important field for missionary operations . . . to be found in the world" than the Union army.[59] According to agency records, by the close of the war a total of nearly 5,000 USCC representatives had distributed an estimated 2.5 million pieces of literature, preached almost 50,000 sermons and held more than 75,000 prayer meetings. In contrast to its rival organization, the United States Sanitary Commission, the main thrust of the USCC was always pietistic and conversionist.[60]

While it insisted that its main work was spiritual, the Christian Commission did in fact care about the temporal needs of soldiers. The commission's purpose statement expressed the relationship between the two: the USCC sought "the spiritual good of the soldiers . . . and *incidentally* their intellectual improvement and social and physical comfort"[61] (italics mine). In an approach increasingly appropriated by evangelicals during the latter nineteenth century, humanitarian concern mattered, but it was incidental to evangelism. As commission chairman George Stuart commented, "there is a good deal of religion in a warm shirt and a good beefsteak."[62] Stuart clearly felt the shirt and steak were important, but he also felt compelled to justify them by citing their effectiveness in promoting religion.

On an individual level, many USCC agents were heroic and genuinely selfless in their expressions of compassion. An agent at Gettysburg won respect when he evacuated severely wounded men from the battlefield by placing them on his back and then crawling on his hands and knees to a place where they could be attended. He apparently saved more than 100 soldiers that way. Others served as nurses, reporting that they had to "dress wounds, strip off filthy garments, wash the blood and dust of hard marches off of the soldiers, cleanse them of vermin, and put upon them clean clothing; dig graves for the dead."[63] Many also comforted the wounded and dying in hospitals and wrote letters home for those unable to do so. By the end of the war, the "practical Christianity" exemplified by many of the delegates was unquestionable. Nonetheless, it tended to be a somewhat individualistic response to the crises of war rather than the expression of a clear humanitarian or benevolent ethic. And the northern view of the conflict as a holy crusade hardly put the popular support for the troops that undergirded the USCC in the category of disinterested or selfless benevolence.

During the immediate postwar years, the social concern of the YMCA reflected a similar "occasional" approach. Officially, the association returned to its focus on "the social, mental, and religious improvement of Young Men" in contrast to the revivalistic stress on general evangelism.[64] Nonetheless, religious activities remained popular, with prayer meetings and Bible classes as featured YMCA functions. In some cities, however, the association also served as a center for community welfare work, often because it was the one interdenominational group in town. In 1867, for example, the Chicago association distributed more than $24,000 to worthy poor families. YMCAs in a number of urban areas established employment bureaus to help returning veterans find work and to provide assistance to association members during the financial depression of the mid-1870s. Associations occasionally became centers for disaster relief, as the New Orleans YMCA did during the yellow fever epidemic of 1878.[65] Such activities demonstrated that revivalistic Protestants did not entirely abandon social action during the postwar period. Even so, most of these efforts focused on amelioration of specific ills that affected urban middle and working classes rather than any concerted attempt at social reform. And the particular legacy of the Revival of 1857–58 continued to be its piety.

At a memorial service in 1900, a YMCA secretary pointed to the parallels between the career of evangelist D. L. Moody and that of Robert R. McBurney, for 30 years secretary of the powerful New York City YMCA. The two were widely acknowledged as the men who exerted the greatest influence on the association during the second half of the nineteenth century. They were born the same year; both came to cities (Moody to Boston and McBurney to New York City) at age 17; both shifted from business careers to Christian service; and they died within a year of one another. They were the ideal, and often idealized, types of the "active layman" who emerged following the Revival of 1857–58.

Both men engaged in a wide range of Christian pursuits during their lifetimes, but their piety made them great in the eyes of admirers: "Each was an evangelist, a preacher of the gospel, a messenger of good tidings and a worker for the extension of the kingdom of the Lord Jesus Christ. . . . Moody was at all times a man of prayer, a student of the Bible, and a personal worker. . . . McBurney never ceased to be a man of prayer, a man of Bible study, a personal worker. . . . These three things . . . sum up the lives of these men."[66]

Holiness, Revivalism, and Reform: Did They Combine in 1857 and 1858?

If revivalism of the YMCA and Moody variety was not strongly reformist, what about those evangelicals who connected revival fervor with Christian perfection?[67] In the first place, although "Pentecostal" terminology became common during the revival, especially among Methodists and New School Presbyterians, the direct links between the awakening and the spread of holiness or perfectionist teachings have been overstated. During the revival itself, specific teachings on sanctification and testimonies of obtaining that experience largely were limited to Methodists, and even in that denomination, the primary emphasis remained on conversion.[68] As chapter 4 pointed out, Phoebe Palmer, the premier holiness figure of the late 1850s, had reservations about the genuineness of the urban union prayer meetings. She felt that meetings where "Christian women were not permitted to open their lips" could not expect to enjoy "blessed outpourings of the Spirit." To Palmer and her followers, such gatherings hardly were evidence of the spread of holiness or a new "Pentecost."[69]

Second, scrutiny of Palmer and other evangelicals most committed to the doctrine of holiness indicates that the connection between those teachings, the Revival of 1857–58, and social reform was never as clear-cut as it may have appeared to later observers. In Palmer's case the demands of the *annus mirabilis* of 1858 actually marked a shift away from community involvement. From then on she would concentrate almost exclusively on preaching and writing to the neglect of the local benevolence that characterized her life in New York City from the 1830s to the late 1850s. Palmer had always been a social conservative who felt that the most useful endeavors involved "the work of bringing sinners to Jesus."[70] Nevertheless, in pursuit of that goal she had visited prisons, distributed tracts, and helped care for orphans.

According to one historian, Palmer's encounter with the poor during tract distribution in the 1840s "drew a compassionate response." "She began taking gifts of money, food, and clothing on her rounds, and eventually affiliated with the New York Female Assistance Society for the Relief and Religious Instruction of the Sick Poor, for whom she served as a 'visitor,' and whose corresponding secretary she became in 1847, filling that office until leaving for England in 1859."[71]

Palmer also initiated efforts to found the Five Points Mission in 1850.[72] As scholars have pointed out, the mission became the site of one of the earliest examples of Protestant institutional work in tenement areas. It has been less recognized that the Five Points Mission began strictly as a religious work and that Palmer and the Methodist women who backed her had little to do with the House of Industry that grew out of it. The mission was located only a few blocks from where the Chatham Street Chapel had been abandoned nine years earlier, and in some ways the area proved just as daunting to Palmer and her friends as it had to Finney and his supporters.

Although it began with adult evangelism and temperance work, throughout the 1850s the actual Five Points Mission focused primarily on children, except for class meetings and Sunday services. Louis Pease, the original city missionary who directed the work, founded an independent House of Industry in May 1851. From that point, two organizations existed side by side: the Mission, sponsored by the Methodist Ladies Home Missionary Society with its large Sabbath school, charity day school for children, and limited religious work among adults; and the House of Industry, sponsored by the Episcopal Church of the Ascension, with workshops, its own day school, job training, and apartments for the poor. Beginning in May 1852, there was an increasing rift between the two institutions.[73]

By the late 1850s, both groups were concentrating on children. They had discovered that in the largely Irish Catholic tenement district children were the group most receptive to Protestant proselytizing. The 1858 Annual Report of the Ladies Home Missionary Society, prepared for the anniversary meetings in May, recorded that 800 children had been "taught and clothed by the mission" during the previous 12 months.[74] The report noted that the religious interest of the winter had reached the Five Points, resulting in increased conversions among a select group of adults: "The subjects of the work were not ordinarily from among the more ignorant and vicious, but were persons of some religious training, who had been dragged down to the Five Points by their poverty, or degraded by intoxicating drinks. . . . Among them are natives of England, Scotland, Ireland, Wales, Germany, France, and America."[75]

During the next decade, the work at the Five Points Mission continued in the same pattern. A guidebook to New York City reported that holidays such as Thanksgiving and Christmas were ideal times to see the fruit of the mission's labor: "From six hundred to a thousand children, homeless, houseless, and orphaned, each with a new suit or dress made by the lady managers and their friends, singing charmingly, exhibiting great proficiency in education and a wonderful knowledge of the Bible, sitting down to a well-laid table, it is touching to see."[76]

The women of the Five Points Mission, inspired by Phoebe Palmer's energy, cared year after year for thousands of street children, at a time when there were approximately 60,000 children of school age in the city who received no formal education at all. However, the Revival of 1857–58 appeared to have little impact on the Mission work other than increased conversions; it did not lead to any marked surge of social reform efforts in the Five Points area. The women had long since scaled back from their initial optimism about working with adults to concentrate on the more productive mission to children. Their relationship with Louis Pease and the House of Industry also indicated that they followed Palmer in considering welfare efforts subservient to evangelism.[77]

In June 1859, Palmer and her husband, Walter, left for England to begin what has been described as a "four-and-one-half-year, almost continual revival campaign." When she returned to the United States in 1863, it was to strengthen holiness adherents within mainstream northern Methodism whose position in the denomination had been undermined by the secession of the holiness-inspired Free Methodists in 1860.[78] In the years until her death in 1874, Palmer continued her career as a revivalist and, as editor of the *Guide to Holiness*, built that magazine into an influential publication. She seems to have had little specific concern for social reform during this period.[79]

A similar pattern was evident in others who later became holiness leaders. Most focused on piety. And some who did hold reformist views before the war were hard-pressed to find popular support among their congregations. At least two leaders of the National Campmeeting Association for the Promotion of Holiness, founded in 1867, had been active as local ministers in the Revival of 1857–58.[80] Benjamin M. Adams, at the time pastor of the Duane Street Methodist Church in New York City, had begun attending Phoebe Palmer's Tuesday meeting in late 1857. Throughout the revival period, Adams's diary reveals his quest for a deeper experience of sanctification.

Sometime after 1858, that desire was fulfilled, and Adams spent the remainder of his years in the Methodist Church as an ardent proponent of holiness teachings. He was a speaker at the first national holiness camp meeting in Vineland, New Jersey, and, until his death in 1902, was a regular preacher and Bible teacher for the holiness cause.[81] Adams's abolitionist tendencies predated his search for sanctification. In 1856, he had combined his preaching with employment as an agent of the New York State Republican Party. During the revival months of 1858 his diary records regular attendance at noon prayer meetings and Palmer's Tuesday meeting, as well as solidarity with the antislavery cause among New York Conference Methodists. In an entry for June 7, 1858, he wrote that one parishioner "took me to task quite severely on my abolition notions." Yet during the ensuing four decades, Adams came to be known chiefly for his preaching and his piety, especially his commitment to prayer, rather than for any political or social activism.[82]

Alfred Cookman, who would win respect in Methodist circles as a popular and powerful preacher, briefly attained what he understood as Christian perfection or "heart purity" in 1847 as a 19-year-old. After some years of doubt about the experience, he decisively embraced holiness views in 1856, 18 months before revival began at the Green Street Church in Philadelphia, where he was the pastor. In a second Philadelphia assignment at Union Church, an influential parish in the city's business district, Cookman experienced conflict with members of the congregation because of his antislavery views.

Although neither was a radical abolitionist, both Cookman and Adams fit the profile of holiness adherents who held antislavery views. The Revival of 1857–58, however, did nothing to rally supporters to their sides, at least not for Cookman in Philadelphia, and apparently not for Adams in New York. During the Civil War, Cookman took a turn as a volunteer Christian Commission agent, when he preached and did pastoral work among the Army of the Potomac. After the war, he was a key figure in the holiness camp meeting movement.[83] As he looked forward to the Vineland camp meeting in 1867, Cookman wrote, "Oh, that, as in 1760, a revival of the work of holiness may begin, that, spreading North, South, East, and West, may wrap the nation, the continent, and the world in a great flame of devotion to Jesus!"[84] A decade after the 1857–58 Revival, Cookman still saw the need for a revival of holiness teachings to *begin* in northern Methodism. His "Golden Age" was not 1858, but the period in English Methodism when hundreds of accounts of instantaneous sanctification convinced John Wesley that deliverance from sin could be immediate. And "devotion to Jesus" centered on holiness rather than involvement in social reform. After his death in 1871, Alfred Cookman's biography became a part of the growing corpus of literature on the "higher life."

A few activists in the 1857–58 Revival did engage in specific efforts to ameliorate social problems in the years immediately following the Civil War. Even in these cases, however, it is difficult to trace the direct connections between revivalism, perfectionism, and social reform. Often mentioned are Episcopalians Stephen H. Tyng, Sr., and his son, Stephen, Jr., along with Unitarian-turned-Episcopalian Frederic Dan Huntington. The elder Tyng, an adherent of what has been described as a "nearly perfectionistic evangelicalism," was a long-time advocate of reform efforts, including support for temperance legislation as well as involvement from 1845 into the postwar period with the American Female Guardian Society and Home for the Friendless.[85] Perfectionistic evangelicalism may have spurred Tyng's concern for indigent women in the 1840s, but during that same period he remained quite conservative on the issue of slavery. He moved into the antislavery camp in the context of the 1857–58 awakening but apparently did so more from a desire to pick up the mantle of his fallen son Dudley than from the ethical influence of revivalism.[86]

During the 15 years following the war, Stephen Tyng, Jr., built Holy Trinity Church, New York City, into "one of the great mission churches in America," combining social concern with aggressive evangelical preaching.[87] In doing so, Tyng, Jr., sought a "return to the ideals of primitive Christianity" but also followed in the footsteps of a Protestant Episcopal church social movement that had begun in the 1850s with increased city missions and support of Pease's House of Industry in New York City and another in Baltimore.[88] Revivalism, evangelical convictions, and a sense of consecration to Christ certainly played a role in the Tyngs' social activism, but the relationship was more complex than a simple cause/effect. Nor is it easy to see a decisive impact from the 1857–58 Revival.

Frederic Dan Huntington, Unitarian chaplain at Harvard University, brought a strong ethical sense with him when he embraced Trinitarian views shortly after the 1858 awakening. However, in a situation somewhat analogous to Alfred Cookman's lonely antislavery stand, Huntington discovered that the revival had not created a kindred ethical spirit among other Unitarian converts to Trinitarian evangelicalism. As a newly ordained Episcopal deacon, Huntington cherished the dream of building a Free "People's Church" in Boston's Back Bay area, but his wealthy potential parishioners refused to support the idea. They might have experienced revival, but they were no more excited about attending a church open to the poor than middle-class Free Church members had been in New York City during the late 1830s. Huntington did go on to organize mission chapels and Sunday schools in tenement areas. After his election in 1869 as the first Episcopal bishop of central New York, he became the president of the Church Association in the Interests of Labor and came to be seen as a forerunner of the Social Gospel movement.[89]

Revivalism without Social Reform

The weight of all of these examples suggests that while some evangelicals maintained and even pioneered specific efforts at social betterment, the Revival of 1857–58 produced no groundswell of ethical concern. Even for evangelicals committed to reform, the revival rarely was the turning point that motivated their involvement. Instead, as this and the previous chapter have argued, the awakening became a different kind of turning point, marking a shift in the public role of revivals in American life. It signaled an end to the dominance of the New England revival tradition, where conversionist piety and community moral reform proceeded in tandem to produce virtue and social harmony. In its place emerged a more socially conservative view of revivalism that stressed the importance of evangelism and shared devotional piety. Any needed social transformation would result from the cumulative personal reforms of regenerate individuals and from the direct, supernatural intervention of God.

Because of their influence as revival apologists and the importance of New York City as the symbolic center of the awakening, conservatives from the Presbyterian camp facilitated this shift, but it signaled a consensus among many middle-class northern Protestants, including Baptists and Methodists. Perhaps to fill a certain void, as reform efforts became more politicized during the 1850s, the social conservatives stepped in to spiritualize public understandings of revival. Their actions anticipated what observers have noted as an increasing "privatization" of revivalism during the years from 1865 to 1900, sometimes described as the transition from a more broadly "Calvinistic" public theology of revivalism to a more "pietistic" view. In some ways, the 1857–58 Revival represented a fusion of the two: the Calvinistic goal of a righteous republic achieved through pietistic means. Socially conservative Calvinists served as mediators in the development of this position.[90]

Of course, continuities and suggestions of connections between the Revival of 1857–58 and postwar evangelicalism must be qualified in light of the immense impact of the Civil War in shaping northern Protestantism's view of religion and the republic during the remainder of the nineteenth century. In *American Apocalypse*, James Moorhead has traced the way eschatological interpretations of the war served to restore Protestants' confidence in themselves and their culture. Northern Protestants viewed the Union victory as God's vindication of his elect. As a result, they collectively reappropriated the New England vision of the republic as a redeemer nation destined to bless the whole world with Christian civilization. This development was in many ways compatible with and related to the changed understanding of revivalism traced in these two chapters. To some people, the war itself vindicated the emphases of the 1857–58 awakening: the conflict was God's cataclysmic intervention to bring about national purification and reformation.[91] The war's outcome also confirmed that conversionist piety had indeed ensured that "the nation was . . . providentially supplied with the moral earnestness and power needed for the terrible conflict."[92] In addition, religious interpretations of both events—the revival and the war—encouraged a passive stance toward social reform. On the one hand, Protestants could retreat from intractable social issues and trust in the efficacy of prayer, evangelism, and divine intervention. On the other, with the resolution of slavery and the absolution of war, northern culture needed little further transformation. Revivalism, laissez-faire economic principles, and personal morality had created a Christian civilization: all that remained was for such principles to be promoted among newly emancipated blacks and around the world.[93] Both stances, in effect, could sanction middle-class social complacency.

These two approaches, a retreat from social issues in favor of conversionist piety and the cultural optimism that assumed conversionist piety somehow had already created a Christian civilization, were both evident among Protestants during the latter nineteenth century, usually adapted to the contexts of pre-and post-millennial views, respectively. Sometimes they could even coexist in the same person, as in the case of D. L. Moody. According to George Marsden, Moody's concern for evangelism lay behind his decision to distance himself from direct social involvement and to embrace a pessimistic premillennial view of culture. At the same time, however, Moody retained a confidence in the cultural impact of revivalistic piety, based on his experiences in the 1857–58 Revival. "Revival," Moody said in an 1899 sermon, "is the only hope for our republic, for I don't believe that a republican form of government can last without righteousness." He continued, "Pentecost isn't over yet. The revival of '57 isn't over yet by a good deal. Some of the best men we have in our churches were brought out in '57. Why shouldn't we have now at the close of this old century a great shaking up and a mighty wave from heaven."[94] Yet, whether Moody was concerned about evangelism or the righteousness necessary for the republic, the key was revivalistic piety, not social reform.

Jeremiah Lanphier, of Fulton Street fame, lived out his days as director of the noon prayer meeting. Even into the 1880s, he was still a permanent fixture at the gathering, praying with newcomers and distributing copies of the Gospel of John.[95] Samuel Irenaeus Prime divided his energies after the war between editorial work and Protestant ecumenical efforts. Henry Ward Beecher, ever the "weather vane" of middle-class trends, spent time after the revival, as he had to a certain extent before, helping his parishioners adapt, guilt-free, to the affluence that urban living offered the successful.[96] Although Harriet Beecher Stowe never completely lost her Yankee moralism, she, too, shifted away from reform efforts after the war, concentrating on her literary career. Stowe advocated her own brand of perfectionist or "higher life" teachings, but they primarily served as sources of comfort in the face of family tragedies and as ideals of piety she regularly set before her grown children.[97] The "great reformation of 1858" that Stowe had called for in March of that year never materialized. The 1857–58 Revival instead marked a transformation in Protestant attitudes toward the role of revivals in American public life, a transformation toward conversionist piety and away from specific moral reforms. Evangelicals never completely rejected social activism at midcentury; rather, the Revival of 1857–58 provided little or no ethical impetus for such activism apart from the imperatives of prayer and evangelism. It was, in that sense, revivalism without social reform.

SEVEN

Legacies of 1857–58

D. L. Moody and the "Revival Generation"

MORE THAN ANY OTHER single person during the second half of the nineteenth century, Dwight L. Moody came to represent a transformed evangelical revival tradition ushered in by the Revival of 1857–58. During the 1870s, supported by religious and secular press coverage, Moody became a national figure and his urban revivalism part of the national popular culture. These postwar revivals reflected the formalism of the earlier establishment Calvinists fused with the emotive, lay-oriented piety of Methodist and Baptist populists and further shaped by the mass commercialism of an urban setting. What emerged was a businesslike, consumer-sensitive approach to revivals that further blurred the line between revivals and mass evangelism. The unusual numbers of conversions and heightened religious concern that had always characterized revivals became more predictable as evangelicals increasingly employed marketing techniques to reach people in densely populated urban settings.

In recent decades, Moody has become a familiar symbol of middle-class Victorian evangelicalism. Critics and admirers alike have recognized the revivalist's appropriation of business techniques and his embrace of commercial culture, in short, his place in the "professionalization" of urban revivals. Yet they have rarely acknowledged his indebtedness to the 1857–58 Revival for much of this style of piety.[1] The connections may have been obscured because Moody, who turned 21 in February 1858, was still a relatively unknown figure in Chicago religious and business circles. Although he was an enthusiastic participant, he played no special role in the Chicago phase of the awakening. He attended church prayer meetings, spoke as a member of the crowd at the downtown noon gatherings, and busied himself expanding his Sunday school work.[2] Not until 1861 when Moody became the first full-time "Y" staff member in Chicago and when he took on wartime duties with the Christian Commission did the impact of the revival on his religious work become most clearly evident. Almost immediately he injected new enthusiasm into the flagging noon prayer meeting, making the lunch-hour gathering and the patterns of piety that had emerged during 1857 and 1858 hallmarks of the Chicago YMCA. Moody's dedication to the noon meeting was legendary. In 1868 Farwell Hall, the first YMCA building in the nation, was destroyed by fire. Association members recalled that even while the building was still in flames Moody had fliers distributed on the street, announcing the new location for the day's prayer meeting.[3]

Moody's later evangelistic "innovations" were in large part systematic recreations of techniques from the prewar spiritual awakening, refined through years of practice with the YMCA. The celebrated Moody campaigns in major American urban centers from 1875 to 1878 appeared to replicate, in intentional rather than spontaneous fashion, the earlier revival ethos. For example, key leaders in many cities issuing invitations to the evangelist had been active in 1857–58, among them William E. Dodge in New York, John Wanamaker and George H. Stuart in Philadelphia, John Farwell in Chicago, and clergyman Theodore Cuyler in Brooklyn. The committees of businessmen and ministers who handled preparatory details and publicity imitated the YMCA organizational approach to the union prayer meetings. Moody recognized the lure of religion as entertainment; he advertised his meetings and sermon topics on the amusement pages of mass-circulation dailies. Apart from the evening preaching services, the most popular aspect of the Moody campaigns was the daily noon prayer meeting, conducted by the evangelist, followed by separate women's meetings. With only a few changes, these gatherings duplicated the earlier businessmen's groups. There may even have been some continuation of gender tensions. In his description of one such 1876 meeting, historian William McLoughlin noted that "[o]stensibly the purpose of the noon prayer meetings were [sic] 'to bring the business men under religious influences at the noon hour.' Usually there were as many women present as men."[4]

In addition, Moody held his religious services in the downtown business districts. In Brooklyn, he preached in a converted skating rink; in Philadelphia, a renovated railroad depot; in New York City, the Hippodrome. As for the revival meetings themselves, the evangelist was famous for his insistence on punctuality and order. In Philadelphia, he informed crowds that the doors would be closed promptly each night at 7:30 PM, "and if the President of the United States comes after that he can't get in." Nor did Moody permit emotional outbursts or interruptions. A shout of "Hallelujah!" meant ushers would ask the offending person to leave.[5] The fast-paced worship and Moody's custom of having people stand for prayer rather than asking them to come forward were also elements of urban mass revivalism drawing from the practices of 1857–58. Although it is more difficult to make specific connections between Moody's personal style and influences from the earlier revival, there were affinities. The evangelist's commitment to a simple gospel message echoed the straightforward "Come to Jesus" theme of the prayer meeting revival, while Moody's well-known aversion to controversy was reminiscent of the prohibition against controverted points.

There were, of course, differences between the Moody approach and the prewar awakening. Most obviously, his urban mass evangelism centered around the personality, initiative, and celebrity status of a single individual. It was a style that both looked back to revivalists such as George Whitefield and Charles Finney and forward to the "personal empire-building" of later evangelicals and fundamentalists.[6] Also, as noted in chapter 4, Moody was able to synthesize Victorian business culture with Victorian sentimentalism to a greater degree than was possible in the 1857–58 Revival. His campaigns were more publicly inclusive; they were revivals organized by businessmen but not businessmen's revivals.[7] Perhaps most important, because of the intentional character of the Moody campaigns, the absence of a powerful clergy/press coalition to canonize their significance, and the increasing pluralism of American society, Moody's efforts were not recognized as evidence of a national awakening in the same league with the events of 1857–58 or earlier in American history.[8]

The "Revival Generation"

Moody was the most visible symbol of a middle-class, public American evangelicalism that emerged in part as a legacy of the Revival of 1857–58, yet he was far from alone. In effect, Moody, Hannah Whitall Smith, John Wanamaker, and many others—some mentioned in chapter 3—whose lives were touched by the awakening constituted a revival generation, loosely analogous to the twentieth-century "sixties generation."[9] They moved almost like a "demographic bump" through Protestant America during the second half of the nineteenth century. The awakening cannot, of course, be seen as the only defining event in their lives; they were, after all, a generation who lived through the Civil War. But neither should it be discounted or downplayed as a formative religious experience.

For most who remained in the evangelical camp, the conversionist emphasis of the revival remained paramount, whether expressed through Sunday school work, urban mass evangelism, or foreign missions. The majority of these young men and women had grown to maturity familiar with traditions of revival as a part of American Protestantism, but the sheer magnitude of the response in 1857–58, dramatized by the crowded urban setting, was something new. Looking back years later, George Stuart viewed the awakening as the moment when he grasped the potential of mass evangelism. For John V. Farwell it brought an epiphany revealing the role urban laymen could play in furthering the cause of Christ.[10] D. L. Pierson, son and biographer of missions leader Arthur Tappan Pierson, credited the Revival of 1857–58 with helping to "mold his [the elder Pierson's] ideals and convictions as to evangelism."[11] As a young New York City seminary student with a Bible class at the Thirteenth Street Presbyterian Church, A. T. Pierson himself wrote during the revival, "I have just begun to realize the true worth of souls and the true secret of living near to Christ. . . . I feel that I have been baptized with the Holy Spirit and am fully resolved never again to pass a day when I cannot feel at its close that I have done something for my Saviour."[12] Pierson's remarks also showed how the intensity of the revival experience helped to create a climate among Protestants conducive to the rapid spread of holiness teachings in the post–Civil War era.[13]

Pierson, a respected missions theorist and educator, was not the only member of the revival generation to include missionary activity within the scope of his concern. Although evidence is fragmentary, enough can be pieced together to suggest that women who had been swept up in the religious intensity of 1857–58 were among the vanguard of the post–Civil War women's mission movement. Lottie Moon, pioneer Southern Baptist missionary to China, was converted during the revival in Charlottesville, Virginia.[14] Laura Askew Haygood, Atlanta teacher and later missionary educator for the Methodist church in China, marked July 28, 1858, as the date of her conversion.[15] The revival also engendered the spirit of interdenominational cooperation that enabled a New York Dutch Reformed woman, Sarah Doremus, to found the Woman's Union Missionary Society in 1861. In the first issue of the group's *Missionary Link* magazine, Doremus offered the missionary cause as "a large field of usefulness" for that "large class of young Christians, who have just crossed the threshold of their holy profession."[16]

John Fretz Funk, a young Mennonite who had left Pennsylvania to work in his uncle's Chicago lumberyard, found his "field of usefulness" closer to home. Funk was converted through revival services in Chicago's Third Presbyterian Church in January 1858. However, he remained deeply influenced by his Mennonite roots and the following winter returned to Bucks County, Pennsylvania, to be baptized. Back in Chicago, Funk stayed in the lumber business for five years, although in January 1864 he began *Herald of Truth*, the first Mennonite periodical in the United States. Ordained in May 1865, Funk went on to pioneer further Mennonite efforts in religious publishing, Sunday schools, and, later in the century, missions. Funk's experience in the revival and his acquaintance with Moody helped to shape his development as a mediator who would introduce evangelical Americanizing influences into the Mennonite church while attempting to retain that denomination's historic distinctiveness.[17]

Identification with the revival generation did not mean, of course, that Victorian Protestants automatically associated themselves with the more overtly evangelical camp. Some, such as Charles A. Briggs and Lyman Abbott, moved toward what would come to be characterized as the modernist or "liberal" side of American Protestantism. In later years, they tended to celebrate the ecumenical focus of the 1857–58 meetings. The distinctions are imprecise—Moody certainly was open to a broad spectrum of Protestants; John Fretz Funk maintained a long friendship with John McMullen, a Chicago Roman Catholic priest. Yet Moody and Funk remained solidly within a revivalistic tradition that prized the evangelism of the prewar awakening. Those with more liberal leanings cherished memories of a unity that broke denominational barriers.

Charles A. Briggs illustrated the difference. In 1904, Briggs, then an Episcopal priest, wrote, "It is doubtless owing to my early experience with devout men of various denominations of Christians in the university [of Virginia] that I have always been a Union man. The reunion of Christendom, which I represent as much as anyone in this country, had its beginning in me, in my religious life at the University."[18] Lyman Abbott, among the liberals, and such moderates as YMCA national secretary Richard C. Morse shared in the revival legacy along with such well-known evangelicals as Moody and Pierson.[19]

However, even for evangelicals unconcerned about denominational ecumenism, the "union" character of the 1857–58 awakening enabled a whole new set of interdenominational Protestant networks that helped like-minded laymen and lay-women to pursue independent religious ventures that caught their attention. These new networks tended to be more fluid and lay-dominated than the earlier extra-ecclesiastical societies of the benevolent empire. They offered evangelical entre-preneurs of the Gilded Age, whether gospel mission pioneers Jerry McAuley and Charles Crittenton or Women's Temperance Crusade leader Annie Wittenmyer, an entirely new field of contacts. The YMCA and the USCC, as well as the va-cation-style holiness camp meetings, were early examples of such networks on a regional and national scale; noon prayer meetings and city Young Men's or Young Women's Associations performed the same functions in local communities. As a result, the legacy from the Revival of 1857–58 to Protestant social activism in the later nineteenth century, a subject discussed in chapters 5 and 6, included patterns of organization and of piety rather than ethical emphases.[20] Two examples were the Women's Temperance Crusade (WTC) and the early urban rescue missions.

The Women's Temperance Crusade of 1873–74 demonstrated that, although evangelical women had been eclipsed in 1857–58, they, too, had developed a national consciousness, as well as strategies that employed many of the patterns of public piety popularized in the awakening. The first mass movement in Amer-ican Protestantism following the Civil War belonged to them. Beginning in De-cember 1873, interdenominational groups of church women in small towns of New York and Ohio began organizing marches against the liquor trade. They invaded saloons, held prayer meetings, and pressured owners to sign a pledge to stop selling alcoholic beverages. When denied permission to enter a saloon, the crusaders would organize prayer meetings on the street in front of the establish-ment. Newspapers picked up the story and helped to turn a few local incidents into a nationwide campaign. By the end of 1874, more than 900 crusades had been held in 32 states and territories, involving between 57,000 and 143,000 women in prayer and nonviolent action against saloons.[21] The WTC made its greatest impact in small midwestern towns rather than large urban areas, sug-gesting that traditional communities remained the power base of "feminized" Prot-estantism.[22] Nevertheless, the crusade provided the grassroots support that led to the formation of the more influential Woman's Christian Temperance Union.

The Women's Temperance Crusade did not begin in imitation of the Revival of 1857–58, but there were numerous hints that influences from the revival con-tributed to its rapid spread. The most obvious was a pervasive commitment to public prayer. Wittenmyer, an activistic Methodist and USCC veteran from the war years, described the temperance crusade as "all of God, in answer to prayer. . . . The temperance question is on the crest of this wonderful tidal wave [of prayer]."[23] The temperance cause provided women with the moral justification for challenging male public space. Stories of WTC work included sensationalistic an-ecdotes with titles such as "The First Saloon Prayer-Meeting," "Fierce Dogs sub-dued by Prayer," "Acquitted—Singing and Praying not Unlawful," and "Every Saloon closed where they held Prayer-Meetings."[24] The appropriation of patterns from the revival was particularly clear in Chicago. After women there were driven from the streets by an angry mob, they regrouped by forming a "daily temperance prayer meeting." Led by Frances Willard, it met at 3:00 PM in Farwell Hall, the

YMCA building, in the same room where association workers continued to hold the noon meeting. Willard's group, open to women and men, was publicized by the women with "large placards of welcome, hand-bills circulated on the streets, notices of the press; [and] accounts of the occurrences at the meeting." It came to serve as a spiritual nerve center for temperance work in the Midwest.[25] The efforts of the temperance women, juxtaposed against those of the YMCA, were just one indication that the patterns of the so-called businessmen's revival had become a part of the voluntaristic lay piety of women and men alike during the second half of the nineteenth century.

Both Jerry McAuley, who began New York City's Water Street Mission in 1872, and Charles Crittenton, founder of the Florence Crittenton homes during the 1880s, were influenced indirectly rather than directly by the events of 1857–58. McAuley, a converted thief and alcoholic, made an initial profession of Christian faith at Sing Sing Prison in the early 1860s after hearing revival celebrity and boxer Orville Gardner speak to the inmates. There was, however, no simple chain of events from Gardner's presentation to McAuley's change of heart to the Water Street Mission. After his release from prison, McAuley relapsed into petty theft and drunkenness a number of times before the friendship of Henry Little, a city missionary, enabled him to stabilize his life. McAuley's decision to open a rescue mission in the slums of New York City derived more from a simple desire to help people like himself than from any formal ethical or perfectionistic convictions.[26] Yet McAuley, a lay person with little or no formal education, let alone any theological training, could supervise his own independent mission because his chapel services resembled nothing so much as the Fulton Street prayer meeting in a more informal atmosphere. They featured prayer, one-minute testimonies, and hymn singing.[27]

In contrast to McAuley, an Irish Catholic immigrant, Charles Crittenton, owner of a successful drug company, epitomized the hard-working country boy who made good in the large city. Crittenton arrived in Manhattan from upstate New York in 1854 to take a job as a office boy. He became a salesman and by 1866 had established his own company, with its office next door to the Fulton Street Church. Despite his close proximity to the action, Crittenton apparently was not affected by the 1857–58 Revival or by the ongoing Fulton Street prayer meeting. Not until the death of his younger daughter, Florence, in 1882, did he undergo a conversion experience. For the next two years the restless businessman, who had been confirmed in the Episcopal church, sampled New York's varied religious life. He attended the Fulton Street group for several months, visited McAuley's mission, consecrated his life at a Methodist camp meeting, and finally settled on a noon prayer gathering at a city mission church on Grand Street with a number of men interested in rescue work. After distributing tracts outside saloons and brothels, Crittenton realized the futility of urging prostitutes to "leave a life of sin" when most literally had nowhere to go. That awareness led to the opening of the Florence Mission, a chapel and home for prostitutes, in 1883. Crittenton spent the rest of his life in rescue work and revival meetings. By 1895, there were 20 Florence Crittenton homes in various cities, a number that more than doubled within a few years, and the chain was incorporated as a national organization.[28] Like

Dwight Moody, Charles Crittenton first began speaking to crowds during noon prayer gatherings and moved from there to conducting his own revival meetings.

Concern for evangelism, interdenominational contacts, and small voluntary groups as apprenticeship settings for new leaders—these patterns came to characterize lay evangelicalism in the wake of the Revival of 1857–58. This orientation toward evangelistic techniques and practices marked a shift away from the more intense inward concern of many early-nineteenth-century revivals. The focus now was on what middle-class businessmen or lay women could "do . . . for the Savior" in an urban setting. Of course, a variety of factors in addition to revivalism shaped popular Protestantism during the last third of the nineteenth century: the holiness movement, dispensationalism, and the intellectual and social challenges of modernity, to name just a few. Even so, as the stories of the revival generation have illustrated, the 1857–58 Revival served in many ways as a prologue to what George Marsden has described as a "new American evangelicalism" that took shape during the 1870s. It certainly helped define the public revival tradition subsequently associated with that movement from Moody through Billy Graham.[29]

Revivalism in a Changing World

The 1857–58 awakening and its interpretations did more than reveal trends and reconfigurations within this northern establishment evangelicalism; they also signaled ways revivalism interacted with other cultural currents in American life, particularly those involving mass print, politics, and gender. In the realm of mass print, the revival was one of a handful of key "media events" in nineteenth-century American Christianity and among the most important in terms of the relationship between popular, middle-class Protestantism and the secular press.[30] It marked the beginning of a shift in the way news about religion was transmitted in the United States and placed revivalism squarely in the midst of the commercial marketplace of industrializing, urban America.

Prior to 1858, the mass print subcultures that shaped American understandings of revival were maintained by religious communications networks, composed of denominational newspapers, the publications of voluntary societies, and books. After 1858, both religious and secular communications channels were involved. Gradually, the secular media came to assume a prominent role in publicizing revivals and most other aspects of popular Protestantism to the general public. Protestants celebrated and encouraged the coverage of the 1857–58 Revival in the popular press as evidence of the Christianization of a powerful social institution. Even as Horace Greeley and James Gordon Bennett were planning their reports, the young men of the "Y" were distributing a press release to encourage the interest.

Yet what looked like Christianization to religious partisans was actually a new phase in the commodification of popular Protestantism. Editors marketed revival news to a mass audience on the same basis that they sold other sensationalistic or human interest stories: as entertainment. Evangelicals, for their part, intuitively grasped the need for publicity if revivals were to become a mass urban phenomenon. In many ways, revivalism was the perfect subject to facilitate the commercialization of religion in the secular press. Evangelicals had long viewed revival reports as legitimate news with a strong human interest appeal; secular dailies quickly grasped the topic's attraction to middle-class readers and its potential for sensationalism. Protestant blindness to any negative implications of commercialization led to a growing accommodation to it after the Civil War. This was particularly true in the case of urban revivals, a form of popular religion closely tied to channels of mass communication.[31]

The influence of the secular press increased as daily newspapers dominated the American scene during the last third of the nineteenth century and religious weeklies lost their function as family newspapers.[32] Modern print journalism became the uncontested interpreter of popular Protestantism to the general public until the advent of the electronic media. Separated from its theological or ecclesiastical context, popular religion was portrayed as the story of revivals and celebrities (Moody, Billy Sunday, Aimee Semple McPherson); of scandals (Beecher's trial for adultery, McPherson's supposed kidnapping); and of tragicomedy (the Scopes trial). Several historians have analyzed changes in both the theological underpinnings and the techniques of revivalism during the nineteenth century. Few have highlighted this transformation in the way revivals were publicized and interpreted.

Changes in communications patterns along with the growing pluralism of American society also may have contributed to the lack of consensus by contemporaries or later historians about whether nationwide awakenings occurred after 1858. Chapters 1 and 2 of this book suggested that widespread revivals or great awakenings "happened" (became public events) when they both captured public attention and attained significance in the historical record. These two things occurred almost simultaneously in 1858 through the collaboration of a powerful Calvinist subculture and the national press to create awareness of the revival. Similar cooperation became much more difficult in the late nineteenth and in the twentieth centuries as mass media became increasingly diffuse, religious print fragmented into a variety of subcultures, and the mainline Protestant establishment turned its attention away from religious awakenings.[33] Ironically, in the wake of the Revival of 1857–58 an evangelical revival tradition had attained a certain national identity and public presence while at the same time revivals were "less able to lend coherence to American culture."[34]

More and more, the agent for coherence was mass politics rather than mass revival. Well before the Civil War, Yankee evangelicals had begun to divert their reformist energy from revivals and channel it into politics. At the same time, the dynamics of the 1857–58 Revival illustrated that urban revivals had become vehicles for evangelization and for middle-class spiritual refreshment rather than agents of cultural transformation. This change in the public role of revivals in American life took place in the context of postmillennial optimism, but the result was a revival tradition that adapted easily to the socially conservative spirit of the Gilded Age and to the rise of dispensational premillennialism among evangelicals. The transformed revivalism of 1857–58 bore a closer affinity to the premillennialist call for "the evangelization of the world in this generation," popularized by A. T. Pierson, than it did to the earlier New England tradition of disinterested benevolence. In addition, the Civil War itself had demonstrated the limits of Christian moral persuasion and of revivals in solving the nation's problems. In the final analysis, politics and federal power rather than revival had arbitrated the basic cultural decisions raised by the conflict. During the postwar years, Victorians were keenly aware of the "competition political activity and symbols offered religion."[35]

The war also confirmed and popularized the values of a nascent corporate America. The "business Christianity" so publicized during the Revival of 1857–58 blended easily with the call for discipline, efficiency, and rational management that undergirded so much of the war effort. During the Gilded Age, the rhetoric and management practices of the business culture were applied to charities and churches, along with other voluntary associations. Literary historians have argued that this widespread move toward professionalization led to a decade of conflict during the 1860s between the successful female novelists who previously had dominated the marketplace and "the rising literary establishment of men who were determined to displace them."[36] Certainly in the public rhetoric and historical interpretations of the 1857–58 awakening, women experienced a similar displacement. In actual practice as well, urban revivals assumed a more masculine character, with their commercial promotion, businesslike organization, and male ushers to direct crowds. The increased respectability or formalization of revivals also worked against women's participation and visibility, since it drew from the more hierarchical Calvinist tradition in contrast to the greater egalitarianism of the populists.

Particularly through the YMCA and Moody's ministry, the impact of the businessmen's revival can be linked to the full-blown manly Christianity of Billy Sunday on the conservative side and also to the more socially oriented Men and Religion Forward Movement of 1911–1912. Fred B. Smith (1865–1936), who directed the Men and Religion Forward campaign, got his start as traveling lay evangelist with the YMCA. By the first decade of the twentieth century, using the proven techniques of newspaper announcements and advertisements on streetcars and buses, Smith was drawing crowds of between 600 and 1,000 men to meetings in theaters or other public halls. He came to be known as "America's greatest speaker to men."[37]

But one should not exaggerate the degree of actual male dominance in American Protestantism during the second half of the nineteenth century.[38] The power of sentimental rhetoric and the domestic ideal endured in sermons and gospel songs. In the broader American culture, the late nineteenth century was a period of expanding public roles for women. Lay Protestant women were involved in positions both of support and leadership in the Women's Christian Temperance Union, various women's missionary movements, and the YWCA in numbers that matched and even exceeded those of the laymen involved in the YMCA, urban revivals, and other evangelical activities. Revivalists such as Moody routinely called on women to distribute tracts or to serve as counselors in inquiry rooms after meetings.[39]

Given that important caveat, it is still true that the public image of the ideal lay Protestant began to shift toward the masculine with the 1857–58 Revival. The shift continued as America "incorporated" during the decades following the Civil

War, and businessmen became the public figures of northern establishment evangelicalism. In addition, the revival marked the beginning point in the development of a particularly American version of muscular Christianity, characterized by a symbiotic relationship between evangelicals and modern sports.[40] The threshold to a greater masculinization of American Protestantism was crossed between 1858 and 1865, not at the close of the century.

In a study of the Victorian middle class and the Civil War, Anne Rose pointed out not one but many Civil Wars: "There was the war that soldiers encountered and the war that touched civilians. There was the war of immediate experience, the war of memory, and even the elusive war of anticipation."[41] The same could be said of most events that catch the attention of historians, certainly of a movement as diffuse and multifaceted as a religious revival. Americans encountered many revivals, both lived and interpreted, during 1857 and 1858: the revival that drew businessmen (and church women) to noon prayer meetings and the revival in small-town churches, the revival on college campuses, and the revival in response to the preaching of Phoebe Palmer. The daily papers reported the "Great Revival" and Calvinist clergy wrote the history of a supernatural act of God. Mass communications, a growing urban population, and the extension of a national transportation system—all in place at a time when evangelicalism was the dominant subculture in American life—helped to link and to multiply these many revivals into a mass awakening of unprecedented scope and clear public identity. The same elements were also constructing a modern, consumer-oriented, national culture. In the context of this awakening, antebellum revival traditions were transformed into a middle-class evangelical revivalism well suited to an emerging modern America. The events of 1857–58 and their interpretation illuminate the ongoing adaptability and vitality of evangelical revivalism but also explain why its influence diminished within the very culture that provided the setting for its transformation.

Appendix A

Chronology of Selected Dates and Events

A S THE TEXT makes clear, mapping the origin and development of the Revival of 1857–58 is a difficult task, complicated by the nature of the revival as a popular, mass movement and by competing interpretive claims. The following is a list of selected dates and events mentioned in different chapters of this book, designed to clarify and to provide a sense of broad trends. It is not intended as a complete chronology of the revival; among other things, for example, the list does not trace the spread of revivals on college campuses or provide a complete chronology of noon prayer meetings. Events noted between 1850 and 1857 as precursors to the revival were those indicated by the primary sources listed in chapters 1 and 2. Readers interested in efforts to provide a more comprehensive compilation of revival activities should consult the books and newspapers cited in those chapters, as well as the secondary works referred to in the introduction.

Before 1857

1850–	Ongoing weekday "union" prayer meeting in Boston's Old South Church.
December 30, 1855–c. late spring 1856	Local revival in Rochester, New York, in response to the preaching of Charles Finney; morning "union" prayer meetings held in participating churches on a rotating basis; Elizabeth Finney organized women's prayer meetings at 3:00 PM daily.
September 1856–summer 1857	New York City YMCA sponsored a noon prayer meeting, daily, then three times a week until early summer, at

the North Reformed Protestant Dutch Church, corner of William and Fulton Streets.

December 7, 1856–April 19, 1857

Finney was guest preacher at Park Street Congregational church in Boston; Elizabeth Finney organized women's prayer meetings.

1857

February 12

"A Laity for the Times," the first of four columns by Phoebe Palmer, appeared in the *Christian Advocate and Journal.*

March 6

Dred Scott v. Sandford. Missouri Compromise declared unconstitutional.

May

American Tract Society published *The Duties of Masters.*

August 24

Collapse of New York branch of the Ohio Life Insurance & Trust Company, initiating a string of bank failures throughout the country.

September

American Tract Society withdrew *The Duties of Masters.*

September 23

Weekly noon prayer meetings for businessmen begun by city missionary Jeremiah Lanphier at the North Dutch Church, William and Fulton Streets, New York City.

September 25, 26

Philadelphia banks suspend payments, evidence of spreading financial panic.

October 7

Fulton Street prayer meeting moved to a daily schedule (except Sunday).

October 8

Phoebe Palmer served as catalyst for local revival in Hamilton, Ontario, Canada, after speaking to large crowds at Canadian camp meetings during summer and early fall.

October 13, 14

Run on New York City banks.

October 14–December 14

Panic of 1857. New York City banks suspend specie payments, leading to nationwide bank suspensions, business failures, and high unemployment in urban centers.

October 23

Lanphier alerted editors of religious press of increasing attendance at the Fulton Street prayer meeting.

November 5	"Revival Extraordinary; The Laity for the Times Exemplified," letter describing Palmer's work in Hamilton appeared in the *Christian Advocate and Journal*.
November 23	Noon prayer meeting organized by Philadelphia YMCA.
December 9	In Congress, Stephen A. Douglas opposed President James Buchanan's support for the proslavery Lecompton constitution in Kansas.
December 2, 1857–April 8, 1858	Finney again in Boston, preaching in various churches; women's prayer meetings organized in Park Street vestry.

1858

January–March	Nationwide recession continued in wake of financial panic.
January 5	Lanphier visited editors of daily papers, requesting coverage of Fulton Street prayer meeting.
January 21	Revivals at the University of Michigan and in Ann Arbor; about this time, brothers Adam and Edwin Spence formed the Student Christian Association.
January 23	Young businessman and future Mennonite leader John Fretz Funk recorded his conversion after revival meetings, Third Presbyterian Church, Chicago.
January 27	*Western Christian Advocate* noted numerous local revivals from late December and early January; similar reports appeared in the *Christian Times*.
January 28	The *Examiner* reported 12,000 "hopeful conversions" during Baptist revivals since January 1 in 20 states, predominantly in New England, the Midwest, and the upper South.
February	Caroline Roberts began a daily women's union prayer meeting at Church of the Puritans, New York City.
February 3	Philadelphia noon prayer meeting moved from Fourth Street Methodist Episcopal Union Church to anteroom of Jayne's Hall.

February 4

New York City YMCA forms devotional committee to organize, sustain, and publicize union prayer meetings; extended list of widespread Methodist revivals reported in *Christian Advocate and Journal*.

c. February 15

New York City YMCA began noon prayer meeting, Ninth Street Dutch Reformed Church.

February 20

YMCA issued a circular letter advertising New York City prayer meetings.

February 21

"Flying Artillery of Heaven," Methodist laymen's prayer/exhortation team, held revival services at the Seventh Street Methodist Episcopal Church, New York City, part of an ongoing Sunday circuit through city Methodist churches. *New York Herald* noted the revival with editorial and brief news item.

February 22

New York City YMCA began additional noon prayer meeting, John Street Methodist Church.

February 24

Brief note in *Western Recorder* of a "refreshing from the Lord" in "several of our Southern States."

February 27

Front page revival coverage, *New York Herald*.

March

Phoebe Palmer in Owego, Binghampton, and Union (upstate New York). J. W. Alexander wrote revival tracts, later published as *The Revival and Its Lessons*.

March 1

Extensive coverage of "The Religious Awakening" in the *New York Tribune*.

March 4

National revival recognized in religious weekly papers: "The Great Revival" (*Examiner*); "The Great Awakening" (*Independent*). Mass rally, New York City, in support of Lecompton constitution for Kansas.

March 5

Tribune reported Orville Gardner's conversion.

March 6

Front page revival coverage, *Philadelphia Press*; *Chicago Daily Journal* reprinted March 1 revival news from *New York Tribune*.

March 8	"Businessmen's" noon prayer meeting organized in Boston. *Philadelphia Inquirer* endorsed Jayne's Hall meeting.
March 8–13	"Pentecost Week" in Philadelphia; attendance at Jayne's Hall noon prayer meeting grew from 300 to approximately 4,000.
March 11	National revival recognized in religious weekly papers: "The Revival" (*New York Observer*); "Great Work of God in the Land" (*Christian Advocate and Journal*). Harriet Beecher Stowe column in the *Independent*, calling for "the great reformation of 1858."
March 11–July 3	Ongoing prayer meetings and revival activities at Henry Ward Beecher's Plymouth Church, Brooklyn.
March 12, 13	Telegraphed greetings exchanged between John Street prayer meeting in New York City and Jayne's Hall in Philadelphia. Fulton Street meetings (total capacity about 600) and John Street meetings (capacity about 2,000) attracted overflow crowds.
March 15	Businessmen's prayer meeting organized in Louisville.
March 17–April 3	Daily noon prayer meetings at Burton's Theater, New York City.
March 22	Metropolitan Hall, Chicago, opened for daily noon prayer; during subsequent weeks John V. Farwell and Dwight L. Moody participated. Organizational meeting held for Chicago YMCA.
March 24	New Orleans noon prayer meeting organized.
March 25	National revival recognized in religious weekly papers: "The Great Revival" (*Watchman and Reflector*). Harriet Olney attended Burton's Theater prayer meeting.
March 26	The *Herald* reported 23 daily prayer meetings in the New York metropolitan area; average total attendance estimated at 6,000.
April–May	Typhoid epidemic at the University of Virginia, 20 students died; subsequent

	preaching of Baptist Pastor John A. Broadus led to local revival in Charlottesville and at the university.
April 3	Revival "Extra," special edition of the *Tribune*.
April 4	Theodore Parker's sermon "A False and True Revival of Religion" delivered in Boston; George Cheever's sermon "A Christian's Duty in Time of Revival" in New York City.
April 4–11	William C. Conant compiled material for *Narratives of Remarkable Conversions*; book was published by the end of the month.
April 7	National revival recognized in religious weekly papers: "The Great Awakening" (*Western Christian Advocate*); "The Times of Refreshing" (*Western Recorder*).
April 8	The *Herald* ended local reports on the revival.
April 10	The *Tribune* shifted from daily revival coverage to weekly summary.
April 11	Theodore Parker's sermon, "The Revival of Religion Which We Need."
April 17	*Louisville Courier* reported "daily union prayer meetings" in St. Louis, Nashville, Mobile, and Charleston.
April 19	Philadelphia Episcopal minister and revival leader Dudley Tyng died; final words inspired poems and hymn, "Stand Up, Stand Up for Jesus."
April 23	"Beecher grandsons" joined Plymouth Church: Frederick W. Stowe, Henry B. Beecher, George B. Beecher.
May	Lyman Abbott participated in prayer meetings at Plymouth Church.
May–August	*Biblical Recorder, Western Recorder*, and other southern denominational papers reported scattered revivals in the lower South.
May 1–c. September 15	Union Tabernacle used for revival meetings in Philadelphia.
May 9–15	Protestant benevolent societies gather in New York City for annual Anniversary Week meetings.

May 11	Horace Bushnell, pastor of North Congregational Church, Hartford, Connecticut, on vacation in New York City, recovering from exhaustion after revival involvement.
May 12	Annual meeting of the American Tract Society; acrimonious debate over editorial policies regarding slavery.
June 1	*New York Tribune* published final report on "The Great Religious Awakening."
June 6	Francis Wayland ended interim pastorate at First Baptist Church, Providence, Rhode Island, in weakened health, in part due to revival participation.
July 17–c. September 30	Tent meetings in Cincinnati, patterned after Philadelphia, organized by Baptist city missionary Joseph Emery.
August 20–September 13	In her diary, Hannah Whitall Smith recorded her "discovery" of Christian faith.
September 23	First anniversary celebration, Fulton Street prayer meeting.
September 25–October 6	Union Tabernacle meetings in Germantown, Pennsylvania.
October 12	YMCA organized at University of Virginia; active members included Charles Augustus Briggs and John William Jones.
November	Caroline Roberts organized Ladies' Christian Association in New York City, precursor to YWCA.
November/December	Books published: James W. Alexander, *The Revival and Its Lessons*; Talbot W. Chambers, *The Noon Prayer Meeting of the North Dutch Church*; Samuel Irenaeus Prime, *The Power of Prayer*; [S. I. Prime, ed.], *The New York Pulpit in the Revival of 1858*.
December 21, 22	In the wake of evangelistic meetings for students, Lottie Moon made a public profession of faith and was baptized at the Charlottesville (Virginia) Baptist Church.

Appendix B

Membership Statistics and Church Growth Rates, 1853–1861

T<small>HE FOLLOWING TABLES</small> illustrate the approximate numerical impact of the 1857–58 Revival on the membership of selected Protestant denominations in the context of church growth rates during the 1850s. Unless otherwise indicated, the growth rates in each table represent the annual net gain or loss expressed as a percentage of total communicants from the previous year. Use of the roughly equivalent terms "communicant" or "member" in the tables follows the preferred style of the group under consideration, based on the primary source reports. Compilers of denominational membership statistics during the 1850s regularly bemoaned the difficulties in securing full and accurate reports from their scattered constituencies. Given that reality, these tables indicate broad trends within and between denominations rather than exact membership totals.

TABLE I. Methodist Episcopal Church and Methodist Episcopal Church, South, Membership and Annual Growth Rates, 1853–61.

Year	Total members,[a] MEC	Percentage growth, MEC	Total members, MEC, South	Percentage growth, MEC, South
1853	751,317[b]	3.28	573,252[c]	5.60
1854	781,930	4.08	596,852	4.12
1855	798,026	2.06	621,135	4.07
1856	798,953	.12	636,714	2.51
1857	819,145	2.53	648,436	1.84
1858	954,997	16.59	691,604	6.66
1859	972,847	1.87	713,185	3.12
1860	988,881[b]	1.65	749,068	5.03
1861	987,114	−.18	—[d]	—

Sources: *Minutes of the Annual Conferences of the Methodist Episcopal Church* (1853–61); *Minutes of the Annual Conferences of the Methodist Episcopal Church, South* (1853–61).

[a]"Members" for both the Methodist Episcopal Church (northern Methodists) and the MEC, South, includes the total of members and probationers reported each year, but does not include ministers. The totals for the MEC also do not include the membership of the church's Liberia conference, customarily listed in the annual "General Recapitulation" of statistics.

[b]MEC totals for 1853 and 1860 are taken from the 1854 and 1861 reports, respectively, when errors for the previous year were corrected.

[c]Until 1859, the MEC, South, published conference minutes from midyear to midyear; for example, statistics listed here for 1853 were published as totals for 1853–54.

[d]The southern church published no summary statistics for 1861; reports from individual conferences for that year are incomplete.

TABLE 2. Membership and Annual Growth Rates for African-American Members of the Methodist Episcopal Church, South, 1853–61.

Year	African-American members, MEC, South	Percentage growth
1853	154,264	4.98
1854	164,584	6.69
1855	170,150	3.38
1856	173,067	1.71
1857	177,919	2.80
1858	188,036	5.69
1859	197,348	4.95
1860	207,766	5.28
1861	—[a]	—

Sources: *Minutes of the Annual Conferences of the Methodist Episcopal Church, South* (1853–61).

[a]The MEC, South, published no summary statistics for 1861; reports from individual conferences for that year are incomplete.

TABLE 3. Regular Baptists in the United States (North and South), Baptized Members and Annual Growth Rates by Region, 1853–61.

Year	Total baptized members, North[a]	Percentage growth	Total baptized members, Border States[b]	Percentage growth	Total baptized members, South[c]	Percentage growth
1853[d]	313,596	1.62	189,566	1.59	305,582	8.72
1854	323,343	3.11	200,063	5.54	318,358	4.18
1855	327,855	1.40	207,947	3.94	333,660	4.81
1856	328,077	.07	214,377	3.09	355,001	6.40
1857	342,532	4.41	223,858	4.42	356,808	.51
1858	386,330	12.79	242,360	8.27	375,930	5.36
1859	380,236	−1.58	236,780	−2.30	403,423	7.31
1860	386,050	1.53	241,753	2.10	408,953	1.37
1861[e]	386,835	.20	241,788	0.01	408,953	0.00

Source: *American Baptist Almanac* (1854–63). As used in the *Almanac*, "Regular Baptist" referred to mainstream revivalistic Baptists, North and South, of broadly Calvinist persuasion. Not included were smaller clusters of churches such as the Anti-Mission Baptists, Free-Will Baptists, General Baptists, and Seventh-Day Baptists, although the *Almanac* provides annual membership figures for these and other groups that practiced believer's baptism. The *Almanac* made no distinction between churches affiliated with northern or southern Baptist conventions and simply listed the number of Regular Baptists in each state.

Numbers are based on state-by-state summaries appearing annually in the *Almanac*. In 1854, the *Almanac* referred to "total communicants"; subsequent years simply listed "totals" of baptized members in the churches.

[a]"North" includes the free states and territories as of 1854, as well as a few hundred Baptists in Nebraska, tabulated from 1858–61.

[b]"Border states" includes Delaware, District of Columbia, Kentucky, Maryland, Missouri, and Virginia.

[c]"South" includes Alabama, Arkansas, Florida, Georgia, Indian Territory, Louisiana, Mississippi, New Mexico, North Carolina, South Carolina, Tennessee, and Texas.

[d]Statistics for any given year appeared in the *Almanac* two years later; figures for 1853, for example, are from the 1855 edition.

[e]Statistics for 1861 are unreliable; most were simply repeated from the previous year's data.

TABLE 4. Regular Baptists in the United States (North and South), Baptized Members and Annual Growth Rates Nationwide, 1853–61.

Year	Total baptized members[a]	Percentage growth
1853	808,744	4.18
1854	841,764	4.08
1855	869,462	3.29
1856	897,455	3.22
1857	923,198	2.87
1858	1,004,620	8.82
1859	1,020,439	1.58
1860	1,036,756	1.60
1861[b]	1,037,576	.08

Source: *American Baptist Almanac* (1854–63).

[a]"Total baptized members" represents the sum of the totals each year for the three regions listed in table 3, based on the numbers published for each state and territory. This amount does not always agree exactly with the number published as the total each year in the *Almanac*, due to occasional errors in the latter figure.

[b]Statistics for 1861 are unreliable; most were simply repeated from the previous year's data.

TABLE 5. Presbyterian Church of the United States of America (Old School), Communicants and Annual Growth Rates by Region, 1853–61.

Year	Total communicants, North[a]	Percentage growth	Total communicants, Border States[b]	Percentage growth	Total communicants, South[c]	Percentage growth
1853[d]	129,922	2.74	43,689	5.17	45,414	5.75
1854	133,856	3.03	44,269	1.33	47,056	3.62
1855	137,899	3.02	44,137	−.30	49,159	4.47
1856	140,297	1.74	43,126	−2.29	50,075	1.86
1857	145,600	3.78	45,922	6.48	53,070	5.98
1858	157,084	7.89	48,151	4.85	53,835	1.44
1859	166,908	6.25	51,930	7.85	60,525	12.43
1860	173,669	4.05	55,516	6.91	63,475	4.87
1861	178,460	2.76	58,028	4.52	64,059	.92

Sources: *Minutes of the General Assembly of the Presbyterian Church in the United States of America*, 1848–58 and 1859–64 (Old School).

[a]"North" includes presbyteries of the free states and territories as of 1854, including a few hundred communicants in California and Oregon.

[b]"Border states" include presbyteries in the District of Columbia, Kentucky, Maryland, Missouri, and Virginia.

[c]"South" includes presbyteries in Alabama, Arkansas, Florida, Georgia, Louisiana, Mississippi, North Carolina, South Carolina, Tennessee, and Texas, as well as Indian mission presbyteries.

[d]The General Assembly usually met in May of each year; statistics listed for 1853, for example, reflect the state of the church as reported at the May 1853 meeting.

TABLE 6. Membership and Annual Growth Rates for African-American Communicants of the Presbyterian Church (Old School), 1853–61.

Year	African-American members, PCUSA (OS)[a]	Percentage growth
1853[b]	8,993	16.67
1854	9,737	8.27
1855	10,412	6.93
1856	10,635	2.14
1857	11,214	5.44
1858	12,115	8.03
1859	13,694	13.03
1860	13,837	1.04
1861	6,935	−49.88

Sources: *Minutes of the General Assembly of the Presbyterian Church in the United States of America*, 1848–58 and 1859–64 (Old School).

[a]During this period, approximately 80 percent of the African-American communicants lived in the South, in the states identified with that region in table 5.

[b]The totals for 1853 represent the total listed in the General Assembly Minutes less 74 people identified as communicants of the India mission. They were not listed in subsequent totals.

TABLE 7. Presbyterian Church of the United States of America (Old School), Communicants and Annual Growth Rates Nationwide, 1853–61.

Year	Total communicants[a]	Percentage growth
1853	219,025	3.83
1854	225,181	2.81
1855	231,195	2.67
1856	233,498	1.00
1857	244,592	4.75
1858	259,070	5.92
1859	279,363	7.83
1860	292,660	4.76
1861	300,547	2.69

Sources: *Minutes of the General Assembly of the Presbyterian Church in the United States of America*, 1848–58 and 1859–64 (Old School).

[a]"Total communicants" reflects the sum of the communicants reported each year in the presbyteries of each region. It does not include numbers from the church's India mission and therefore is a few hundred less each year than the number listed in official church records.

TABLE 8. Presbyterian Church of the United States of America (New School), Communicants and Annual Growth Rates, 1851–61.

Year	Total communicants, nationwide[a]	Percentage growth	Total communicants, North[b]	Percentage growth, North
1851	140,076	.20	125,150	.03
1852	140,652	.41	125,487	.27
1853	140,452	−.14	124,980	−.40
1854	141,477	.73	126,137	.93
1855	143,029	1.10	127,142	.80
1856	138,760[c]	−2.99	122,738[c]	−3.46
1857	139,115	.26	122,978	.20
1858	143,410[d]	3.09	127,273	3.49
1859	137,990	−3.78	131,451	3.28
	[145,866][e]	[1.71]		
1860	134,933	−2.22	134,157	2.06
	[146,867]	[.69]		
1861	134,760	−.13	133,832	−.24

Sources: *Minutes of the General Assembly of the Presbyterian Church in the United States of America, 1838–58* and *1859–69* (New School); *Presbyterian Reunion: A Memorial Volume, 1837–1871* (New York, 1870); Joseph M. Wilson, *The Presbyterian Historical Almanac and Annual Remembrancer of the Church*, vols. 1–4 (1858–59, 1860–1862).

Two additional years of New School statistics (1851, 1852) are included to provide a better perspective on fluctuations in the denomination's membership nationwide, fluctuations affected in part by the abrogation of the Plan of Union with the Congregationalists in 1852 and the withdrawal of six southern synods (21 presbyteries) in 1857.

[a]The "Total communicants nationwide" data is included for comparative purposes; however, it is flawed from 1858 to 1861 due to the withdrawal of the southern synods in a dispute over denominational pronouncements on slavery.

[b]The majority of New School churches, representing between 88 and 89 percent of total church membership during this period, were located in the North. The columns listing communicants and growth rates from the northern synods (Albany, Utica, Geneva, Onondaga, Susquehanna, Genesee, New York, and New Jersey, Pennsylvania, W. Pennsylvania, Michigan, Western Reserve, Ohio, Cincinnati, Indiana, Wabash, Illinois, Peoria, Wisconsin, Iowa, and Alta California) provide a more consistent and accurate measure of the impact of the 1857–58 Revival than the nationwide totals.

[c]The decline in communicants between 1855 and 1856, most sharply reflected in denominational losses in New York state, may reflect in part the ongoing impact and rancor from the breakup of the Plan of Union.

[d]The 1858 statistics simply repeat 1857 numbers for the six absent southern synods; of them, two (Virginia and Missouri) are included in 1858 although they sent no commissioners to the General Assembly. After 1858 the absent synods are not included in the annual reports, except for the Missouri synod, which returned to the New School in 1860.

[e]The figures in brackets reflect New School totals adjusted to include annual statistics published in 1859 and 1860 in the *Presbyterian Historical Almanac* for the former southern synods, which had formed a separate group, the United Synod of the Presbyterian Church, representing four of the six absent synods. The United Synod listed 12,125 communicants in 1859 and 11,934 in 1860. Both the New School and the United Synod counted Virginia in 1859, and the total in brackets was adjusted to avoid that duplication.

TABLE 9. Protestant Episcopal Church, Communicants and
Triennial Growth Rates, 1847–62.

Year	Number of dioceses	Total communicants	Percentage growth
1847	27	67,550	−6.31
1850	28	79,802	18.14
1853	30	105,136	31.75
1856	31	119,540	13.70
1859	33	139,611	16.79
1862	23	125,829	−9.87
			[10.31][a]

Sources: Data from 1847 to 1859 are from the appendix of the *Journal of the Proceedings of the Bishops, Clergy, and Laity of the Protestant Episcopal Church . . . Assembled in a General Convention, . . . 1859.* Statistics for 1862, as well as a comparative extrapolation of communicants in the 23 dioceses for 1859 are from the appendix of the *Journal* for 1862, p. 226. On p. 227, an alternative total for 1862 of 124,340 is given for the communicants in 23 dioceses.

The General Convention of the Protestant Episcopal Church met and published statistics triennially; the growth rates in this table represent the cumulative net gain or loss expressed as a percentage of total communicants reported by the convention three years earlier.

[a]Records for 1862 show sharp membership losses because 10 of the 33 dioceses were unable to submit reports due to disruptions from the Civil War. The growth rate in brackets represents the rate for the 23 dioceses reporting, based on a total number of communicants for those dioceses in 1859 of 114,068.

TABLE 10. Congregational Churches in North America,
Members and Annual Growth Rates, 1857–61.

Year	Total members[a]	Percentage growth
1857	232,549	—[b]
1858	239,586	3.03
1859	257,634	7.53
1860	260,389	1.07
1861	259,119	−.49

Sources: The *Congregational Yearbook* (1855–58); the *Congregational Quarterly* (1859–62).

Although church membership statistics were printed in the *Congregational Yearbook*, 1854–58, they were incomplete and unreliable. Editors blamed ministerial laxity in keeping accurate church records, the lack of functioning state associations for the churches of this decentralized group, and the effects of the Plan of Union, making it difficult even during the years following 1852 to sort out who was a Congregationalist and who was a Presbyterian. The unreliability and variations in the numbers prior to 1857 led to the reduced character of this chart.

[a]Membership numbers are based on a set of revised statistics for 1857–60, published in the January 1861 *Congregational Quarterly*, followed by the figure for 1861 from the January 1862 *Quarterly*. Totals were for North America, including a few thousand Congregationalists in Canada and a few hundred in Jamaica.

[b]The rate of growth for 1857 is not included because the 1856 numbers are incomplete.

TABLE 11. Methodist and Baptist Annual Growth Rates, Compared, 1853–61.

Methodist Episcopal Church, North and South			Regular Baptists in the United States		
Year	Total members	Percentage growth	Year	Total members	Percentage growth
1853	1,324,569	4.27	1853	808,744	4.18
1854	1,378,782	4.09	1854	841,764	4.08
1855	1,419,161	2.93	1855	869,462	3.29
1856	1,435,667	1.16	1856	897,455	3.22
1857	1,467,581	2.22	1857	923,198	2.87
1858	1,646,601	12.20	1858	1,004,620	8.82
1859	1,686,032	2.40	1859	1,020,439	1.58
1860	1,737,949	3.08	1860	1,036,756	1.60
1861	—	—	1861	1,037,576	.08

Sources: *American Baptist Almanac* (1854–63); *Minutes of the Annual Conferences of the Methodist Episcopal Church* (1853–61); *Minutes of the Annual Conferences of the Methodist Episcopal Church, South* (1853–61).

TABLE 12. Increase in Net Membership for Major Denominations, 1853–56 and 1856–59.

Denominational group	Net membership increase, 1853–56	Net membership increase, 1856–59
Methodist, North and South	111,098	250,365
Regular Baptist	88,711	122,984
Presbyterian, OS/NS	12,781	52,971[a]
Episcopal	14,404	20,071
Total net increase	226,994	446,391
Congregational (1857–60)[b]		27,840
Total		474,231[c]

Sources: Numbers are based on the following sources, as developed in previous tables: *American Baptist Almanac* (1854–63); *Congregational Quarterly* (1859–62); *Journal of the Proceedings of the Bishops, Clergy, and Laity of the Protestant Episcopal Church . . . Assembled in a General Convention* (1859); *Minutes of the Annual Conferences of the Methodist Episcopal Church* (1853–61); *Minutes of the Annual Conferences of the Methodist Episcopal Church, South* (1853–61); *Minutes of the General Assembly of the Presbyterian Church in the United States of America*, 1838–58 and 1859–69 (New School); *Minutes of the General Assembly of the Presbyterian Church in the United States of America*, 1848–58 and 1859–64 (Old School); Joseph M. Wilson, *The Presbyterian Historical Almanac, . . . for 1860* (Philadelphia, 1860).

[a]The bracketed figure for 1859 in table 8 was used in calculating Presbyterian net increase in order to include both the New School and the United Synod in the totals.

[b]Comparable period for net Congregational increase. See table 10 for an explanation of difficulties surrounding statistics from this group.

[c]Approximate net increase among major denominational groupings for the three-year period including the 1857–58 Revival.

Notes

Introduction

1. *Examiner*, March 4, 1858; Talbot W. Chambers, *The Noon Prayer Meeting of the North Dutch Church* (New York: Board of Publication, Reformed Protestant Dutch Church, 1858), 285; James W. Alexander, *The Revival and Its Lessons* (New York: American Tract Society, 1858), 14.

2. The first noon-hour prayer meeting at the North Dutch Church on Fulton Street in lower Manhattan, often considered the beginning of the revival, was held September 23, 1857. The connection between Graham's visit and the 1857–58 Revival is based on conversations with local organizers.

3. See, for example, "The Time for Prayer: the Third Great Awakening," *Christian History* 8; 23 (1989): 32–33, and Iain H. Murray, *Revival and Revivalism: The Making and Marring of American Evangelicalism 1750–1858* (Edinburgh: Banner of Truth Trust, 1994), 331–53.

4. Joseph Conforti, "The Invention of the Great Awakening, 1795–1842," *Early American Literature* 26 (1991): 99. Conforti's essay has been adapted as chapter 1 of his *Jonathan Edwards, Religious Tradition, and American Culture* (Chapel Hill: University of North Carolina Press, 1995). Richard Carwardine, "The Second Great Awakening in Comparative Perspective: Revivals and Culture in the United States and Britain," in *Modern Christian Revivals*, ed. Edith L. Blumhofer and Randall Balmer (Urbana: University of Illinois Press, 1993), provides a perceptive summary of recent interpretive approaches to the second awakening. For a summary of the currents of academic inquiry surrounding the colonial revivals, see Jon Butler, "Enthusiasm Described and Decried: The Great Awakening as Interpretive Fiction," *The Journal of American History* 69 (September 1982): 305 and passim.

5. Kathryn T. Long, "The Power of Interpretation: The Revival of 1857–58 and the Historiography of Revivalism in America," *Religion and American Culture* 4 (Winter 1994): 77–105, or Long, "The Revival of 1857–58: The Power of Interpretation" (Ph.D. dissertation, Duke University, 1993), chapter 1.

6. Works that suggest some relationship between the 1857–58 Revival and the

Civil War, although they do not focus on that relationship, include Perry Miller, *The Life of the Mind in America from the Revolution to the Civil War: Books One Through Three* (New York: Harcourt, Brace, 1965); James H. Moorhead, *American Apocalypse: Yankee Protestants and the Civil War, 1860-1869* (New Haven: Yale University Press, 1978); and Leonard I. Sweet, " 'A Nation Born Again': The Union Prayer Meeting Revival and Cultural Revitalization," in *The Great Tradition: In Honor of Winthrop S. Hudson, Essays on Pluralism, Voluntarism, and Revivalism*, ed. Joseph D. Ban and Paul R. Dekar (Valley Forge, Penn.: Judson Press, 1982): 193-221. The standard work on nineteenth-century "feminization" remains Ann Douglas, *The Feminization of American Culture* (New York: Alfred A. Knopf, 1977).

7. Examples of monographs that include brief, summary treatments are Richard J. Carwardine, *Evangelicals and Politics in Antebellum America* (New Haven: Yale University Press, 1993); Melvin Easterday Dieter, *The Holiness Revival of the Nineteenth Century* (Metuchen, N.J.: Scarecrow Press, 1980); William G. McLoughlin, *Modern Revivalism: Charles Grandison Finney to Billy Graham* (New York: Ronald Press, 1959) and McLoughlin, *Revivals, Awakenings, and Reform: An Essay on Religion and Social Change in America, 1607-1977* (Chicago: University of Chicago Press, 1978); Moorhead, *American Apocalypse*; Kenneth M. Stampp, *America in 1857: A Nation on the Brink* (New York: Oxford University Press, 1990); and Harold E. Raser, *Phoebe Palmer, Her Life and Thought* (Lewiston, N.Y.: Edwin Mellen Press, 1987).

8. *Annus mirabilis* ("year of wonder") was the title of chapter 4 in Timothy L. Smith, *Revivalism and Social Reform: American Protestantism on the Eve of the Civil War* (Nashville: Abingdon Press, 1957). Smith also devoted a portion of chapter 9, "Revivalism and Perfection," to the revival. The phrase *annus mirabilis* was first used by editor Richard Wheatley to describe Phoebe Palmer's revivalistic ministry during 1857. See Wheatley, *The Life and Letters of Mrs. Phoebe Palmer* (New York: Walter C. Palmer, Jr., 1876; reprint, Garland, 1984), 315.

9. Smith, *Revivalism and Social Reform*; Richard Carwardine, *Transatlantic Revivalism: Popular Evangelicalism in Britain and America, 1790-1865* (Westport, Conn.: Greenwood Press, 1978); also Carwardine, "The Religious Revival of 1857-8 in the United States," in *Religious Motivation: Biographical and Sociological Problems for the Church Historian*, ed. Derek Baker (Oxford: Basil Blackwell, 1978); Sandra Sizer [Frankiel], *Gospel Hymns and Social Religion: The Rhetoric of Nineteenth-Century Revivalism* (Philadelphia: Temple University Press, 1978); also Sizer [Frankiel], "Politics and Apolitical Religion: The Great Urban Revivals of the Late Nineteenth Century," *Church History* 48 (March 1979): 81-98; J. Edwin Orr, *The Event of the Century: The 1857-1858 Awakening*, ed. Richard Owen Roberts (Wheaton, Ill.: International Awakening Press, 1989). Orr, a British scholar and confessional historian with an evangelical readership, was the most persistent advocate of the revival's significance for nearly a half century, through works including *The Fervent Prayer: The Worldwide Impact of the Great Awakening of 1858* (Chicago: Moody Press, 1974); *The Light of Nations: Evangelical Renewal and Advance in the Nineteenth Century* (Grand Rapids: Eerdmans, 1965); "The Millionfold Awakening in America, 1857-58" (D.Th. diss., Northern Baptist Theological Seminary, Chicago, 1943); and *The Second Evangelical Awakening in Britain* (London: Marshall, Morgan and Scott, 1949).

10. Sweet, "The Union Prayer Meeting Revival," 194.

11. Discussions of revival traditions and their interpretations that have informed my comments here include Carwardine, "Second Great Awakening in Comparative Perspective"; Nathan O. Hatch, *The Democratization of American Christianity* (New

Haven: Yale University Press, 1989), 220–26; George A. Rawlyk, "Writing about Canadian Religious Revivals," in *Modern Christian Revivals*, ed. Edith L. Blumhofer and Randall Balmer (Urbana: University of Illinois, 1993), 208–26; and John Walsh, " 'Methodism' and the Origins of English-Speaking Evangelicalism," in *Evangelicalism: Comparative Studies of Popular Protestantism in North America, the British Isles, and Beyond, 1700–1990*, ed. Mark A. Noll, David W. Bebbington, and George A. Rawlyk (New York: Oxford University Press, 1994), 19–37.

12. Perry Miller, "From the Covenant to the Revival," in *Religion in American Life*, vol. 1, *The Shaping of American Religion*, ed. James Ward Smith and A. Leland Jamison, (Princeton: Princeton University Press, 1961), 354; Carwardine, "Second Great Awakening in Comparative Perspective," 86.

13. Samuel Irenaeus Prime, *Autobiography and Memorials*, ed. Wendall Prime (New York: Anson D. F. Randolph, 1888), 205. Recent works highlighting various revival traditions include Michael J. Crawford, *Seasons of Grace: Colonial New England's Revival Tradition in Its British Context* (New York: Oxford University Press, 1991); David W. Kling, *A Field of Divine Wonders: The New Divinity and Village Revivals in Northwestern Connecticut, 1792–1822* (University Park: Pennsylvania State University Press, 1993); G. A. Rawlyk, *The Canada Fire: Radical Evangelicalism in British North America 1775–1812* (Kingston and Montreal: McGill-Queen's University Press, 1994); and Leigh Eric Schmidt, *Holy Fairs: Scottish Communions and American Revivals in the Early Modern Period* (Princeton: Princeton University Press, 1989). See also the collection of essays in *Modern Christian Revivals*, eds. Blumhofer and Balmer, particularly Randall Balmer, "Eschewing the 'Routine of Religion': Eighteenth-Century Pietism and the Revival Tradition in America," 1–16, on the assimilation of the pietist tradition; and Edith L. Blumhofer, "Restoration as Revival: Early American Pentecostalism," 145–60, for the emergence of a particular Pentecostal revival tradition during the early twentieth century.

14. See W. R. Ward, *The Protestant Evangelical Awakening* (Cambridge: Cambridge University Press, 1992) for the eighteenth century; also Carwardine, "Second Great Awakening in Comparative Perspective," 91–95, for parallel revival patterns in the context of nineteenth-century American and British social, political, and economic settings.

15. Carwardine, "Second Great Awakening in Comparative Perspective," 88.

16. For the formalist/antiformalist distinction, see Curtis D. Johnson, *Redeeming America: Evangelicals and the Road to Civil War* (Chicago: Ivan R. Dee, 1993), 7–9. I am indebted to his explanation of the contrasts between formalists and antiformalists; Johnson also recognizes African Americans as a third major grouping of antebellum evangelicals. Hatch, *Democratization*, distinguishes between elites and popular or populist evangelicals. Rawlyk, *Canada Fire*, describes Canadian populists of the late eighteenth century as "radical evangelicals."

17. See Murray, *Revival and Revivalism*, 138–39, and *passim* for examples. Murray's book is in part an extensively researched confessional history of Calvinist revivals in America, 1750–1858; many of those revivals exemplified the formalist side of the paradigm.

18. Daniel Walker Howe, "Religion and Politics in the Antebellum North," in *Religion and American Politics: From the Colonial Period to the 1980s*, ed. Mark A. Noll (New York: Oxford University Press, 1990), 121–45, makes the distinction between "hard" and "soft" evangelicalism. A often-cited study reflecting the "hard" side of formalist revivals is Paul E. Johnson, *A Shopkeeper's Millennium: Society and Revivals in Rochester, New York, 1815–1837* (New York: Hill and Wang, 1978).

19. Donald G. Mathews, "The Second Great Awakening as an Organizing Process, 1780–1830: An Hypothesis," *American Quarterly*, 21 (Spring 1969): 27. There were, as Mathews himself emphasized, impulses toward order and organization among the populists as well as the formalists. Recurring tensions between fragmentation and order, freedom and control existed within both groups. The categorizations represent the major tendencies of each.

20. Curtis D. Johnson, *Redeeming America*, 8. The most influential recent study of populist evangelicals is Hatch, *Democratization*.

21. The dynamic between tendencies toward integration and fragmentation in American evangelicalism is a complex one; as this study of the 1857–58 Revival will show, practices of piety were becoming more standardized even while differentiation within denominations and between North and South was increasing, cf. Hatch, *Democratization*, 205.

22. Hatch, *Democratization*, 193–209. For the "cultural symbiosis" between evangelicalism and politics as part of the move toward "a discernibly modern mass democracy," see Carwardine, *Evangelicals and Politics*, 320 and *passim*; Carwardine also traces the rise of a sectional evangelicalism during the years prior to the war. R. Laurence Moore, *Selling God: American Religion in the Marketplace of Culture* (New York: Oxford University Press, 1994), chronicles a similar symbiosis between religion and commercial culture.

23. A list of the 32 largest cities in the United States according to the 1850 Census, locations ranging in population from about ten thousand inhabitants to more than half a million, indicated that 21 were located in the North and Old Northwest; six in the Middle States or Upper South; four in the Lower South and one in the West. Bureau of the Census, *Seventh Census of the United States: 1850* (Washington, D.C.: Government Printing Office, 1853), table 34.

24. Appendix B, tables 1, 3, and 5. Baptists were particularly strong in the southern and border states, as Timothy Smith pointed out in *Revivalism and Social Reform*, 22, n. 12. Regular Baptists in these two regions were growing at an average of 4.3 percent between 1853 and 1857, twice the rate of those in the North. If the Border States were not included in the comparison, the contrast between the growth of Baptists in the North and in the South would be even greater. During the same period, Southern Methodists grew at an average of 3.6 percent per year, while those in the North averaged a growth rate of 2.4 percent. Old School Presbyterians in the lower South averaged about 4.3 percent per year between 1853 and 1857, in contrast to Old School churches in the North, which grew at an average of 2.9 percent per year. The contrast is less significant, however, if the net growth of Old School churches in the Border States is added to those in the South, resulting in an average annual growth rate for the combined group of 3.2 percent.

25. Joel Carpenter, "Is 'Evangelical' a Yankee Word? Relations Between Northern Evangelicals and the Southern Baptist Convention in the Twentieth Century," in *Southern Baptists and American Evangelicals: The Conversation Continues*, ed. David S. Dockery, (Nashville: Broadman and Holman, 1993), 83. Carpenter used the term "Yankee evangelicalism" to refer to the cultural particularities of the transdenominational, evangelical coalition that emerged from northern Fundamentalism after World War II in contrast to the cultural patterns of evangelicals in the South, particularly those affiliated with the Southern Baptist Convention. Analogously, the Revival of 1857–58 helped to shape a particularly northern style of evangelicalism that emerged during the second half of the nineteenth century.

26. Carwardine, *Transatlantic Revivalism*, 169–97. Most notable among the Brit-

ish revivals was an explosive popular movement in Ulster during 1859 that spread to the west of Scotland. See William Gibson, *The Year of Grace: A History of the Ulster Revival of 1859* (Edinburgh: Andrew Elliot, 1860); David Hempton and Myrtle Hill, *Evangelical Protestantism in Ulster Society 1740–1890* (London: Routledge, 1992); and Janice Holmes, "The 'world turned upside down': Women in the Ulster Revival of 1859," in *Coming into the Light: The Work, Politics, and Religion of Women in Ulster, 1840–1940*, ed. Janice Holmes and Diane Urquhart (Belfast: Queen's University of Belfast, 1994), 126–53. Wales also experienced widespread revival, while religious fervor in England was more erratic and generally the result of efforts by visiting American evangelists. Authors of some popular histories of the revival, for example, Orr, *Fervent Prayer*, point to its impact on other parts of the world within the scope of Anglo-American evangelical influence.

27. Robert Baird, *Religion in the United States of America* (Glasgow: W. G. Blackie, 1844; reprint New York: Arno Press, 1969), 442. Baird was a Presbyterian; nineteenth-century Methodists described revivals in a similar fashion as "seasons of refreshing, . . . [where] souls were converted," quoted in Samuel A. Seaman, *Annals of New York Methodism* (New York: Hunt and Eaton, 1892), 79. Both denominations credited the Spirit of God as the ultimate agent behind such occasions.

28. In *Modern Revivalism*, William G. McLoughlin used "revival" and "revivalism" interchangeably but defined "modern revivalism" as the anthropomorphic, manufactured process of mass evangelism inaugurated by Charles Finney. See pp. 1–11. For a recent argument in favor of a theological distinction between the two words, see Murray, *Revival and Revivalism*.

29. Studies both of George Whitefield and of the evangelical communications network during the mid-eighteenth-century awakening have highlighted the innovative methods that accompanied what traditionally have been considered spontaneous revivals. For "letter days," the evangelical network, and a caution to historians about creating too great a contrast "between the spontaneity of the mid-eighteenth-century revivals and the professionalization of those in the nineteenth century," see Susan O'Brien, "A Transatlantic Community of Saints: The Great Awakening and the First Evangelical Network, 1735–1755," *American Historical Review* 91 (October 1986): 815, 825–29. Frank Lambert, *"Pedlar in Divinity": George Whitefield and the Transatlantic Revivals* (Princeton: Princeton University Press, 1994) and Harry S. Stout, *The Divine Dramatist: George Whitefield and the Rise of Modern Evangelicalism* (Grand Rapids: Eerdmans, 1991) examine Whitefield's methods.

30. Points made by George Marsden in "Forum: The Decade Ahead in Scholarship," *Religion and American Culture* 3 (Winter 1993): 11–12, provided a framework for these comments.

31. Daniel Walker Howe, "Victorian Culture in America," in *Victorian America*, ed. Daniel Walker Howe (Philadelphia: University of Pennsylvania Press, 1976), 21, noted the discomfort of scholars with certain aspects of Victorian culture; also Sizer [Frankiel], "Politics and Apolitical Religion," 81.

One: The Revival Takes Shape as History

1. *Christian Advocate and Journal*, September 30, 1858.

2. Samuel Irenaeus Prime, *The Power of Prayer, Illustrated in the Wonderful Displays of Divine Grace at the Fulton Street and Other Meetings*, (New York: Scribner, 1858), 47; Talbot W. Chambers, *The Noon Prayer Meeting of the North Dutch Church* (New York: Board of Publication, Reformed Protestant Dutch Church, 1858);

William C. Conant, *Narratives of Remarkable Conversions and Revival Incidents* (New York: Derby and Jackson, 1858).

3. James W. Alexander, *The Revival and Its Lessons* (New York: American Tract Society, 1858); and [Samuel Irenaeus Prime, ed.], *The New York Pulpit in the Revival of 1858: A Memorial Volume of Sermons* (New York: Sheldon, Blakeman, 1858). Although no editor is listed on the title page of *The New York Pulpit*, Prime wrote "gathered and edited by S. I. Prime" in a copy catalogued with his papers at the Speer Library, Princeton Theological Seminary.

4. These ministers stood within a Calvinist revival tradition that emerged in Britain and the American colonies during the seventeenth and eighteenth centuries, a tradition explored in Michael J. Crawford, *Seasons of Grace: Colonial New England's Revival Tradition in Its British Context* (New York: Oxford University Press, 1991). Joseph Conforti locates the tradition more narrowly, finding it in the "New Divinity men" who transformed "the New England revival experience into a great, general, and formative American historical event." Joseph Conforti, "Invention of the Great Awakening, 1795–1842," *Early American Literature* 26 (1991): 113.

5. Robert Ellis Thompson made the often quoted remark that the rise of revivalism "terminated the Puritan and inaugurated the Pietist or Methodist age of American church history." See Thompson, *A History of the Presbyterian Churches in the United States of America*, American Church History Series, vol. 6 (New York: Scribner's, 1907 [1895]), 34.

6. In neither of these cases was there a formal alliance; rather my groupings refer to theological and social like-mindedness. The Congregationalists and New School Presbyterians had been united until the former abrogated the Plan of Union in 1852. For a detailed study of the Old School/New School Presbyterian split and the differences in the groups, see George M. Marsden, *The Evangelical Mind and the New School Presbyterian Experience: A Case Study of Thought and Theology in Nineteenth-Century America* (New Haven: Yale University Press, 1970). Marsden divides the Old School party into "the moderates of Princeton" and the "strict confessionalists of Philadelphia" (p. 42). The Old Schoolers in New York who "claimed" the revival, such as Prime and Alexander, were Princetonians. In general, they were theologically moderate and socially conservative.

7. Ibid., 75–79.

8. Richard Carwardine, "The Second Great Awakening in Comparative Perspective: Revivals and Culture in the United States and Britain," in *Modern Christian Revivals*, ed. Edith L. Blumhofer and Randall Balmer (Urbana: University of Illinois Press, 1993), 85, 87, 89. Talbot W. Chambers, *The Noon Prayer Meeting of the North Dutch Church* (New York: Board of Publication, Reformed Protestant Dutch Church, 1858), 36–38, provides one illustration of the activist style of the conservatives.

9. Marsden, *Evangelical Mind*, 155.

10. Prime, *Power of Prayer*, 18, 38. The church, a Dutch Reformed congregation, was often referred to simply as the Fulton Street church.

11. Ibid., chapter subtitle, 18. *The Power of Prayer*, 18–29, and Chambers, *Noon Prayer Meeting*, 39–44, provide background on Lanphier. Chambers's work also is one of the few primary sources with illustrations of revival activities, focusing, of course, on the Fulton Street prayer meeting.

12. In a later interview, Lanphier did acknowledge that a woman was first to arrive, apparently early in the hour, but was turned away. None of the revival accounts noted the incident. See chapter 5, n. 88.

13. Prime, *Power of Prayer*, 47.

14. Ibid.

15. In early 1857 the New York City YMCA split in a bitter controversy over questions concerning slavery and the role of the association as a political group. About 150 prominent, socially conservative young men left the group. L. L. Doggett, *Life of Robert R. McBurney* (Cleveland: F. M. Barton, 1902), 40–42.

16. Charles P. McIlvaine, *Bishop McIlvaine's Address to the Convention of the Diocese of Ohio, on the Revival of Religion* (Cincinnati: C. F. Bradley, 1858), 6; cf. *Noon Prayer Meeting*, 287, and *Power of Prayer*, 46.

17. Conant wrote his version of the revival during the first week in April 1858, the week after Greeley had published a special Easter weekend edition of the *Tribune*, solely devoted to the revival. See *Narratives*, 394, for Conant's acknowledgment of his source.

18. Ibid., 414.

19. Ibid., 426–35. Conant briefly acknowledged revivals in Maryland, Kentucky, and Tennessee.

20. A letter to the editor of the *Tribune*, April 24, 1858, from the "Beaufort District," South Carolina, criticizing the paper's report that the revival "appears to have affected only in a very slight and hardly perceptible degree, the entire South," together with an account of blacks and whites together in plantation worship, indicated that southerners were getting this message. The definitive statement of it did not occur until Charles G. Finney's *Memoirs*, including an account of the revival, were published in 1876. Charles G. Finney, *The Memoirs of Charles G. Finney: The Complete Restored Text*, ed. Garth M. Rosell and Richard A. G. Dupuis (Grand Rapids: Academic Books/ Zondervan, 1989).

21. Conant, *Narratives*, 1, 415, for the supernatural and the natural; 416, for democratization; and 359, for revivalism. As a populist group concerned about religious liberty, the Baptists traditionally had opposed the religious hegemony and community reform efforts of the Calvinist formalists. However, by the late 1850s many northern Baptists, Conant among them, had become part of the religious formalist/ Republican camp. Richard Carwardine, *Evangelicals and Politics in Antebellum America* (New Haven: Yale University Press, 1993), 273, explores these shifts. Other Baptists prominent in the 1857–58 Revival, such as Francis Wayland and Henry Clay Fish, also shared the Whig, later Republican, values of a Christian Republic.

22. Conant, *Narratives*, 359.

23. *Power of Prayer*, 38. Fifteen years later when Prime rewrote the narrative, the focus had become more ecumenical. The same four groups were represented at the first prayer meeting, but the story added that a week later men from two other denominations arrived, "the Methodist and Episcopalian." Samuel Irenaeus Prime, *Fifteen Years of Prayer in the Fulton Street Meeting* (New York: Scribner, Armstrong, 1872), 18.

24. Ibid., 106.

25. Conant, *Narratives*, title page. Alexander, *Revival and Its Lessons*, 14, also put what he described as "our American awakening" in the context of a series of "times of refreshing" from the first century up through the Reformation, the Pietists, the "prodigious revolution" in eighteenth-century Great Britain and the colonies and, finally, the New England revivals of Asahel Nettleton.

26. Due to its wide distribution, the most important early publication from a city outside New York was *Pentecost; or, The Work of God in Philadelphia, A.D. 1858* (Philadelphia: Parry and McMillan, 1859), a pamphlet produced by the Philadelphia YMCA, probably by George Duffield, Jr. See Chambers, *Noon Prayer Meeting*, x. Not

as widely circulated but still important were *The Old South Chapel Prayer Meeting* (Boston: Tilton, 1859) and *Memorial of the Revival in Plymouth Church, Brooklyn, [Rev. Henry Ward Beecher] During the Early Part of the Year 1858: Comprising Incidents and Narratives, and also Fragments of Sermons, Lectures, Etc., By the Pastor*, written by a member of the church (New York: Clark, Austin and Smith, 1859). The latter book sought to emphasize Plymouth Church's influence rather than that of Fulton Street.

27. Conforti, "Invention of the Great Awakening," 99.

28. Jonathan Edwards, *A History of the Work of Redemption*, ed. John F. Wilson, *Works of Jonathan Edwards*, vol. 9 (New Haven: Yale University Press, 1989), 143, cf. 457, 460. Other eighteenth-century Calvinists who articulated the same idea included William Cooper in New England and John Gillies in Scotland. See Crawford, *Seasons of Grace*, 223-26, 248.

29. William B. Sprague, *Lectures on Revivals of Religion* (Albany: J. P. Haven and J. Leavitt, 1832), 4. Sprague also made a brief survey of the history of revivals from the Old Testament to the Reformation to the eighteenth-century evangelical awakenings in order to refute charges from opponents that revivals were of "modern origin" and therefore spurious (pp. 33-34).

30. Ibid., *passim*; note especially remarks by Princetonians Archibald Alexander, appendix, 4, and Samuel Miller, appendix, 24-44; also Charles McIlvaine's thinly veiled reference to Finney in the context of "pious frauds," Appendix (p. 90).

31. Sprague, *Lectures on Revivals*, 3.

32. For other references to ebbs and flows of revivals during this period, see Joseph Tracy, *The Great Awakening: A History of the Revival of Religion in the Time of Edwards and Whitefield* (Boston: Tappan and Dennet, 1842), chapter 1; D. MacFarlan, *The Revivals of the Eighteenth Century* (London: John Johnstone, [1847]), 9-13; and Henry Clay Fish, *Primitive Piety Revived* (Boston: Congregational Board of Publication, 1855), 236-40. Tracy placed the "ebb" before the First Great Awakening in the context of the Puritan understanding of New England spiritual decline; Fish introduced a primitivist interpretation, that revivals restored various aspects of pure, primitive piety to the church. Millennialist, "jeremiadic," and primitivist interpretive approaches often blended in antebellum historical analyses of revival, depending on the optimism or pessimism of the interpreter in assessing different events.

33. Conforti has suggested that New Divinity leaders and some Presbyterians during this period were engaged in a broad effort to deradicalize "the revivalistic legacy of Edwards and the mid-eighteenth-century awakening" so that the colonial tradition as exemplified in New England could be contrasted to the excesses of frontier revivals, as well as to those of Finney and of the Methodist preachers who had begun to invade New England. See "Invention of the Great Awakening," 101.

34. Archibald Alexander, "Letter I" in Sprague, *Lectures*, Appendix, 4-5.

35. Humphrey and Marvin stood in the New Divinity wing of Congregationalism. Both were careful to distance themselves from Finney and the western revivals, and they evinced a certain social conservatism.

36. Chapter 1 covered revivals in biblical times and the early church; chapter 2, "The Great Reformation" of the sixteenth and seventeenth centuries; chapter 3, "The Great Awakening" in Scotland, England, and America; and chapters 4-7, the first half of the nineteenth century, including the Revival of 1857-58. Heman Humphrey, *Revival Sketches and Manual* (New York: American Tract Society, 1859).

37. Ibid., 206, 209.

38. Ibid., 118-205.

39. Humphrey did mention western revivalism, though only briefly. He noted the extensive revivals in central and western New York and devoted a few pages to "some things to be regretted," but did not name Finney. Humphrey, *Revival Sketches,* 263–67.

40. Nelson R. Burr, *A Critical Bibliography of Religion in America,* vol. 4 of *Religion in American Life,* ed. James Ward Smith and A. Leland Jamison (Princeton: Princeton University Press, 1961), 181–82.

41. A. P. Marvin, "Three Eras of Revival in the United States," *Bibliotheca Sacra* 16 (April 1859): 279, 298.

42. Ibid., 298, 284.

43. Ibid., 279. See also Conant, *Narratives,* title page, and Humphrey, *Revival Sketches,* 3. For the "Invention of the Great Awakening," culminating in the publication of Tracy's *Great Awakening,* see Conforti's essay with that title.

44. Marvin, "Three Eras of Revival," 291. Obviously, 1857–58 was the backdrop for the entire article. See, for example, Marvin's comparison of responses to the "Awakening of 1740" and "the present special religious interest," 282.

45. Ibid., 291, 293, 299. From Marvin's New England perspective, "it was not heresy, nor intemperance, nor licentiousness, nor Sabbath desecration, nor war, nor slavery even. . . . The sin of the times was worldliness" (p. 293).

46. Prime, *Power of Prayer,* v. The "prayer of faith" was the popular term for Finney's teaching that believers could count on specific, often immediate, results from prayers based on faith in Scriptural promises. See Charles G. Finney, *Lectures on Revivals of Religion,* ed., William G. McLoughlin (Cambridge: Harvard University Press, 1960), chapters 5 and 6; also Finney, *Memoirs,* 72, n. 43; 168, n. 55.

47. Newman Hall, *Come to Jesus!* Tract no. 107 (Philadelphia: Presbyterian Board of Publication, n.d.), 24. The tract by Hall, an Anglican, was widely distributed during the revival; cf. James W. Alexander, "Looking Unto Jesus," *Revival and Its Lessons,* especially p. 83, where sinners were urged to "come at once to the Cross." Alexander and Hall used a strategy the Reformed had employed for years in writing for the tract societies: eschew complex theology and present the message via biblical texts. Hymns such as "Just as I Am," written by Charlotte Elliott in 1836, and its corollary, "Just as Thou Art," reinforced the message. See *Union Prayer Meeting Hymns* (Philadelphia: American Sunday-School Union, 1859), 53, 54. For comments on mid-nineteenth-century evangelical biblicism, see Timothy L. Smith, "History, Social Theory, and the Vision of the American Religious Past, 1955–1980," new afterword in Smith, *Revivalism and Social Reform: American Protestantism on the Eve of the Civil War* (Baltimore: Johns Hopkins University Press, 1980 [1957]), 258, 260.

48. There were still "hard cases," people who struggled days or longer to experience conversion but many others "came to Jesus" almost instantly through prayer. Prime, *Power of Prayer,* 129–33, 146–47, and *passim,* contains examples of both.

49. Methodists did, as I have indicated earlier, cover the revival extensively in their periodicals. This silence referred to here is to the lack of books on the subject.

50. An editorial note, "The Great Revival," in the *Pittsburgh Christian Advocate* (March 23, 1858) reflected this dynamic: "We have been specially gratified to see less dread of revivals . . . than was formerly evinced by our 'order' loving friends."

51. G. A. Reeder, "The Cleveland Revival," *Western Christian Advocate,* April 28, 1858.

52. Nathan Bangs, *A History of the Methodist Episcopal Church,* vol. 1 (New York: Carlton and Porter, 1840 [1838–41]), 362–63, referring to the official guide for church practice. See also historian Richard Carwardine's comparison of Methodists

and Calvinists in the late 1840s: "The Methodists' understanding of their obligation as a church often seemed to go no further than saving the largest number of souls, whereas revival-conscious Calvinists pressed ahead to establish the kingdom of God by redeeming society," *Evangelicals and Politics* (pp. 125–26).

53. Russell E. Richey, "History as a Bearer of Denominational Identity: Methodism as a Case Study," in *Beyond Establishment: Protestant Identity in a Post-Protestant Age*, ed. Jackson W. Carroll and Wade Clark Roof (Louisville: Westminster/John Knox Press, 1993), 273–74, 276. Edith L. Blumhofer, "Restoration as Revival: Early American Pentecostalism," in *Modern Christian Revivals*, ed. Edith L. Blumhofer and Randall A. Balmer (Urbana: University of Illinois Press, 1993), 146, has discerned a similar perspective in twentieth-century Pentecostalism.

54. Crawford, *Seasons of Grace*, 183–90, 242–43, discusses the "revival narrative" as a product of New England and British Calvinism; for Methodist communications patterns, see Russell E. Richey, *Early American Methodism* (Bloomington: Indiana University Press, 1991), 93.

55. I am indebted to Russell E. Richey of the Divinity School, Duke University, for this insight.

56. Bangs, *History*, 2: 116.

57. John Abernathy Smith, "How Methodism Became a National Church," *Methodist History*, 20 (October 1981): 15, citing Jesse Lee, *A Short History of the Methodists in the United States of America* (Baltimore: Magill and Clime, 1810), cf. Bangs, *History*, vol. 1: 89–97.

58. Bangs, *History*, vol. 1: 244, 273; Carwardine, *Transatlantic Revivalism*, 46–49.

59. The Methodist Episcopal Church, the northern denomination, gained more than 135,000 members during 1858 for a stunning one-year growth rate of 16.6 percent. Appendix B, table 1.

60. Sydney E. Ahlstrom, *A Religious History of the American People* (New Haven: Yale University Press, 1972), 9.

61. Daniel Dorchester, *Christianity in the United States from the First Settlement Down to the Present Time* (New York: Hunt and Eaton, 1889), 694. Other important late-nineteenth-century books that contained favorable treatments of the revival included Edward Norris Kirk, *Lectures on Revivals*, ed. David O. Mears (Boston: Congregational Publishing Society, 1875), and Henry Clay Fish, *Handbook of Revivals for the Use of Winners of Souls* (Boston: James H. Earle, 1879).

62. Ahlstrom, *Religious History*, 9. Ahlstrom described Dorchester as the first "historian-laureate" of the post–Civil War era and judged his book as "probably the finest work of its kind ever published." Not until Ahlstrom's own tome would it be surpassed for thoroughness.

63. Dorchester, *Christianity in the United States*, 372. Dorchester went on to comment, "The Methodist and Baptist churches, if their record could be fully sketched, would show still more numerous and powerful revivals and greater accessions" (p. 373). Dorchester's tactic anticipated the way historians would incorporate Methodism into general surveys of Christianity in America for years to come.

64. Ibid., 694. Dorchester's figures seem fairly accurate if taken for the northern branch of the denomination during 1858 alone. From 1856–59, Methodists, North and South, accounted for a little more than 50 percent of net membership gains among major Protestant denominations. See appendix B, tables 1 and 12.

65. Leonard Woolsey Bacon, *A History of American Christianity*, American Church History Series, vol. 13 (New York: Scribner's, 1925 [1897]), 230. Bacon's was

the first history of American Christianity to class what were seen as mid-eighteenth- and early-nineteenth-century revival periods as first and second "Awakenings," an interpretive convention that became accepted practice among later historians. Dorchester had followed Reformed historiography in casting the early National era (1776–1800) as a "dark period" of infidelity and spiritual decline, but he did not use cyclical revivalism as an interpretive framework.

66. Bacon, *History of American Christianity*, 344.

67. Denominational historians during this period were preoccupied with other issues. Of the 12 volumes in the American Church History Series, only Williston Walker, *A History of the Congregational Churches in the United States* (New York: Christian Literature, 1894), mentioned the 1857–58 Revival.

68. Among them were George Brown, *The Lady Preacher: or, The Life and Labors of Mrs. Hannah Reeves* (Philadelphia: Daughaday and Backer, 1870; reprint, New York: Garland, 1987); Mary B. Cheney, *The Life and Letters of Horace Bushnell* (New York: Harper, 1880); D. Stuart Dodge, *Memorials of William E. Dodge* (New York: Randolph, 1887); John O. Foster, *Life and Labors of Mrs. Maggie Newton Van Cott* (Cincinnati: Hitchcock and Walden, 1872); Asa Mahan, *Autobiography: Intellectual, Moral and Spiritual* (London: T. Woolmer, 1882); George H. Stuart, *The Life of George H. Stuart* (Philadelphia: J. M. Stoddart, 1890).

69. The first edition of Finney's *Memoirs*, 2,500 copies, sold out within a month, and a second was immediately issued. See Finney, *Memoirs of Charles G. Finney*, xx–xxiv, xlii. The book was reprinted in 1878 and 1903, before the 1989 critical edition. Numerous British editions also appeared. Richard Wheatley, *The Life and Letters of Mrs. Phoebe Palmer* (New York: Walter C. Palmer, Jr.) was reprinted in 1881, in 1884, and in the 1984 Garland edition (New York).

70. Finney, *Memoirs*, 562–63.

71. Ibid., 565. Finney's analysis of the situation in the South reflected both his opposition to slavery and the fact that the revival was less sensational in the southern states. As noted earlier, however, church growth statistics suggest that evangelicalism was spreading more rapidly in the South than in the North during the two decades prior to the Civil War. Concerning antecedents, during a sermon preached in 1859, Finney had pushed the roots of the 1857–58 Revival back to a revival in response to his preaching in Rochester, New York, during the winter and spring of 1856. Charles G. Finney, *The Prevailing Prayer-Meeting* (London: Ward, 1859), 24, 25.

72. Finney, *Memoirs*, 564–65. In some editions of the *Memoirs*, "male and female" was changed to "men and women" or deleted.

73. Ibid., 561. Rosell and Dupuis identify the opponent from the original text of the *Memoirs* as Congregationalist Edward Kirk. Finney did conclude that "Ministers nowhere opposed it [the Revival]" (p. 565). He also noted the positive response of Boston Unitarians.

74. Wheatley, *Life and Letters*, 315. Wheatley may have selected the title based on Palmer's letter to her sister, dated October 14th, 1857, where she wrote of "God's wonder-working power, in sanctifying believers, and saving sinners" (p. 330).

75. Ibid., 332.

76. Hamilton was one of eight urban centers in Canada with a population of 10,000 or more at that time. Peter George Bush, "James Caughey, Phoebe and Walter Palmer and the Methodist Revival Experience in Canada West, 1850–1858" (master of arts thesis, Queen's University, Kingston, Ontario, Canada, 1985), 126–38, and *passim*, provides an analysis of the Hamilton revival, as well as the Palmers' other revival work in Canada.

77. Wheatley, *Life and Letters*, 330–31. During February and March, 1857, Palmer had written "A Laity for the Times," a series of columns for the *Christian Advocate and Journal* offering her vision of ideal Methodist piety. She thought the Hamilton revival confirmed the principles she had advocated.

78. "From our Canadian Correspondent," *Guide to Holiness*, vol. 32 (July 1857–January 1858), 186; "Revival Extraordinary," *Christian Advocate and Journal*, November 5, 1857. The revival also was mentioned in the Canadian *Christian Guardian* but received much less acclaim than it did in the two U.S. periodicals. See Bush, "The Methodist Revival Experience in Canada West," 130, 136.

79. Palmer did not emphasize her role as a woman and public figure in the revival though she did note with obvious surprise that *both* she and Walter were invited to speak to the morning union prayer meeting at the Old South Chapel when they visited Boston in July (they were not invited to the businessmen's noon meeting). Wheatley, *Life and Letters*, 377.

80. One dissertation was written on the Revival in the 1930s by Carl Lloyd Spicer, "The Great Awakening of 1857 and 1858" (Ph.D. diss., Ohio State University, 1935). Spicer viewed revivals from an instrumental perspective and argued for the social benefits of the 1857–58 Revival. His was the first scholarly investigation of the awakening, valuable mainly for the fresh primary sources it cited. The dissertation apparently went unnoticed in the broader academic arena.

81. Histories include Frank G. Beardsley, *A History of American Revivals* (New York: American Tract Society, 1912); Warren A. Candler, *Great Revivals and the Great Republic* (Nashville: Methodist Episcopal Church, South, 1904); among biographies and autobiographies were Lyman Abbott, *Reminiscences* (Boston: Houghton Mifflin, 1923 [1915]); Charles R. Erdman, *D. L. Moody: His Message for Today* (New York: Fleming H. Revell, 1928); L. L. Doggett, *Life of Robert R. McBurney* (Cleveland: F. M. Barton, 1902); William R. Moody, *The Life of Dwight L. Moody* (Chicago: Fleming H. Revell, 1900); Hannah Whitall Smith, *The Unselfishness of God and How I Discovered It* (New York: Fleming H. Revell, 1903). For the YMCA, see L. L. Doggett, *History of the Young Men's Christian Association*, Parts 1 and 2 (New York: Association Press, 1922).

82. In *Life of McBurney*, L. L. Doggett, a YMCA historian, stressed the role of the "Y" in promoting union prayer meetings. He downplayed Lanphier's importance and claimed that "the first noon prayer-meeting was held in September, 1856" (p. 43), spearheaded by a young man named L. L. Deane.

83. Erdman, *Moody*, 36. Biographies did not emphasize the revival as a pivotal point in Moody's life, but they did agree that it was the event that linked him with the YMCA and the Christian Commission and so provided a broader arena for his energies.

84. Mark A. Noll, "How We Remember Revivals: The virtues and vices of tribal history," *Christianity Today*, April 24, 1995, 34.

85. Smith, *Revivalism and Social Reform*, 60, 62. Looking back a quarter of a century later, Smith explicitly affirmed that intention. See Timothy L. Smith, "Response of Professor Smith on Cycles of National Awakenings," *Sociological Analysis* 44 (1983): 121.

86. Smith, *Revivalism and Social Reform*, 92.

87. In later years, Smith softened this stance, finding common ground for nineteenth-century evangelicals in their biblicism rather than their affirmation of a particular theological framework. See "History, Social Theory, and the Vision of the American Religious Past, 1955–1980," Afterword in *Revivalism and Social Reform*:

American Protestantism on the Eve of the Civil War (Baltimore: Johns Hopkins University Press, 1980), 259.

88. These included such people as Phoebe Palmer, Boston Unitarian Frederic Dan Huntington, and New York abolitionist George Cheever, none of whom were favorites of socially conservative Calvinists. Smith, *Revivalism and Social Reform*, 65, 68, 70.

89. In addition to fresh primary sources, Smith also tapped information from two neglected doctoral dissertations on the subject: Russell E. Francis, "Pentecost: 1858," (Ph.D. diss., The University of Pennsylvania, 1948), and Spicer, "The Great Awakening of 1857 and 1858."

90. Smith incorporated periodical accounts into his narrative as well, although his principal source was the Baptist *Watchman and Reflector*, rather than the Methodist press.

91. In his follow-up chapter on the revival, "The Fruits of Fervor," in *Revivalism and Social Reform*, for instance, Smith wrote of an interdenominational meeting of laymen and ministers to discuss continuing means of promoting the revival as an example of "the absence of sectarian bigotry" and of concern for the poor. Yet there is no evidence that anything came of the meeting. He also spoke of the "businessmen's noonday prayer meetings" being "thrown open to the ladies," an exaggeration at best (pp. 82, 84–85).

92. "The Upstart Sects Win America, 1776–1850," chapter 3 in Roger Finke and Rodney Stark, *The Churching of America, 1776–1990: Winners and Losers in Our Religious Economy* (New Brunswick: Rutgers University Press, 1992), 55, and *passim*. The percentages refer to religious adherents rather than church members and represent a portion of a total that includes Catholics as well as Protestants. Although he did not distinguish regional variations, Richard Carwardine identified a rhythmic pattern of continued church growth among the Methodists with five discernible peak periods from 1780 to 1858, *Transatlantic Revivalism*, 46–47, 49. For Methodist growth measured in numbers of congregations, see Carwardine, " 'Antinomians' *and* 'Arminians': Methodists and the Market Revolution," in *The Market Revolution in America: Social, Political, and Religious Expressions, 1800–1880*, ed. Melvyn Stokes and Stephen Conway (Charlottesville: University Press of Virginia, 1996), 290.

93. I am indebted to Joel Carpenter for his observation about the "losers" writing the history. See Joel A. Carpenter, "The Scope of American Evangelicalism; Some Comments on the Dayton-Marsden Exchange," *Christian Scholar's Review* 23 (September 1993): 59–60, for his comments in the context of contemporary interpretive debates. Conforti, "Invention of the Great Awakening," 100, suggests that the creation of the Great Awakening construct was an effort to contain the popular religious movements of the early republic. By 1858, as those movements were becoming respectable, the effort had become more one of assimilation.

Two. Revivalism in the News

1. *New York Herald*, February 27, 1858. This account was not the first time the revival had been mentioned in the secular dailies. For example, the *New York Daily Tribune* had run a brief note, "The Hour of Prayer," February 10, 1858; and under the headline, "Extensive 'Revival' in New York City," the *Evening Post*, February 11, 1858, had reprinted a two-paragraph report from the *New York Evangelist*. Indeed, Bennett had signaled his intentions with an editorial, "A Religious Revolution," and a few news notes in his Sunday paper, February 21. Nonetheless, the page one position, flamboyant headlines, and extensive coverage February 27 marked a new stage: the

recognition of the revival as a major news story. Bennett's competitors, who rushed to follow his lead in covering the event, clearly got that message.

2. In addition to eastern seaboard cities, coverage was most intense in the Old Northwest and the Upper South—in such cities as Chicago, Cincinnati, Louisville, Richmond, and St. Louis. However, newspapers in the Lower South, including those in Charleston and New Orleans, printed articles and editorials about the event.

3. Bureau of the Census, "The Public Press," *Eighth Census of the United States: 1860*, vol. 4. (Washington, D.C.: Government Printing Office, 1860), 319. Estimates of newspapers and circulation figures are based on the 1850 census as reported in J. C. G. Kennedy, "Catalogue of the Newspapers and Periodicals Published in the United States," *Livingston's Law Register for 1852* (New York: John Livingston, 1852). Editors estimated that each subscription represented from four to six actual readers; the circulation total represents a conservative estimate. About 70 of the Protestant weeklies represented denominations sympathetic to the 1857–58 Revival.

4. These were the *Christian Advocate and Journal*, New York City; the *Nashville Christian Advocate*; the *North-Western Christian Advocate*, Chicago; the *Southern Christian Advocate*, Charleston; and the *Western Christian Advocate*, Cincinnati. The *Advocates* represented either the Methodist Episcopal Church or the MEC, South, respectively, depending on their regional location. See James Penn Pilkington, *The Methodist Publishing House: A History*, vol. 1 (Nashville: Abingdon Press, 1968), 386.

5. Kennedy, "Catalogue," 30. Circulation figures for the *Observer* and the *Evangelist* are based on the 1850 census and probably were higher in 1858. Wesley Norton has estimated that religious periodicals in the Old Northwest had a combined circulation of "well over 200,000 by 1860." See Norton, *Religious Newspapers in the Old Northwest to 1861: A History, Bibliography, and Record of Opinion* (Athens: Ohio University Press, 1977), 5.

6. "The Revival in Troy," *New York Daily Tribune*, March 24, 1858.

7. For the *Herald* and the dynamics of the "cash and carry" press, see James L. Crouthamel, *Bennett's New York Herald and the Rise of the Popular Press* (Syracuse: Syracuse University Press, 1989), chapter 2; for the *Tribune*, see Frank Luther Mott, *American Journalism* (New York: Macmillan, 1950), 268–78. Michael Schudson, *Discovering the News: A Social History of American Newspapers* (New York: Basic Books, 1978), provides a broad overview of the consumer revolution in news brought about by the rise of the mass circulation dailies.

8. Harry S. Stout, *The Divine Dramatist: George Whitefield and the Rise of Modern Evangelicalism* (Grand Rapids: Eerdmans, 1991), 35. See also Frank Lambert, " 'Pedlar in Divinity': George Whitefield and the Great Awakening, 1737-1745," *Journal of American History* 77 (December 1990): 812–37, and the more extensive treatment in Lambert, *"Pedlar in Divinity": George Whitefield and the Transatlantic Revivals*, 1737–1770 (Princeton: Princeton University Press, 1994). Studies of nineteenth-century Protestants include R. Laurence Moore, *Selling God: American Religion in the Marketplace of Culture* (New York: Oxford University Press, 1994), and Peter J. Wosh, *Spreading the Word: The Bible Business in Nineteenth-Century America* (Ithaca: Cornell University Press, 1994).

9. There is no evidence, for example, that George Whitefield reaped any significant personal profit from his preaching. See Lambert, *Whitefield and Transatlantic Revivals*, 181–82. Nathan O. Hatch, *The Democratization of American Christianity* (New Haven: Yale University Press, 1989), chapter 5, *passim*, highlights the populist religious entrepreneurs of the early nineteenth century. Moore, *Selling God*, suggests a profit motive for Mason Locke Weems, an early purveyor of "moral sensationalism,"

but prior to 1858 few people profited from revival news. William G. McLoughlin, *Modern Revivalism: Charles Grandison Finney to Billy Graham* (New York: Ronald Press, 1959), 87, 98, 138, notes the early use of advertising techniques.

10. Lambert, "George Whitefield and the Great Awakening," 814, notes this "creative tension" in Whitefield's life, although he also acknowledges Whitefield's personal openness to consumer goods and his sense that commerce and religion could be compatible, 834–36. See also Michael Zuckerman, "Holy Wars, Civil Wars: Religion and Economics in Nineteenth-Century America," *Prospects: An Annual of American Cultural Studies* 16 (1991): 219–24.

11. For Whitefield's ability to "manipulate the press," see Stout, *Divine Dramatist*, 47. Lambert, *Whitefield and Transatlantic Revivals*, 110–29, has demonstrated that Benjamin Franklin and other commercial printers viewed Whitefield as "good business." However, Whitefield remained his own most important publicist.

12. Moore, *Selling God*, 5–7. While Whitefield was an important forerunner of this commercialization, the colonial press was not yet a mass medium in the modern sense, nor did secular papers maintain any significant revival coverage during the century following the grand itinerant's visits.

13. Stout, *Divine Dramatist*, 146–50. For detailed information on the eighteenth-century evangelical press, consult Frank Lambert, "The Great Awakening as Artifact: George Whitefield and the Construction of Intercolonial Revival, 1739–1745," *Church History* 60 (June 1991): 223–46; Susan Durden [O'Brien], "A Study of the First Evangelical Magazines, 1740–1748," *Journal of Ecclesiastical History* 27 (July 1974): 255–75; Susan O'Brien, "A Transatlantic Community of Saints: The Great Awakening and the First Evangelical Network, 1735–1755," *American Historical Review* 91 (October 1986): 811–32; and O'Brien, "Eighteenth-Century Publishing Networks in the First Years of Transatlantic Evangelicalism" in *Evangelicalism: Comparative Studies of Popular Protestantism in North America, the British Isles, and Beyond, 1700–1990*, ed. Mark A. Noll, David W. Bebbington, and George A. Rawlyk, 38–57; as well as Roberta J. Moore, "The Beginning and Development of Protestant Journalism in the United States, 1743–1850" (Ph.D. diss., Syracuse University, 1968), chapter 2.

14. See, for example, sources cited by John B. Boles, *The Great Revival 1787–1805: The Origins of the Southern Evangelical Mind* (Lexington: University of Kentucky Press, 1972), 64, n. 50, or Paul K. Conkin, *Cane Ridge: America's Pentecost* (Madison: University of Wisconsin Press, 1990), 56, n. 19, and 97, n. 22, in their respective reconstructions of the event.

15. No comprehensive study exists of religion in the secular press during this period; however, sources cited in scholarly monographs reflect little evidence of attention to revivals. For example, recent studies of Finney, including the biography by Keith J. Hardman, and the heavily documented, annotated edition of the *Memoirs*, contain extensive citations from religious periodicals but nothing from the secular press concerning Finney prior to 1858. See Keith J. Hardman, *Charles Grandison Finney, 1792–1875* (Syracuse, N.Y.: Syracuse University Press, 1987) and Charles Grandison Finney, *The Memoirs of Charles G. Finney: The Complete Restored Text*, ed. Garth M. Rosell and Richard A. G. Dupuis (Grand Rapids: Academic Books/Zodervan, 1989). Note also the contrast observed in McLoughlin, *Modern Revivalism*, 219, between the secular press treatment of Moody and Sankey and its lack of interest in Finney. Other monographs on revivalism reviewed for citations from the secular press included Boles, *The Great Revival*; Carwardine, *Transatlantic Revivalism: Popular Evangelicalism in Britain and America, 1760–1865* (Westport, Conn.: Greenwood Press, 1978); Timothy L. Smith, *Revivalism and Social Reform: American Protestant-*

ism on the Eve of the Civil War (Nashville: Abingdon Press, 1957); and Bernard A. Weisberger, *They Gathered at the River: The Story of the Great Revivalists and their Impact upon Religion in America* (Boston: Little, Brown, 1958). The only secular sources cited were in Boles, *Great Revival*: occasional references to the *Georgia Analytical Repository* and the *Raleigh Register* and *North-Carolina State Gazette* for letters or other information on early southern revivalism.

16. Cited in Finney, *Memoirs*, 293, n. 55.

17. James F. Findlay, *Dwight L. Moody: American Evangelist, 1837–1899* (Chicago: University of Chicago Press, 1969), 190. Findlay points to the role of the religious press in piquing the interest of the secular dailies. The exchange of information between religious and secular periodicals that began in 1858 continued in the second half of the century; evangelical sophistication in public relations developed during that period as well.

18. Quoted in Frank Luther Mott, *American Journalism* (New York: Macmillan, 1950), 697–98. Roger A. Bruns, *Preacher: Billy Sunday and Big-Time American Evangelicalism* (New York: W. W. Norton, 1992), 211–12, and Lyle W. Dorsett, *Billy Sunday and the Redemption of Urban America* (Grand Rapids: Eerdmans, 1991), 99–100, also examine press coverage of the Sunday revivals. Although he includes no specific analysis of the print media and revivalism, William McLoughlin comments frequently on the press and revivalists such as Moody, Edward Payson Hammond, Sam Jones, Fay Mills, and Billy Graham in *Modern Revivalism*, 156, 232–33, 333–34, and *passim*.

19. Daniel Walker Howe, *Political Culture of the American Whigs* (Chicago: University of Chicago Press, 1979), 185. Although awareness of secular press involvement is common, few historians have attempted any focused analysis of its significance. In his 1948 dissertation, Russell E. Francis offered a somewhat cursory examination of the Bennett/Greeley rivalry, suggesting that each editor was motivated by political concerns. Francis viewed the extensive coverage in the *Tribune* as evidence of Greeley's effort, ultimately futile, to coopt the revival in service to the Republican cause and the antislavery movement. See Francis, "Pentecost: 1858, A Study in Religious Revivalism" (Ph.D. diss., University of Pennsylvania, 1948), 75. More recently, in a brief but perceptive analysis, James Moorhead placed the roles of press and telegraph during the revival in the context of antebellum Protestant eschatology. James H. Moorhead, "The Millennium and the Media," in *Communication and Change in American Religious History* ed. Leonard I. Sweet (Grand Rapids: Eerdmans, 1993): 222–23.

20. Schudson, *Discovering the News*, chapter 1, provides the best brief account of modern journalism as part of an emerging "democratic market society" in antebellum America.

21. *New York Herald*, May 5, 1835, quoted in Crouthamel, *Bennett's New York Herald*, 20.

22. *New York Herald*, February 12, 1858.

23. Crouthamel, *Bennett's New York Herald*, provided most of the background for my discussion of Bennett as a journalist. See especially chapter 2, *passim*.

24. Judith M. Buddenbaum, " 'Judge . . . What Their Acts Will Justify': The Religion Journalism of James Gordon Bennett," *Journalism History* 14 (Summer/Autumn 1987): 55. An early proponent of this view was Bennett's managing editor, Frederic Hudson, in his *Journalism in the United States from 1690 to 1872* (New York: Harper, 1873), 453–54. See also Crouthamel, *Bennett's New York Herald*, 34–37, 42. Moore, *Selling God*, chapters 1 and 5, notes Bennett's skill at marketing sensationalism and

controversy concerning religion. Some evidence indicates that secular weeklies in the early republic printed occasional news items about religion, especially when they existed in competition with religious weeklies. See, for example, the comment by Sidney Morse, *New York Observer*, June 23, 1849, quoted in Moore, "Protestant Journalism in the United States," 102. Still, Bennett's place as the most important early popularizer of religion news in a mass-circulation daily seems secure.

25. Buddenbaum, "Religion Journalism," 66, n. 52, 62. Monk's *Awful Disclosures of the Hotel Dieu Nunnery in Montreal* (New York: Hoisington and Trow, 1836) contained lurid, but bogus, anti-Catholic revelations.

26. *New York Herald*, May 27, 1840, quoted in Crouthamel, *Bennett's New York Herald*, 35. Bennett was raised in a strict Catholic home in predominantly Presbyterian Scotland. He adopted a cynical stance toward organized religion though he professed respect for the Bible and "real Christianity." Nonetheless, Bennett was married in a Catholic service and died in communion with the church. See Crouthamel, *Bennett's New York Herald*, 4, 5, 36, 155; also Buddenbaum, "Religion Journalism," 60, 64–65.

27. Most historians center their discussion of Bennett's religion on the Anniversary Meetings and the subsequent Moral War, although there also is general agreement that the "war" was motivated by political and business rivalries along with moral issues. Hudson, *Journalism in the United States*, 453–54, 456–62; Crouthamel, *Bennett's New York Herald*, 34–37; Buddenbaum, "Religion Journalism," 60–61, 63–64. Most assessments emphasize the satire and sensationalism of the *Herald's* religion coverage, although Buddenbaum attempts a revisionist argument based on a random content analysis that Bennett's coverage was "essentially secular and even-handed." For Bennett's wealth, see Crouthamel, 53–54.

28. Buddenbaum, "Religion Journalism," 62; Crouthamel, *Bennett's New York Herald*, 42. Hatch, *Democratization*, 145, treats the publicity campaign and media coverage surrounding Miller.

29. *New York Daily Tribune*, May 12, 1858.

30. Crouthamel, *Bennett's New York Herald*, 161.

31. *Christian Advocate and Journal*, November 26, 1857.

32. For Greeley as a Whig, see Howe, *Political Culture*, 184–97. Apart from Howe's treatment, Greeley has received little critical scholarly attention. For the *Tribune*, see Hudson, *Journalism in the United States*, chapter 33; Mott, *American Journalism*, 267–78; and Glyndon G. Van Deusen, *Horace Greeley* (Philadelphia: University of Pennsylvania, 1953), chapter 5 and *passim*.

33. Horace Greeley, *New York Daily Tribune*, quoted in Hudson, *Journalism in the United States*, 523; *Tribune*, April 19, 1841, quoted in Mott, *American Journalism*, 271.

34. *New York Daily Tribune*, December 3, 1845, quoted in Van Deusen, *Greeley*, 51.

35. Quoted in Hudson, *Journalism in the United States*, 526.

36. Howe, *Political Culture*, 188, 355, n. 26.

37. *New York Daily Tribune*, April 4, 1856, cited in Clifford E. Clark, Jr., *Henry Ward Beecher: Spokesman for a Middle-Class America* (Urbana: University of Illinois Press, 1978), 123, n. 56; *Tribune*, April 18, 1857, cited in Robert M. York, "George B. Cheever, Religious and Social Reformer," *University of Maine Bulletin* (April 1955) in *University of Maine Studies*, 2nd. ser., no. 69, 149, n. 6.

38. *New York Daily Tribune*, June 8, 1850, cited in Ann Braude, *Radical Spirits: Spiritualism and Women's Rights in Nineteenth-Century America* (Boston: Beacon

Press, 1989), 16, n. 13. Horace Greeley and his wife, Molly, investigated spiritualism in the early 1850s in attempts to communicate with a recently deceased son.

39. *Christian Advocate and Journal*, March 25, 1858; the same editorial, written in the midst of the revival, suggested that the *Tribune* "has been steadily advancing nearer and nearer to the stand-point of Christianity, embodied and brought into action in the evangelical Churches of the country."

40. Constance Rourke, *Trumpets of Jubilee: Henry Ward Beecher, Harriet Beecher Stowe, Lyman Beecher, Horace Greeley, P. T. Barnum* (New York: Harcourt, Brace, 1927), 314. See also Mott, *American Journalism*, 276–77. Circulation of the *Weekly Tribune* reached 100,000 during the presidential campaign of 1856 when it supported the Republican John C. Frémont. Greeley's antislavery "onslaught" during 1857, as well as the panic that year, resulted in a heavy circulation loss, although probably not half of all subscribers, as James Gordon Bennett suggested. By 1860, most analysts agree the *Weekly Tribune* had reached a high of 200,000. See Alfred McClung Lee, *The Daily Newspaper in America* (New York: Macmillan, 1937), 384, and Van Deusen, *Horace Greeley*, 216, 229–30.

41. For circulation figures, see the *New York Herald*, March 4, 1858. Crouthamel, *Bennett's New York Herald*, has commented that the *Herald* was "the North's most prosouthern newspaper." See p. 69.

42. For example, during the first full weeks of February and March, 1858, the *Tribune* averaged about two pages, six columns each, of advertising. By April, with spring sales underway, the average was close to three pages per issue. See the *Daily Tribune*, February 1–6, March 1–6, and April 5–10, 1858. Bennett made a backhanded acknowledgment of similar problems in the *Herald*, March 18, 1858.

43. Donald Lewis Shaw, "At the Crossroads: Change and Continuity in American Press News 1820–1860," *Journalism History* 8 (Summer 1981): 43.

44. In his diary, Lanphier noted, "Called to converse with some of the editors of the daily papers in regard to having some of the incidents, which occur from day to day in the prayer-meetings, inserted in them." Quoted in Samuel Irenaeus Prime, *The Power of Prayer: Illustrated in the Wonderful Displays of Divine Grace at the Fulton Street and Other Meetings* (New York: Scribner, 1858), 35. Lanphier did not specify which newspapers he visited, although it is probable that the *Tribune*, at least, was among them.

45. *New York Examiner*, February 4 and 11, 1858; Lee, *Daily Newspaper in America*, 394.

46. *New York Herald*, February 21, 1858. Bennett reinforced the images of class distinction by also describing women at prayer in uptown churches as "daughters of fashion, in all the pomp of sables, and velvets, and . . . crinoline." Opposition to Sabbath observance would continue to be a subtext in the *Herald's* revival coverage. See the *Herald*, February 27 and March 21, 1858. Mention of the Sabbath Committee does not appear in evangelical accounts of the revival nor did its activities seem affected by the religious excitement. See the *New York Daily Tribune*, March 18, 1858.

47. "Revivals in the Churches," *New York Herald*, February 21, 1858. As Catholics voiced their disapproval of the revival, Bennett quietly dropped this strategy, *New York Herald*, March 2, 1858, and April 4, 1858.

48. Ibid., February 21, 1858, for a reproduction of the Fulton Street card. The YMCA circular was reprinted in the *New York Evening Post*, March 11, 1858.

49. *New York Herald*, March 14, 1858.

50. Ibid., February 21, 1858.

51. Ibid., February 27, 1858.

52. Charles Finney, who had been in Brooklyn in April 1858, later told audiences that Greeley "employed a special and able Christian editor to collect and arrange the revival intelligence." Finney, *The Prevailing Prayer-Meeting* (London-Ward, 1859), 26–27. William Conant, whose revival book, *Narratives of Remarkable Conversions and Revival Incidents* (New York: Derby and Jackson, 1858), would draw heavily from the *Tribune*, had journalistic aspirations and was editing a small religious paper, *The Message*, when the revival began. See the Baptist *Examiner*, March 4, 1858. Because his book used so much *Tribune* material and was heavily advertised in the paper, it seems likely he was the editor employed.

53. This is not to say the *Tribune's* coverage stopped on April 3. There was a "recap" of revival prayer meetings as late as June 1, 1858. But coverage tapered off noticeably after the "Extra."

54. *New York Daily Tribune*, March 1, 1858.

55. *New York Herald*, February 27, 1858.

56. *New York Daily Tribune*, March 6, 1858.

57. Ibid.

58. Ibid., April 7, 1858.

59. Apart from his publication strategy, one indication that Greeley had an intentional marketing plan was the questionnaire the *Tribune* apparently mailed to pastors in early March requesting revival information for the "Extra," April 3, 1858.

60. Ibid., March 13, 1858, for Olney and Lloyd.

61. *Boston Post*, February 3, 1858; J. W. Alexander noted 100,000 copies of a collection of sermons by British preacher Charles Haddon Spurgeon had sold during early spring 1858. Alexander, *Forty Years' Familiar Letters of James W. Alexander*, ed. John Hall (New York: Scribner, 1860), 2: 277.

62. Prime, *Power of Prayer*, 310.

63. *New York Daily Tribune*, March 6, 1858.

64. Ibid., letter to the editor. Other letters noted the *Tribune's* role in the formation of prayer meetings. *New York Daily Tribune*, April 24, 1858.

65. Ibid., March 13, 1858.

66. Finney made the comments in a sermon before a British audience. Finney had mailed several copies of the *Tribune* to England and credited them with helping to stimulate prayer for revival in that country. Finney, *Prevailing Prayer-Meeting*, 27.

67. *Boston Post*, April 9, 1858.

68. The *Tribune*, most responsible for the naming, began calling the event, "The Religious Awakening," but quickly shifted to the "The Religious Revival" as a standing headline for revival reports. *New York Daily Tribune*, March 1 and 2, 1858, and subsequent issues. "The Religious Revival," "The Religious Awakening," and "The Great Revival" seemed to be the most popular designations for this much-named event.

69. "Great Work of God in the Land," *Christian Advocate and Journal* (Methodist), March 11, 1858; "The Great Revival," *Examiner* (Baptist), March 4, 1858; "The Great Awakening," *Independent* (Congregational), March 4, 1858; "The Revival," *New York Observer* (Presbyterian, OS), March 11, 1858; "The Great Revival," *Watchman and Reflector* (Baptist), March 25, 1858; "The Great Awakening," *Western Christian Advocate* (Methodist), April 7, 1858; and "The Times of Refreshing," *Western Recorder* (Baptist), April 7, 1858.

70. Interdenominational ("union") prayer meetings had taken place prior to 1857–58, as well as prayer meetings predominantly for men, although these usually were scheduled in the early morning. What was new about the Fulton Street meeting was its location in the center of an urban area, its time—obviously tailored to busi-

nessmen—and the ongoing support it received from men. The New York City YMCA had experimented with noon meetings prior to 1857 but could not find the personnel, interest, or publicity to sustain them.

71. The John Street meeting apparently began Monday, February 22, and the other YMCA meeting a week earlier at the Ninth Street Dutch Reformed Church. While still highly structured, the "Y" meetings tended to be less formal and more attractive to young people, as well as to Methodists and New School Presbyterians of all ages, than the more conservative Fulton Street meeting. *New York Daily Tribune*, March 1, 1858.

72. *Pentecost; or, the Work of God in Philadelphia*, 9. For the press coverage, see Russell E. Francis, "The Religious Revival of 1858 in Philadelphia," *Pennsylvania Magazine of History and Biography* 70 (1946): 63–65. The *Philadelphia Inquirer* had endorsed the Jayne's Hall meeting Monday morning, March 8, and the papers continued their coverage that week.

73. Not all the meetings met at noon—the Louisville gathering took place from 8:00-9:00 AM—but all were inspired by stories of New York City, Philadelphia, and elsewhere. No comprehensive list exists of the meetings or of dates they began. For Boston, see *The Old South Chapel Prayer Meeting* (Boston: Titton, 1859), 121; for Louisville, the *Louisville Daily Courier*, March 29, 1858; for Chicago, the *Chicago Tribune*, March 28, 1858; for New Orleans, the *Daily Picayune*, March 24, 1858.

74. A political cartoon from the 1850s shows a newsboy trying to sell a *Tribune* to a southerner. The response in the caption was, "No, curse your Tribune—don't you see I'm a *white* man [italics in original]." Reproduced in Van Deusen, *Greeley*, 217.

75. *Charleston Daily Courier*, March 24, 1858. Church membership statistics indicate an unusual increase during 1857 among Old School Presbyterians in the border states and in the lower South, as well as some positive change for Baptists in the border states, but no other widespread signs of increased religious interest. See appendix B, tables 3 and 5.

76. *Louisville Daily Courier*, April 17, 1858.

77. In Philadelphia, for example, the organizational and public relations abilities of John Wanamaker, full-time secretary of the Philadelphia YMCA, also contributed to the success of the noon meetings. Francis, "Religious Revival in Philadelphia," 62–63.

78. For a discussion of the "contagious diffusion" of news that accompanied exceptional circumstances in eighteenth- and nineteenth-century America, see Richard D. Brown, *Knowledge Is Power: The Diffusion of Information in Early America, 1700–1865* (New York: Oxford University Press, 1989), chapter 10.

79. *Louisville Daily Courier*, March 27, 1858.

80. *New York Daily Tribune*, March 16, 1858. Eddy's comments also illustrate how Protestants continued practices similar to those of the eighteenth-century "letter days," now powerfully reinforced by press publicity.

81. *New York Herald*, March 28, 1858.

82. Ibid., March 26, 1858. See also tables published March 24 and 26.

83. Ibid., April 6, 1858, cf. March 6 and March 18.

84. *Evening Transcript*, April 6, 1858.

85. Quentin J. Schultze, "Keeping the Faith: American Evangelicals and the Mass Media," in *American Evangelicals and the Mass Media*, ed. Quentin J. Schultze (Grand Rapids: Zondervan, 1990), 28.

86. *Christian Advocate and Journal*, March 25, 1858; see a similar comment in the *Western Recorder* (Louisville), July 14, 1858, citing the *Boston Recorder*.

87. *New York Observer*, March 25, 1858, also April 1.

88. Moorhead, "The Millennium and the Media," 223.

89. These were the *New York World*, founded in June 1860, and the *Sun*, purchased for the same purpose, also in summer 1860. Both were financial disasters. Mott, *American Journalism*, 350–51, 373. Mott commented, "This emphasis on religion was doubtless an effect of the Great Revival of 1858" (p. 373).

90. *Examiner*, April 8, 1858.

91. Moore, *Selling God*, 271.

92. *Western Recorder*, April 21, 1858.

93. The paper's circulation was listed in the 1850s census as 1,500, although there were indications it had increased by late in the decade. The *Post* had begun as a Democratic paper, switched to Free Soil in 1848, and then gone to the Republican party. Although small, it was respected and influential. See Mott, *American Journalism*, 257–58, and Kennedy, "Catalogue of Newspapers and Periodicals," 29.

94. *Evening Post*, March 11, 1858. However, the *Post* soon softened its stance toward revival coverage and embraced some of the same strategies it criticized here.

95. *New York Daily Tribune*, March 8, 1858; similar items appeared in the *Chicago Daily Democrat*, March 17, 1858, reprinted from the *Evening Post*; and in the *Cincinnati Daily Enquirer*, March 12, 1858.

96. Headline in the *Cincinnati Daily Enquirer*, March 13, 1858. Even in the respectable *Tribune*, revival news never completely eclipsed stories such as "Alleged Wife Murder," March 5, 1858.

97. What R. Laurence Moore describes as "moral sensationalism" was a literary genre that had developed during the first half of the nineteenth century, as evident in a variety of tracts and books. Moore, "Religion, Secularization, and the Shaping of the Culture Industry in Antebellum America," *American Quarterly* 41 (June 1989): 225, also *Selling God*, chapter 1. Revivals, however, had not previously been marketed in this fashion in the secular press, nor, in general, had mainstream popular Protestantism.

98. "Orville Gardner Insane," *New York Times*, March 20, 1889. The story reported an application to have Gardner, by then about 60 years old, committed to the New Jersey state insane asylum.

99. Unless otherwise indicated, the information on prizefighting in the following paragraphs is based on Elliott J. Gorn's fine cultural study, *The Manly Art: Bare-Knuckle Prizefighting in America* (Ithaca: Cornell University Press, 1986).

100. From comments by Horace Greeley after the 1842 Lilly-McCoy fight in Hastings, New York, which ended in the death of Tom McCoy, quoted in Gorn, *The Manly Art*, 79.

101. Ibid., 82, also 121.

102. *American Fistiania, Showing the Progress of Pugilism in the United States, from 1816 to 1873* (New York: Robert M. DeWitt, 1873), 16.

103. "A Terrible Affray Among Pugilists," *New York Times*, October 15, 1853; "Arrest of 'Awful Gardner,'" *Times*, October 17, 1853; "Caught at Last," *Times*, September 18, 1855; and "Awful Gardner Sentenced for Six Months," *Times*, October 3, 1855.

104. "Revival," *New York Sun*, March 4, 1858.

105. Although he does not mention Gardner, James A. Mathisen, "From Muscular

Christians to Jocks for Jesus," *Christian Century*, January 1-8, 1992, 11-15, provides a brief history of the relationship between sports and Christianity in the United States.

106. *New York Daily Tribune*, March 5, 1858.

107. Ibid., March 8, 1858.

108. Ibid., March 13, 1858.

109. *Richmond Whig*, April 5, 1858; *Boston Post*, March 11, 1858.

110. See, for example, the *Louisville Daily Journal*, March 25, 1858; the *Charleston Daily Courier*, March 24, 1858; the *Chicago Tribune*, April 5, 1858; the *Examiner*, March 25, 1858; the *Pittsburgh Christian Advocate*, March 23, 1858; and the *Nashville Christian Advocate*, March 25, 1858. Some of these are accounts by correspondents; others are reprints of articles from the New York City papers.

111. George Templeton Strong, *The Diary of George Templeton Strong*, vol. 2, *The Turbulent Fifties, 1850-1859*, ed. Allan Nevins and Milton Halsey Thomas (New York: Macmillan, 1952), 391.

112. Letter to "My dear cousin" from "May," New York, January 21, 1858. Cheever family papers, American Antiquarian Society, Worcester, Mass. From the contents of the letter, "May" apparently was a Boston cousin of the Cheever clan.

113. See, for example, an English observer's evaluation of the top American preachers in "A Spurgeon in New-York," *Christian Advocate and Journal*, October 1, 1857.

114. Editorial in the *Louisville Daily Journal*, citing the *New York Courier and Enquirer*, April 9, 1858.

115. Stout, *Divine Dramatist*, 146.

116. Quoted in Norris Magnuson, *Salvation in the Slums: Evangelical Social Work, 1865-1920* (Metuchen, N.J.: Scarecrow Press, 1977), 138.

117. McLoughlin, *Modern Revivalism*, 489-91. The exact tie between the publicity centered on these "celebrities" and William Randolph Hearst's November 1949 directive to "puff" Graham is unclear; however the conversions of Hamblen, Zamperini, and Vaus were the focus of the publicity in Los Angeles.

118. *New York Daily Tribune*, March 31, 1858.

119. James D. Hart, *The Popular Book: A History of America's Literary Taste* (Berkeley: University of California Press, 1950), 109. See also Moore, *Selling God*, 29.

120. Moore, *Selling God*, 44-45.

121. *New York Daily Tribune*, March 8, 1858.

122. Peter Buckley, "To the Opera House: Culture and Society in New York City, 1820-1860," (Ph.D. diss., SUNY Stony Brook, 1984), 495-538, quoted in Moore, "The Culture Industry," 231. Buckley was referring to P. T. Barnum's success in marketing Jenny Lind as a paragon of Protestant values during her 1850 American tour; the same dynamic holds true for Greeley and Bennett in 1858.

123. This understanding of secularization is based on discussions by George M. Marsden in *Religion and American Culture* (San Diego: Harcourt Brace Jovanovich, 1990), 6, and in George M. Marsden and Bradley J. Longfield, eds., *The Secularization of the Academy* (New York: Oxford University Press, 1992), 5.

124. Often noted in discussions of the rise of the consumer culture is Richard Wrightman Fox and T. J. Jackson Lears, eds., *The Culture of Consumption: Critical Essays in American History, 1880-1980* (New York: Pantheon Books). For negative assessments of the relationship between revivals and consumer culture, see George A. Rawlyk, "Writing about Canadian Religious Revivals," in *Modern Christian Revivals*, ed. Edith L. Blumhofer and Randall Balmer (Urbana: University of Illinois Press, 1993), 219-24; also Douglas W. Frank, *Less than Conquerors: How Evangelicals Entered

the Twentieth Century (Grand Rapids: Eerdmans, 1986), 167–231. Moore, *Selling God*, views the symbiotic relationship forged during the nineteenth century between religion and commercial in a generally more positive light.

125. *New York Herald*, March 26, 1858, quoting the New York *Examiner*.

126. Ibid., quoting the *New York Observer*.

127. Thomas W. Higginson, "Saints, and their Bodies," *Atlantic Monthly* 1 (March 1858), 592.

128. Mathisen, "Muscular Christians," 11–12.

129. The line was based on the text of one of Dudley Tyng's final sermons. Henry Wilder Foote, *Three Centuries of American Hymnody* (Cambridge, Mass.: Harvard University Press, 1940), 212–13.

130. *New York Evening Post*, March 30, 1858. For other examples of humor, see the *New York Sun*, April 6, 1858, and the *Chicago Daily Democrat*, April 20, 1858.

131. *Charleston Daily Courier*, April 19, 1858.

132. *Boston Evening Transcript*, April 6, 1858.

Three. Personal Perspectives on the Revival

1. *Pentecost; or, The Work of God in Philadelphia, A.D. 1858* (Philadelphia: Parry and McMillan, 1859), 10, cf., Samuel Irenaeus Prime, *The Power of Prayer, Illustrated in the Wonderful Displays of Divine Grace at the Fulton Street and Other Meetings* (New York: Scribner, 1858), 53, and Talbot W. Chambers, *The Noon Prayer Meeting of the North Dutch Church* (New York: Board of Publication, Reformed Protestant Dutch Church, 1858), 285.

2. George Brown, *The Lady Preacher: or, The Life and Labors of Mrs. Hannah Reeves* (Philadelphia: Daughaday and Backer, 1870; reprint New York: Garland, 1987), 299–301. Reeves (1800–1868) was known for her preaching and benevolent efforts. She began preaching at age 19 and after her marriage 12 years later shared her husband's appointments in the Methodist Protestant Church.

3. Ibid., 302.

4. Lyman Abbott, *Reminiscences* (Boston: Houghton Mifflin, 1923), 125, 127–32. Edward Abbott later became an Episcopal priest.

5. Hannah Whitall Smith (1832–1911), *The Unselfishness of God and How I Discovered It* (New York: Fleming H. Ravell, 1903; reprint, New York: Garland, 1985), 172.

6. Ibid., 177–78.

7. Gilbert Robbins, *The Christian Patriot, A Biography of James E. McClellen* (1838–1863) (Worcester, Mass.: Grout and Bigelow, 1865), 17.

8. Ibid., *passim*, especially 24, 33–40, 53, 83, 86.

9. Appendix B, table 12. This is a conservative figure, reflecting net membership gains among major Protestant denominations. A three-year period was chosen for measuring the revival's impact because different denominations compiled membership statistics at different times of the year, making it difficult to measure precise gains among different denominations for the calendar year 1858 or from mid-1857 to mid-1858.

10. Others included Sunday school organizer and businessman B. F. Jacobs and YMCA leaders Richard Morse and Robert Weidensall. For more on this group, see chapter 7.

11. Wayland (1796–1895) had in 1857 assumed an interim pastorate at the First Baptist Church in Providence, Rhode Island; Bushnell (1802–1876) continued as pas-

tor of the North Church in Hartford, Connecticut; and Broadus (1827–1895), a Southern Baptist preacher and educator, held a pastorate in Charlottesville, Virginia.

12. Harold P. Shelley, "Borne of the Current of Revivalism: Origin of the Bible Fellowship Church," *Mennonite Quarterly Review* 63 (July 1989): 265–84, offers an example of the revival's impact on the Mennonites. Information on blacks during the revival is sketchy. Membership statistics for African Americans in the Methodist Episcopal Church, South, reflect no dramatic increase during the revival years. Instead, except for a slump in 1856 and 1857, there was a continuation of already healthy growth rates, a pattern similar to that of white Southern Methodists. However, blacks in the southern Presbyterian church, a much smaller group, did show dramatic gains during 1858 and 1859. See appendix B, tables 2 and 6. Southern Baptist records did not indicate the race of those baptized. For comments on revivals among blacks, see the *Western Recorder*, April 21, 1858, and June 23, 1858; the *Nashville Christian Advocate and Journal*, September 30, 1858; *Chicago Weekly Press*, April 3, 1858. J. Edwin Orr, *The Event of the Century: The 1857–58 Awakening*, ed. Robert Owen Roberts (Wheaton, Ill.: Interdenominational Awakening Press, 1989), 195–97, argues for extensive church growth among black Baptists and Methodists in the South. Some northern press reports indicate discomfort or condescension toward exuberant styles of black worship in the midst of a revival celebrated for its controlled character. The *New York Daily Tribune*, March 15, 1858, for example, contains such comments regarding black churches in New Bedford, Massachusetts.

13. Based on church membership statistics listed in the tables of appendix B, especially tables 1, 4, 5, 7, and 12, for the following churches: Methodist Episcopal, Regular Baptist, New and Old School Presbyterian, Episcopal, and Congregational. Denominational totals for 1856 included figures from 1857 for Congregationalists since reliable numbers for 1856 were not available.

According to a table compiled by Richard Carwardine in *Evangelicals and Politics in Antebellum America* (New Haven: Yale University Press, 1993), 6, in 1855 Methodist Episcopal churches (North and South) and Regular Baptists (North and South) together constituted about 60 percent of the total membership of the 18 largest Protestant denominations in the United States. If the growth of all denominations in this group were accurately measured, the Methodist/Baptist gains from 1856–1859 would probably represent about two thirds of the total or a little less.

Other estimates of the numerical impact of the 1857–58 Revival have ranged from 300,000 to one million converts. Variations depend in part on the chronological boundaries placed on the revival, on the number of denominations included, and on whether the numbers reflect an attempt to measure the gross numerical impact (a tally of all professed conversions and additions to church membership rolls during the revival period) or an attempt to determine net church growth (taking losses as well as gains into account). Other decisions can affect final totals as well, for example, whether Methodist figures include (1) only full members, or (2) members and probationers, or (3) members, probationers, and ministers. To avoid double counting and to provide as careful a comparative measure as possible, all tables in appendix B are based on net church growth. For statistics on gross church growth showing a total of 1,043,881 for two years from mid-1857 to mid-1859, see Orr, *Event of the Century*, 326, 327. Orr's data is generally substantiated by Roy J. Fish's earlier total of 996,379 for two years. See Fish, "The Awakening of 1858 and Its Effects on Baptists in the United States," (D.Th. diss., Southwestern Baptist Theological Seminary, 1963), 226. In *Event of the Century*, 321–26, 371–72, Orr also provided figures for net increases during the same two-year period that more closely correspond to those listed in appendix B, table 12. The revival did not result in unusual long-term increase in Protestant church growth, but it did help to maintain the evangelical percentage of the total population at more than 10 percent (sometimes the approximation is as high as 15 percent), a figure that held steady between 1840–60 in the face of the first waves of large-scale Catholic immigration. See Carwardine, *Evangelicals and Politics*, 4–6.

14. Appendix B, tables 1, 3, and 5. Between 1856–59, the growth rates for Baptists in the North ran significantly higher than for those in the South, particularly, again, if Border States growth is included in the totals. However, this was in contrast to overall trends during the 1840s and 1850s. Fish, "Awakening of 1858 and Baptists," 153–54, contrasts the explosive growth of Baptists in the South (an increase of more than 200,000 members in the upper and lower South) between 1843 and 1857 with the much slower growth of northern Baptist churches. See also Timothy L. Smith, *Revivalism and Social Reform: American Protestantism on The Eve of the Civil War* (Nashville: Abingdon, 1957), 22, n. 12.

15. Appendix B, tables 8 and 12; Roger Finke and Rodney Stark, *The Churching of America 1776–1990: Winners and Losers in Our Religious Economy* (New Brunswick: Rutgers University Press, 1992), chapter 3. Presbyterians (Old and New Schools combined) gained about 11 percent of the total net membership increase as measured in table 12; Congregationalists gained nearly 6 percent.

16. In their study of Pentecostalism and of the Black Power movement, anthropologists Luther P. Gerlach and Virginia H. Hine stress the role of personal relationships in the recruitment ("conversion") of people to social movements. Although the 1857–58 Revival would not fulfill all of Gerlach and Hine's definition of a movement of social transformation, it does illustrate the relational dynamics they discuss. See chapter 4, "Recruitment," in Gerlach and Hines, *People, Power, Change: Movements of Social Transformation* (Indianapolis: Bobbs-Merrill, 1970), 79–97.

17. Patterns of participatory, lay piety among American evangelicals had European roots in the Pietist "conventicles," Scottish "praying societies," Puritan family worship, and Methodist class meetings. For more on the European background of this piety, see Ted A. Campbell, *The Religion of the Heart: A Study of European Religious Life in the Seventeenth and Eighteenth Centuries* (Columbia: University of South Carolina Press, 1991), chapters 3–5; also David Martin, *Tongues of Fire: The Explosion of Protestantism in Latin America* (Oxford: Basil Blackwell, 1990), 14–23.

18. Phoebe Palmer, *The Promise of the Father; or, A Neglected Specialty of the Last Days* (New York: W. C. Palmer, Jr., 1872 [1859]), 254–55; see also Richard Wheatley, *The Life and Letters of Mrs. Phoebe Palmer* (New York: Walter C. Palmer, Jr., 1876; reprint, New York: Garland, 1984), 328–34; and the *Christian Guardian* (Canada), March 31, 1858, quoted in Peter George Bush, "James Caughey, Phoebe and Walter Palmer and the Methodist Revival Experience in Canada West, 1850–1858" (Master of Arts thesis, Queen's University, Kingston, Ontario, Canada, 1985), 126. Bush's research suggests that the social and relational patterns of this revival reflected those of traditional Methodist camp meetings adapted to an urban setting.

19. Sandra Sizer [Frankiel], *Gospel Hymns and Social Religion: The Rhetoric of Nineteenth-Century Revivalism* (Philadelphia: Temple University Press, 1978), was one of the early works stressing the role of communal piety in nineteenth century revivals. Other works which reveal the communal element in a variety of revival traditions include Gerald F. Moran, "Christian Revivalism and Culture in Early America: Puritan New England as a Case Study," in *Modern Christian Revivals*, especially pp. 50–53; Russell E. Richey, *Early American Methodism* (Bloomington: Indiana University Press, 1991); Mary P. Ryan, *Cradle of the Middle Class: The Family in Oneida County, New*

York, 1790–1865 (New York: Cambridge University Press, 1981); and Leigh Eric Schmidt, *Holy Fairs: Scottish Communions and American Revivals in the Early Modern Period* (Princeton: Princeton University Press, 1989).

20. Chambers, *Noon Prayer Meeting*, xi, xii.

21. Richard Carwardine notes the balance and tension between communal piety and "individualism, self-discipline and self-improvement" among Methodists in Carwardine, " 'Antinomians' *and* 'Arminians'; Methodists and the Market Revolution," in *The Market Revolution in America: Social, Political, and Religious Expressions, 1800–1880,* ed. Melvyn Stokes and Stephen Conway (Charlottesville: University Press of Virginia, 1996), 292; cf. Carwardine, "The Second Great Awakening in Comparative Perspective: Revivals and Culture in the United States and Britain," in *Modern Christian Revivals,* ed. Edith L. Blumhofer and Randall Balmer (Urbana: University of Illinois Press, 1993), 94–95.

22. Richard J. Carwardine, *Transatlantic Revivalism: Popular Evangelicalism in Britain and America, 1790–1865* (Westport, Conn.: Greenwood Press, 1978), 56.

23. Schmidt, *Holy Fairs,* 205–6. *Selections from the Religious and Literary Writings of John H. Bocock, D. D.,* edited by his widow (Richmond: Whittet and Shepperson, 1891), 398–402, provides a contemporary account of this style of revivalism; cf. the story of a similar "sacramental meeting" in Louisiana, Missouri, in the *New York Observer,* September 24, 1857.

24. Richey, *Early American Methodism,* 21–32, discusses Methodist adoption of the camp meeting as a foundation for revivalism. Accounts in the *Western Christian Advocate,* January 13 and 27, 1858, illustrate the persistence of the watch night and quarterly meeting as revival occasions.

25. Jacob Knapp, *Autobiography of Elder Jacob Knapp* (New York: Sheldon, 1868), v, vi. John B. Boles, "Revivalism, Renewal, and Social Mediation in the Old South," in *Modern Christian Revivals,* ed. Blumhofer and Balmer, 64, provides a succinct summary of the various patterns of revivalism among southern churches.

26. Crises such as epidemic diseases, economic downturns, political conflicts, and even denominational schisms influenced revivals, though not always in a predictable fashion. Carwardine, *Transatlantic Revivalism,* 54–56. For popular antebellum attitudes toward the concept of providence, see Lewis O. Saum, *The Popular Mood of Pre-Civil War America* (Westport, Conn.: Greenwood Press, 1980), 3–26.

27. A writer in the *Southern Presbyterian Review* listed "the commercial panic, the efforts of the Young Men's Christian Association, the ordinary labors of the ministry, the activities of private Christians" as "preparatory processes" but insisted that the "efficient cause" was God alone. See "The Religious Awakening of 1858," *Southern Presbyterian Review* 11 (July 1858), 253. The opening paragraphs of Leonard I. Sweet, " 'A Nation Born Again': The Union Prayer Meeting Revival and Cultural Revitalization," in *The Great Tradition: In Honor of Winthrop S. Hudson, Essays on Pluralism, Voluntarism, and Revivalism,* ed. Joseph D. Ban and Paul R. Dekar (Valley Forge, Penn.: Judson Press, 1982), 193, provide a succinct summary of debates over the revival's origins.

28. Walt Whitman, *I Sit and Look Out,* ed. Emory Hollywood and Vernolian Schwarz (New York: Columbia University Press, 1932), 72.

29. George Templeton Strong, *The Diary of George Templeton Strong,* vol. 2, *The Turbulent Fifties, 1850–1859,* ed. Allan Nevins and Milton Halsey Thomas (New York: Macmillan, 1952), 361.

30. George W. Van Vleck, *The Panic of 1857* (New York: AMS Press, 1967 [1943]), 28. Van Vleck provided a succinct overview of the panic, stressing interna-

tional as well as national factors. Recent treatments of the panic include James L. Huston, *The Panic of 1857 and the Coming of the Civil War* (Baton Rouge: Louisiana State University Press, 1987) and chapter 8 in Kenneth M. Stampp, *America in 1857: A Nation on the Brink* (New York: Oxford University Press, 1990).

31. An article in the Washington County (Wisconsin) *Democrat*, December 20, 1857, estimated that between 2,000 and 3,000 small farms in Wisconsin were mortgaged to railroads. Cited in Van Vleck, *Panic*, 84. See also Stampp, *America in 1857*, 215.

32. Van Vleck, *Panic*, 64–73, provided a detailed chronology of events. A few banks—the Chemical Bank in New York City, the Indiana State Bank, Kentucky banks, and four New Orleans banks—managed to stay open and maintain specie payment. Otherwise, the system was in collapse throughout the nation. See p. 73, n. 17.

33. Entry for October 3, 1857, in Tappan Papers, reel no. 2, journals and notebooks, April 19, 1855–May 23, 1869, at the Library of Congress.

34. Stampp, *America in 1857*, 226.

35. *Journal of Commerce*, November 26 and December 2, 1857, cited in Van Vleck, *Panic*, 107.

36. Van Vleck, *Panic*, 5, n. 17. The broad impact resulted from various factors: a dramatic growth in commercial agriculture and imports during the 1840s and 1850s meant that many more Americans were dependent on the market than even in the 1830s; weaknesses in the banking system were nationwide; and flush times had tempted many people into some sort of speculation.

37. Peter Lesley to Lydia M. Child, October 11, 1857, in *Life and Letters of Peter and Susan Lesley*, ed. Mary Lesley Ames, vol. 1 (New York, 1909), 351, cited in Huston, *Panic of 1857*, 25.

38. Benjamin M. Adams Diary, October 8, 1857, in Benjamin M. Adams Journal and Papers, Methodist Archives and History Center, Drew University, Madison, N.J.

39. Peter Woods, "Autobiography," 147–48. Manuscript, Methodist Archives and History Center.

40. "Revival Correspondence" in the January 13 and 27 issues of the *Western Christian Advocate*; the *Christian Times*, January 27, 1858, and February 2, 1858; also note citations in "Chicago and Hinterland," Orr, *Event of the Century*, 131–37.

41. Letter from Rev. D. Coble, *Christian Advocate and Journal*, February 28, 1858.

42. Stampp, *America in 1857*, 36–43, provides a discussion of these two social problems. Stampp identified fear of slave insurrection as a third major social tension of the 1850s. Chapter 7 in Richard Carwardine, *Evangelicals and Politics*, also contains an excellent discussion of the political responses among antebellum Protestants to "drink, social tension, and immigrant culture."

43. "Police Report of District No. 3, North Division—From the 18th of March, 1857, to the 18th of March, 1858," *Chicago Daily Democrat*, March 24, 1858. Of the 2,579 people charged, 383 were identified as Germans, 1,746 as Irish, and 290 as native-born Americans. The remainder were listed as English, Scottish, Norwegian, Swedish, Danish, and African. The bulk of the arrests were for disorderly conduct, fighting or drunkenness, larceny, and vagrancy.

44. Charles Augustus Briggs, age 16, to his Uncle Marvin Briggs, November 9, 1856, Briggs Transcript III [letters transcribed by Emilie Grace Briggs], 15–16, cited in Max Gray Rogers, "Charles Augustus Briggs, Conservative Heretic" (Ph.D. dissertation, Columbia University, 1964), 4.

45. The original Five Points referred to an open space formed by the intersection of Cross, Anthony, Little Water, Orange, and Mulberry streets in lower Manhattan. The poverty and vice that came to characterize the locale were given notoriety in Charles Dickens's *American Notes*. See Herbert Asbury, *The Gangs of New York: An Informal History of the Underworld* (New York and London: Alfred A. Knopf, 1928), 5–20.

46. Abbott, *Reminiscences*, 33–36. For a more recent account of the July 4, 1857, riots, see Edward K. Spann, *The New Metropolis* (New York: Columbia University Press, 1981), 393–94.

47. Huston, *Panic of 1857*, 24–27; Stampp, *America in 1857*, 228–29; Strong, *Diary*, 369–70.

48. For an example of an immigrant Catholic conversion narrative, see Prime, *Power of Prayer*, 211–19.

49. Huston, *Panic of 1857*, 14; Van Vleck, *Panic of 1857*, 65.

50. "New York Correspondence," *Nashville Christian Advocate*, October 22, 1857; also, the *Episcopal Recorder*, October 17, 1857, cited in Russell E. Francis, "The Religious Revival of 1858 in Philadelphia," *Pennsylvania Magazine of History and Biography* 70 (1946) 53. The actual amount of Porter's embezzlement apparently turned out to be less than originally reported and was repaid by his friends. Even so, the reputation of Christian businessmen had been tarnished.

51. Note of such a lecture is recorded in the diary of John F. Funk, a young Mennonite working as a bookkeeper in Chicago. See "John F. Funk, Early Diary, Etc.," "Tuesday morning" [Jan. 5, 1858], Archives of the Mennonite Church, Goshen, Indiana. Funk recorded a conversion experience about three weeks later. Cf. Horace Bushnell's sermons to Hartford businessmen, Mary Bushnell Cheney, *The Life and Letters of Horace Bushnell* (New York: Scribner's, 1905), 410–11. For a sample of straightforward conversion sermons preached during the same period, see sermon titles listed in the diary of John Summerfield Coit, a New Jersey Methodist minister, during "extra meetings," held October 7–November 18, 1857, and for January 1858. John Summerfield Coit Diary, Methodist Archives.

52. "Letter from Missouri," *Christian Advocate and Journal*, March 18, 1858. For a discussion of revivals as occasions of "anti-structural liminality," based on the work of Victor Turner, see George A. Rawlyk, "Writing about Canadian Revivals," in *Modern Christian Revivals*, ed. Edith L. Blumhofer and Randall Balmer (Urbana: University of Illinois Press), 212–13.

53. "Letter From New-England," *Christian Advocate and Journal*, February 4, 1858; "Letter from Illinois," *Pittsburgh Christian Advocate*, March 2, 1858. For conditions in Cincinnati a year earlier, see "From Cincinnati," *Pittsburgh Christian Advocate*, February 3, 1857; cf. account of bitter weather in 1857 along the Atlantic seaboard from New England to the Carolinas in Stampp, *America in 1857*, 17, 33–34.

54. Stampp, *America in 1857*, 32; R. Laurence Moore, *Selling God: American Religion in the Marketplace of Culture* (New York: Oxford University Press, 1994), 44–45.

55. Richard Carwardine, *Evangelicals and Politics*, 11–12, cites antebellum evangelicals' own expressions of concern over this difficulty. In *Transatlantic Revivalism*, 55, Carwardine pointed out the uncertainty in the relationship between party politics and revivals. Evangelicals blamed partisan debates surrounding the War of 1812 and the Mexican War for dampening religious fervor. Revivals flourished during the political campaigns of 1828 and 1840, although they did not enjoy the nationwide pub-

licity in the secular press that contributed to the momentum of the 1857–58 Revival. See *Transatlantic Revivalism*, 55. One contributing factor to the uncertainty is the role of women. Denied the vote, could they, less affected than their male counterparts by the attractions and demands of politics, sustain religious fervor?

56. Quoted in Carwardine, *Evangelicals and Politics*, 259. For the decline in church growth rates, see appendix B, tables 1, 3, 5, and 8.

57. This is not to say that politics completely disappeared; Lecompton, for example, remained an issue until the constitution was rejected for a third and final time in August 1858. Nonetheless, compared with previous and subsequent periods, the first six months of 1858 were relatively quiet.

58. For comments on the popular sense of the presence of God, see "A Revival Prayer Meeting" (March 11, 1858) in Whitman, *I Sit and Look Out*, 79; also extract of a letter from Mrs. B. W. Merriam, April 15, 1858, quoted in John B. Hill, "A Missouri Missionary Faces Obstacles, More Extracts from the Diary of Timothy Hill 1851–1860," *Journal of the Presbyterian Historical Society* 25 (September 1947), 185.

59. John F. Funk, "Early Diary," Jan. 17, 1858. Of the day's activities, Funk recorded, "Went to prayer meeting at 9 ½ [9:30], church 10 ½, Sunday School 12 to 1, Church of Atonement 3 o'clock, 3rd Presbyterian 7 ½ p.m." Funk's distress was compounded by loneliness for the family home in Pennsylvania after eight months in Chicago and for a young woman, also in Pennsylvania, who would later become his wife.

60. Prime, *Power of Prayer*, 69.

61. *Work of God in Philadelphia*, 11.

62. Among studies on nineteenth-century attitudes toward death are essays by Ann Douglas, Stanley French, and Lewis O. Saum in David E. Stannerd, ed., *Death in America* (Philadelphia: University of Pennsylvania Press, 1974); James Moorhead, " 'As Though Nothing at All Had Happened': Death and Afterlife in Protestant Thought, 1840–1925," *Soundings* 67, no. 4 (Winter 1984); and Martha Pike, "In Memory Of: Artifacts Relating to Mourning in Nineteenth Century America," in *American Material Culture*, ed. Edith Mayo (Bowling Green, Ohio: Bowling Green State University Popular Press, 1984). Essays by Douglas, Moorhead, and Saum include discussions of attitudes toward heaven and hell.

63. Most of the popular best sellers of consolation literature such as Elizabeth Stuart Phelps's *Gates Ajar* (1868), Elizabeth Payson Prentiss's *Stepping Heavenward* (1869), and Theodore Cuyler's *The Empty Crib* (1873) were post–Civil War works. See Ann Douglas, "Heaven our Home: Consolation Literature in the Northern United States, 1830–1880" in *Death in America*, 49–68.

64. The three hymns on heaven are from J. W. Dadmun, *Revival Melodies: A Collection of Some of the Most Popular Hymns and Tunes* (Boston: n.p., 1858), 4, 12, 24. The two warning hymns were from *Union Prayer Meeting Hymns* (Philadelphia: American Sunday-School Union, 1859), 50–51, 124–25. Printed sermons and tracts indicated that ministers were more concerned to retain the "warning" note than were lay people in the prayer meetings. See, for example, "The Unawakened" in James W. Alexander, *The Revival and Its Lessons* (New York: American Tract Society, 1858), also such sermons as "Past Feeling" by Theodore L. Cuyler and "Why Will Ye Die?" by Benjamin F. Cutler in [Samuel Irenaeus Prime, ed.], *The New York Pulpit in the Revival of 1858: A Memorial Volume of Sermons* (New York: Sheldon, Blakeman, 1858).

65. Harriet Beecher Stowe, *Uncle Tom's Cabin* (New York: Bantam Books, 1981), 259.

66. Annie Fields, *Life and Letters of Harriet Beecher Stowe* (Boston and New York: Houghton, Mifflin, 1897), 244. A letter from Harriet Beecher Stowe to Henry Ellis Stowe, December 16, 1855, cited in Marie Caskey, *Chariot of Fire: Religion and the Beecher Family* (New Haven: Yale University Press, 1978), 178–79, illustrates Stowe's concern for Henry's spiritual growth.

67. Caskey, *Chariot of Fire*, 65, and chapter 7, *passim*, categorized Stowe with brothers Henry Ward and Thomas Kinnicut as "Christocentric liberals," children of New England theology who "came to argue that religious sensibility and effective experience were surer guides to truth."

68. For Stowe's role as an "informal minister" within the women's culture of mid-nineteenth-century America, see Joan D. Hedrick, *Harriet Beecher Stowe: A Life* (New York: Oxford University Press, 1994), 278.

69. *Memorial of the Revival in Plymouth Church, Brooklyn, [Rev. Henry Ward Beecher] During the Early Part of the Year 1858* (New York: Clark, Austin and Smith, 1859), 37.

70. Ibid., 41, All were Lyman Beecher's grandsons. Stowe also joined Plymouth Church sometime later during this same period, p. 46. See also "Alphabetical List of Members of Plymouth Church," *Manual of Plymouth Church* (New York: Baker and Godwin, 1867), 48, 61.

71. In 1856, Tyng had taken a forcible stand against slavery from the pulpit of the Church of the Epiphany in Philadelphia. Requested to resign, he later accepted a call from the new Church of the Covenant, formed by parishioners who had left Church of the Epiphany over the dispute. Francis, "The Religious Revival of 1858 in Philadelphia," 69. For more on Tyng, see Diana Hochstedt Butler, *Standing Against the Whirlwind: Evangelical Episcopalians in Nineteenth-Century America* (New York: Oxford University Press, 1995), 136–37.

72. Taken from accounts of Tyng's death as described in the funeral sermon by his father, Stephen H. Tyng, in the *New York Observer*, April 29, 1858, and the Chicago *Daily Democrat*, May 3, 1858, reprinted from the Philadelphia *Evening Bulletin*. See also the *Independent*, April 22, 1858, and the *New York Daily Tribune*, April 23, 1858.

73. "Letter from Philadelphia," *Watchman and Reflector*, April 29, 1858.

74. The past 25 years have seen numerous studies on the moral and spiritual influence of the Victorian "true woman." For a helpful treatment of evangelical women and revivals in an emerging middle-class society, see Ryan, *Cradle of the Middle Class*, 83–104. Cf. Sizer [Frankiel], *Gospel Hymns and Social Religion*, chapter 4, and Leonard I. Sweet, *The Minister's Wife: Her Role in Nineteenth-Century American Evangelicalism* (Philadelphia: Temple University Press, 1983), chapter 2.

75. In New York City, for example, more than 1,000 women crowded an uptown church near Madison Square for a late-afternoon prayer meeting, reported in the *Daily Tribune*, March 2, 1858. The specific role of women in the 1857–58 Revival is addressed in chapter 4.

76. Chambers, *Noon Prayer Meeting*, 196–97. For an additional example of prayer requests from women see the sampling of "typical requests" from an April prayer meeting in the *New York Observer*, May 6, 1858. They were from sisters, a step sister, a mother, and "two aged widows."

77. Charles A. Briggs to "sister," Briggs Transcript, III (n.d., though the letter is in a sequence of correspondence Briggs wrote from the University of Virginia during the revival period), 44, #183b, quoted in Max Gray Rogers, "Charles Augustus Briggs," 7–8.

78. Levi Countryman Diary, Levi N. Countryman Papers (Minnesota Historical Society), quoted in Saum, *Popular Mood of Pre-Civil War America*, 64–65, 76.

79. Letter dated March 16, 1858, in William David Stuart, *Memoir of William David Stuart, 1840–1863* (Philadelphia: Printed for private circulation, 1865), 221–22. The elder Stuart was a banker active in benevolent work and instrumental in founding the Philadelphia YMCA. His son, a student at the University of Pennsylvania during the revival, suffered from chronically poor health and died shortly after his marriage to Johnson.

80. Ibid., 135.

81. Ibid., 224, 230.

82. For example, according to the U.S. Census, between 1800 and 1840, some 4.3 million people settled in the states created from the Northwest Territory; more than 80 percent of them were native-born. See Bureau of the Census, *A Century of Population Growth in the United States, 1790–1900* (Washington, D.C.: Government Printing Office, 1909), chapter 12, table 54, table 9, n.p.

83. The relationships between church, family, and religious socialization is a complex one. Nonetheless, the decline of Calvinist notions of total depravity and human inability, the rise of the voluntary church principle, and the influence of aggressive Methodist and Baptist proselytization all contributed to a rise in family religious activism. For similar observations regarding such shifts in early nineteenth-century America, see Curtis D. Johnson, *Islands of Holiness: Rural Religion in Upstate New York, 1790–1860* (Ithaca: Cornell University Press, 1989), 65–66; Ryan, *Cradle of the Middle Class*, chapter 2, *passim*; and Schmidt, *Holy Fairs*, 203.

84. "New Hampshire," *Watchman and Reflector*, March 25, 1858.

85. The celebrated Cane Ridge camp meeting revival, for example, drew Methodists and Baptists, as well as the Presbyterian organizers. See Sydney E. Ahlstrom, *A Religious History of the American People* (New Haven: Yale University Press, 1972), 432–35. Anne C. Loveland, "Presbyterians and Revivalism in the Old South," *Journal of Presbyterian History* 57 (Spring 1979): 40, discussed cooperative efforts in the South during the 1830s. Carwardine, *Evangelicals and Politics*, 273, treats evangelical unity against Catholics and, in the North, against slavery. Examples of local union revivals prior to the autumn of 1857 include "Union in Christian Effort," *Christian Advocate and Journal*, March 20, 1856, and "Revival in Fincastle, Va.," *Nashville Christian Advocate*, April 23, 1857.

86. Clifford E. Clark, Jr., *Henry Ward Beecher: Spokesman for a Middle-Class America* (Urbana: University of Illinois Press, 1978), 132.

87. Francis Wayland and H. L. Wayland, *A Memoir of the Life and Labors of Francis Wayland*, (New York: Sheldon, 1867), 2:215. Wayland (1796–1865) served as president of Brown University from 1827–1855. His *Elements of Moral Science* (1835) was a classic American exposition of Common Sense philosophy.

88. "Thomas Gilbert Osborn [1820–1888]," *Minutes of the New York East Annual Conference of the Methodist Episcopal Church* (New York: Phillips and Hunt, 1888), 70. Twenty-Seventh Street Church grew from 336 members in 1857 to 708 in 1858. Samuel A. Seaman, *Annals of New York Methodism*, (New York: Hunt and Eaton, 1892), 302–5.

89. C. R. Vaughan, "Biographical Sketch" in *John H. Bocock*, xv. Bocock (1813–1870) was an Old School Presbyterian, born in Buckingham County, Virginia.

90. From "Revivals of Religion," cited in Cheney, *Life and Letters*, 83.

91. Cheney, *Life and Letters*, 413, quoting Bushnell (1802–1876). Cheney herself commented, "Ministers, and all those who took an active part in the direction of the

great and frequent meetings of the people, were called to make unwonted exertions, and were themselves kept at a sustained pitch or strain of feeling that was more exhausting than the work" (p. 412). In the summer of 1858, Bushnell published *Sermons for the New Life*, a popular collection that suggested to many of his theological opponents that the revival had nudged him toward a more conservative position. Cheney, 417–18. More accurately, the book reflected the difference between Bushnell's "practical" preaching and his theological treatises, as the publication of *Nature and the Supernatural* a few months later made clear.

92. For this reason, perhaps, some historians view the revival as having taken place in 1858. Smith, *Revivalism and Social Reform*, 63–67, describes it as the "awakening of 1858," although he mentions the Palmers' 1857 successes in Canada and other antecedents, cf. John D. Hannah, "The Layman's Prayer Revival of 1858," *Bibliotheca Sacra* 134 (January–March 1977): 59–73, and Howard Fenimore Shipps, "The Revival of 1858 in Mid-America," *Methodist History* 16 (April 1978): 139–50. Orr, *Event of the Century*, 39–42, and *passim*, claims that there were widespread revivals during the fall of 1857. Earlier, Charles G. Finney had reported that "a spirit of revival had been growing for several years," demonstrated by his 1856 revival in Rochester, New York, and its gradual effect on New England. See Charles G. Finney, *The Prevailing Prayer-Meeting* (London: Ward, 1859), 24, and Finney, *The Memoirs of Charles G. Finney: The Complete Restored Text*, ed. Garth M. Rosell and Richard A. G. Dupuis (Grand Rapids: Academie Books/Zondervan, 1989), 560, n. 6. In *A Passion for Souls: The Life of D. L. Moody* (Chicago: Moody Press, 1997), Lyle W. Dorsett cites comments from Moody's letters as evidence of local church revivals in Chicago prior to the 1857 panic. Such differences point to the difficulty of assigning a specific beginning point to the 1857–58 Revival.

93. See, for example, the *Christian Advocate and Journal*, January 28, 1858; February 4, 1858; the *Examiner*, January 24, 1858; *Nashville Christian Advocate*, February 11, 1858; *Pittsburgh Christian Advocate*, February 23, 1858; *Watchman and Reflector*, January 7, 1858; *Western Christian Advocate*, January 27, 1858; *Western Recorder*, February 24, 1858.

94. The *New York Observer*, May 13, 1858, contains notices that provide a sampling of some such meetings.

95. Lyman Abbott, ed., *Henry Ward Beecher* (New York: Funk and Wagnalls, 1883), 272.

96. For examples of this trend in New York City churches, see a *History of the Stanton Street Baptist Church in the City of New York* (New York: Sheldon, 1860), 148. From September 1852 to December 1859 the church added 474 members, 204 by baptism, 152 by letter of transfer, and 118 by "experience and restoration." During the same period, 454 people left the church, 230 by letter, 29 through death, 46 by expulsion, and 149 were dropped. In 1857, the Fourteenth Street Presbyterian Church received 65 new members but dismissed 39 with letters of transfer. "New York City. Fourteenth Street Presbyterian Church Session Minutes, 1851–1874," Philadelphia: Presbyterian Historical Society.

97. *Forty Years of Methodism in Eighty-Sixth-Street, City of New York* [pamphlet] (New York: Nelson and Phillips, 1877), 21.

98. Ibid., 22. For membership statistics and the building dedication, see Seaman, *Annals of New York Methodism*, 311–12.

99. Clark, *Henry Ward Beecher*, 133. Although Beecher spoke at one widely publicized union prayer meeting in Burton's Theater, during most of the revival he directed his energies to his own church.

100. Chambers, *Noon Prayer Meeting*, 304.

101. The standard history of the YMCA continues to be C. Howard Hopkins, *History of the Y.M.C.A. in North America* (New York: Association Press, 1951).

102. Martin, *Tongues of Fire*, 13, 43, discusses the connections between the spread of evangelical religion and the process of differentiation. For more on the YMCA and the masculine dimension of urban revivalism, see chapter 4.

103. William Chauncy Langdon, "The Early Story of the Confederation of the Young Men's Christian Associations, *1888 Yearbook of the Young Men's Christian Associations* (New York: YMCA International Committee, 1888), 55; L. L. Doggett, *History of the Young Men's Christian Association, Part 1, The Founding of the Association, 1844–1855; Part 2, The Confederation Period, 1855–1861* (New York: Association Press, 1922), 284–85. John V. Farwell, *Early Recollections of Dwight L. Moody* (Chicago: Winona, 1907), 34–35, 173, is a later example of YMCA supporters' uneasiness with denominational "sectarianism."

104. The circular was published verbatim in *Guide to Holiness* 33 (January–July, 1858), 127. Excerpts appeared in many newspapers.

105. The revival affected many colleges in the country, including such places as Amherst, Dartmouth, Brown, and Yale in the North and the University of Georgia, the University of North Carolina, and Davidson College in the South. For specific examples, see E. Merton Coalter, *College Life in the Old South* (New York: Macmillan, 1928), 212–13; and Cornelia Rebekah Shaw, *Davidson College* (New York: Fleming H. Revell, 1923), 84–85. Many schools had formal church connections, and church and family continued to play the pivotal roles in conversion. For a survey of institutions where revivals were reported, see Orr, *Event of the Century*, chapters 19 and 20, *passim*.

106. Earlier religious influences at the University of Virginia are traced in Milton Robert Allen, "A History of the Young men's Christian Association at the University of Virginia" (Ph.D. dissertation, University of Virginia, 1946); for the University of Michigan, see C. Grey Austin, *A Century of Religion at the University of Michigan* (Ann Arbor: University of Michigan, 1957), and Victor Wilbee, "The Religious Dimensions of Three Presidencies in a State University" (Ph.D. dissertation, University of Michigan, 1967); Clarence P. Shedd, *Two Centuries of Student Christian Movements* (New York: Association Press, 1934), also is helpful.

107. John L. Johnson, "Reminiscences of the Y.M.C.A.," *Alumni Bulletin of the University of Virginia*, third series, vol. 2 (1909): 64. Johnson was elected first president of the university's YMCA.

108. Broadus was later a faculty member and second president of the first Southern Baptist seminary. See *DAB*, s.v. "John Albert Broadus." His preaching gifts and reputation for piety attracted a sizable contingent of Baptist students to the University of Virginia during the 1850s. Nearly a third of the 92 charter members of the YMCA were Baptist.

109. Hugh M. McIlhany, "Founding of the First Young Men's Christian Association among Students," *Alumni Bulletin of the University of Virginia*, third series, vol. 2 (1909): 50. For notice of the community YMCA, see Doggett, *Young Men's Christian Association*, 302.

110. Among the charter members who listed denominational affiliation were 29 Episcopalians, 27 Baptists, 18 Presbyterians, and five Methodists, "Madison Hall Ledger Book, YMCA Membership, Sessions 1858–1893," Manuscripts Department, Alderman Library, University of Virginia. For years chaplains had been frustrated over the haphazard approach to religious activity at the university. In 1856, Broadus com-

plained, "nobody expects immediate results, and . . . there is no organized body of believers." Archibald Thomas Robertson, *Life and Letters of John A. Broadus* (Philadelphia: American Baptist Publication Society, 1901), 134.

111. "Second Annual Catalogue of the Young Men's Christian Association of the University of Virginia, 1859–60" [pamphlet, n.d.], 5, from collection 2993-d, "YMCA Constitution and Bylaws," Manuscripts Department, Alderman Library, University of Virginia.

112. Ibid.

113. Charles A. Briggs (1841–1913) spent three years at the University of Virginia (1857–60). He later became a Presbyterian minister and professor of Hebrew and Cognate languages at Union Theological Seminary in New York. In 1893, Briggs was ousted from the Presbyterian church for his embrace of higher criticism and controversial views concerning biblical authority. See *Dictionary of Christianity in America* (Downers Grove, Ill.: Intervarsity Press, 1990), s.v. "Briggs, Charles Augustus." For the story of Briggs's conversion and citations from several letters in the Briggs Transcript concerning the experience, see Rogers, "Charles Augustus Briggs," 6–8.

114. Rogers, "Charles Augustus Briggs," 8.

115. *Dictionary of American Biography*, s.v., "John William Jones"; also, J. William Jones, *Christ in the Camp, or, Religion in Lee's Army* (Richmond: B. F. Johnson, 1887). Other chaplains included W. P. Dubose, association vice president, and Thomas Hume, secretary. Many other YMCA students served as officers or soldiers in the Confederacy.

116. Jones, *Christ in the Camp*, 261.

117. Adam Knight Spence, "A History of the Founding of the Young Men's Christian Association at the University of Michigan," cited in Wilbee, "The Religious Dimensions," 119.

118. Clarence P. Shedd, *Two Centuries*, 95. There has been a long debate over the original name of the Michigan association. The organizers clearly took their idea from the YMCA model, but the earliest documented name (1859) was Students' Christian Association. It is unclear whether the students changed the name when a constitution was written or if it was known as the SCA from the beginning.

119. "Revival in Ann Arbor," *Evangelist*, May 20, 1858. This letter from Ann Arbor contains a recap of events beginning early winter 1858.

120. January 21, 1858, in George Beck Diary, Michigan Historical Collections, Bentley Historical Library, University of Michigan, Ann Arbor, Michigan.

121. Ibid., February 24, 1858.

122. "Revival in Ann Arbor." There continued to be a connection between campus and community religious interest. During a revival period in 1874, people from daily union meetings in Ann Arbor would join students for Sunday afternoon sessions with then president E. O. Haven, in crowds of up to 3,000 people. Wilbee, "The Religious Dimensions," 192.

123. Wilbee, "The Religious Dimensions," 114, 116. See also Bradley J. Longfield, "From Evangelicalism to Liberalism: Public Midwestern Universities in Nineteenth-Century America," in *The Secularization of the Academy*, ed. George M. Marsden and Bradley J. Longfield, (New York: Oxford University Press, 1992) 54.

124. Shedd, *Two Centuries*, 113.

125. *Western Recorder*, August 25, 1858, for Natchez, and the *Biblical Recorder*, August 12, 1858, for Columbus, cited in Fish, "The Awakening of 1858 and Its Effects on Baptists," 151, 149. Though heavily weighted toward Baptists and short on interpretation, Fish has one of the best factual summaries of the revival in the South, based

on a survey of religious periodicals and on church membership statistics. See chapter 5, *passim*.

126. Smith, *Unselfishness of God*, 174.

127. Though common in the early nineteenth century, Smith's individualistic, unmediated approach to the Bible and salvation was an anomaly in the relational context of the 1857–58 Revival, although even in Smith's case a houseguest provided needed assistance. For an analysis of conversion patterns similar to Smith's, see Nathan O. Hatch, "Sola Scriptura and Novus Ordo Seclorum," in *The Bible in America*, ed. Nathan O. Hatch and Mark A. Noll (New York: Oxford University Press, 1982), 66–71.

128. Strong, *Diary*, 396.

129. Stephen E. Slocum, Jr. "The American Tract Society: 1825–1975" (Ph.D. diss., New York University, 1975), 107–28, provides a summary account of this dispute. For more, see chapter 6.

130. Plymouth Church provided a classic illustration of this pattern: the church revival ran from March 11 to July 3, when Henry Ward Beecher left for the country on vacation after a final Sunday communion service. See *Memorial of the Revival in Plymouth Church*, 82–85. The session minutes of the Thirteenth Street Presbyterian Church offer a similar example. The session met repeatedly in March, April, and May to examine applicants for church membership (Mar. 2, 4, 6, 9, 10, 11; April 7, 14, 22, 28; May 5, 6). However, after one meeting in June and in July, no further meetings were held until September 8. "New York City. Thirteenth St. Presbyterian Church, Session Minutes, 1846–," Presbyterian Historical Society, Philadelphia. A "History of the 13th St. Presbyterian Church by its first pastor—Rev. S. D. Burchard" at the beginning of the minute book mentioned the church's participation in the revival.

131. "Note from the Sea Side," *Christian Advocate and Journal*, June 3, 1858.

132. Most notable was a prayer meeting in Bedford Springs, a Pennsylvania resort near the home of President James Buchanan. The meeting was remembered chiefly because Buchanan made an appearance over the summer. Brief notices were also made of prayer meetings at Saratoga, Cape May, and Atlantic City. See Orr, *The Event of the Century*, 280, citing the *Western Recorder*, August 25 and September 15, 1858.

133. Nathan Bangs, "The Recent Revival," *Christian Advocate and Journal*, July 29, 1858; also August 5, 1858. The elderly Bangs (1778–1862), a Methodist itinerant preacher, minister, and editor, had retired in New York City.

134. "Revival Incidents," *New York Observer* (September 16, 1858).

135. During March, an estimated 1,000 men had crowded the vestry and various rooms of the Old South Church for prayer. By summer, the meeting was drawing 30 or 40 regulars. Participation increased again in the fall, though not to former levels. See *Old South Prayer-Meeting*, 122, and Charles G. Finney, *Memoirs*, 564, n. 21, citing the *Boston Morning Journal*. Charles and Elizabeth Finney had left Boston April 8 while the revival was, in Finney's words, "in its full strength" (p. 571).

136. For example, large-scale efforts by the Philadelphia "Y" did not begin until March; the Chicago YMCA did not even hold an organizational meeting until March 22, the day of the first downtown prayer meeting in that city. See F. Roger Dunn, "Formative Years of the Chicago Y.M.C.A.," *Journal of the Illinois State Historical Society*, 37 (December, 1944): 338.

137. The Union Tabernacle was the brainchild of a German Reformed minister, Edwin M. Long, from Norristown, Pennsylvania. Long had worked as an itinerant preacher and tract missionary in the small towns and rural areas of southeastern Pennsylvania. Portable tents had been used in religious work before; Finney, for example,

had one at Oberlin. But the practice was unusual until after the Civil War. For background on the Union Tabernacle, see Edwin M. Long, *The Union Tabernacle, or, Movable Tent-Church: Showing in its Rise and Success a New Department of Christian Enterprise* (Philadelphia: Parry and McMillan, 1859), 90–110; also, *Pentecost; or, The Work of God in Philadelphia*, 20–30.

138. Tent superintendent Long and other workers in Philadelphia increasingly shifted their energy to child evangelism. By summer, the children who flocked to the tent were the most responsive audience. The tent evangelists also were trying to appeal to "the masses"—the poor, German-speaking immigrants and some Roman Catholics—groups traditionally more resistant to evangelical appeals than the revival's primary audience of native-born Americans of Protestant heritage. Long, *Union Tabernacle*, 91–92, 107. The response of pious children in the wake of the 1857–58 Revival was a part of the lore not only of the tent meetings in Philadelphia and Cincinnati but also of the Fulton Street prayer meetings. City missionary Joseph Emery described Cincinnati tent meetings in *Thirty-five Years Among the Poor and the Public Institutions of Cincinnati* (Cincinnati: Elm Street, 1887), 148, 149, 155. For Philadelphia, see Edwin M. Long, *The Children of the Tent, or, The Work of God among the Young at the Union Tabernacle* (Philadelphia: Parry and McMillan, 1859, bound with *The Union Tabernacle*); also comments by George H. Stuart, *The Life of George H. Stuart*, ed. Robert Ellis Thompson (Philadelphia: J. M. Stoddart, 1890), 113. For a sample of the later Fulton Street emphasis, see [Bingham, Luther Goodyear], *Memoir of Scovell Hayens McCollum* (New York: Board of Publications of the Reformed Protestant Dutch Church, 1861). Investigation remains to be done on the response of children to modern revivalism and its significance.

139. Frances Willard, Diary, April 4, 1859, quoted in Ruth Bordin, *Frances Willard* (Chapel Hill: University of North Carolina Press, 1986), 27. Willard (1839–1898) had struggled with religious doubts since arriving at the college during spring 1858. She was torn between an intellectual tendency toward skepticism and, as an earnest young Methodist, the desire for a heartfelt experience of Christ's presence. Serious illness during summer 1859 brought Willard's crisis to a head. For a discussion of her subsequent journey toward a public profession of faith as an expression of her lifelong identification with Methodist piety and moral endeavor, see Carolyn De Swarte Gifford, " 'My Own Methodist Hive': Frances Willard's Faith as Disclosed in Her Journal, 1855–1870," in *Spirituality and Social Responsibility: Vocational Vision of Women in the United Methodist Tradition*, ed. Rosemary Skinner Keller (Nashville: Abingdon Press, 1993), 81–97.

140. W. K. McClee to George Richard Crooks, May 8, 1858, George Richard Crooks Correspondence, Methodist Archives and History Center, Drew University, Madison, New Jersey.

141. The experiences of McClee and others may point to the move away from conversionist piety to alternate, more profane views of the world that Anne Rose finds in her analysis of Victorian culture. Yet the vigor of evangelical piety of the kind popularized in the 1857–58 Revival that continued during the post–Civil War years among significant segments of the middle class, however accommodated to Victorian culture it may have been, suggests that Rose's subjects may not adequately represent the religious mores of Victorian America. See Anne Rose, *Victorian America and the Civil War* (Cambridge: Cambridge University Press, 1992), 25, 63; also discussion of the "revival generation" in chapter 7.

142. Ellen Weiss, *City in the Woods: The Life and Design of an American Camp Meeting on Martha's Vineyard* (New York: Oxford, 1987), 30.

Four. Gender Tensions and the Masculinization of Urban Piety

1. For the view of women as conduits of redemptive power, see the discussion of "evangelical domesticity" in Sandra Sizer [Frankiel], *Gospel Hymns and Social Religion* (Philadelphia: Temple University Press, 1978), 87; also, Leonard Sweet, *The Minister's Wife: Her Role in Nineteenth-Century American Evangelicalism* (Philadelphia: Temple University Press, 1983), chapter 2, and William G. McLoughlin, ed., *The American Evangelicals* (Gloucester, Mass.: Peter Smith, 1976), 17–19. Historians trace recognition of the ideology of separate spheres back to de Toqueville's *Democracy in America*; in the 1960s the ideology was popularized as an interpretive framework through Barbara Welter's influential article, "The Cult of True Womanhood: 1820–1860," *American Quarterly* 18 (Summer 1966): 151–74. Linda K. Kerber, "Separate Spheres, Female Worlds, Woman's Place: The Rhetoric of Women's History, *Journal of American History* 75 (June 1988): 9–39, provides a summary of historiography concerning the metaphor of separate spheres for the first two decades after Welter, as well as a skillful exploration of the complexities of the concept. The idea of women's religious exceptionalism was strongest among members of the northern Whig/evangelical subculture that shaped so much of the Victorian ethos; in contrast, for example, holiness proponents in Methodist churches based religious "exceptionalism" on the nongender-specific experience of sanctification. Nancy A. Hardesty, "Minister As Prophet? or As Mother? Two Nineteenth-Century Models," in *Women in New Worlds: Historical Perspectives on the Wesleyan Tradition*, ed. Hilah F. Thomas and Rosemary Skinner Keller (Nashville: Abingdon Press, 1981): 88–101.

2. *Christian Advocate and Journal*, March 11, 1858. There were many similar comments, for example, in the *New York Daily Tribune*, March 1, 1858.

3. The *New York Daily Tribune*, March 29, 1858, carried an extensive report of what was billed as the "largest congregation in America," a Sunday evening service (on what would have been Palm Sunday for Catholics) for more than 1,500 New York City firemen and their families. Politicians as well as ministers shared the dais and listened to a sermon by Methodist minister W. P. Corbit. See also William C. Conant, *Narratives of Remarkable Conversions and Revival Incidents* (New York: Derby and Jackson, 1858), 401–07; *Pentecost, or The Work of God in Philadelphia, A.D. 1858* (Philadelphia: Parry and McMillan, 1859), 31–37; and Samuel Irenaeus Prime, *The Power of Prayer, Illustrated in the Wonderful Displays of Divine Grace at the Fulton Street and Other Meetings* (New York: Scribner, 1858), 220–52.

4. Prime, *Power of Prayer*, 59.

5. Ibid., 57.

6. Conant, *Narratives*, 414.

7. Leonard Woolsey Bacon, *A History of American Christianity* (New York: Scribner's, 1925 [1897]), 344; cf. Henry Clay Fish, *Handbook of Revivals for the Use of Winners of Souls* (Boston: James H. Earle, 1879), 70, 327–28; and Daniel Dorchester, *Christianity in the United States* (New York: Hunt and Eaton, 1889), 695.

8. Mark A. Noll, *A History of Christianity in the United States and Canada* (Grand Rapids: Eerdmans, 1992), 287–88, is one example.

9. See Ann Douglas, *The Feminization of American Culture* (New York: Anchor Press, 1988), in addition to the works already cited.

10. Gail Bederman, " 'The Women Have Had Charge of the Church Work Long Enough': The Men and Religion Forward Movement of 1911–1912 and the Masculinization of Middle-Class Protestantism," *American Quarterly* 41 (September 1989): 436. Although Bederman's article is primarily concerned with religion in the Progres-

sive Era, she provides a succinct summary, along with certain revisions, of conventional scholarly wisdom first articulated by Nancy F. Cott, Ann Douglas, and others regarding feminized Protestantism and entrepreneurial capitalism during the early Republic and midcentury years.

11. Anne C. Rose, *Victorian America and the Civil War* (Cambridge: Cambridge University Press, 1992), 183, points out that, in colonial America and the early republic, families acted as corporate units to support public religion. By the Victorian generation, while family ties remained emotionally strong, the corporate sense had given way to more individual autonomy. This interpretation is compatible with my suggestion that the revival marked the emergence of a new group, businessmen, as the bulwarks of public religion.

12. Leonard I. Sweet, " 'A Nation Born Again': The Union Prayer Meeting Revival," in *The Great Tradition, In Honor of Winthrop S. Hudson, Essays on Pluralism, Voluntarism, and Revivalism*, ed. Joseph D. Ban and Paul R. Dekar (Valley Forge, Penn.: Judson Press, 1982), 194.

13. For more on the YWCA, see below. The best recent work on the Women's Temperance Crusade is Jack S. Blocker, Jr., *"Give to the Winds Thy Fears:" The Women's Temperance Crusade, 1873–1874* (Westport, Conn.: Greenwood Press, 1985).

14. Donald G. Mathews, *Religion in the Old South* (Chicago: University of Chicago Press, 1977), 104. Although the amount of release women found from constraints and stereotypes based on gender varied in different revival traditions, there is evidence that, however temporarily, in the eighteenth century and first half of the nineteenth, revivals in general were a setting of spiritual equality and empowerment for women. Gerald F. Moran, "Christian Revivalism and Culture in Early America: Puritan New England as a Case Study," in *Modern Christian Revivals*, ed. Edith L. Blumhofer and Randall Balmer (Urbana: University of Illinois Press, 1993), 52–53; George A. Rawlyk, "Writing about Canadian Religious Revivals," in *Modern Christian Revivals*, 224; and Stephen R. Grossbart, "Seeking the Divine Favor: Conversion and Church Admission in Eastern Connecticut, 1711–1832," *William and Mary Quarterly* 46 (October 1989): 739. This is not to say that men did not also find spiritual release, rather that in some cases at least, "women, men, and children were all one in Christ and were seen as spiritual equals," (p. 224), Rawlyk, "Canadian Revivals."

15. *New York Daily Tribune*, March 2, 1858, cf. the *New York Herald*, February 27, 1857. It is possible that combined attendance at the Fulton Street and John Street businessmen's meetings during the first week of March topped 1000, although estimates for John Street at that time were not given. At its peak in mid-March, there were reports that the John Street meeting drew 2,000 people and that the Fulton Street Church was overflowing. Conant, *Narratives*, 361; *New York Daily Tribune*, March 9 and 13, 1858. During the last week in March, with more than 20 other daily prayer meetings in New York City proper, the *Herald* estimated that the Fulton Street meeting averaged 300 people; John Street, 600; and Burton's Theater, 1,200. The estimates probably were low because of the newspaper's lack of sympathy toward the revival. *Herald*, March 26, 1858.

16. *New York Daily Tribune*, March 13 and March 15, 1858; see also the *Herald*, March 2, 1858.

17. *New York Daily Tribune*, March 15, 1858; also Prime, *Power of Prayer*, 45.

18. *New York Evening Post*, March 23 and 25, 1858.

19. Charles G. Finney, *The Memoirs of Charles G. Finney*, ed. Garth M. Rosell and Richard A. G. Dupuis (Grand Rapids: Academie Books/Zondervan, 1989), 564.

See also n. 22 on the same page. Elizabeth Finney actually had begun similar meetings a year earlier when Finney also preached in Boston. Leonard Sweet discusses Elizabeth Finney's ministry, including her efforts during the 1857–58 Revival in *Minister's Wife*, 186–93.

20. Charles G. Finney, *The Prevailing Prayer-Meeting* (London: Ward, 1859), 29. At the time of the sermon, Finney's wife, Elizabeth, was working with Helen Bruce Kirk, a minister's wife in Edinburgh, Scotland, to organize public women's prayer meetings in conjunction with Charles Finney's efforts in 1859 to help spread the revival from the United States to Britain. This may have been part of the reason for Finney's emphasis on women's role in the revival. Finney, *Memoirs*, 594.

21. Although daily prayer meetings were held in various Boston churches, the focal point during the 1857–58 Revival was the Old South Chapel where the ongoing union prayer meeting was held from 8:00–9:00 AM; the women's meeting from 9:00–10:00 AM; and the noon businessmen's meeting from 12:00–1:00 PM. By the time Phoebe and Walter Palmer visited Boston in July 1858, a meeting for people interested in holiness teachings had been organized from 10:00–12:00. Richard Wheatley, *The Life and Letters of Mrs. Phoebe Palmer* (New York: Walter C. Palmer, Jr., 1876; reprint New York: Garland, 1984), 337. Later accounts that mentioned the role of women in Boston were Finney's *Memoirs*, chapter 33, and *The Old South Chapel Prayer Meeting* (Boston: Tilton, 1859), 54–55, 62.

22. John Weiss, *Life and Correspondence of Theodore Parker* (New York: D. Appleton, 1864), 2: 251–52; cf. Finney, *Memoirs*, 566–68. For more on the Parker incident, see chapter 6.

23. Churches selected were those that claimed to have participated in the 1857–58 Revival and that had lists of members or probationers available for 1858. Statistics were as follows: Plymouth Church, 350 total new members, including 211 women and 139 men; Forsyth Street Church (Methodist Episcopal), 99 new members, 60 women, 39 men; Second Street Church (Methodist Episcopal), 235 new members, 117 women, 118 men; Stanton Street Baptist Church, 61 new members, 37 women, 24 men; and Thirteenth Street Presbyterian Church, 296 new members, 199 women, 97 men. Sources were *Manual of Plymouth Church* (New York: Baker and Goodwin, 1867), 47–64; Methodist Episcopal Church, Church Records, New York City; Forsyth Street Church, list of probationers, 1858; Second Street Church, list of probationers, 1858, Manuscript Division, New York City Public Library; *A History of the Stanton Street Baptist Church in the City of New York* (New York: Sheldon, 1860), 152–220; New York City, Thirteenth St. Presbyterian Church Register, 1846–1892, Presbyterian Historical Society, Philadelphia. For the Second Street Church and the Flying Artillery, see *Church Records, Second Street Methodist Episcopal Church, New York City* (New York: Nelson and Phillips, 1871) and *New York Daily Tribune*, March 1, 1858.

24. Conant, *Narratives*, 426–27, 430–33, contains examples of such usage.

25. *New York Observer*, July 22, 1858. See the similar wording in a report from a Baptist church in Beverly, Massachusetts, in the same issue. "Heads of families" referred to married adults in contrast to young, unmarried people. For an example of confusion surrounding the term, see Sweet, "Union Prayer Meeting Revival," 194. Richard J. Carwardine, *Transatlantic Revivalism: Popular Evangelicalism in Britain and America, 1790–1865* (Westport, Conn.: Greenwood Press, 1978), 164, placed the phrase in an inclusive context, although he still assumed that the majority of the adult converts were men.

26. Mary P. Ryan suggests that this period spanned about 1840–1870. Prior to 1840 the boundaries between the household and the marketplace were much more

fluid; after 1870, a significant portion of urban public space was set apart specifically for women. Ryan, *Women in Public: Between Banners and Ballots, 1825–1880* (Baltimore: Johns Hopkins University Press, 1990), 64, 68, 76, and *passim*. For other discussions of women and urban public space in the nineteenth century, see Glenna Matthews, *The Rise of the Public Woman: Woman's Power and Woman's Place in the United States 1630–1970* (New York: Oxford University Press, 1992) and Christine Stansell, *City of Women: Sex and Class in New York, 1789–1860* (New York: Alfred A. Knopf, 1988).

27. Ryan, *Women in Public*, and others caution against simplistic dualisms between public/private and male/female, noting among other things that gender boundaries were also shaped by issues of class and ethnicity. Nonetheless, there were discernible dualisms established by and for middle- and upper-class urbanites at mid-century.

28. I am not saying that men and women had no shared social world in antebellum America; chapter 3 demonstrated the importance of relational ties in family and church. Nonetheless, there were gender-based and location-specific "subcultures" for the emerging middle class within that broader social world. For the female subculture, see Carroll Smith-Rosenberg, "The Female World of Love and Ritual: Relations Between Women in Nineteenth-Century America," in *Disorderly Conduct: Visions of Gender in Victorian America* (New York: Oxford University Press, 1985), 53–76; also Daniel Walker Howe, "Victorian Culture in America," in *Victorian America*, ed. Daniel Walker Howe (Philadelphia: University of Pennsylvania Press, 1976), 26–27.

29. Matthews, *Public Woman*, 4.

30. For an explanation of changes in New York City residential patterns during the first half of the nineteenth century, see Allan Stanley Horlick, *Country Boys and Merchant Princes: The Social Control of Young Men in New York* (Lewisburg, Penn.: Bucknell University Press, 1975), 26–34. By 1860, almost half of the city's population, the wealthier half, lived north of Fourteenth Street. In contrast, the most popular union prayer meetings were in the business district south of Canal Street.

31. *New York Herald*, February 21, 1858.

32. As chapter 2 noted, this was the case for the *Herald* and the Fulton Street meeting.

33. Conant, *Narratives*, 414.

34. *New York Daily Tribune*, March 2, 1858.

35. Ibid., March 1, 1858.

36. *New York Herald*, March 26, 1858.

37. Talbot W. Chambers, *The Noon Prayer Meeting of the North Dutch Church* (New York: Board of Publication, Reformed Protestant Dutch Church, 1858), 71. "Sound of many waters" appears in visionary passages of the Bible to refer both to the voice of God and to the praises of redeemed humanity in the context of the final judgment. See Ezekiel 43:2; Revelation 1:15; 14:2, and 19:6.

38. For an illustration of such piety, see the request from "an anxious mother" in Prime, *Power of Prayer*, 157–58, who had prayed for her 35-year-old son "since his birth up to the present time."

39. Ibid., 69.

40. Chambers, *Noon Prayer Meeting*, 57.

41. Ibid., 307.

42. James H. Moorhead, "The Millennium and the Media," in *Communications and Change in American Religious History*, ed. Leonard I. Sweet (Grand Rapids: Eerdmans, 1993), Conant, *Narratives*, 394–96.

43. For an expression of the Methodist position in the late 1850s, see "Rights and Duties of Christian Women in Religious Assemblies," *Christian Advocate and Journal*, July 9, 1857. See also Sweet, *Minister's Wife*, 115–16.

44. Keith J. Hardman, *Charles Grandison Finney* (Syracuse N.Y.: Syracuse University Press, 1987), 136–38. See also, Sizer [Frankie] *Gospel Hymns and Social Religion*, 55, 62.

45. Presbyterian Church in the U.S.A., General Assembly, *Minutes*, 1832, quoted in Janet Harbison Penfield, "Women in the Presbyterian Church—An Historical Overview," *Journal of Presbyterian History* 55 (Summer 1977): 109.

46. *New York Herald*, February 27, 1858.

47. Prime, *Power of Prayer*, 56 (italics in the original).

48. Palmer made her position clear in her critique of "the union meeting" as it was organized in the 1857–58 Revival. Phoebe Palmer, *The Promise of the Father; or, A Neglected Specialty of the Last Days* (New York: W. C. Palmer, Jr., 1872 [1859]), chapter 11. Palmer's "Tuesday Meeting for the Promotion of Holiness" began as a Methodist "female prayer meeting" in 1835. In 1840, men began to attend, and during the 1840s and 1850s people from a variety of denominations who were interested in holiness teachings found their ways to the meeting. See Harold E. Raser, *Phoebe Palmer, Her Life and Thought* (Lewiston, N.Y.: Edwin Mellen Press, 1987), 79–101.

49. *New York Daily Tribune*, March 9, 1858.

50. Ibid., March 11, 1858.

51. Ibid., March 31, 1858. Early Methodist churches had seated men and women separately, although space was divided evenly between the two groups. Mixed seating was introduced in New York City in 1837; see Samuel A. Seaman, *Annals of New York Methodism* (New York: Hunt and Eaton, 1892), 239, 268–69.

52. *New York Daily Tribune*, March 17, 1858. "The body of the church is reserved for men, and ladies occupy the wall pews and galleries."

53. For Philadelphia, see reports on the Jayne's Hall meeting in *New York Daily Tribune* March 15 and 17, 1858. A reporter for the Chicago *Daily Democrat* at the Metropolitan Hall in that city wrote on March 27, "The ladies who were backward at the outset, are now out in full strength." Leonard I. Sweet cites the Cincinnati *Daily Gazette*, March 1, 12, and 15, 1858, for similar patterns in that city. Sweet correctly notes that women remained in the minority at the downtown noon meetings. However, while he interprets the male majority as evidence of the "sheer numbers of men" involved in the revival or that "women stayed away in droves," I view the significant female presence as evidence of the spiritual interest that drove women to overcome logistical obstacles and social conventions to arrive in the business district in the numbers that they did. Sweet, "Union Prayer Meeting Revival," 215, n. 11.

54. *New York Daily Tribune*, March 22, 1858.

55. See, for example, *Pentecost; or, the Work of God in Philadelphia*, 12, 16, 40, 51, for examples of and quotations from women participating in socially acceptable ways.

56. Leonard I. Sweet is the only historian who has noted Olney's participation in the revival, and his research was hampered by lack of access to the main source of information on Olney's life, her book, *The Old Way of Holiness, With a Sketch of the Christian Experience of Harriet Olney* (New York: Published by the Author, 1857). The one extant copy is located at the Library of Congress. It was missing at the time of Sweet's work. See Sweet, *Minister's Wife*, 128; and "Union Prayer Meeting Revival," 215, n. 11.

57. Olney, *Old Way of Holiness*, 20, 43, 64, 73, 81, and *passim*. Olney also

appears on the membership and class lists of the Seventh Street Methodist Episcopal Church, New York City in the 1850s, "Class No. 6, Thursday evening," in "Seventh Street Church—Classes 1837–64," and "Seventh St. Church Members, 1840–1860," Microfilm, Manuscript Division, New York City Public Library. Olney's membership was "remov'd by certificate" in 1863.

58. *New York Daily Tribune*, March 17, 1858.

59. Ibid.

60. Ibid., March 13, 1858.

61. Ibid., March 17, 1858. In a letter to the editor, Olney wrote, "I am not in the least astonished, nor would I have been had they called me the 'Old Harry,' for it would only have been what my Divine Master was called when on earth."

62. Ibid., March 17 and 19, 1858. The title suggests that the pamphlet was an excerpt from her book. There is no record of extant copies.

63. Ibid., March 18, 1858. For roots of this evangelical attitude in the British nonconformist tradition, see Harry S. Stout, *The Divine Dramatist: George Whitefield and the Rise of Modern Evangelicalism* (Grand Rapids: Eerdmans, 1991), 22–23. The noon prayer meetings at Burton's were held from March 17 to April 3. They began at a point when reporters were beginning to look for fresh news and quickly joined the Orville Gardner story as a featured item in the New York City papers. Regional papers that reprinted the story included the *New Orleans Daily Picayune*, March 25, 1858; the *Charleston Daily Courier*, March 29; the *Louisville Daily Courier*, March 27; and the *Cincinnati Daily Enquirer*, April 18.

64. *New York Daily Tribune* March 24, 1858.

65. Ibid.

66. Timothy J. Gilfoyle, "The Urban Geography of Commercial Sex: Prostitution in New York City, 1790–1860," *Journal of Urban History* 14 (August 1987): 387. Although the "Third Tier" trade had been banned by midcentury, the notoriety remained and business simply moved to nearby streets.

67. For a description of Stewart's as a public space for women, see Ryan, *Women in Public*, 76–77.

68. *New York Daily Tribune*, March 25, 1858.

69. Ibid., March 26, 1858.

70. Ibid.

71. Ibid., March 15 and 29, 1858; *New York Herald*, March 22, 1858. The *Herald* story may have referred to another occasion when Olney spoke, although she was not identified by name. Of the published narratives of the revival by clergy, only Conant, *Narratives*, 386, included an account of a woman speaking (a mother) at Burton's, taken from the *Tribune*, March 29.

72. Palmer and her husband, Walter, were in New York City from late October 1857 to early March 1858. She used the Tuesday meeting to spread word of the revival in Hamilton, Ontario, and to urge the formation of "Christian Vigilance Bands" ("Bands of Soul-Savers") who would engage in revivalistic activity. Palmer, *Promise of the Father*, 262–69, also *Christian Advocate and Journal*, November 5, 1857. The Benjamin M. Adams Diary, October 1857 to March 1858, includes notes by one Methodist minister of his participation in the Tuesday meeting during this time.

73. Palmer, *Promise of the Father*, 13, see also p. 1. Harold Raser, in his helpful study of Palmer's life and thought, describes Phoebe and Walter Palmer as "highly visible promoters" of the Revival of 1857–58, yet both were invisible as far as the public phase of the New York City revival was concerned. Phoebe Palmer's greatest revival successes took place during the summer months of 1857 and 1858 in Canada

(the provinces of Ontario and the Maritimes), outside the pale of interest for revival publicists in the United States. See Raser, *Phoebe Palmer*, 120–26.

74. Palmer, *Promise of the Father*, 4–6 and *passim*.

75. Ibid., 255. Palmer viewed the Hamilton revival, together with the catalyst of the financial panic, as the beginning of the 1857–58 Revival.

76. Wheatley, *Life and Letters* 334.

77. She may have done so at Methodist churches and simply not mentioned the meetings. The accounts Palmer left of her work in the three towns is sketchy. Wheatley, *Life and Letters*, 334–36, and Palmer, *Promise of the Father*, 269–73.

78. Palmer, *Promise of the Father*, 270.

79. Sweet's research in *Minister's Wife*, 121, also 276, n. 71, supports this perception: "By the 1860s ... the Presbyterian and Congregational prejudice against women praying and speaking had so faded, especially in rural areas, that some congregations 'seem quite astonished when told that it is anti-scriptural, anti-Presbyterian, and unprofitable.' "

80. Palmer, *Promise of the Father*, 273.

81. The book was more than simply a response to the revival. Palmer first mentioned the idea in 1856, and she needed to write the book as an apologetic for her own activities and as a corollary for her teaching that all, men *and* women, who experienced sanctification should tell of the experience in public religious meetings. Yet Palmer did write the *Promise of the Father* during and in the immediate aftermath of the revival. The book's message, its dedication to Dudley Tyng, the chapter critiquing "Union Prayer Meetings," and the narration of Palmer's revival activities all link it with the events of 1857–58. For background on the book, see "Preface," *Promise of the Father*, n.p.; Wheatley, *Life and Letters*, 336; Raser, *Phoebe Palmer*, 201–02.

82. Palmer's argument for women's right to "preach" was used by some later writers to support arguments for women's ordination, but Palmer disclaimed any desire to promote women as ministers in a technical or formal sense. Her central concern was for female involvement in lay ministry activities, which could include informal preaching, as practiced by Palmer herself. However, there was a thin line between "preaching, technically so called" and Palmer's revivalistic activities. *Promise of the Father*, 34. Monographs that give attention to *Promise of the Father* include Donald Dayton, *Discovering an Evangelical Heritage* (New York: Harper and Row, 1976); Nancy A. Hardesty, *Women Called to Witness: Evangelical Feminism in the 19th Century* (Nashville: Abingdon Press, 1984); Janette Hassey, *No Time for Silence: Evangelical Women in Public Ministry Around the Turn of the Century* (Grand Rapids: Zondervan, 1986); and Raser, *Phoebe Palmer*.

83. "A Laity for the Times" was the standing headline given to a series of epistolary articles written by Palmer for the *Christian Advocate and Journal*, February 12, 19, 26, and March 12, 1857, advocating evangelistic activism by church members, men and women, as a sign of genuine revival.

84. This summary of Palmer's "Pentecostal argument" is based on Raser, *Phoebe Palmer*, 202–04.

85. See Hardesty, *Women Called to Witness*, 162–64, for a chronological listing of "Defenses of Woman's Ministry."

86. *Christian Advocate and Journal*, February 19, 1857.

87. Palmer, *Promise of the Father*, 227–28, 230.

88. Ibid., 231.

89. Ibid., 259–69. On other occasions Palmer called the groups "Christian Vigilance Bands."

90. The same circumstances and attitudes that forced Palmer to the periphery of public revivalism in 1858 operated against widespread acceptance of her book. Palmer attempted to position the work within mainstream revivalistic piety by dedicating it to the memory of Dudley Tyng and his challenge to "stand up for Jesus" and by seeking the support of respected clergymen such as Francis Wayland. Wheatley, *Life and Letters*, 336. However, the impact of the book's inclusive ideal was limited mostly to the holiness churches and voluntary associations that embraced Palmer's teaching. For its influence on Salvation Army leader Catherine Booth, see Hardesty, *Women Called to Witness*, 66.

91. Although little research has been done on women and the press, secular newspapers were a male public arena where "women appear irregularly and surrounded with the most distortion," (p. 17), Ryan, *Women in Public*. The prescriptions for what it meant to be a "lady" in public did not include newspaper notoriety. This may have been another reason Phoebe Palmer avoided lower Manhattan and, throughout her life, orchestrated her own publicity as much as possible.

92. Doremus (1802–1877), founded the Woman's Union Missionary Society in November, 1860.

93. Like the American YMCA, the YWCA has debates over origins. Roberts's group, founded in 1858, receives first mention in two standard YWCA histories, but the Boston YWCA, founded in 1866, was the first to use the full YWCA name. See Mary S. Sims, *The Natural History of a Social Institution: The Young Women's Christian Association* (New York: Little and Ives, 1935); and Elizabeth Wilson, *Fifty Years of Association Work Among Young Women* (New York: National Board of the Young Women's Christian Associations, 1916). Little scholarly research has been done on the early YWCA; unless indicated, the account that follows is based on Sims and Wilson.

94. *DAB*, s.v. "Marshall O. Roberts." After 1856, Marshall Roberts was a leading contributor to the Republican party. He augmented his fortune through profiteering during the Civil War and narrowly lost the 1865 mayoral race in New York City.

95. Wilson, *Fifty Years*, 23. A brief report on the New York City association also appears under its name during the 1860s, "Ladies' Christian Union of the City of New York" in Henry J. Cammann and Hugh N. Camp, *The Charities of New York, Brooklyn, and Staten Island* (New York: Hurd and Houghton, 1868).

96. Wilson, *Fifty Years*, 103–04. Earlier, Wilson listed three "outstanding characteristics" of the "historic American revival of 1857–58," including "the large place filled by women as leaders of organized Christian forces" (p. 22).

97. The Boston YWCA, first in the nation to bear that specific name, was founded in 1866; in 1867, Roberts once again was instrumental in founding the third association, in Hartford, Connecticut. As in New York City, it grew out of a "Ladies Union prayer meeting." There are also connections between other YWCAs founded in the decade after the Civil War and revival participants, male and female. The revival was not the sole factor behind the growth of the YWCA, but it was an important early influence. See Wilson, *Fifty Years*, 50–54; and Kathryn Teresa Long. "The Revival of 1857–58: The Power of Interpretation" (Ph.D. diss., Duke University, 1993), 299–300. Anne Firor Scott, *Natural Allies, Women's Associations in American History* (Urbana: University of Illinois Press, 1991) noted that by the late 1870s, as student YWCAs proliferated in the Midwest, "the students . . . tended to be evangelical and conservative, while the middle-aged women in the East tended to be liberal in their religious views" (p. 108). Such a distinction was less clear in the decade immediately following the Civil War.

98. Stuart, *Life*, 23.

99. *New York Daily Tribune*, March 13 and 15, 1858; cf., Conant, *Narratives*, 395–96, and the *Examiner*, March 18, 1858.

100. Stuart, *Life*, 131.

101. Ibid., 145–46.

102. Ibid., 170.

103. Studies of the "masculinization" of late-century Protestantism include Bederman, " 'The Women Have Had Charge' "; Susan Curtis, "The Son of Man and God the Father: The Social Gospel and Victorian Masculinity," in *Meanings for Manhood, Constructions of Masculinity in Victorian America*, ed. Mark C. Carnes and Clyde Griffen (Chicago: University of Chicago Press, 1990), 67–78; Susan Curtis, *A Consuming Faith: The Social Gospel and Modern American Culture* (Baltimore: Johns Hopkins University Press, 1991); James H. Moorhead, "Presbyterians and the Mystique of Organizational Efficiency, 1870–1936," in *Reimagining Denominationalism: Interpretive Essays*, ed. Robert Bruce Mullin and Russell E. Richey (New York: Oxford University Press, 1994), 264–87; and Louis Weeks, "The Incorporation of American Religion: The Case of the Presbyterians," *Religion and American Culture* 1 (Winter 1991): 101–18. Through her study of the rhetoric of hymnody and prayer in late-century urban revivalism, Sandra Sizer [Frankiel] has been influential in emphasizing the ongoing influence of evangelical domesticity. Her insights into "social religion" and the role of sentiment are astute; however, in stressing domesticity, she tends to isolate the rhetoric of hymnody from the broader milieu of urban revivalism, particularly its commercial context. See Sizer, *Gospel Hymns*, chapters 5 and 6.

104. *Independent*, April 8, 1858, from a column written by Harriet Beecher Stowe.

105. Prime, *Power of Prayer*, 179. Prime devoted chapter 14 of his book to the effect of the revival in encouraging men to "do their business upon Christian principles."

106. Conant, *Narratives*, 366.

107. Edward Anthony Rotundo, "Manhood in America: The Northern Middle Class 1770–1920," (Ph.D. diss., Brandeis University, 1982), 270–72, discusses the urgency surrounding time and work among midcentury men; in contrast, the nature of middle-class women's activities in the home meant their work continued to be more task-oriented.

108. *New York Daily Tribune*, March 11, 1858. The *Tribune* reprinted the card that served as a guide for the John Street meeting. Most of the YMCA-sponsored meetings followed similar guidelines; others were somewhat more flexible. See also Conant, *Narratives*, 380–82.

109. *Louisville Daily Courier*, April 5, 1858. The Philadelphia publicity was spearheaded by John Wanamaker, YMCA secretary at the time.

110. Theodore Parker, *A False and True Revival of Religion* (Boston: William L. Kent, 1858), 10. For a description of the promotional activities in New York City, see the *Tribune*, March 2, 1858.

111. Finney, *Prevailing Prayer-Meeting*, 25, 19. Finney viewed the revival as a vindication of the principles in his *Lectures on Revivals* and singled out S. I. Prime and other Old Schoolers for their unwillingness to acknowledge the use of means.

112. The family as a "little church" was particularly a Puritan ideal, as Edmund Sears Morgan discussed in the classic treatment of the subject, *The Puritan Family: Religion and Domestic Relations in Seventeenth-Century New England* (New York: Harper and Row, 1966 [1944]). However, with increasing emphasis on the family in the nineteenth century and as part of their biblicism, all evangelical denominations invested a certain formal status in the father as religious leader of the family.

113. Robert Burns, "The Cotter's Saturday Night," quoted in Albert Barnes, *Prayers for the Use of Families* (Philadelphia: Thomas, Cowperthwait, 1850), 48–49, italics in original. See Leigh Eric Schmidt, *Holy Fairs: Scottish Communions and American Revivals in the Early Modern Period* (Princeton: Princeton University Press), 200–01, for a discussion of the poem as one symbol of privatization of Scottish revival piety during the nineteenth century.

114. Martha T. Blauvelt, "The Mechanics of Revival: New Jersey Presbyterians During the Second Awakening," in *Religion in New Jersey Life Before the Civil War*, ed. Mary R. Murrin (Trenton: New Jersey Historical Commission, 1985), 94–95. Blauvelt notes that "by 1800 the male lay role had been institutionalized in the office of church elder. Although many Presbyterian congregations had elders before 1740, the office did not become a staple in church life until after the First Awakening." For a contemporary example of the role of church elder, in addition to those given by Blauvelt, see Samuel Irenaeus Prime, *Autobiography and Memorials*, ed. Wendell Prime (New York: Anson D. F. Randolph, 1888), 91, 103.

115. Roger Finke and Rodney Stark, *The Churching of America, 1776–1990: Winners and Losers in Our Religious Economy* (New Brunswick: Rutgers University Press, 1992), 73; also Emory Stevens Bucke, ed., *History of American Methodism: In Three Volumes*, vol. 2 (New York: Abingdon Press, 1964), *passim*, for a discussion of various lay representation movements.

116. Heman Humphrey, *Revival Sketches and Manual* (New York: American Tract Society, 1859), 199.

117. Titles in the series of tracts published by the American Tract Society illustrate the situation. Titles extolling lay female piety far outnumber those devoted to men. A sampling includes, "A Dying Mother's Counsel to her Only Son," "To Mothers," "A Word to Mothers," "Letters on Christian Education" ("chiefly addressed to mothers"), "The Praying Mother," "The Mother's Last Prayer," "The Mother of St. Augustine," and "My Mother." Three titles were devoted to fathers. Most tracts focused specifically on men were aimed at promoting temperance and warning young men to avoid worldly temptations. See "Sketch of the Origin and Character of the Principal Series of Tracts of the American Tract Society," *American Tract Society Documents, 1824–1925* (New York: Arno Press, 1972).

118. Anthony Rotundo, in his study of northern manhood, has suggested typologies for this period that he describes as the "Christian gentleman" and the "Christian soldier." Both are composites rather than types appealed to by evangelical men. Rotundo, "Manhood in America," 148–62.

119. Carwardine, *Transatlantic Revivalism*, 255, n. 14, cites a number of such works, including James W. Alexander et al., *The Man of Business Considered in his Various Relations* (New York: Anson D. F. Randolph, 1857); Henry Clay Fish, *Primitive Piety Revived* (Boston: Congregational Board of Publication, 1855); and William Arthur, *The Successful Merchant* (London: Hamilton, Adams, 1852). There also were regular articles in the religious press. See, for example, "Men of Business" in the *Christian Advocate and Journal*, May 14 and July 2, 1857.

120. Fish, *Primitive Piety Revived*, 48–49.

121. Ibid., 56, 50. Italics in the original.

122. Ibid., 43. Phoebe Palmer's soul-saving bands cited the "divine injunction, 'Diligent in business,'" as their justification for making "every earthly consideration, whether it be secular business or domestic avocations, specifically subservient to the service of Christ." See *Promise of the Father*, 263. It apparently came from the New Testament directive, "[Be] not slothful in business," Romans 12:11.

123. Quoted in John S. Gilkeson, Jr., *Middle-Class Providence, 1820–1940* (Princeton: Princeton University Press, 1986), 74.

124. James F. Findlay, *Dwight L. Moody: American Evangelist, 1837–1899* (Chicago: University of Chicago Press, 1969), 83.

125. Walt Whitman, *I Sit and Look Out: Editorials from the Brooklyn Daily Times*, ed. Emory Holloway and Vernolian Schwartz (New York: Columbia University Press, 1932), 77.

126. "Extracts from John V. Farwell's Diary" in *Reminiscences of John V. Farwell by His Elder Daughter*, vol. 1 (Chicago: Ralph Fletcher Seymour, 1928).

127. John V. Farwell, Jr., ed., *Some Recollections of John V. Farwell* (Chicago: R. R. Donnelley, 1911), 102.

128. Ibid., 103.

129. L. L. Doggett, *History of the Young Men's Christian Association: Part I, the Founding of the Association, 1844–1855; Part II, the Confederation Period, 1855–1861* (New York: Association Press, 1922), 289.

130. For example, in 1852 northern Methodist clergy had voted against opening the Annual and General Conferences to lay representation, a vote not overruled until 1868. In the late 1850s, there was fear among conservatives that increased lay influence within Methodism would upset the precarious church stance toward slavery. It was fueled by the Genesee radicals, who held a series of annual "Laymen's Conventions" in upstate New York from 1858–1860. They were countered by the conservative "Ministers' and Laymen's Union," formed in 1859 in the New York Conference. See Bucke, *History of American Methodism*, 2: 187, 202, 350–52. On a more pedestrian level, laymen still faced some church scrutiny of their personal and business practices, although church discipline had eased considerably by midcentury. See Session Minutes, Thirteenth St. Presbyterian Church, New York City, April 7, 1858, for a call for a vote over accepting a letter of transfer from James C. Coleman because he was "engaged in the milk business and in the habit of supplying his customers on the Sabbath day." The vote was four to one in favor of receiving Coleman into membership.

131. The Fulton Street prayer meeting, which became a New York City establishment, was a much more localized institutional legacy of the revival. Although the prayer meeting itself always was interdenominational, it operated under the auspices of the Dutch Reformed church. In addition to *Power of Prayer*, a whole corpus of pious literature on prayer came out of the Fulton Street meeting. See Samuel Irenaeus Prime, *Five Years of Prayer, With the Answers* (New York: Harper, 1864), *Fifteen Years of Prayer in the Fulton Street Meeting* (New York: Scribner, Armstrong, 1872), and *Prayer and Its Answer Illustrated in the First Twenty-five Years of the Fulton Street Prayer Meeting* (New York: Scribner, 1882); J. C. Lanphier, *Alone with Jesus* (New York: Tibbals, 1872); and Thomas C. Strong, *Living Words from Living Men: Experiences of Converted Infidels* (New York: Board of Publications, Reformed Protestant Dutch Church, 1863).

132. *Pentecost; or Work of God in Philadelphia*, 31–47; C. Howard Hopkins, *History of the Y.M.C.A. in North America* (New York: Association Press, 1951), 26. Doggett, *Young Men's Christian Association*, 244.

133. These points are in part based on assessments of the USCC found in Hopkins, *History of the Y.M.C.A.*, 85–92, and Findlay, *Moody*, 101–3.

134. The most complete account of the USCC is Lemuel Moss, *Annals of the United States Christian Commission* (Philadelphia: J. B. Lippincott, 1868). See also Cephas Brainerd, "The Work of the Army Committee of the New York Young Men's Christian Association" (New York: John Mendole, printer, 1866); Owen E. Pence,

"Meet Vincent Colyer" [typescript], main collection, Library of Congress, Washington, D.C.; and Stuart, *Life*, 128–72. For Moody, see Emmett Dedmon, *Great Enterprises* (New York: Rand McNally, 1957), 44; also Theodore J. Karamanski, *Rally 'Round the Flag: Chicago and the Civil War* (Chicago: Nelson-Hall, 1993), 120–24.

135. Manierre was president of the New York City YMCA in 1858; for his participation in the John Street prayer meeting, see *New York Daily Tribune*, March 13, 1858. John V. Farwell and H. Thane Miller also were committee members with known experience in the revival. Other activists—Edward Colgate, Cephas Brainerd, and John Wanamaker—were delegates to the organizational meeting. See Moss, *Annals*, 103, 104.

136. Charles R. Erdman, *D. L. Moody: His Message for Today* (New York: Fleming H. Revell, 1928), 36.

137. Findlay, *Moody*, 103.

138. Stuart, *Life*, 133, 141. The anecdote also reflected the wealth of northern merchants during the war years, and the distance many could maintain between their lifestyles and the battlefield.

139. Farwell, *Recollections*, 74.

140. Moss, *Annals*, 548, italics in the original.

141. The publicity given the delegates as well as the male USCC executive committee also overshadowed the many women who provided supplies and other support services for the group. For women as initiators of the war relief work, see Moss, 73–77. Scholarly works investigating the war efforts of northern women include Scott, *Natural Allies*, and Lori D. Ginzberg, *Women and the Work of Benevolence: Morality, Politics, and Class in the 19th Century United States* (New Haven: Yale University Press, 1990).

142. Moss, *Annals*, 93, 574.

143. Hopkins, *History of the Y.M.C.A.*, 91–92.

144. The essentials of this common evangelicalism were reflected in an anecdote about an encounter between a USCC delegate and a pious Catholic soldier. The delegate asked the soldier a series of questions, "Do you love God? . . . Have you faith in Christ, trusting in him as *your* Saviour? . . . Do you pray to God through Jesus Christ? . . . Do you truly repent of sin, seeking pardon, acceptance, and salvation through the merit of Christ? . . . And do you find comfort in prayer and communion with God?" When all were answered in the affirmative, the delegate assured the soldier that he was, indeed, a true Christian, regardless of his Romanist affiliation. Moss, *Annals*, 584. Of course, requests by troops for "*good* Catholic books" and "Douay [*sic*] Testaments" gave evidence of the distinct Catholic piety that coexisted alongside the more public evangelicalism of the Christian Commission. Brainerd, *Work of the Army Committee*, 14, 36–37.

145. Bederman, " 'The Women Have Had Change,' " 441, 447.

146. A few YMCAs owned modest structures in the early 1860s; a distinctive "Association architecture" began in 1869 with the dedication of YMCA buildings in Washington, D.C., San Francisco, and New York City. See Hopkins, *History of the Y.M.C.A.*, 150–51.

147. William Warren Sweet, *The Story of Religion in America* (New York: Harper, 1939 [1930]), 501.

148. Bucke, *History of American Methodism*, 2: 273–75.

149. *The Development of the Sunday School, 1780–1905* (Boston: Executive Committee of the International Sunday School Association, 1905), 41.

150. William R. Glass, "Liberal Means to Conservative Ends: Bethany Presbyterian Church, John Wanamaker and the Institutional Church Movement," *American*

Presbyterian 68 (Fall 1990): 185; Herbert Adams Gibbons, *John Wanamaker* (New York: Harper, 1926), 1: 191–92. Wanamaker's promotion of the *Sunday School Times* at the 1876 Centennial Exhibition in Philadelphia demonstrated both his marketing abilities and the way businessmen used their public connections to further conversionist piety. He secured a handwritten letter of endorsement from Ulysses Grant and reproduced a facsimile of it on the cover of the *Times*, June 6, 1876. Together with a subscription coupon, the issue was distributed free to interested Centennial visitors.

151. For the role of the Confederate soldier in shaping postwar southern evangelicalism, see Harry S. Stout, "The Confederate Jeremiad in Defeat," lecture 3 of "The Life and Death of the Confederate Jeremiad" (James A. Gray Lectures, Duke Divinity School, October 1992), 21–24.

152. Recent analyses of the staying power of modern evangelicalism have stressed the movement's adaptability and flexibility. Robert H. Handy, "Trans-Atlantic Evangelicalism in Historical Perspective," *Evangelical Studies Bulletin* 11 (Fall 1994): 1–4.

153. *First Annual Report with the Constitution and By-Laws* [Richmond, VA, Young Men's Christian Association] (Richmond: William H. Clemmit, 1856), 7.

154. Moss, *Annals*, 672. For a biographical sketch of Wittenmyer, see *Notable American Women* 3, s.v. "Wittenmyer, Annie Turner."

155. This pattern began to break down in the late nineteenth century in the context of growing conservative/liberal tensions within Protestantism, the rise of the Bible Institute movement, and a general weakening of nineteenth-century gender restrictions.

156. Scott, *Natural Allies*, 93.

157. Quoted in Findlay, *Moody*, 219, 178; the description of Sankey is based on Findlay's assessment, 209. With the onset of middle age and increasing weight, Moody was generally seen as "portly" rather than muscular.

158. Sizer [Frankiel], *Gospel Hymns and Social Religion*, 119–21, 134.

Five. The Privatization of Northern Revivalism

1. "The Revival," *Independent*, March 11, 1858.

2. Ibid.

3. "Revival Incidents," *National Anti-Slavery Standard*, April 3, 1858. For Stowe's subsequent editorials, see the *Independent*, March 25, 1858, and April 8, 1858.

4. Letter from William Goodell to Charles Hicks, April 29, 1858. Cheever Family Papers, American Antiquarian Society, Worcester, Mass.

5. John B. Boles, *The Great Revival, 1787–1805: The Origins of the Southern Evangelical Mind* (Lexington: University of Kentucky Press, 1972), 182. According to Presbyterian theologian James Henley Thornwell, the "spirituality of the church" meant that the church was a "spiritual body . . . whose purposes are only the dispensation of eternal salvation, and not the creation of morality, decency and good order, which may . . . be secured without faith in the Redeemer." Quoted in Gardiner H. Shattuck, *A Shield and Hiding Place: The Religious Life of the Civil War Armies* (Macon, Ga.: Mercer University Press, 1987), 3. E. Brooks Holifield and others have pointed out that, despite such doctrinal disclaimers, southern clergymen were, in fact, deeply involved in addressing the issues of southern life. Holifield, *The Gentlemen Theologians: American Theology in Southern Culture, 1795–1860* (Durham: Duke University Press, 1978), 154. The point here is that arguments in the South over revivalism were confined to debates about appropriate means and levels of enthusiasm.

6. Richard J. Carwardine, *Evangelicals and Politics in Antebellum America* (New Haven: Yale University Press, 1993), 322.

7. James H. Moorhead, "Social Reform and the Divided Conscience of Antebellum Protestantism," *Church History* 48 (December 1979): 416; also Moorhead, *American Apocalypse: Yankee Protestants and the Civil War, 1860–1869* (New Haven: Yale University Press, 1978), 11–14.

8. For the Manichean perspective fostered by revivalism that viewed "the world as a battle-ground between two moral orders," of good and evil, see Richard Carwardine, "Religious Revival and Political Renewal in Antebellum America," in *Revival and Religion Since 1700: Essays for John Walsh*, ed. Jane Garnett and Colin Matthew (London: Hambledon Press, 1993), 141; also *Evangelicals and Politics*, 8–9.

9. Carwardine, *Evangelicals and Politics*, 147–48, 176–86.

10. George B. Cheever, "The Fire and Hammer of God's Word Upon Slavery and Its Abettors," *National Anti-Slavery Standard*, May 22, 1858.

11. "Political Praying," *New York Observer*, April 15, 1858.

12. Again, labels are difficult for these groups. What I have described as a moderate, Old School/Dutch Reformed coalition was theologically moderate but socially conservative. The New School/Congregationalist "progressives" often were progressive both theologically and socially, though particularly in urban areas they could blend a progressive attitude toward theology with social moderation or conservatism.

13. The most influential advocate of the link has been Timothy L. Smith, *Revivalism and Social Reform: American Protestantism on the Eve of the Civil War* (Nashville: Abingdon Press, 1957). Carwardine, *Evangelicals and Politics*, also suggested that "the revival generated a highly charged sense of social responsibility in many of its converts" (p. 294). Various challenges to this perspective include William G. McLoughlin, *Modern Revivalism: Charles Grandison Finney to Billy Graham* (New York: Ronald Press, 1959); Carroll Smith-Rosenberg, *Religion and the Rise of the American City: The New York City Mission Movement, 1812–1870* (Ithaca: Cornell University Press, 1971); and John R. McKivigan, *The War against Proslavery Religion: Abolitionism and the Northern Churches, 1830–1865* (Ithaca: Cornell University Press, 1984).

14. Carwardine, *Evangelicals and Politics*, 216–18, 277–78.

15. Moorhead, *American Apocalypse*, 125–28, has noted a social passivity, particularly toward racial issues, that arose from the "culture-Protestantism" of the Civil War years; George Marsden, *Fundamentalism and American Culture: The Shaping of Twentieth-Century Evangelicalism, 1870–1925* (New York: Oxford University Press, 1980), 36–37, points to D. L. Moody's rejection of social reform in favor of evangelism as a characteristic of the middle-class "new American evangelicalism" during the latter third of the nineteenth century. Most historians agree that a more militant rejection of social reform did not occur until the "great reversal" of the early twentieth century. See Marsden, 85–86, for a brief summary of this complicated issue. Jean Miller Schmidt, *Souls or the Social Order: The Two-Party System in American Protestantism* (Brooklyn: Carlson, 1991), is a recently published monograph containing Schmidt's pivotal work on the subject from a much earlier dissertation. My concern in this chapter is not evangelicals and social reform in general but the relationship of revivals and social reform.

16. Leonard I. Sweet, " 'A Nation Born Again': The Union Prayer Meeting Revival and Cultural Revitalization," in *The Great Tradition, In Honor of Winthrop S. Hudson, Essays on Pluralism, Voluntarism, and Revivalism*, ed. Joseph D. Ban and Paul R. Dekar (Valley Forge, Penn.: Judson Press, 1982), 193–221, argues, in contrast

to McLoughlin, that the revival was an attempt at cultural revitalization, an effort to forge a new national unity that would avert a sectional split and war. The effort, however, failed, "shipwrecked on the revival's shallowness and immateriality." Sandra Sizer [Frankiel], "Politics and Apolitical Religion," *Church History* 48 (March 1979): 81–98, sees revival efforts to create community as a social response to threats to Victorian cultural hegemony. I am indebted to both studies in forming my own interpretation.

17. "The Religious Revival: Burton's Theater—A Midday Prayer-Meeting," *New York Daily Tribune*, March 18, 1858. Cf. William C. Conant, *Narratives of Remarkable Conversions and Revival Incidents* (New York: Derby and Jackson, 1858), 362–63. In his description, Conant conflates two *Tribune* accounts, from March 18 and March 22, 1858. Theodore Cuyler was not entirely correct in his reference to 1831. Negotiations had begun that year, but the Chatham Street Theater was leased in 1832. Finney began preaching there April 23, 1832, and was installed as pastor October 5. Finney conducted his first New York City revivals in a rented church building from autumn 1829 to mid-1830. In 1831, New Englander and Finney associate Joel Parker was continuing that work as pastor of the First Free Presbyterian Church.

18. *New York Daily Tribune*, March 18, 1858.

19. Conant, *Narratives*, 362. The meetings were canceled when the federal government took possession of the building due to a previous lease with the owner. At that point, the peak revival period had passed and a couple of smaller rooms were rented.

20. "The Religious Revival: The Meeting at Burton's Theater on Saturday," *New York Daily Tribune*, March 22, 1858.

21. See Bertram Wyatt-Brown, *Lewis Tappan and the Evangelical War Against Slavery* (Cleveland: The Press of Case Western Reserve University, 1969), 104–06.

22. As the prayer meetings became more widely publicized, antislavery advocates apparently submitted written prayer requests from slaves to test the "no controversy" policy. Two were read at Burton's Theater and one at the John Street Methodist Church before the policy was reaffirmed and no further such requests admitted. See the *National Anti-Slavery Standard*, April 3, 1858, and April 10, 1858.

23. "The Religious Revival: Saturday at the Old Theater," *New York Daily Tribune*, March 29, 1858. Beecher did pray for the slave, as part of a closing prayer before the meeting was dismissed. Occasionally during the revival he included prayers for an end to slavery as part of Sunday services before his own congregation; even so, the thrust of the Plymouth Church revival was clearly devotional. See *Memorial of the Revival in Plymouth Church, Brooklyn, [Rev. Henry Ward Beecher] During the Early part of the Year 1858* (New York: Clark, Austin and Smith, 1859), 139, 144, and *passim*.

24. Schmidt, *Souls or the Social Order*, 19, argues that a common evangelicalism, shaped by Methodism and with a consensus attitude toward revivalism and social reform, was in place by 1837, with the exception of debates over slavery. The exception, perhaps, should call into question the assumption of consensus. Also, Carwardine, *Evangelicals and Politics*; Daniel Walker Howe, *The Political Culture of the American Whigs* (Chicago: University of Chicago Press, 1979); and Moorhead, "Social Reform and the Divided Conscience," paint a more nuanced picture of evangelicalism during the decades prior to the revival.

25. For background on the Free Church movement, see Charles C. Cole, Jr., "The Free Church Movement in New York City," *New York History* 34 (July 1953): 284–97; Keith J. Hardman, "Charles G. Finney, the Benevolent Empire, and the Free

Church Movement in New York City," *New York History* 67 (October 1986): 411–35; also Hardman, *Charles Grandison Finney* (Syracuse: Syracuse University Press, 1987), chapters 9 and 12; and Wyatt-Brown, *Lewis Tappan*, chapter 4.

26. This group included Anson G. Phelps, David Low Dodge, Eleazar Lord, Knowles Taylor, Zachariah Lewis, Silas Holmes, Peletiah Perit, Jonas Platt, Zephaniah Platt, and Moses Allen. See Wyatt-Brown, *Lewis Tappan*, 61.

27. Ibid., 71.

28. Lewis Tappan to Charles Finney, March 16, 1832, quoted in Cole, "Free Church Movement," 291.

29. Lewis Tappan to S. D. Hastings, April 11, 1841, quoted in Cole, "Free Church Movement," 295.

30. Smith-Rosenberg, *Religion and the American City*, 80–81, and 102–04.

31. Wyatt-Brown, *Lewis Tappan*, 71. For more on the national evangelical societies that made up the "benevolent empire," see Charles I. Foster, *An Errand of Mercy: The Evangelical United Front, 1790–1837* (Chapel Hill: University of North Carolina Press, 1960); Clifford S. Griffin, *Their Brothers' Keepers: Moral Stewardship in the United States, 1800–1865* (New Brunswick: Rutgers University Press, 1960); and John W. Kuykendall, *Southern Enterprize: The Work of National Evangelical Societies in the Antebellum South* (Westport, Conn.: Greenwood Press, 1982).

32. Michael J. Crawford, *Seasons of Grace: Colonial New England's Revival Tradition in Its British Context* (New York: Oxford University Press, 1991), 50–51, 165.

33. William B. Sprague, *Lectures on Revivals of Religion* (Albany: J. P. Haven and J. Leavitt, 1832), 261. Although an opponent of new measures, Sprague was a New Englander and his social vision clearly reflected that tradition. See "Results of Revivals," chapter 9 of the *Lectures, passim*.

34. Ibid., 266–67. Jonathan Edwards, *A Faithful Narrative of the Surprising Work of God* in *The Great Awakening*, ed. C. C. Goen, vol. 4, *Works of Jonathan Edwards* (New Haven: Yale University Press, 1972), had helped to establish a narrative pattern linking individual conversions to community reformation in his contrast between the "licentiousness" and "lewd practices" of the Northampton youth and the "glorious alteration in the town" during the revival of 1735 (pp. 146, 151). For more on New England revival narratives that follow Edwards's pattern, see Crawford, *Seasons of Grace*, 183–90.

35. Kuykendall, *Southern Enterprize*, 9, based on Samuel Hopkins, "An Inquiry into the Nature of True Holiness," *The Works of Samuel Hopkins, D. D.*, vol. 3 (Boston: Doctrinal Tract and Book Society, 1854), 16, 28–29.

36. Moorhead, "Social Reform and the Divided Conscience," 417. Moorhead applies his analysis to Charles Finney, but the comment would apply equally to Beecher.

37. Charles G. Finney, *Lectures on Revivals of Religion*, ed. William G. McLoughlin (Cambridge: Harvard University Press, 1960), 404.

38. Postmillennialism, as well as the perfectionist impulses of the era, also contributed to the moral energy of these projects. For a brief explanation of the influence of such emphases, along with benevolence and revivalism, on antislavery thought, see McKivigan, *War Against Proslavery Religion*, 19–20.

39. Howe, *Political Culture of the American Whigs*, 36. Throughout, Howe stressed the compatibility of Whig values with New England evangelicals and described the Northeast as the "homeland of Whig culture" (p. 5).

40. See, for example, Charles Finney's comment in *Lectures* that if young converts

were "well grounded in gospel principles," they would have "but one heart and one soul in regard to every question of duty that occurs," (p. 426).

41. John L. Hammond studied these classic representatives of New England revivalism in *Politics of Benevolence: Revival Religion and American Voting Behavior* (Norwood, N.J.: Ablex, 1979), an analysis of Finney-inspired abolitionists in Ohio and upstate New York, 1825–1835.

42. The population in New York City increased from about 200,000 to 800,000 from 1830 to 1860. Overall urban population in the United States during the same period grew from about 500,000 to 3.8 million, more than a sevenfold increase. Much of the increase came from German and Irish immigration: during the peak famine years of 1847–1854, 1.2 million Irish immigrants arrived. See Paul Boyer, *Urban Masses and Moral Order in America, 1820–1920* (Cambridge: Harvard University Press, 1978), 67.

43. Theodore Fiske Savage, *The Presbyterian Church in New York City* (New York: Presbytery of New York, 1949), 31.

44. Finney opposed slavery but did not advocate the "amalgamation" of blacks and whites. His dispute with Tappan paralleled similar debates with Theodore Weld at Oberlin. Lawrence Thomas Lesick, "The Lane Rebels: Evangelicalism and Antislavery in Antebellum America" (Ph.D. diss., Syracuse University, 1968), 218–27.

45. Lewis Tappan to S. D. Hastings, April 11, 1841, quoted in Cole, "Free Church Movement," 295.

46. Ibid.

47. Finney, *Lectures*, 303. The most comprehensive study of the ties between New York City commercial interests and the South is still Philip S. Foner, *Business and Slavery; the New York Merchants and the Irrepressible Conflict* (Chapel Hill: University of North Carolina Press, 1941).

48. *The Courier and Enquirer*, July 8, 1833, quoted in Hardman, "Finney and the Free Church Movement," 429.

49. For the identification of a number of Free churches and their leaders with the antislavery cause, see Cole, "Free Church Movement," 293–94. McKivigan, *War Against Proslavery Religion*, concluded that "the bitterness of the debate in the churches during the 1830s between the abolitionists and other northerners who regarded themselves as genuine opponents of slavery produced such a polarization of attitudes that subsequent concessions by either side seemed almost impossible" (p. 54).

50. S. D. Burchard, "History of the 13th St. Presbyterian Church by its first pastor," in New York City. Thirteenth St. Presbyterian Church Session Minutes, 1846–, Presbyterian Historical Society, Philadelphia.

51. Ibid.

52. Hardman, "Finney and the Free Church Movement," lists the need for a better location and a building "whose acoustics and appearance would be first-rate" as major reasons for the new church (p. 434).

53. For example, the First Free Presbyterian Church was dissolved in 1838; Chatham Chapel in 1841 (it became Congregational and moved locations); most of the Third Free Church moved to Thirteenth Street in 1846, though a remnant struggled in the old location until 1858; and the Fourth Free Church disbanded in 1842. See Savage, *Presbyterian Church*, 159–62.

54. Carwardine, *Evangelicals and Politics*, 320–22, and *passim*; Lori D. Ginzberg, *Women and the Work of Benevolence: Morality, Politics, and Class in the Nineteenth-Century United States* (New Haven: Yale University Press, 1990), chapter 4, chronicles

the increasing shift from moral influence to political activism among Protestant reformers during the 1840s and 1850s.

55. For Beecher's activities on behalf of prohibition and later Frémont, see Carwardine, *Evangelicals and Politics*, 216, 268. The *National Anti-Slavery Standard*, April 10, 1858, registered its disapproval of Beecher's pietistic stance during the revival.

56. Clifford E. Clark, Jr., *Henry Ward Beecher: Spokesman for a Middle-Class America* (Urbana: University of Illinois Press, 1978), 135.

57. William G. McLoughlin, *The Meaning of Henry Ward Beecher: An Essay on the Shifting Values of Mid-Victorian America, 1840–1870* (New York: Knopf, 1970), 112–13. Historians are divided in their assessments of Beecher's involvement in social reform. The point here is that by 1858 he clearly had separated reform from revivalism.

58. For examples of early opposition, see Wyatt-Brown, *Lewis Tappan*, 60–68.

59. Robert M. York, "George B. Cheever, Religious and Social Reformer," *University of Maine Bulletin* (April 1955) in *University of Maine Studies*, 2nd. ser., no. 69, 127. Both the *Evangelist and Independent* newspapers were founded in part to defend Yankee interests in the face of the *Observer* and the New York establishment. When I speak of an "establishment," I am referring to the *New York Observer* and, in the late 1850s, such social conservatives as Presbyterians Gardiner Spring, S. I. Prime, J. W. Alexander, and Dutch Reformed ministers Thomas De Witt and George W. Bethune.

60. "The Revival," *Harper's Weekly* 2 (April 3, 1858): 210. Two and sometimes three prayer meetings met in lecture rooms on different floors of the North Dutch Church consistory building, next to the sanctuary.

61. Ibid.

62. Apart from those coordinated by the YMCA, revival prayer meetings generally were organized independently by churches, groups of ministers, or laypeople. It is very difficult to determine the actual number of meetings even in New York City at any given time. Estimates for urban New York range from 20 to 150. The lower figure, cited by Timothy Smith, *Revivalism and Social Reform*, 64, probably is a good estimate for the number of noon meetings in the city at the height of the revival; the higher figure, from Samuel Irenaeus Prime, *The Power of Prayer, Illustrated in the Wonderful Displays of Divine Grace at the Fulton Street and Other Meetings* (New York: Scribner, 1858), 46, could approximate the total number of prayer meetings held throughout the revival period in both New York City and Brooklyn.

63. *New York Observer*, April 22, 1858.

64. Ibid.

65. For Prime's role at the *Observer*, see Samuel Irenaeus Prime, *Autobiography and Memorials*, ed. Wendell Prime (New York: Anson D. F. Randolph, 1888), 231–35.

66. Lois Banner, "Religious Benevolence as Social Control: A Critique of an Interpretation," *Journal of American History*, 60 (June 1973): 27. Also, the moderate Presbyterian linkage between pure revivals and a true doctrine made it difficult to conceptualize a genuine spiritual awakening among people who had not been catechized.

67. Sprague, "Appendix," *Lectures on Revivals*, 1–8, 22–44.

68. Ibid., 62–63.

69. Ibid., 4–5.

70. James W. Alexander, "The Holy Flock," in [Samuel Irenaeus Prime, ed.,] *The*

New York Pulpit in the Revival of 1858: A Memorial Volume of Sermons (New York: Sheldon, Blakeman, 1858), 15.

71. Ibid., 28–29.

72. See, for example, the contrast Charles Hodge made between the salutary moral influence of true doctrines and the pernicious influence of false ones in his analysis of abolitionism. Hodge, "Abolitionism," *Biblical Repertory and Princeton Review*, 2nd ser., 16 (1844), 550.

73. In response to the Compromise of 1850 and the Fugitive Slave Law, appeal to conscience and a "higher [divine] law" became an increasingly powerful argument among "free-soil evangelicals" in the early 1850s. Carwardine, *Evangelicals and Politics*, 176–80.

74. Hodge, "Abolitionism," 554. Hodge did acknowledge that the laws regulating slavery and their application could be evil, (pp. 572–81). I am indebted to Robert Bruce Mullin for his analysis of the retreat from "moral considerations" by scholars at Princeton and Andover seminaries in their concern to protect the authority of the biblical text from the influence of Unitarian rationalism and the related social conservatism of their stances toward slavery. See Mullin, "Biblical Critics and the Battle Over Slavery, *Journal of Presbyterian History* 61 (Summer 1983): 210–26.

75. Samuel Irenaeus Prime, "Only Two Parties," *New York Observer*, February 25, 1858. Prime's stress on constitutionalism was in part a reference to the tract society controversy. See chapter 6, pp. 114–17.

76. These "Unionist evangelicals" identified respect for law and the constitution with respect for the God-ordained American Union. Carwardine, *Evangelicals and Politics*, 182–83.

77. Conant, *Narratives*, 380–82, reprints one such guide.

78. Talbot W. Chambers, *The Noon Prayer Meeting of the North Dutch Church* (New York: Board of Publication, Reformed Protestant Dutch Church, 1858), 47.

79. S. May, *Some Recollections of the Anti-Slavery Conflict*, 127–28, quoted in Foner, *Business and Slavery*, 14; see also, Carwardine, *Evangelicals and Politics*, 180–81.

80. For Presbyterian influence in these groups, see Clifford S. Griffin, *Their Brothers' Keepers: Moral Stewardship in the United States, 1800–1865* (New Brunswick: Rutgers University Press, 1960), 46–47, also Banner, "Religious Benevolence," 27.

81. Kuykendall, *Southern Enterprize*, 123, quoting the *Twenty-eighth Annual Report, American Tract Society*, 1853.

82. Social conservatives in both Old and New School Presbyterian denominations shared this pride, although the focus here is on the Old School conservatives. Carwardine, *Evangelicals and Politics*, 186.

83. Kuykendall, *Southern Enterprize*, 147, quoting the *Thirty-third Annual Report, American Sunday School Union*, 1857.

84. Prime, *Power of Prayer*, 56. The Fulton Street prayer meeting remained the most prominent symbol of the 1857–58 Revival at least until Prime's death in 1885, due in no small measure to the publicity he gave the ongoing meeting in the pages of the *Observer* and through the four books, *Power of Prayer* (1858), *Five Years of Prayer* (1864), *Fifteen Years of Prayer in the Fulton Street Meeting* (1872), and *Prayer and Its Answer* (1882), that he wrote from those accounts. According to Marvin D. Hoff, "The Fulton Street Prayer Meeting," *Reformed Review* 17 (September 1963): 37, the Fulton Street prayer meeting survived in various locations, sometimes struggling, until 1960.

85. Chambers, *Noon Prayer Meeting*, 34. At the time he was hired, Lanphier was a member of the Nineteenth Street Presbyterian Church (Old School), where J. W. Alexander was pastor. Born in 1809, Lanphier had come to New York City in the late 1830s to pursue a business career. In 1842, he made a public profession of Christian faith at the Broadway Tabernacle.

86. Ibid., 35. By 1858, with the exception of such landmarks as Trinity Church (Episcopal) and Methodism's historic John Street Church, many Protestant churches, including the prestigious Brick Presbyterian and the Broadway Tabernacle, had followed their parishioners out of lower Manhattan.

87. Ibid., 35, 38.

88. "The Origin and Methods of the Fulton Street Prayer-Meeting—An Interview with the Founder and Manager, J. C. Lamphier [sic]," *The Preacher and Homiletic Monthly* 3 (October 1878 to September 1879), 225. Lanphier had distributed a flier throughout the downtown area that indicated the meeting was "to give merchants, mechanics, clerks, strangers and business men generally" an opportunity to pray at midday. Chambers, *Noon Prayer Meeting*, 42.

89. John O. Foster, *Life and Labors of Mrs. Maggie Newton Van Cott* (Cincinnati: Hitchcock and Waldon, 1872), 58–60. Based on the sequence of events in Van Cott's biography, this incident probably took place in the early 1860s. However, it was not an isolated occurrence. As chapter 4 indicated, part of the problem at Fulton Street was an ambivalence among the public over whether the meeting was a businessmen's prayer meeting or a union prayer meeting open to all. See Chambers, *Noon Prayer Meeting*, 41; cf. partial listing of prayer meetings in Prime, *Power of Prayer*, 45. A few meetings were designated for "ladies," "colored," "workingmen," and "merchants," though Fulton Street was not so identified.

90. *New York Daily Tribune*, March 27, 1858. Of course, the *Tribune*'s editor, Horace Greeley, was sympathetic to blacks and antagonistic to the city's conservative establishment, including Prime, the *Observer*, and the businessmen of the Fulton Street meeting. It was not surprising he printed the letter. I have found no other evidence of such incidents at Fulton Street, although accounts of similarly rigid treatment of women lend credibility to the letter.

91. Prime, *Power of Prayer*, 48, 52.

92. Ibid., 52, 55.

93. Charles P. McIlvaine, *Bishop McIlvaine's Address to the Convention of the Diocese of Ohio, on the Revival of Religion* (Cincinnati: C. F. Bradley, 1858), 21–23, 26. For more on McIlvaine's millennial hopes in connection with the 1857–58 Revival, see Diana Hochsted Butler, *Standing Against the Whirlwind: Evangelical Episcopalians in Nineteenth-Century America* (New York: Oxford University Press, 1995), 158–63.

94. James W. Alexander, "The Holy Flock," in *New York Pulpit*, 32.

95. Richard Carwardine, *Evangelicals and Politics*, 14, 124–26, has emphasized that, although "conservative pietists" were common in these denominations, members of the northern branches in particular represented a spectrum of social and political views. However, the successful urbanites most identified with the 1857–58 Revival, such as Francis Wayland for the Baptists and Phoebe Palmer, Nathan Bangs, and Abel Stevens for the Methodists, did represent the conservative pietist wing of these churches.

96. Henry Clay Fish, *Primitive Piety Revived* (Boston: Congregational Board of Publication, 1855), 195, quoted in Moorhead, *American Apocalypse*, 11–12.

97. *The Doctrines and Discipline of the Methodist Episcopal Church* (New York: Carlton and Porter, 1856), iv. This is not to deny the political activism of a significant

number in a denomination as large as the Methodists. Still the pietistic Methodist heritage proved compatible with social conservatism for those who might be classified as "Unionist evangelicals" as the denomination became more prosperous.

98. Richey, "History as a Bearer of Denominational Identity: Methodism as a Case Study," in *Beyond Establishment: Protestant Identity in a Post-Protestant Age*, ed. Jackson W. Carroll and Wade Clark Roof (Louisville: Westminster/John Knox Press, 1993), 276, based on an analysis of Nathan Bangs. For a detailed exploration of Methodists and politics during the antebellum years, see Carwardine, *Evangelicals and Politics*. The enduring affinity of many grassroots Methodists for the Democratic party, with its essentially laissez-faire philosophy, reflected the denomination's pietistic heritage and distrust of imperialistic Yankee Calvinists. *Evangelicals and Politics*, 113, 273–76, and *passim*.

99. "A Laity for the Times," *Christian Advocate and Journal*, February 12, 1857, and March 12, 1857.

100. Smith, *Revivalism and Social Reform*, 192.

101. Chambers, *Noon Prayer Meeting*, 246. Bangs shared the platform with a group of ministers who exemplified the generally conservative tenor of the Fulton Street meeting: Dutch Reformed minister Thomas De Witt; Old School Presbyterians John M. Krebs and Gardiner Spring; New School Presbyterians Asa D. Smith and William Adams; and Baptist A. D. Gillette.

102. Richard E. Herrmann, "Nathan Bangs: Apologist for American Methodism," (Ph.D. diss., Emory University, 1973), 205.

103. Abel Stevens, "American Slavery—Its Progress and Prospects," *Methodist Review* 39 (1857), 460. Stevens (1815–1897) considered slavery essentially a southern problem; gradual emancipation could be achieved first in the Border States, then in the deep South if the North would moderate its self-righteous attacks. See also Smith, *Revivalism and Social Reform*, 192–93; McKivigan, *War Against Proslavery Religion*, 171.

104. C. Howard Hopkins, *History of the Y.M.C.A. in North America* (New York: Association Press, 1951), 76–77, also Smith, *Revivalism and Social Reform*, 193. During his speech in Paris, Stevens expressed the hope that a union of YMCAs would promote Christian unity in the United States despite abolitionist agitation.

105. *Christian Advocate and Journal*, April 15, 1858.

106. See, for example, Chambers, *Noon Prayer Meeting*, 281–308, passim; McIlvaine, *Bishop McIlvaine's Address*, 12–16; *Christian Advocate and Journal*, March 25, 1858, April 1, 1858, and April 15, 1858; *New York Observer*, April 1, 1858; and *Watchman and Reflector*, March 25, 1858.

107. Butler, *Standing Against the Whirlwind*, 175, n. 133, makes a similar point in her analysis of McIlvaine's evaluation of the revival. As Butler observes, the shift away from Edwards reflected the pervasive and often unrecognized influence of Finney's "objective" and "scientific" approach to revivalism. However, in 1857–58 it also reflected the influence of the press in shaping public perceptions of the revival: these were characteristics that could be observed by eager religious and secular reporters.

108. I am referring to the American branch of the Evangelical Alliance, formed in 1867. Interest in Protestant unity as well as the original British call for such an Alliance predated the revival by more than a decade and was affected by many factors. Even so, the unity enjoyed in 1857–58 did contribute to the establishment of the American branch.

109. Prime, *Power of Prayer*, 54.

110. Alexander, "The Holy Flock," 32.

111. Sweet, " 'A Nation Born Again,' " 210.

112. *Watchman and Reflector*, March 25, 1858.

Six. Critiques of the Revival's Social Impact

1. There also was some criticism of the northern revival among southerners, usually those who thought northern clergy were trying to politicize the revival or use it as an evidence of Yankee superiority. See, for example, the *Charleston Daily Courier*, May 6, 1858; also Russell E. Francis, "Pentecost: 1858, A Study in Religious Revivalism" (Ph. D. diss., University of Pennsylvania, 1948), chapter 6, nn. 7–10.

2. Timothy L. Smith, *Revivalism and Social Reform: American Protestantism on the Eve of the Civil War* (Nashville: Abingdon Press, 1957), 86–87, 215, dismissed Parker and claimed Cheever as a socially involved evangelical but ignored his criticism of the revival. Leonard I. Sweet, " 'A Nation Born Again': The Union Prayer Meeting Revival and Cultural Revitalization" in *The Great Tradition: In Honor of Winthrop S. Hudson, Essays on Pluralism, Voluntarism, and Revivalism*, ed. Joseph D. Ban and Paul R. Dekar (Valley Forge, Penn.: Judson, 1982), 210, was more balanced in his treatment of Cheever but did not mention Parker.

3. Theodore Parker, *A False and True Revival of Religion* (Boston: W. L. Kent, 1858), 10.

4. Ibid., 11.

5. Theodore Parker, *The Revival of Religion Which We Need* (Boston: W. L. Kent, 1858), 6.

6. Sydney E. Ahlstrom, *A Religious History of the American People* (New Haven: Yale University Press, 1972), 606–07.

7. Smith, *Revivalism and Social Reform*, 86–87.

8. Parker, *Revival of Religion*, 11. For Adams, see Robert Cholerton Senior, "New England Congregationalists and the Anti-Slavery Movement, 1830–1860" (Ph.D. diss., Yale University, 1954), 392–94, also *New York Observer*, April 1, 1858. Parker did not mention Adams by name, but the reference was clear.

9. John Weiss, *Life and Correspondence of Theodore Parker*, vol. 2 (New York: D. Appleton, 1864), 250–52. The most complete accounts of this incident are found in Parker's journal, cited by Weiss and by Octavius Brooks Frothingham, *Theodore Parker* (New York: G. P. Putnam's Sons, 1886), 494–96. Charles Finney, who apparently was the first to encourage public prayer for Parker during his visit to Boston in spring 1857, related a version of the incident in his memoirs, though it was deleted by his editor from the 1876 edition. Finney's comments reflected the tacit evangelical conviction that Parker's death in May 1860 vindicated their prayers. See restored text and notes in Charles G. Finney, *The Memoirs of Charles G. Finney*, ed. Garth M. Rosell and Richard A. G. Dupuis (Grand Rapids: Academic Books/Zondervan, 1989), 566–68. See also *National Anti-Slavery Standard*, April 10, 1858.

10. For an explanation of this view, see George M. Marsden, *Fundamentalism and American Culture: The Shaping of Twentieth-Century Evangelicalism, 1870–1925* (New York: Oxford University Press, 1980), 50.

11. For example, evangelical members of the American Peace Society or of the American Female Moral Reform Society.

12. For examples of such incidents in Boston, similar to those in New York City, see "Prayer and the Card-Table" and "Drunkard Converted," *The Old South Chapel Prayer Meeting* (Boston: Tilton, 1859), 140–41, 154–55.

13. The *Boston Evening Transcript*, March 27, 1858, reported an incident when

a city missionary, probably a Unitarian, spoke in one of the prayer meetings. Immediately following, "one of the more zealous brethren . . . announced to the meeting that the last speaker was not a 'Bible Christian,' and proposed prayers for his conversion."

14. Cheever (1807–1890) was the son of Nathaniel Cheever, a trader and publisher in Hallowell, Maine, and Charlotte Barrell Cheever, both from respected New England families. The best source of information on Cheever is Robert M. York, "George B. Cheever, Religious and Social Reformer," *University of Maine Bulletin* (April 1955), in *University of Main Studies*, 2nd. ser., no. 69, 1–237.

15. *Evangelist*, June 19, 1845. See also Hugh Davis, "The New York *Evangelist*, New School Presbyterians and Slavery, 1837–1857," *American Presbyterian* 68 (Spring 1990), 20.

16. George B. Cheever, *The Christian's Duty, in a Time of Revival* (New York: Dunn Brothers, 1858). A Christian's duty, according to Cheever, p. 22, was to pray fervently and to act fervently for the salvation of souls. Cheever followed the Puritan custom of preaching "regular" (pietistic) sermons on Sunday mornings and "social" (societal) sermons Sunday evenings and during midweek lectures. This was his morning sermon, April 4, 1858.

17. *National Anti-Slavery Standard*, May 22, 1858.

18. York, "Cheever," 156. Cheever had promised Franklin Pierce, a former college mate, a "warm reception in hell" for his prosouthern actions in the Kansas conflict; he insinuated that Chief Justice Roger B. Taney, a Catholic, was part of a "Papal conspiracy to steal the people's liberties" for his decision in the Dred Scott case; and he described wealthy members of his congregation who disagreed with his antislavery preaching as "hypocrites," and "white sepulchres, full of dead men's bones and all uncleanliness." Quotations regarding Pierce and Taney are from York, 144, 148. Quotations regarding the congregation are citations in York, 154, from *A Narrative of Recent Occurrences* by the ousted church members.

19. The letter requesting Cheever's resignation was presented April 27, 1857, on the heels of his Dred Scott lectures. At issue were both Cheever's political preaching and his high-handed methods. A bitter church dispute continued for the next four years, both sides making their cases in private and in the religious press. Cheever never stepped down, but Church of the Puritans was weakened beyond recovery and effectively ceased to exist when the church property was sold in 1867. York, "Cheever," 150–56, 204–05.

20. George B. Cheever to Elizabeth B. Cheever, April 17, 1858, Cheever family papers. Cheever never completely repudiated the revival. In addition to his personal commitment to revival piety, religious fervor both in his church and in his brother Henry's church in Jewett City, Connecticut, validated the spirituality of both men for fellow evangelicals in spite of their antislavery activities.

21. *Independent*, June 3, 1858. These points are based on an analysis of Cheever's major sermons during spring and early summer 1858 that dealt with the public role of revivalism. They included, "The Two Revivals," *Independent*, March 4, 1858; "The Fire and Hammer of God's Word Upon Slavery and Its Abettors," *National Anti-Slavery Standard*, May 22, 1858; "Rev. Dr. Cheever on the Tract Society," *Independent*, June 3, 1858; and George B. Cheever, *The Commission from God Against the Sin of Slavery* (Boston: 1858).

22. Philip S. Foner, *Business and Slavery: the New York Merchants and the Irrepressible Conflict* (Chapel Hill: University of North Carolina Press, 1941), 150–53. Foner attributed the surge of support to (1) the merchants' desire in the wake of the

financial panic to conclude the Kansas controversy so that economic issues could be faced, and (2) their particular need to cultivate southern trade during the weak economic climate.

23. *Independent*, March 4, 1858.

24. Ibid.

25. Ibid.

26. *Independent*, June 3, 1858. Of course, this position vindicated Cheever's own actions as a minister; also, embroiled as he was in conflict with lay leaders in his church, he was in no mood to extol laity.

27. Cheever, *Commission from God*, 13.

28. Except as otherwise indicated, my narrative of the ATS conflict is based on Clifford S. Griffin, "The Abolitionists and the Benevolent Societies, 1831–1861," *Journal of Negro History*, 44 (July 1959): 195–216, and John R. McKivigan, *The War Against Proslavery Religion: Abolitionism and the Northern Churches, 1830–1865* (Ithaca: Cornell University Press, 1984), 119–22.

29. For example, "Debauchery of Conscience by the Policy of the Tract Society," Cheever's editorial in the *Independent*, February 4, 1858.

30. John W. Kuykendall, *Southern Enterprize: The Work of National Evangelical Societies in the Antebellum South* (Westport, Conn.: Greenwood Press, 1982), 137–38.

31. *National Anti-Slavery Standard*, June 5, 1858. The analysis in this paragraph is based largely on a report in the *Standard* of a preliminary meeting by the "reformers" of the ATS two days before the anniversary. It is safe to assume that many of those attending participated in the revival. A range of antislavery views was expressed with representatives from New England (Maine, Massachusetts) and the West (Illinois) most strongly abolitionist, certainly in contrast to the urban conservatives who have been the subject of this chapter. The *Standard* gave a detailed, if critical, account of the meeting, including participants and the range of opinions expressed.

32. Once again, the breakdown between reformers and conservatives paralleled that between "conscience evangelicals" and "unionist evangelicals."

33. Women as well as men could be either lifetime "directors" of the organization for a contribution of 50 dollars or more or lifetime members for 20 dollars. Women, however, were not allowed to vote. Because the stakes were so high, only voting members were given tickets to enter the 1858 meeting.

34. *National Anti-Slavery Standard*, May 22, 1858. The *Independent*, May 13, 1858, described the scene as "such uproar as is more appropriate to Tammany Hall than to a house of worship." Both sources, of course, were biased against the majority, but transcripts indicated the meeting did get out of hand. Cf. *New York Daily Tribune*, May 13, 1858.

35. For an example of such criticism, see comments by William T. Eustis, *Independent*, May 20, 1858. Foner, *Business and Slavery*, 100–105, 143–48, provided support for this analysis although he did not specifically discuss the ATS meeting. Of course, many delegates also shared the commitment of their ministers to the ideal of preserving Christian unity and the national Union. However, since William Jay's 1853 attack in *Letter to the American Tract Society*, the ATS had been seen by Christian abolitionists as a tool of its wealthy supporters, both southerners and northern merchants.

36. Because the meeting lasted more than six hours, most published reports are selective and designed to support the side represented by the publishing agency. My account is based on reports in the *New York Daily Tribune*, May 13, 1858; the *Na-*

tional Anti-Slavery Standard, May 22, 1858; the *Independent*, May 13, 1858; and the *Thirty-Third Annual Report of the American Tract Society* (New York: American Tract Society, 1858).

37. "Bishop McIlvaine's Address," *Thirty-Third Annual Report*, 199, 201.

38. Cf. [Samuel Irenaeus Prime, ed.], *The New York Pulpit in the Revival of 1858: A Memorial Volume of Sermons* (New York: Sheldon, Blakeman, 1858), 61, 171, 382.

39. *Independent*, May 20, 1858.

40. Cheever, *Commission from God*, 22.

41. *Independent*, June 3, 1858. On May 4, 1858, Congress had passed a compromise bill that would admit Kansas to the Union if the state would ratify the Lecompton constitution. Kansans rejected the constitution in August, and the state was not admitted to the Union until 1861.

42. Cheever, *Commission from God*, 22. An anonymous author, thought by some to be Theodore Parker, made a similar allusion in "The American Tract Society," *Atlantic* (July 1858): 248.

43. The ATS constitution stated its purpose as "to diffuse a knowledge of our Lord Jesus Christ as the Redeemer of sinners, and to promote the interests of vital godliness and sound morality" (p. 249), *Thirty-Third Annual Report*. For the doctrines set forth as "the basis of our union" when the organization was formed in 1825, see *Address of the Executive Committee*, cited in Stephen E. Slocum, Jr., "The American Tract Society: 1825–1975: An Evangelical Effort to Influence the Religious and Moral Life of the United States" (Ph.D. diss., New York University, 1975), 47–48.

44. I refer to Moody's often-quoted statement: "I look on this world as a wrecked vessel. God has given me a life-boat, and said to me, 'Moody, save all you can.'" From *New Sermons, Addresses, and Prayers*, quoted in James F. Findlay, *Dwight L. Moody: American Evangelist, 1837–1899* (Chicago: University of Chicago Press, 1969), 253. The intense concern for evangelism fostered by the 1857–58 Revival probably helped create a climate among northern evangelicals conducive to the spread of premillennial ideas. See Findlay, 253, n. 54.

45. Sweet, " 'A Nation Born Again,' " commented, "Whereas the first phase of the revival witnessed religion helping to revitalize American culture, the conclusion of the revival helped to send two sections toward their gruesome collision, bathing the ensuing carnage with God's blessing and benediction" (p. 212). I differ from Sweet in my argument that the revival originally was a de facto retreat from culture but agree with his analysis of its role in the sectional conflict. See also a similar assessment of the revival eventually hardening sectional lines in Richard J. Carwardine, *Evangelicals and Politics in Antebellum America* (New Haven: Yale University Press, 1993), 294–95.

46. James A. Thome, *Prayer for the Oppressed* (Boston: American Tract Society: [1859], 21.

47. The Church Anti-Slavery Society, formed by George and Henry Cheever, was an interdenominational abolitionist association exclusively for Protestant church members. Although heavily dominated by Congregationalists, it did serve as a central clearinghouse for Protestant abolitionist activities immediately before and during the Civil War. See McKivigan, *War Against Proslavery Religion*, 137–41.

48. Ibid., 140.

49. In an intriguing statement, seemingly revising his previous work, Timothy Smith seemed to make this suggestion. He commented that the social impact of the publicized events of 1858 "actually ran counter to the reformist tendencies that the steady growth of revivalism in congregational and regional settings had generated

and sustained across the previous fifty years. And widespread occurrences of local revivals continued to nurture these reformist tendencies during the succeeding three decades, when Dwight Moody's international fame served to obscure the currents of spirituality and moral commitment that were stirring at congregational levels" (p. 120), "Response of Professor Smith on Cycles of National Awakenings," *Sociological Analysis* 44 (1983). Smith offered no specific evidence of such a grassroots phenomenon.

50. Marsden, *Fundamentalism and American Culture*, 86.

51. Carwardine, *Evangelicals and Politics*, 297–303. Anti-Catholicism, as Carwardine noted earlier in the same work, was closely tied in evangelical minds to the social problems associated with the influx of immigration, including the Catholic/immigrant challenge to "Protestant" public education and to temperance.

52. Although the issue of slavery popularized the use of the "gag rule" in politics as well as religion, a tacit prohibition on controversial issues had long been the rule in evangelical benevolent societies, particularly the more conservative ones, such as the tract society and the American Bible Society, which, for example, had always emphasized its commitment to publish and distribute Bibles "without note or comment" (p. 47), quoted in Slocum, "The American Tract Society." For evangelical opposition to proslavery gag laws in the U.S. Congress, see Carwardine, *Evangelicals and Politics*, 135, 137, 143.

53. In a revival as diffuse as that of 1857–58, there certainly were a few such ministers, especially in the New England states, but they rarely had an impact on the broader, public revival. By "radical holiness," I mean the "Nazarites" in the Genesee Conference of Northern Methodism during the 1840s and 1850s, who associated holiness with abolition and a return to primitive Methodist simplicity. Their withdrawal in 1860 to form the Free Methodist Church apparently had as much to do with Methodist discipline, church politics, and personalities as holiness. The 1857–58 Revival seemingly had little impact on events leading up to the schism; it certainly did not lead to an accord on the social implications of sanctification. Smith makes no connection between the Nazarites and the revival, *Revivalism and Social Reform*, 129–33; cf. Walter W. Benjamin, "The Free Methodists," in Emory Stephens Bucke, ed., *The History of American Methodism: In Three Volumes*, vol. 2 (New York: Abingdon Press, 1964), 339–60.

54. William Boardman's *The Higher Christian Life* (Boston: Henry Hoyt, 1858), a popular exposition of "Reformed" holiness teachings written in the midst of the 1857–58 Revival, itself carried little ethical emphasis. Picking up on revival themes, Boardman stressed the "unity, activity and spirituality" that would come from full trust in Jesus, but the "activity" he had in mind primarily was increased evangelization. See, for example, pp. 232–33. There is no record of any role Boardman played in the 1857–58 Revival; apparently he was writing *Higher Christian Life* during that period. Mrs. W. E. Boardman, *Life and Labors of the Rev. W. E. Boardman* (New York: D. Appleton, 1887), 101–05. Marsden, *Fundamentalism and American Culture*, 72–80, provides a summary of the spread of holiness teachings during the last third of the nineteenth century.

55. William R. Glass, "Liberal Means to Conservative Ends: Bethany Presbyterian Church, John Wanamaker and the Institutional Church Movement" *American Presbyterian* 68 (Fall 1990), 189. The YWCA "directed its main energies to supplying the needs of middle-class women" (p. 45), Aaron Abell, *The Urban Impact on American Protestantism, 1865–1900* (Cambridge: Harvard University Press, 1943). Even A. B. Simpson, whose Christian and Missionary Alliance sponsored a wide range of urban

programs, insisted that his initial Gospel Tabernacle Church, begun in the early 1880s in New York City, "was not designed as a mission to the lowest and vicious classes, but as a self-supporting work among the middle classes, who have no church home" (p. 94), A. E. Thompson, *A. B. Simpson: His Life and Work* (Harrisburg, Penn.: Christian Publications, 1960).

56. C. Howard Hopkins, *History of the Y.M.C.A. in North America* (New York: Association Press, 1951), 83–84, quoting the *Young Men's Christian Journal* 4 (May 1859), 118–19, and the *Young Men's Magazine* 2 (November 1858), 328–29.

57. Hopkins, *History of the Y.M.C.A.*, 69, 17–18.

58. Lemuel Moss, *Annals of the United States Christian Commission* (Philadelphia: J. B. Lippincott, 1868), 81. Moss dedicated his 752-page history to "the Young Men's Christian Associations of the United States, by whose action the United States Christian Commission was constituted." See also [W. E. Boardman, et. al.], *Christ in the Army* (Philadelphia: J. B. Rogers, 1865), 17–20.

59. Minutes of the Executive Committee (14 April 1864) in United States Christian Commission Records, Record Group 94, no. 753, National Archives, Washington, D.C., quoted in Gardiner H. Shattuck, *A Shield and Hiding Place: The Religious Life of the Civil War Armies* (Macon, Ga.: Mercer University Press, 1987), 26.

60. "Table V—Summary of Labors and Distributions," Moss, *Annals*, 729. The Table lists 39 million pages of tracts distributed. To estimate the actual number of tracts, the number of pages was divided by 16, the length of an average tract. For an account of the experiences of a Methodist minister, active in the 1857–58 Revival, who served in the USCC, see Henry B. Ridgaway, *The Life of the Rev. Alfred Cookman* (London: Hodder and Stoughton, 1873), 258–74.

61. Moss, *Annals*, 107.

62. George H. Stuart, *The Life of George H. Stuart*, ed. Robert Ellis Thompson (Philadelphia: J. M. Stoddart, 1890), 129.

63. James O. Henry, "The United States Christian Commission in the Civil War," *Civil War History* 6 (1960): 383, quoting Charles Demond, *Address Before the Society of Alumni of Williams College* (Boston: 1865), 24, and the USCC *First Annual Report*, 21.

64. Hopkins, *History of the Y.M.C.A.*, 113, quoting the YMCA Convention 1866, pp. 19–20.

65. Ibid., 190–93. Hopkins provides a detailed account of such activities.

66. Ibid., 189, quoting *Association Men*, 25 (July 1, 1900), 340–41.

67. "Christian perfection," "holiness," "perfect love," and "sanctification" were all terms that in Wesleyan circles referred to a religious experience after conversion that brought with it an awareness of being constantly saved or kept from all sin.

68. Phoebe Palmer, Harriet Olney, and other women drew from Pentecostal imagery, as discussed in chapter 4; see also *Pentecost; or the Work of God in Philadelphia* (Philadelphia: Parry and McMillan, 1859). Proponents of the awakening as a holiness revival include Smith, *Revivalism and Social Reform*, chapter 9, *passim*; Melvin Easterday Dieter, *The Holiness Revival of the Nineteenth Century* (Metuchen, N.J.: Scarecrow Press, 1980), 58–59; see also Donald Dayton, "From 'Christian Perfection' to the 'Baptism of the Holy Ghost' " in *Aspects of Pentecostal-Charismatic Origins*, ed. Vinson Synan (Plainfield, N.J.: Logos International, 1975), 41–54. For examples of Methodist revival accounts that mentioned "sanctification" or "perfect love," see the *Christian Advocate and Journal*, December 3, 1857, and the *Western Christian Advocate*, February 17, 1858. An editorial in an influential holiness periodical, while celebrating the growing acceptance of holiness teaching during the revival, noted only

five weekly meetings for holiness in New York City at a time when there may have been as many as 100 daily prayer meetings. "Editors' Drawer," *Guide to Holiness* 34 (July to December, 1858), 94. Martha M. Goetzman, "Anomalous Features in the Chicago Prayer Meeting Revival of 1858: The Nature of the Revival as Revealed in Contemporary Newspaper Accounts" (master of arts thesis, Trinity Evangelical Divinity School, Deerfield, Illinois, 1985), 129, notes the absence of references to the doctrine of sanctification in newspaper accounts of the revival in Chicago, both secular and religious.

69. Phoebe Palmer, *The Promise of the Father, or, A Neglected Specialty of the Last Days* (New York: W. C. Palmer, Jr., 1872 [1859]), 155–56. As previously noted, however, Palmer was enthusiastic about the revival in the context of her own meetings in Canada and upstate New York.

70. Harold E. Raser, *Phoebe Palmer, Her Life and Thought* (Lewiston, N.Y.: Edwin Mellen Press, 1987), 212.

71. Ibid., 216.

72. Ibid., 369, n.195. Raser observed that the initial motivation behind Palmer's activities was not so much ethical as psychological, tied into complex nineteenth-century attitudes toward death. She got the idea for the Five Points Mission while riding through the tenement area on the way to her father's burial service in 1847. As Raser pointed out, Palmer responded to the deaths of those close to her by increased activity in service to God.

73. The best account of the initial mission work and the development of the House of Industry is Carroll Smith-Rosenberg, *Religion and the Rise of the American City: The New York City Mission Movement, 1812–1870* (Ithaca: Cornell University Press, 1984), chapter 8. My summary is based on her account. See also Smith, *Revivalism and Social Reform*, 170–71, and Raser, *Phoebe Palmer*, 215.

74. "Anniversary of the Ladies' Home Missionary Society," *Christian Advocate*, May 20, 1858. The report added that "15,000 garments, 704 pairs of shoes, 604 hats, 462 quilts and 285 other articles of bedding have been distributed; 162 children and 155 adults have been placed in good homes." "Placing" adults and children usually meant sending them to live with rural Protestant families. Smith-Rosenberg, *Religion and the City*, 235.

75. "Anniversary," *Christian Advocate*, May 20, 1858.

76. Matthew Hale Smith, *Sunshine and Shadows in New York* (Hartford: J. B. Burr, 1868), 207.

77. Smith-Rosenberg, *Religion and the City*, 232, 235, n. 14.

78. See n. 53 above.

79. Raser, *Phoebe Palmer*, 128, 141–148.

80. For the National Campmeeting Association, see Timothy L. Smith, *Called Unto Holiness, The Story of the Nazarenes: The Formative Years* (Kansas City: Nazarene Publishing House, 1962), 15–18.; also A. McLean and J. W. Eaton, *Penuel, or Face to Face with God* (New York: W. C. Palmer, Jr., 1869), 3–14.

81. Information on Adams (1824?–1902) is from Benjamin M. Adams Diary, 1857, 1858; see also Adams' obituary in *Minutes of the New York East Conference* (New York: Eaton and Mains, 1903): 127–30. Adams's piety, particularly his prayer life, was extolled.

82. Benjamin M. Adams Diary, comments about a "Miss A E." For examples of Adams's revival activities, see the Diary, entries for February 11, 23, 28, as well as April 5 and 6, 1858. On May 12, 1858, Adams noted disagreements in the New York Conference "committee on slavery."

83. This summary of Cookman's life is based on Ridgaway, *Life of the Rev. Alfred Cookman*; see especially 120, 126, 194–202, 218–19, 225–26, 258–74.

84. Ibid., 316; cf. 123.

85. Smith, *Revivalism and Social Reform*, 172, n. 30; see also Marsden, *Fundamentalism and American Culture*, 82. For Tyng's part in supporting New York's 1854 prohibition law, see Carwardine, *Evangelicals and Politics*, 216.

86. Diana Hochstedt Butler, *Standing Against the Whirlwind: Evangelical Episcopalians in Nineteenth-Century America* (New York: Oxford University Press, 1995), 154–55, considers Tyng's conservatism. She notes that in 1853 he referred to *Uncle Tom's Cabin* as "the Stowe farce."

87. Abell, *Urban Impact*, 28.

88. Ibid., 28, 39.

89. Smith, *Revivalism and Social Reform*, 101–02, 159. Smith downplays the recalcitrance of Huntington's parishioners as well as the contribution of Huntington's Unitarian background to his ethical sensitivity.

90. For a discussion of these trends, see Marsden, *Fundamentalism and American Culture*, 85–87. Marsden distinguished in broad terms between the New England "Calvinistic" tradition in its attitude toward the use of politics to advance social reform and the " 'pietistic' view of political action as no more than a means to restrain evil."

91. James H. Moorhead, *American Apocalypse: Yankee Protestants and the Civil War, 1860–1869* (New Haven: Yale University Press, 1978), 80–81, and *passim*.

92. Moss, *Annals*, 63.

93. Moorhead, *American Apocalypse*, 125, 196, 201, 216, noted the social passivity of this "culture-Protestantism."

94. "Revivals," *Moody's Latest Sermons* (Chicago, 1900), 106, 125–26, quoted in Marsden, *Fundamentalism and American Culture*, 38.

95. See, for example, Charles N. Crittenton, *Brother of Girls: The Life Story of Charles N. Crittenton as Told by Himself* (Chicago: World Events, 1910), 72–73.

96. Beecher's novel *Norwood* (New York, 1868), 209–14, contained a classic statement of Beecher's approach to this issue. See William G. McLoughlin, *The Meaning of Henry Ward Beecher: An Essay on the Shifting Values of Mid-Victorian America, 1840–1870* (New York: Alfred A. Knopf, 1970), 112–17; also Marsden, *Fundamentalism and American Culture*, 22–23.

97. Stowe serves as an example of the lingering commitment to social activism, greatly tempered by family and career concerns. See Forrest Wilson, *Crusader in Crinoline: The Life of Harriet Beecher Stowe* (Philadelphia: J. B. Lippincott, 1941), 506–31; also Joan D. Hedrick, *Harriet Beecher Stowe: A Life* (New York: Oxford University Press, 1994), chapter 25. Marie Caskey, *Chariot of Fire: Religion and the Beecher Family* (New Haven Yale University Press, 1993), 195, quoted Stowe's thoughts on the "higher life."

Seven. D. L. Moody and the "Revival Generation"

1. William G. McLoughlin, *Modern Revivalism: Charles Grandison Finney to Billy Graham* (New York: Ronald Press, 1959): 217–233, 239, was one of the first to explore critically the commercial and professional side of the Moody revivals. For more recent appraisals, see George M. Marsden, *Fundamentalism and American Culture: The Shaping of Twentieth-Century Evangelicalism, 1870–1925* (New York: Oxford University Press, 1980), 32–39; Douglas W. Frank, *Less than Conquerors: How Evan-*

gelicals Entered the Twentieth Century (Grand Rapids: Eerdmans, 1986), 169–80; and R. Laurence Moore, *Selling God: American Religion in the Marketplace of Culture* (New York: Oxford University Press, 1994), 184–88. George A. Rawlyk, "Writing about Canadian Religious Revivals," in *Modern Christian Revivals*, ed. Edith L. Blumhofer and Randall Balmer (Urbana: University of Illinois Press, 1993), does not mention Moody, but his criticism of the consumerism and masculinization evident in the Billy Sunday revivals would also apply in a less extreme fashion to Moody. Although he does not emphasize the 1857–58 Revival, Moody biographer James F. Findlay does trace Moody's techniques from his participation in the 1857–58 meetings through a period of refinement during Moody's years as a full-time YMCA staff member to his revival activities of the 1870s. Moody did begin to modify his revivals significantly in 1878, although as late as 1893 continuities could be observed between the patterns of 1858 and Moody's campaign during the Chicago World's Fair. See James F. Findlay, *Dwight L. Moody: American Evangelist, 1837–1899* (Chicago: University of Chicago Press, 1969), 112–15, 303; and, for the World's Fair campaign, James Gilbert, *Perfect Cities: Chicago's Utopias of 1893* (Chicago: University of Chicago Press, 1991), chapter 6.

2. Findlay, *Moody*, 72–74, traced Moody's Sunday school work among poor children. Information about Moody's participation in the revival is sparse, although letters from Moody to various family members during 1857 provide details about religious fervor in Chicago and reflect Moody's enthusiasm for church prayer meetings. See Lyle W. Dorsett, *A Passion for Souls: The Life of D. L. Moody* (Chicago: Moody Press, 1997), chapter 3, and Findlay, *Moody*, 63. For Moody's presence at the urban prayer meetings of 1858, see W. H. Daniels, *D. L. Moody and his Work* (Hartford: American, 1875), 76–77; and John Villiers Farwell, *Early Recollections of Dwight L. Moody* (Chicago: Winona, 1907), 25–26.

3. Although he probably joined earlier, Moody's membership in the YMCA was not officially recorded until 1862, when he was elected a life member. During the 1860s, Moody served as a volunteer "agent" and later president of the Chicago Association. He depended on private contributions for his living expenses. See Findlay *Moody*, 72, n. 37, 101, also 114–15, for Moody and the YMCA noon meeting. Numerous contemporaries credited Moody with the long-term success of the Chicago noon prayer meeting after it had languished when revival enthusiasm dimmed. See, for example, Charles R. Erdman, *D. L. Moody: His Message for Today* (New York: Fleming H. Revell, 1928), 36, and comments of the *Association Men* issue devoted to Moody, vol. 40, no. 5 (February 1915), 234, 238; also William W. R. Moody, *The Life of Dwight L. Moody*, 94.

4. McLoughlin, *Modern Revivalism*, 231.

5. George H. Stuart, *The Life of George H. Stuart*, ed. Robert Ellis Thompson (Philadelphia: J. M. Stoddart, 1890), 280–81.

6. For Moody as a transitional figure in the trend toward "personal empire-building," see Marsden, *Fundamentalism and American Culture*, 34.

7. As evident in the many published conversion narratives, an element of sentimentality was present in the 1857–58 Revival, but it was neither as intense or as publicized as that associated with Moody and Sankey. Later in his career Moody began differentiating between different segments of the urban population based on a range of criteria in addition to gender. During the World's Fair campaign, for example, there were special services for children, young people, young men, foreign tourists, Civil War veterans, and others. See Gilbert, *Perfect Cities*, 186.

8. Most historians of religion in America, both academic and confessional writers, do recognize the popularity and widespread influence of the Moody/Sankey urban revivals, particularly the campaigns between 1875 and 1879. McLoughlin, *Modern Revivalism*, 8, 10, viewed them as one aspect of a third "great awakening" period (1875–1915), a position he later revised in *Revivals, Awakenings, and Reform: An Essay on Religion and Social Change in America, 1607–1977* (Chicago: University of Chicago Press, 1978), 141–45, where the dates of the "Third Great Awakening" were 1890–1920. Post–Civil War revivals, however, have not served as interpretive "markers" or been identified as general or national awakenings in the same way the earlier awakenings were. See n. 33 below.

9. This group represents a different segment of middle-class American culture than the subjects studied by Anne C. Rose in *Victorian America and the Civil War* (Cambridge: Cambridge University Press, 1992), one more clearly northern and evangelical. In contrast to Rose's subjects, many of these young people retained at least some commitment to the revival tradition and mass evangelism as its offspring. Most were young adults at the time of the 1857–58 Revival. In addition to Moody, Smith, and Wanamaker, examples include Lyman Abbott, C. A. Briggs, J. F. Funk, B. F. Jacobs, Lottie Moon, Richard Morse, A. T. Pierson, H. C. Trumbull, and Robert Weidensall. The group also would include a few people who were older but for whom the event was a turning point that decisively affected many of their later activities. John V. Farwell, Samuel Irenaeus Prime, and George H. Stuart would fall in this category.

10. John V. Farwell, Jr., ed., *Some Recollections of Farwell* (Chicago: R. R. Donnelly, 1911), 102–03; Stuart, *Life*, 111–13.

11. Delavan Leonard Pierson, *Arthur T. Pierson* (London: James Nisbit, 1912), 64. A. T. Pierson (1837–1911) was a missions leader, theorist, and educator who popularized the Student Volunteer Movement's "watchword": "The Evangelization of the World in this Generation." See William R. Hutchison, *Errand to the World: American Protestant Thought and Foreign Missions* (Chicago: University of Chicago Press, 1987), 99, n. 11, 113–20.

12. Pierson, *A. T. Pierson*, 66. Pierson was enrolled at Union Theological Seminary at the time, along with William J. Erdman and future Presbyterian missions leader Arthur Mitchell.

13. Ibid., 67, 130. Pierson's own case illustrated the common pattern noted in chapters 3 and 6: he personally sensed a special experience with the Holy Spirit during the revival, but his major concern was "over the unconverted members of his own family and among his friends." Pierson himself did not embrace specific holiness teachings until 1874, when, under the influence of Moody evangelists D. W. Whittle and P. P. Bliss, he placed himself "unreservedly in the hands of God."

14. "Lottie Digges Moon [1840–1912]," *Notable American Women*, 2: 570–71; see also Catherine B. Allen, *The New Lottie Moon Story* (Nashville: Broadman Press, 1980), 34–35.

15. Oswald Eugene Brown and Anna Muse Brown, *Life and Letters of Laura Askew Haygood* [1845–1900], (Nashville: Publishing House of the M. E. Church, South, 1904; reprint New York: Garland, 1987), 21.

16. Sarah Doremus, "First number for the Woman's Union Missionary Society of America, for Heathen Lands," *Missionary Link [Crumbs]* (January 1861), 16–17.

17. For Funk's conversion, see "John F. Funk, Early Diary," January 23, 1858. For later activities, Aaron C. Kolb, "John Fretz Funk, 1835–1930: An Appreciation," *Mennonite Quarterly Review*, 6 (July 1932): 144–55; (October 1932): 251–63; also

Funk's biography by Helen Kolb Gates et al., *Bless the Lord O My Soul: A Biography of Bishop John Fretz Funk, 1835–1930* (Scottdale, Penn.: Herald Press, 1964). In 1892, Funk was ordained a bishop in the Mennonite church.

18. Letter from C. A. Briggs to C. A. Kent, October 11, 1905, cited in Milton Robert Allen, "A History of the Young Men's Christian Association at the University of Virginia," (Ph.D. diss., University of Virginia 1946), 127–28.

19. Richard C. Morse (1841–1926) was converted at Andover during the revival. Robert Weidensall (1836–1922), a key early organizer of American student YMCAs, was also deeply affected by the event. See C. Howard Hopkins, *History of the Y.M.C.A. in North America* (New York: Association Press, 1951), 120–22; also Hopkins, *John R. Mott, 1865–1955: A Biography* (Grand Rapids: Eerdmans, 1979), 53.

20. In making these points, I am indebted to George Marsden, *Fundamentalism and American Culture*, 34, for his discussion of "religion structured according to the free enterprise system" during the Gilded Age.

21. Jack S. Blocker, Jr., *"Give to the Winds Thy Fears:"* The Women's Temperance Crusade, 1873–1874 (Westport, Conn.: Greenwood Press, 1985), 12, 24.

22. Ibid., 90.

23. Annie Wittenmyer, *History of the Woman's Temperance Crusade* (St. Louis: H. M. Brockstedt, 1878), 405. In November 1874, Wittenmyer was elected first president of the Woman's Christian Temperance Union, the institutionalization of the WTC. In 1879, she was defeated by Frances Willard.

24. Ibid., 7–9.

25. Ibid., 407–8.

26. McAuley credited the inspiration to a "sort of trance or vision . . . It seemed as if I was working for the Lord down in the Fourth Ward. I had a house and people were coming in. There was a bath, and as they came in I washed and cleansed them outside, and the Lord cleansed them inside" (p. 37), Robert M. Offord, *Jerry McAuley, His Life and Work* (New York: *New York Observer* [c. 1885]). The Water Street Mission was a model for many of the rescue missions opened in American cities in the 1880s and 1890s. Middle-class evangelicals helped to support these efforts, but most were run by converted criminals or alcoholics: men and women who themselves had been "rescued." See Norris Magnuson, *Salvation in the Slums: Evangelical Social Work, 1865–1920* (Metuchen, N.J.: Scarecrow Press, 1977), 10–13.

27. Offord, *Life*, 183–208. Women as well as men participated freely at Water Street. Of course, such meetings for prayer, testimony, and singing also resembled gatherings at Methodist camp meetings, as well as the holiness meetings popularized by Phoebe Palmer. Through the widespread publicity, the 1857–58 Revival gave legitimacy to the role of laity in organizing and supervising such gatherings.

28. Based on Charles N. Crittenton's autobiography, *The Brother of Girls* (Chicago: World Events, 1910), and Magnuson, *Salvation in the Slums*, 79–81.

29. Marsden, *Fundamentalism and American Culture*, 32–39. There were, of course, in the 1870s as well as today, varieties of American evangelicalism. The 1857–58 Revival most visibly affected what I have described as middle-class, northern "establishment" evangelicals, roughly the same group that was the subject of the Marsden volume. The heirs of this group were northern Fundamentalists and the later neo-evangelicals, or, "Yankee evangelicals," as Joel Carpenter described them. Through his involvement with "Youth for Christ" and later revival work, Southern Baptist preacher Billy Graham penetrated this northern coalition and made it his own. Joel A. Carpenter, "Is 'Evangelical' a Yankee Word?" in *Southern Baptists and American Evangelicals*, ed. David S. Dockery (Nashville: Broadman and Holman, 1993), 87.

30. Other such events in antebellum America might include the Millerite excitement and the publication of *Uncle Tom's Cabin*. Moore, *Selling God*, chapter 5, explores the "market for religious controversy," particularly controversies concerning people or movements outside the Protestant main stream.

31. Ibid., 185. As R. Laurence Moore has pointed out, D. L. Moody "was not the tool of his business sponsors [nor, one might add, of the press], but he was their ideological companion."

32. Frank Luther Mott, *American Journalism* (New York: Macmillan, 1950), 513.

33. "Third" and "Fourth" American Awakenings have been suggested for the Progressive Era and post–World War II period, most forcefully by McLoughlin, *Revivals, Awakenings and Reform*, xiii and *passim*, although he distinguishes between "revivals" as "Protestant rituals" and "awakenings" as "periods of cultural revitalization." There is no consensus on definition, chronological boundaries, or on the extent to which awakenings took place. For a more detailed discussion of the relationship between press coverage and clergy interpretations of the 1857–58 Revival, see Kathryn Teresa Long, "The Revival of 1857–58: The Power of Interpretation" (Ph.D. diss., Duke University, 1993), 259–62; also, Timothy L. Smith, "My Rejection of a Cyclical View of 'Great Awakenings,'" *Sociological Analysis* 44 (1983), 98.

34. Rose, *Victorian America, 34,* n. 40. Edith Blumhofer, "Restoration as Revival: Early American Pentecostalism," in *Modern Christian Revivals*, ed. Edith L. Blumhofer and Randall Balmer (Urbana: University of Illinois Press, 1993), 150–52, notes the sense of worldwide awakening among evangelicals between 1905 and 1907 as news spread of revivals in Wales, India, and in the United States at the Pentecostal Azusa Street Mission in Los Angeles. News of such events, however, remained primarily within the channels of evangelical press networks.

35. Rose, *Victorian America,* 66; see also Mark A. Noll, *A History of Christianity in the United States and Canada* (Grand Rapids: Eerdmans, 1992), 330. The evangelization motto was the watchword of the Student Volunteer Movement; see n. 11.

36. Joan D. Hedrick, *Harriet Beecher Stowe: A Life* (New York: Oxford University Press, 1994), ix.

37. Smith made no secret of his indebtedness to Moody, Sankey, and another Moody associate, D. W. Whittle. See *DAB*, s.v. "Fred Buton Smith"; and Fred B. Smith, *I Remember* (New York: Fleming H. Revell, 1936), 129–36.

38. Michael S. Hamilton, "Women, Public Ministry, and American Fundamentalism, 1920–1950," *Religion and American Culture* 3 (Summer 1993): 172–73, cautions historians against the tendency to confuse prescribed gender roles found in male rhetorical sources with what men and women actually did.

39. By the 1890s, the Woman's Christian Temperance Union and its auxiliaries had a membership of more than 200,000; by 1896 the women's missionary movement had mobilized an estimated 600,000 women, a figure that would quadruple during the next 20 years. Ruth Bordin, *Woman and Temperance: The Quest for Power and Liberty, 1873–1900* (Philadelphia: Temple University Press, 1981), 3–4: and Patricia R. Hill, *The World Their Household: The American Woman's Foreign Mission Movement and Cultural Transformation, 1870–1920* (Ann Arbor: The University of Michigan Press, 1985), 195, n. 1. In 1895, the North American YMCA reported 263,000 members, a small percentage of whom may have been women, Hopkins, *History of the Y.M.C.A.,* 409. For the continuing role of the domestic ideal and women in urban revivals, see Sandra Sizer, [Frankiel], *Gospel Hymns and Social Religion: The Rhetoric of Nineteenth-Century Revivalism* (Philadelphia: Temple University Press, 1978), chapters 5 and 6; and Theckla Ellen Joiner Caldwell, "Women, Men, and Revival: The

Third Awakening in Chicago" (Ph.D. diss., University of Illinois at Chicago, 1991), 74–75, 119–31.

40. See the discussion of Orville Gardner in chapter 2. The argument for a uniquely American "muscular Christianity," shaped by revivalistic Protestants and the dynamics of modern sport, is developed in Tony Ladd and James A. Mathisen, *Muscular Christians: Evangelical Protestants and the Development of American Sport* (forthcoming).

41. Rose, *Victorian America and the Civil War*, 2.

Selected Bibliography

Primary Sources

Manuscripts

Benjamin M. Adams Journal and Papers, Methodist Archives and History Center, Drew University, Madison, New Jersey.

George Beck Diary, Michigan Historical Collections, Bentley Historical Library, University of Michigan, Ann Arbor, Michigan.

Cheever Family Papers, American Antiquarian Society, Worcester, Massachusetts.

John Summerfield Coit Diary, Methodist Archives and History Center, Drew University, Madison, New Jersey.

George Richard Crooks Correspondence, Methodist Archives and History Center, Drew University, Madison, New Jersey.

Forsyth Street Methodist Episcopal Church Records, New York City [microfilm], Manuscript Division, New York City Public Library.

Fourteenth Street Presbyterian Church [New York City] Session Minutes, 1851–1874. Presbyterian Historical Society, Philadelphia, Pennsylvania.

John F. Funk Early Diary, Archives of the Mennonite Church, Goshen, Indiana.

Second Street Methodist Episcopal Church Records, New York City [microfilm], Manuscript Division, New York City Public Library.

Seventh Street Methodist Episcopal Church Records, New York City [microfilm], Manuscript Division, New York City Public Library.

Lewis Tappan Papers [microfilm], Manuscript Division, Library of Congress, Washington, D.C.

Thirteenth St. Presbyterian Church [New York City], Session Minutes, 1846–, Presbyterian Historical Society, Philadelphia, Pennsylvania.

Peter Woods Autobiography, Methodist Archives and History Center, Drew University, Madison, New Jersey.

Periodicals

NEWSPAPERS

Boston Evening Transcript, January–June 1858.
Boston Post, January–June 1858.
Charleston Daily Courier, January–June 1858.
Chicago Daily Democrat, January–June 1858.
Chicago Daily Tribune, January–June 1858.
Chicago Times, January–June 1858.
Cincinnati Daily Enquirer, January–June 1858.
Louisville Daily Courier, January–June 1858.
Louisville Daily Journal, January–June 1858.
New Orleans Daily Picayune, January–June 1858.
New-York Daily Tribune, 1858.
New York Evening Post, January–June 1858.
New York Herald, 1858.
New York Sun, January–June 1858.
New York Times, January–June 1858.
Richmond Enquirer, January–June 1858.
Richmond Whig, January–August 1858.
Savannah Daily Morning News, January–June 1858.

RELIGIOUS WEEKLY PAPERS

Notation in parentheses indicates place of publication and denominational sympathy of the periodical. Not all had official denominational affiliation.

Christian Advocate and Journal (New York City, Methodist), 1856–58.
Christian Times (Chicago, Baptist), August 1857–June 1858.
The Evangelist (New York City, New School Presbyterian), February–July 1858.
The Examiner (New York City, Baptist), 1858.
The Independent (New York City, Congregational), January–June 1858.
Nashville Christian Advocate (MEC, South), 1858.
New York Observer (Old School Presbyterian), 1858.
Pittsburgh Christian Advocate (Methodist), August 1857–June 1858.
Religious Herald (Richmond, Baptist), 1858.
Watchman and Reflector (Boston, Baptist), December 1857–May, 1858.
Western Christian Advocate (Cincinnati, Methodist), December 1857–June 1858.
Western Recorder (Louisville, Baptist), January–October 1858.

OTHER PERIODICALS

American Baptist Almanac (1854–63).
The Congregational Quarterly 1–4 (1859–62).
Journal of the Proceedings of the Bishops, Clergy, and Laity of the Protestant Episcopal Church in the United States of America: Assembled in a General Convention (1859, 1862).

Books

Abbott, Lyman, ed. *Henry Ward Beecher*. New York: Funk and Wagnalls, 1883.

———. *Reminiscences*. Boston: Houghton Mifflin, 1923.

Alexander, James W. *Forty Years' Familiar Letters of James W. Alexander*. Edited by John Hall. New York: Scribner, 1860.

———. *The Revival and Its Lessons*. New York: American Tract Society, 1858.

American Fistiana, Showing the Progress of Pugilism in the United States, from 1816 to 1873. New York: Robert M. DeWitt, 1873.

Baird, Robert. *Religion in the United States of America*. Glasgow: W. G. Blackie, 1844; reprint, New York: Arno Press, 1969.

Bangs, Nathan. *A History of the Methodist Episcopal Church*. Vols. 1, 2. New York: Carlton and Porter, 1840.

Barnes, Albert. *Prayers for the Use of Families*. Philadelphia: Thomas, Cowperthwait, 1850.

[Bingham, Luther Goodyear]. *Memoir of Scovell Hayens McCollum*. New York: Board of Publications of the Reformed Protestant Dutch Church, 1861.

Boardman, Mrs. W. E. *Life and Labors of Rev. W. E. Boardman*. New York: D. Appleton, 1887.

[Boardman, W. E., et al.]. *Christ in the Army*. Philadelphia: J. B. Rogers, 1865.

Boardman, William. *The Higher Christian Life*. Boston: Henry Hoyt, 1858.

Bocock, Sarah Margaret, ed. *Selections from the Religious and Literary Writings of John H. Bocock*. Richmond: Whittet and Shepperson, 1891.

Bureau of the Census. *Seventh Census of the United States: 1850*. Washington, D.C.: Government Printing Office, 1853.

Cammann, Henry J., and Hugh N. Camp. *The Charities of New York, Brooklyn, and Staten Island*. New York: Hurd and Houghton, 1868.

Chambers, Talbot W. *The Noon Prayer Meeting of the North Dutch Church*. New York: Board of Publication, Reformed Protestant Dutch Church, 1858.

Cheney, Mary Bushnell. *The Life and Letters of Horace Bushnell*. New York: Scribner's, 1905.

Conant, William C. *Narratives of Remarkable Conversions and Revival Incidents*. New York: Derby and Jackson, 1858.

Congregational Yearbook. Vols. 2–5. New York: American Congregational Union, 1855–58.

Crittenton, Charles N. *The Brother of Girls: The Life Story of Charles N. Crittenton as Told by Himself*. Chicago: World Events, 1910.

Dadmun, J. W. *Revival Melodies: A Collection of Some of the Most Popular Hymns and Tunes*. Boston: n.p., 1858.

Daniels, W. H. *D. L. Moody and his Work*. Hartford: American, 1875.

The Doctrines and Discipline of the Methodist Episcopal Church. New York: Carlton and Porter, 1856.

Edwards, Jonathan. *A Faithful Narrative of the Surprising Work of God. In The Great Awakening*, ed. C. C. Goen. Vol. 4, *Works of Jonathan Edwards*. New Haven: Yale University Press, 1972.

———. *A History of the Work of Redemption*. Edited by John F. Wilson. Vol. 9, *Works of Jonathan Edwards*. New Haven: Yale University Press, 1989.

Emery, Joseph. *Thirty-five Years Among the Poor and the Public Institutions of Cincinnati*. Cincinnati: Elm Street, 1887.

Farwell, John Villiers. *Early Recollections of Dwight L. Moody*. Chicago: Winona, 1907.

Finney, Charles Grandison. *Lectures on Revivals of Religion*. Edited by William G. McLoughlin. Cambridge: Harvard University Press, 1960.

———. *The Memoirs of Charles G. Finney: The Complete Restored Text*. Edited by Garth M. Rosell and Richard A. G. Dupuis. Grand Rapids: Academie Books/Zondervan, 1989.

Fish, Henry Clay. *Handbook of Revivals for the Use of Winners of Souls*. Boston: James H. Earle, 1879.

———. *Primitive Piety Revived*. Boston: Congregational Board of Publication, 1855.

Gibson, William. *The Year of Grace: A History of the Ulster Revival of 1859*. Edinburgh: Andrew Elliot, 1860.

A History of the Stanton Street Baptist Church in the City of New York. New York: Sheldon, 1860.

Humphrey, Heman. *Revival Sketches and Manual*. New York: American Tract Society, 1859.

Jones, J. William. *Christ in the Camp, or, Religion in Lee's Army*. Richmond: B. F. Johnson, 1887.

Kirk, Edward Norris. *Lectures on Revivals*. Edited by David O. Mears. Boston: Congregational Publishing Society, 1875.

Knapp, Jacob. *Autobiography of Elder Jacob Knapp*. New York: Sheldon, 1868.

Lanphier, J. C. *Alone With Jesus*. New York: Tibbals, 1872.

Long, Edwin M. *The Children of the Tent, or, The Work of God among the Young at the Union Tabernacle*. Philadelphia: Parry and McMillan, 1859. Bound with *The Union Tabernacle*.

———. *The Union Tabernacle, or, Movable Tent-church: Showing in its Rise and Success a new Department of Christian Enterprise*. Philadelphia: Parry and McMillan, 1859.

MacFarlan, D. *The Revivals of the Eighteenth Century*. London and Edinburgh: John Johnstone, [1847].

Mahan, Asa. *Autobiography: Intellectual, Moral and Spiritual*. London: T. Woolmer, 1882.

Manual of Plymouth Church. New York: Baker and Godwin, 1867.

McLean, A., and J. W. Eaton. *Penuel, or, Face to Face with God*. New York: W. C. Palmer, Jr., 1869.

Memorial of the Revival in Plymouth Church, Brooklyn, [Rev. Henry Ward Beecher] During the Early Part of the Year 1858. New York: Clark, Austin and Smith, 1859.

Minutes of the Annual Conferences of the Methodist Episcopal Church. New York, 1853–61.

Minutes of the Annual Conferences of the Methodist Episcopal Church, South. Nashville, 1854–62.

Minutes of the General Assembly of the Presbyterian Church in the United States of America, 1838–1858; 1859–1869. (New School). 2 vols. New York: Published by the Stated Clerks, 1838–58, 1859–69; reprint, Philadelphia: Presbyterian Board of Publication and Sabbath-School Work, 1894.

Minutes of the General Assembly of the Presbyterian Church in the United States of America, 1848–1858; 1859–1864 (Old School). Philadelphia: Presbyterian Board of Publication and Sabbath-School Work, n.d.

Moss, Lemuel. *Annals of the United States Christian Commission*. Philadelphia: J. B. Lippincott, 1868.

The Old South Chapel Prayer Meeting. Boston: Tilton, 1859.

Olney, Harriet. *The Old Way of Holiness, With a Sketch of the Christian Experience of Harriet Olney*. New York: Published by the author, 1857.

Palmer, Phoebe. *The Promise of the Father; or, A Neglected Specialty of the Last Days*. New York: W. C. Palmer, Jr., 1872 [1859].

Presbyterian Reunion: A Memorial Volume, 1837–1871. New York: De Witt C. Lent, 1870.

Prime, Samuel Irenaeus. *Autobiography and Memorials*. Edited by Wendall Prime. New York: Anson D. F. Randolph, 1888.

———. *Fifteen Years of Prayer in the Fulton Street Meeting*. New York: Scribner, Armstrong, 1872.

———. *Five Years of Prayer, With the Answers*. New York: Harper, 1864.

———. *The Power of Prayer, Illustrated in the Wonderful Displays of Divine Grace at the Fulton Street and Other Meetings*. New York: Scribner, 1858.

———. *Prayer and Its Answer Illustrated in the First Twenty-five Years of the Fulton Street Prayer Meeting*. New York: Scribner, 1882.

[Prime, Samuel Irenaeus, ed.]. *The New York Pulpit in the Revival of 1858: A Memorial Volume of Sermons*. New York: Sheldon, Blakeman, 1858.

Robbins, Gilbert. *The Christian Patriot, A Biography of James E. McClellen*. Worcester, Mass.: Grout and Bigelow, 1865.

Smith, Fred B. *I Remember*. New York: Fleming H. Revell, 1936.

Smith, Hannah Whitall. *The Unselfishness of God and How I Discovered It*. New York: F. H. Revell, 1903; reprint, New York: Garland, 1985.

Smith, Matthew Hale. *Sunshine and Shadows in New York*. Hartford: J. B. Burr, 1868.

Sprague, William B. *Lectures on Revivals of Religion*. Albany: J. P. Haven and J. Leavitt, 1832.

Stowe, Harriet Beecher. *Uncle Tom's Cabin*. New York: Bantam Books, 1981.

Strong, George Templeton. *The Diary of George Templeton Strong*. Vol. 2, *The Turbulent Fifties, 1850–1859*. Edited by Allan Nevins and Milton Halsey Thomas. New York: Macmillan, 1952.

Strong, Thomas C. *Living Words from Living Men: Experiences of Converted Infidels*. New York: Board of Publications, Reformed Protestant Dutch Church, 1863.

Stuart, George H. *The Life of George H. Stuart*. Edited by Robert Ellis Thompson. Philadelphia: J. M. Stoddart, 1890.

Stuart, William David. *Memoir of William David Stuart, 1840–1863*. Philadelphia: Printed for private circulation, 1865.

Tracy, Joseph. *The Great Awakening: A History of the Revival of Religion in the Time of Edwards and Whitefield*. Boston: Tappan and Dennet, 1842.

Union Prayer Meeting Hymns. Philadelphia: American Sunday-School Union, 1859.

Weiss, John. *Life and Correspondence of Theodore Parker*. 2 vols. New York: D. Appleton, 1864.

Wheatley, Richard. *The Life and Letters of Mrs. Phoebe Palmer*. New York: Walter C. Palmer, Jr., 1876; reprint, New York: Garland, 1984.

Whitman, Walt. *I Sit and Look Out: Editorials from the Brooklyn Daily Times*. Edited by Emory Holloway and Vernolian Schwartz. New York: Columbia University Press, 1932.

Wilson, Joseph M. *The Presbyterian Historical Almanac and Annual Remembrancer of the Church*. Vols. 1–4. Philadelphia: Joseph M. Wilson, 1859–62.

Wittenmyer, Annie. *History of the Woman's Temperance Crusade*. St. Louis: H. M. Brockstedt, 1878.

Articles

"The American Tract Society." *Atlantic Monthly* 1 (July 1858): 246–51.

Association Men 40, no. 5 (February 1915). [Issue devoted to Dwight L. Moody.]

"Benjamin M. Adams." In *Minutes of the New York East Annual Conference of the Methodist Episcopal Church*, 127–30. New York: Eaton and Mains, 1903.

Bureau of the Census. "The Public Press." *Eighth Census of the United States: 1860.* Vol. 4:319. Washington, D.C.: Government Printing Office, 1860.

Doremus, Sarah. "First Number for the Woman's Union Missionary Society of America, for Heathen Lands." *Missionary Link [Crumbs]* (January 1861).

"The Fulton-Street Prayer-Meeting." *Harper's Weekly*, September 30, 1871, supplement.

Higginson, Thomas W. "Saints and their Bodies." *Atlantic Monthly* 1 (March 1858): 582–95.

Hodge, Charles. "Abolitionism [review essay]." *Biblical Reperatory and Princeton Review*, 2nd ser., 16 (1844): 545–81.

Johnson, John L. "Reminiscences of the Y.M.C.A. II." *Alumni Bulletin of the University of Virginia*, 3rd ser., Vol. 2 (1909): 61–66.

Kennedy, J. C. G. "Catalogue of the Newspapers and Periodicals Published in the United States." In *Livingston's Law Register for 1852*, 3–56. New York: John Livingston, 1852.

Lamphier [*sic*], J. C. "The Origin and Methods of the Fulton Street Prayer-Meeting—An Interview with the Founder and Manager." *The Preacher and Homiletic Monthly* 3 (October 1878 to September 1879): 224–26.

Langdon, William Chauncy. "The Early Story of the Confederation of the Young Men's Christian Associations." In *1888 Yearbook of the Young Men's Christian Associations*, 17–58. New York: YMCA International Committee, 1888.

Marvin, A. P. "Three Eras of Revival in the United States." *Bibliotheca Sacra* 16 (April 1859): 279–301.

McIlhany, Hugh M. "Founding of the First Young Men's Christian Association Among Students." *Alumni Bulletin of the University of Virginia*, 3rd ser., no. 2 (1909): 48–56.

Pence, Owen E. "Meet Vincent Colyer." Typescript, main collection. Library of Congress, Washington, D.C.

"The Religious Awakening of 1858." *Southern Presbyterian Review* 11 (July 1858): 246–63.

Stevens, Abel. "American Slavery—Its Progress and Prospects." *Methodist Review* 39 (1857): 437–64.

"Thomas Gilbert Osborn." In *Minutes of the New York East Annual Conference of the Methodist Episcopal Church*, 70–71. New York: Phillips and Hunt, 1888.

Pamphlets, Sermons, Tracts

American Tract Society. *Thirty-Third Annual Report of the American Tract Society*. New York: 1858.

————. *Twenty-Seventh Annual Report of the American Tract Society*. New York: 1852.

Brainerd, Cephas. *The Work of the Army Committee of the New York Young Men's Christian Association*. New York: John Mendole, printer, 1866.

Cheever, George B. *The Christian's Duty, in a Time of Revival*. New York: Dunn Brothers, 1858.

————. *The Commission from God Against the Sin of Slavery*. Boston: 1858.

Finney, Charles G. *The Prevailing Prayer-Meeting*. London: Ward, 1859.

First Annual Report with the Constitution and By-Laws [Richmond, Va., Young Men's Christian Association]. Richmond: William H. Clemmit, 1856.

Forty Years of Methodism in Eighty-Sixth-Street, City of New York. New York: Nelson and Phillips, 1877.

Hall, Newman. *Come to Jesus!* Tract no. 107. Philadelphia: Presbyterian Board of Publication, n.d.

McIlvaine, Charles P. *Bishop McIlvaine's Address to the Convention of the Diocese of Ohio, on the Revival of Religion*. Cincinnati: C. F. Bradley, 1858.

Parker, Theodore. *A False and True Revival of Religion*. Boston: W. L. Kent, 1858.

————. *The Revival of Religion Which We Need*. Boston: W. L. Kent, 1858.

Pentecost; or, The Work of God in Philadelphia, A.D. 1858. Philadelphia: Parry and McMillan, 1859.

Second Annual Catalogue of the Young Men's Christian Association of the University of Virginia, 1859–60. (n.p.) From collection 2993-d, "YMCA Constitution and Bylaws." Manuscripts Department, Alderman Library, University of Virginia, Charlottesville, Virginia.

Thome, James A. *Prayer for the Oppressed*. Boston: American Tract Society, [1859].

Secondary Sources

Books

Abell, Aaron. *The Urban Impact on American Protestantism, 1865–1900*. Cambridge: Harvard University Press, 1943.

Ahlstrom, Sydney E. *A Religious History of the American People*. New Haven: Yale University Press, 1972.

Allen, Catherine B. *The New Lottie Moon Story*. Nashville: Broadman, 1980.

Asbury, Herbert. *The Gangs of New York: An Informal History of the Underworld*. New York: Alfred A. Knopf, 1928.

Austin, C. Grey. *A Century of Religion at the University of Michigan*. Ann Arbor: University of Michigan, 1957.

Bacon, Leonard Woolsey. *A History of American Christianity*. Vol. 13. American Church History Series. New York: Scribner's, 1925 [1897].

Beardsley, Frank G. *A History of American Revivals*. New York: American Tract Society, 1912.

Blocker, Jack S., Jr. *"Give to the Winds Thy Fears:" The Women's Temperance Crusade, 1873–1874*. Westport, Conn.: Greenwood Press, 1985.

Boles, John B. *The Great Revival 1787–1805: The Origins of the Southern Evangelical Mind*. Lexington: University of Kentucky Press, 1972.

Bordin, Ruth. *Frances Willard: A Biography*. Chapel Hill: University of North Carolina Press, 1986.

————. *Woman and Temperance: The Quest for Power and Liberty, 1873–1900*. Philadelphia: Temple University Press, 1981.

Boyer, Paul. *Urban Masses and Moral Order in America, 1820–1920*. Cambridge: Harvard University Press, 1978.

Braude, Ann. *Radical Spirits, Spiritualism and Women's Rights in Nineteenth-Century America*. Boston: Beacon Press, 1989.

Brown, George. *The Lady Preacher: or, The Life and Labors of Mrs. Hannah Reeves*. Philadelphia: Daughaday and Backer, 1870; reprint, New York: Garland, 1987.

Brown, Oswald Eugene, and Anna Muse Brown. *Life and Letters of Laura Askew Haygood*. Nashville: Publishing House of the M. E. Church, South, 1904; reprint, New York: Garland, 1987.

Brown, Richard D. *Knowledge Is Power: The Diffusion of Information in Early America, 1700–1865*. New York: Oxford University Press, 1989.

Bruns, Roger A. *Preacher: Billy Sunday and Big-Time American Evangelicalism*. New York: W.W. Norton, 1992.

Bucke, Emory Stevens, ed. *The History of American Methodism: In Three Volumes*. New York: Abingdon Press, 1964.

Bureau of the Census. *A Century of Population Growth in the United States, 1790–1900*. Washington, D.C.: Government Printing Office, 1909.

Butler, Diana Hochsted. *Standing Against the Whirlwind: Evangelical Episcopalians in Nineteenth-Century America*. New York: Oxford University Press, 1995.

Campbell, Ted A. *The Religion of the Heart: A Study of European Religious Life in the Seventeenth and Eighteenth Centuries*. Columbia: University of South Carolina Press, 1991.

Candler, Warren A. *Great Revivals and the Great Republic*. Nashville: Methodist Episcopal Church, South, 1904.

Carnes, Mark C., and Clyde Griffen, eds. *Meanings for Manhood: Constructions of Masculinity in Victorian America*. Chicago: University of Chicago Press, 1990.

Carwardine, Richard J. *Evangelicals and Politics in Antebellum America*. New Haven: Yale University Press, 1993.

————. *Transatlantic Revivalism: Popular Evangelicalism in Britain and America, 1790–1865*. Westport, Conn.: Greenwood Press, 1978.

Caskey, Marie. *Chariot of Fire: Religion and the Beecher Family*. New Haven: Yale University Press, 1978.

Clark, Clifford E., Jr. *Henry Ward Beecher: Spokesman for a Middle-Class America*. Urbana: University of Illinois Press, 1978.

Coalter, E. Merton. *College Life in the Old South*. New York: Macmillan, 1928.

Conforti, Joseph A. *Jonathan Edwards, Religious Tradition, and American Culture*. Chapel Hill: University of North Carolina Press, 1995.

Conkin, Paul K. *Cane Ridge: America's Pentecost*. Madison: University of Wisconsin Press, 1990.

Crawford, Michael J. *Seasons of Grace: Colonial New England's Revival Tradition in Its British Context*. New York: Oxford University Press, 1991.

Crouthamel, James L. *Bennett's New York Herald and the Rise of the Popular Press*. Syracuse: Syracuse University Press, 1989.

Curtis, Susan. *A Consuming Faith: The Social Gospel and Modern American Culture*. Baltimore: Johns Hopkins University Press, 1991.

Dayton, Donald. *Discovering an Evangelical Heritage*. New York: Harper and Row, 1976.

Dedmon, Emmett. *Great Enterprises: 100 Years of the YMCA of Metropolitan Chicago.* New York: Rand McNally, 1957.

The Development of the Sunday School, 1780–1905. Boston: Executive Committee of the International Sunday School Association, 1905.

Dieter, Melvin Easterday. *The Holiness Revival of the Nineteenth Century.* Metuchen, N.J.: Scarecrow Press, 1980.

Dodge, D. Stuart. *Memorials of William E. Dodge.* New York: Randolph, 1887.

Doggett, L. L. *History of the Young Men's Christian Association: Part I, the Founding of the Association, 1844–1855; Part II, the Confederation Period, 1855–1861.* New York: Association Press, 1922.

———. *Life of Robert R. McBurney.* Cleveland: F. M. Barton, 1902.

Dorchester, Daniel. *Christianity in the United States from the First Settlement Down to the Present Time.* New York: Hunt and Eaton, 1889.

Dorsett, Lyle W. *Billy Sunday and the Redemption of Urban America.* Grand Rapids: Eerdmans, 1991.

———. *A Passion for Souls: The Life of D. L. Moody.* Chicago: Moody Press, 1997.

Douglas, Ann. *The Feminization of American Culture.* New York: Alfred A. Knopf, 1977; reprint, New York: Anchor Press, 1988.

Erdman, Charles R. *D. L. Moody: His Message for Today.* New York: Fleming H. Revell, 1928.

Farwell, John V., Jr., ed. *Some Recollections of John V. Farwell.* Chicago: R. R. Donnelley, 1911.

Fields, Annie. *Life and Letters of Harriet Beecher Stowe.* Boston and New York: Houghton, Mifflin, 1897.

Findlay, James F. *Dwight L. Moody: American Evangelist, 1837–1899.* Chicago: University of Chicago Press, 1969.

Finke, Roger, and Rodney Stark. *The Churching of America, 1776–1990: Winners and Losers in Our Religious Economy.* New Brunswick: Rutgers University Press, 1992.

Foner, Philip S. *Business and Slavery; the New York Merchants and the Irrepressible Conflict.* Chapel Hill: University of North Carolina Press, 1941.

Foote, Henry Wilder. *Three Centuries of American Hymnody.* Cambridge: Harvard University Press, 1940.

Foster, Charles I. *An Errand of Mercy: The Evangelical United Front, 1790–1837.* Chapel Hill: University of North Carolina Press, 1960.

Foster, John O. *Life and Labors of Mrs. Maggie Newton Van Cott.* Cincinnati: Hitchcock and Waldon, 1872.

Fox, Richard Wrightman and T. J. Jackson Lears, eds. *The Culture of Consumption: Critical Essays in American History, 1880–1980.* New York: Pantheon Books, 1983.

Frank, Douglas W. *Less than Conquerors: How Evangelicals Entered the Twentieth Century.* Grand Rapids: Eerdmans, 1986.

Frothingham, Octavius Brooks. *Theodore Parker: A Biography.* New York: G. P. Putnam's Sons, 1886.

Gates, Helen Kolb, et al. *Bless the Lord O My Soul: A Biography of Bishop John Fretz Funk, 1835–1930.* Scottdale, Penn.: Herald Press, 1964.

Gerlach, Luther P., and Virginia H. Hine. *People, Power, Change: Movements of Social Transformation.* Indianapolis: Bobbs-Merrill, 1970.

Gibbons, Herbert Adams. *John Wanamaker.* New York: Harper, 1926.

Gilbert, James. *Perfect Cities: Chicago's Utopias of 1893*. Chicago: University of Chicago Press, 1991.

Gilkeson, John S., Jr. *Middle-Class Providence, 1820–1940*. Princeton: Princeton University Press, 1986.

Ginzberg, Lori D. *Women and the Work of Benevolence: Morality, Politics, and Class in the Nineteenth-Century United States*. New Haven: Yale University Press, 1990.

Gorn, Elliott J. *The Manly Art: Bare-knuckle Prize Fighting in America*. Ithaca: Cornell University Press, 1986.

Griffin, Clifford S. *Their Brothers' Keepers: Moral Stewardship in the United States, 1800–1865*. New Brunswick: Rutgers University Press, 1960.

Hammond, John L. *The Politics of Benevolence: Revival Religion and American Voting Behavior*. Norwood, N. J.: Ablex, 1979.

Hardesty, Nancy A. *Women Called to Witness: Evangelical Feminism in the 19th Century*. Nashville: Abingdon Press, 1984.

Hardman, Keith J. *Charles Grandison Finney, 1792–1875*. Syracuse: Syracuse University Press, 1987.

Hart, James D. *The Popular Book: A History of America's Literary Taste*. Berkeley: University of California Press, 1950.

Hassey, Janette. *No Time for Silence: Evangelical Women in Public Ministry Around the Turn of the Century*. Grand Rapids: Zondervan, 1986.

Hatch, Nathan O. *The Democratization of American Christianity*. New Haven: Yale University Press, 1989.

Hedrick, Joan D. *Harriet Beecher Stowe: A Life*. New York: Oxford University Press, 1994.

Hempton, David, and Myrtle Hill. *Evangelical Protestantism in Ulster Society 1740–1890*. London: Routledge, 1992.

Hill, Patricia R. *The World Their Household: The American Woman's Foreign Mission Movement and Cultural Transformation, 1870–1920*. Ann Arbor: The University of Michigan Press, 1985.

Holifield, E. Brooks. *The Gentlemen Theologians: American Theology in Southern Culture, 1795–1860*. Durham, N.C.: Duke University Press, 1978.

Hopkins, C. Howard. *History of the Y.M.C.A. in North America*. New York: Association Press, 1951.

———. *John R. Mott, 1865–1955: A Biography*. Grand Rapids: Eerdmans, 1979.

Horlick, Allan Stanley. *Country Boys and Merchant Princes: The Social Control of Young Men in New York*. Lewisburg, Penn.: Bucknell University Press, 1975.

Howe, Daniel Walker. *The Political Culture of the American Whigs*. Chicago: University of Chicago Press, 1979.

Hudson, Frederic. *Journalism in the United States from 1690 to 1872*. New York: Harper, 1873.

Huston, James L. *The Panic of 1857 and the Coming of the Civil War*. Baton Rouge: Louisiana State University Press, 1987.

Hutchison, William R. *Errand to the World: American Protestant Thought and Foreign Missions*. Chicago: University of Chicago Press, 1987.

Johnson, Curtis D. *Islands of Holiness: Rural Religion in Upstate New York, 1790–1860*. Ithaca: Cornell University Press, 1989.

———. *Redeeming America: Evangelicals and the Road to Civil War*. Chicago: Ivan R. Dee, 1993.

Johnson, Paul E. *A Shopkeeper's Millennium: Society and Revivals in Rochester, New York, 1815–1837*. New York: Hill and Wang, 1978.

Karamanski, Theodore J. *Rally 'Round the Flag: Chicago and the Civil War*. Chicago: Nelson-Hall, 1993.

Kling, David W. *A Field of Divine Wonders: The New Divinity and Village Revivals in Northwestern Connecticut, 1792–1822*. University Park: Pennsylvania State University Press, 1993.

Kuykendall, John W. *Southern Enterprize: The Work of National Evangelical Societies in the Antebellum South*. Westport, Conn.: Greenwood Press, 1982.

Lambert, Frank. *"Pedlar in Divinity": George Whitefield and the Transatlantic Revivals, 1737–1770*. Princeton: Princeton University Press, 1994.

Lee, Alfred McClung. *The Daily Newspaper in America: The Evolution of a Social Instrument*. New York: Macmillan, 1937.

Magnuson, Norris. *Salvation in the Slums: Evangelical Social Work, 1865–1920*. Metuchen, N.J.: Scarecrow Press, 1977.

Marsden, George M. *The Evangelical Mind and the New School Presbyterian Experience: A Case Study of Thought and Theology in Nineteenth-Century America*. New Haven: Yale University Press, 1970.

———. *Fundamentalism and American Culture: The Shaping of Twentieth-Century Evangelicalism, 1870–1925*. New York: Oxford University Press, 1980.

———. *Religion and American Culture*. San Diego: Harcourt Brace Jovanovich, 1990.

Marsden, George M. and Bradley J. Long Field, eds. *The Secularization of the Academy*. New York: Oxford University Press, 1992.

Martin, David. *Tongues of Fire: The Explosion of Protestantism in Latin America*. Oxford: Basil Blackwell, 1990.

Mathews, Donald G. *Religion in the Old South*. Chicago: University of Chicago Press, 1977.

Matthews, Glenna. *The Rise of the Public Woman: Woman's Power and Woman's Place in the United States 1630–1970*. New York: Oxford University Press, 1992.

McKivigan, John R. *The War Against Proslavery Religion: Abolitionism and the Northern Churches, 1830–1865*. Ithaca: Cornell University Press, 1984.

McLoughlin, William G. *The Meaning of Henry Ward Beecher: An Essay on the Shifting Values of Mid-Victorian America, 1840–1870*. New York: Alfred A. Knopf, 1970.

———. *Modern Revivalism: Charles Grandison Finney to Billy Graham*. New York: Ronald Press, 1959.

———. *Revivals, Awakenings, and Reform: An Essay on Religion and Social Change in America, 1607–1977*. Chicago: University of Chicago Press, 1978.

———. ed. *The American Evangelicals, 1800–1900: An Anthology*. Gloucester, Mass: Peter Smith, 1976.

Miller, Perry. *The Life of the Mind in America from the Revolution to the Civil War: Books One through Three*. New York: Harcourt, Brace, 1965.

Moody, William R. *The Life of Dwight L. Moody*. Chicago: Fleming H. Revell, 1900.

Moore, R. Laurence. *Selling God: American Religion in the Marketplace of Culture*. New York: Oxford University Press, 1994.

Moorhead, James H. *American Apocalypse: Yankee Protestants and the Civil War, 1860–1869*. New Haven: Yale University Press, 1978.

Morgan, Edmund Sears. *The Puritan Family: Religion and Domestic Relations in Seventeenth-Century New England*. New York: Harper and Row, 1966 [1944].

Mott, Frank Luther. *American Journalism*. New York: Macmillan, 1950.

Murray, Iain H. *Revival and Revivalism: The Making and Marring of American Evangelicalism 1750–1858*. Edinburgh: Banner of Truth Trust, 1994.

Noll, Mark A. *A History of Christianity in the United States and Canada.* Grand Rapids: Eerdmans, 1992.

Norton, Wesley. *Religious Newspapers in the Old Northwest to 1861: A History, Bibliography, and Record of Opinion.* Athens: Ohio University Press, 1977.

Offord, Robert M. *Jerry McAuley, His Life and Work.* New York: New York Observer, [c. 1885].

Orr, J. Edwin. *The Event of the Century: The 1857–1858 Awakening.* Edited by Richard Owen Roberts. Wheaton, Ill.: International Awakening Press, 1989.

———. *The Fervent Prayer: The Worldwide Impact of the Great Awakening of 1858.* Chicago: Moody Press, 1974.

———. *The Light of Nations: Evangelical Renewal and Advance in the Nineteenth Century.* Grand Rapids: Eerdmans, 1965.

———. *The Second Evangelical Awakening in Britain.* London: Marshall, Morgan and Scott, 1949.

Pierson, Delavan Leonard. *Arthur T. Pierson: A Biography.* London: James Nisbit, 1912.

Pilkington, James Penn. *The Methodist Publishing House: A History.* 2 vols. Nashville: Abington Press, 1968.

Raser, Harold E. *Phoebe Palmer, Her Life and Thought.* Lewiston, N.Y.: Edwin Mellen Press, 1987.

Rawlyk, G. A. *The Canada Fire: Radical Evangelicalism in British North America 1775–1812.* Kingston and Montreal: McGill-Queen's University Press, 1994.

Reminiscences of John V. Farwell by His Elder Daughter. 2 vols. Chicago: Ralph Fletcher Seymour, 1928.

Richey, Russell E. *Early American Methodism.* Bloomington: Indiana University Press, 1991.

Ridgaway, Henry B. *The Life of the Rev. Alfred Cookman.* London: Hodder and Stoughton, 1873.

Robertson, Archibald Thomas. *Life and Letters of John A. Broadus.* Philadelphia: American Baptist Publication Society, 1901.

Rose, Anne C. *Victorian America and the Civil War.* Cambridge: Cambridge University Press, 1992.

Rourke, Constance. *Trumpets of Jubilee: Henry Ward Beecher, Harriet Beecher Stowe, Lyman Beecher, Horace Greeley, P. T. Barnum.* New York: Harcourt, Brace, 1927.

Ryan, Mary P. *Cradle of the Middle Class: The Family in Oneida County, New York, 1790–1865.* New York: Cambridge University Press, 1981.

———. *Women in Public: Between Banners and Ballots, 1825–1880.* Baltimore: Johns Hopkins University Press, 1990.

Saum, Lewis O. *The Popular Mood of Pre-Civil War America.* Westport, Conn.: Greenwood Press, 1980.

Savage, Theodore Fiske. *The Presbyterian Church in New York City.* New York: Presbytery of New York, 1949.

Schmidt, Jean Miller. *Souls or the Social Order: The Two-Party System in American Protestantism.* Brooklyn: Carlson, 1991.

Schmidt, Leigh Eric. *Holy Fairs: Scottish Communions and American Revivals in the Early Modern Period.* Princeton: Princeton University Press, 1989.

Schudson, Michael. *Discovering the News: A Social History of American Newspapers.* New York: Basic Books, 1978.

Scott, Anne Firor. *Natural Allies, Women's Associations in American History*. Urbana: University of Illinois Press, 1991.

Seaman, Samuel A. *Annals of New York Methodism*. New York: Hunt and Eaton, 1892.

Shattuck, Gardiner H. *A Shield and Hiding Place: The Religious Life of the Civil War Armies*. Macon, Ga.: Mercer University Press, 1987.

Shaw, Cornelia Rebekah. *Davidson College*. New York: Fleming H. Revell, 1923.

Shedd, Clarence P. *Two Centuries of Student Christian Movements: Their Origin and Intercollegiate Life*. New York: Association Press, 1934.

Sims, Mary S. *The Natural History of a Social Institution: The Young Women's Christian Association*. New York: Little and Ives, 1935.

Sizer [Frankiel], Sandra. *Gospel Hymns and Social Religion: The Rhetoric of Nineteenth-Century Revivalism*. Philadelphia: Temple University Press, 1978.

Smith, James Ward, and A. Leland Jamison, eds. *Religion in American Life*. Vol. 4. *A Critical Bibliography of Religion in America*. Edited by Nelson R. Burr. Princeton: Princeton University Press, 1961.

Smith, Timothy L. *Called Unto Holiness, the Story of the Nazarenes: The Formative Years*. Kansas City: Nazarene Publishing House, 1962.

———. *Revivalism and Social Reform: American Protestantism on the Eve of the Civil War*. Nashville: Abingdon Press, 1957.

Smith-Rosenberg, Carroll. *Religion and the Rise of the American City: The New York City Mission Movement, 1812–1870*. Ithaca: Cornell University Press, 1984.

Spann, Edward K. *The New Metropolis: New York City, 1840–1857*. New York: Columbia University Press, 1981.

Stampp, Kenneth M. *America in 1857: A Nation on the Brink*. New York: Oxford University Press, 1990.

Stannerd, David E., ed. *Death in America*. Philadelphia: University of Pennsylvania Press, 1974.

Stansell, Christine. *City of Women: Sex and Class in New York, 1789–1860*. New York: Alfred A. Knopf, 1988.

Stout, Harry S. *The Divine Dramatist: George Whitefield and the Rise of Modern Evangelicalism*. Grand Rapids: Eerdmans, 1991.

Sweet, Leonard I. *The Minister's Wife: Her Role in Nineteenth-Century American Evangelicalism*. Philadelphia: Temple University Press, 1983.

Sweet, William Warren. *Revivalism in America: Its Origin, Growth and Decline*. New York: Scribner's, 1945.

———. *The Story of Religion in America*. New York: Harper, 1939 [1930].

Thompson. A. E. *A. B. Simpson: His Life and Work*. Harrisburg, Penn.: Christian Publications, 1960.

Thompson, Robert Ellis. *A History of the Presbyterian Churches in the United States of America*. Vol. 6. American Church History Series. New York: Scribner's, 1907 [1895].

Van Deusen, Glyndon G. *Horace Greeley: Nineteenth-Century Crusader*. Philadelphia: University of Pennsylvania, 1953.

Van Vleck, George W. *The Panic of 1857*. New York: AMS Press, 1967.

Walker, Williston. *A History of the Congregational Churches in the United States*. New York: Christian Literature, 1894.

Ward, W. R. *The Protestant Evangelical Awakening*. Cambridge: Cambridge University Press, 1992.

Wayland, Francis, and H. L. Wayland. *A Memoir of the Life and Labors of Francis Wayland*. 2 vols. New York: Sheldon, 1867.

Weisberger, Bernard A. *They Gathered at the River: The Story of the Great Revivalists and Their Impact upon Religion in America*. Boston: Little, Brown, 1958.

Weiss, Ellen. *City in the Woods: The Life and Design of an American Camp Meeting on Martha's Vineyard*. New York: Oxford University Press, 1987.

Wilson, Elizabeth. *Fifty Years of Association Work Among Young Women*. New York: National Board of the Young Women's Christian Associations, 1916.

Wilson, Robert Forrest. *Crusader in Crinoline: The Life of Harriet Beecher Stowe*. Philadelphia: J. B. Lippincott, 1941.

Wosh, Peter J. *Spreading the Word: The Bible Business in Nineteenth-Century America*. Ithaca: Cornell University Press, 1994.

Wyatt-Brown, Bertram. *Lewis Tappan and the Evangelical War Against Slavery*. Cleveland: The Press of Case Western Reserve University, 1969.

Component Parts of Books

Balmer, Randall. "Eschewing the 'Routine of Religion': Eighteenth-Century Pietism and the Revival Tradition in America." In *Modern Christian Revivals*, ed. Edith L. Blumhofer and Randall Balmer, 1–16. Urbana: University of Illinois Press, 1993.

Benjamin, Walter W. "The Free Methodists." In *History of American Methodism: In Three Volumes*, ed. Emory Stevens Bucke, 2: 339–60. New York: Abingdon Press, 1964.

Blauvelt, Martha T. "The Mechanics of Revival: New Jersey Presbyterians During the Second Awakening." In *Religion in New Jersey Life Before the Civil War*, ed. Mary R. Murrin, 88–103. Trenton: New Jersey Historical Commission, 1985.

Blumhofer, Edith L. "Restoration as Revival: Early American Pentecostalism." In *Modern Christian Revivals*, ed. Edith L. Blumhofer and Randall Balmer, 145–60. Urbana: University of Illinois Press, 1993.

Boles, John B. "Revivalism, Renewal, and Social Mediation in the Old South." In *Modern Christian Revivals*, ed. Edith L. Blumhofer and Randall Balmer, 42–59. Urbana: University of Illinois Press, 1993.

Carpenter, Joel A. "Is 'Evangelical' a Yankee Word? Relations Between Northern Evangelicals and the Southern Baptist Convention in the Twentieth Century." In *Southern Baptists and American Evangelicals: The Conversation Continues*, ed. David S. Dockery, 78–99. Nashville: Broadman and Holman, 1993.

Carwardine, Richard. " 'Antinomians' and 'Arminians': Methodists and the Market Revolution." In *The Market Revolution in America: Social, Political, and Religious Expressions, 1800–1880*, ed. Melvyn Stokes and Stephen Conway, 282–307. Charlottesville and London: University Press of Virginia, 1996.

———. "Religious Revival and Political Renewal in Antebellum America." In *Revival and Religion Since 1700: Essays for John Walsh*, ed. Jane Garnett and Colin Matthew, 127–52. London: Hambledon Press, 1993.

———. "The Religious Revival of 1857–58 in the United States." In *Religious Motivation: Biographical and Sociological Problems for the Church Historian*, ed. Derek Baker, 393–406. Oxford: Basil Blackwell, 1978.

———. "The Second Great Awakening in Comparative Perspective: Revivals and Culture in the United States and Britain." In *Modern Christian Revivals*, ed. Edith L. Blumhofer and Randall Balmer, 84–100. Urbana: University of Illinois Press, 1993.

Dayton, Donald. "From 'Christian Perfection' to the 'Baptism of the Holy Spirit.' " In *Aspects of Pentecostal-Charismatic Origins*, ed. Vinson Synan, 41–54. Plainfield, N.J.: Logos International, 1975.

Gifford, Carolyn De Swarte. " 'My Own Methodist Hive': Frances Willard's Faith as Disclosed in Her Journal, 1855–1870." In *Spirituality and Social Responsibility: Vocational Vision of Women in The United Methodist Tradition*, ed. Rosemary Skinner Keller, 81–98. Nashville: Abingdon Press, 1993.

Hatch, Nathan O. "Sola Scriptura and Novus Ordo Seclorum." In *The Bible in America*, ed. Nathan O. Hatch and Mark A. Noll, 59–78. New York: Oxford University Press, 1982.

Hardesty, Nancy A. "Minister As Prophet? Or As Mother? Two Nineteenth Century Models." In *Women in New Worlds: Historical Perspectives on the Wesleyan Tradition*, ed. Hilah F. Thomas and Rosemary Skinner Keller, 88–101. Nashville: Abingdon Press, 1981.

Holmes, Janice. "The 'world turned upside down': Women in the Ulster Revival of 1859." In *Coming into the Light: The Work, Politics, and Religion of Women in Ulster, 1840–1940*, ed. Janice Holmes and Diane Urquhart, 126–53. Belfast: Queen's University of Belfast, 1994.

Howe, Daniel Walker. "Religion and Politics in the Antebellum North." In *Religion and American Politics, From the Colonial Period to the 1980s*, ed. Mark A. Noll, 121–45. New York: Oxford University Press, 1990.

———. "Victorian Culture in America." In *Victorian America*, ed. Daniel Walker Howe, 3–28. Philadelphia: University of Pennsylvania Press, 1976.

Longfield, Bradley J. "From Evangelicalism to Liberalism: Public Midwestern Universities in Nineteenth-Century America." In *The Secularization of the Academy*, ed. George M. Marsden and Bradley J. Longfield, 46–73. New York: Oxford University Press, 1992.

Miller, Perry. "From the Covenant to the Revival." In *Religion in American Life*. Vol. 1. *The Shaping of American Religion*, ed. James Ward Smith and A. Leland Jamison, 322–368. Princeton: Princeton University Press, 1961.

Moorhead, James H. "The Millennium and the Media." In *Communication and Change in American Religious History*, ed. Leonard I. Sweet, 216–38. Grand Rapids: Eerdmans, 1993.

———. "Presbyterians and the Mystique of Organizational Efficiency, 1870–1936." In *Reimagining Denominationalism*, ed. Robert Bruce Mullin and Russell E. Richey, 264–287. New York: Oxford University Press, 1994.

Moran, Gerald F. "Christian Revivalism and Culture in Early America: Puritan New England as a Case Study." In *Modern Christian Revivals*, ed. Edith L. Blumhofer and Randall Balmer, 42–59. Urbana: University of Illinois Press, 1993.

O'Brien, Susan. "Eighteenth-Century Publishing Networks in the First Years of Transatlantic Evangelicalism." In *Evangelicalism: Comparative Studies of Popular Protestantism in North America, the British Isles, and Beyond, 1700–1990*, ed. Mark A. Noll, David W. Bebbington, and George A. Rawlyk, 38–57. New York: Oxford University Press, 1994.

Pike, Martha. "In Memory Of: Artifacts Relating to Mourning in Nineteenth Century America." In *American Material Culture*, ed. Edith Mayo, 48–65. Bowling Green, Ohio: Bowling Green State University Popular Press, 1984.

Rawlyk, George A. "Writing about Canadian Religious Revivals." In *Modern Christian Revivals*, ed. Edith L. Blumhofer and Randall Balmer, 208–226. Urbana: University of Illinois, 1993.

Richey, Russell E. "History as a Bearer of Denominational Identity: Methodism as a Case Study." In *Beyond Establishment: Protestant Identity in a Post-Protestant Age*, ed. Jackson W. Carroll and Wade Clark Roof, 270–95. Louisville: Westminster/John Knox Press, 1993.

Schultze, Quentin J. "Keeping the Faith: American Evangelicals and the Mass Media." In *American Evangelicals and the Mass Media*, ed. Quentin J. Schultze, 23–45. Grand Rapids: Academie Books/Zondervan, 1990.

"Sketch of the Origin and Character of the Principal Series of Tracts of the American Tract Society." In *American Tract Society Documents, 1824–1925*. New York: Arno Press, 1972.

Smith, Timothy. "History, Social Theory, and the Vision of the American Religious Past, 1955–1980." Afterword in *Revivalism and Social Reform: American Protestantism on the Eve of the Civil War*, 249–61. Baltimore: Johns Hopkins University Press, 1980.

Smith-Rosenberg, Carroll. "The Female World of Love and Ritual: Relations Between Women in Nineteenth-Century America." In Part One of *Disorderly Conduct: Visions of Gender in Victorian America*, 53–76. New York: Oxford University Press, 1985.

Sweet, Leonard I. " 'A Nation Born Again': The Union Prayer Meeting Revival and Cultural Revitalization." In *The Great Tradition: In Honor of Winthrop S. Hudson, Essays on Pluralism, Voluntarism, and Revivalism*, ed. Joseph D. Ban and Paul R. Dekar, 193–221. Valley Forge, Penn.: Judson Press, 1982.

Walsh, John. " 'Methodism' and the Origins of English-Speaking Evangelicalism." In *Evangelicalism: Comparative Studies of Popular Protestantism in North America, the British Isles, and Beyond, 1700–1990*, ed. Mark A. Noll, David W. Bebbington, and George A. Rawlyk, 19–37. New York: Oxford University Press, 1994.

Welter, Barbara. "The Feminization of American Religion: 1800–1860." In *Clio's Consciousness Raised: New Perspectives on the History of Women*, ed. Mary S. Hartman and Lois Banner, 137–57. New York: Octagon Books, 1974.

York, Robert M. "George B. Cheever, Religious and Social Reformer." *University of Maine Bulletin* (April 1955): 1–237. In *University of Main Studies*, 2nd. ser., no. 69.

Articles

Banner, Lois. "Religious Benevolence as Social Control: A Critique of an Interpretation." *Journal of American History* 60 (June 1973): 23–41.

Bederman, Gail. " 'The Women Have Had Charge of the Church Work Long Enough': The Men and Religion Forward Movement of 1911–1912 and the Masculinization of Middle-Class Protestantism." *American Quarterly* 41 (September 1989): 432–65.

Buddenbaum, Judith M. " 'Judge . . . What Their Acts Will Justify': The Religion Journalism of James Gordon Bennett." *Journalism History*, 14 (Summer/Autumn 1987): 54–67.

Butler, Jon. "Enthusiasm Described and Decried: The Great Awakening as Interpretative Fiction." *The Journal of American History* 69 (September 1982): 305–25.

Carpenter, Joel A. "The Scope of American Evangelicalism: Some Comments on the Dayton-Marsden Exchange." *Christian Scholar's Review* 23 (September 1993): 53–61.

Carwardine, Richard. "The Second Great Awakening in Urban Centers: An Examination of Methodism and the 'New Measures.' " *Journal of American History* 59 (September 1972): 327–40.

Cole, Charles C., Jr. "The Free Church Movement in New York City." *New York History* 34 (July 1953): 284–97.

Conforti, Joseph. "The Invention of the Great Awakening, 1795–1842." *Early American Literature* 26 (1991): 99–111.

Davis, Hugh. "The New York Evangelist, New School Presbyterians and Slavery, 1837–1857." *American Presbyterian* 68 (Spring 1990): 14–23.

Dunn, F. Roger. "Formative Years of the Chicago Y.M.C.A." *Journal of the Illinois State Historical Society* 37 (December 1944): 329–50.

Durden [O'Brien], Susan. "A Study of the First Evangelical Magazines, 1740–1748." *Journal of Ecclesiastical History* 27 (July 1974): 255–75.

Francis, Russell E. "The Religious Revival of 1858 in Philadelphia." *Pennsylvania Magazine of History and Biography* 70 (1946): 52–77.

Gilfoyle, Timothy J. "The Urban Geography of Commercial Sex: Prostitution in New York City, 1790–1860." *Journal of Urban History* 14 (August 1987): 371–93.

Glass, William R. "Liberal Means to Conservative Ends: Bethany Presbyterian Church, John Wanamaker and the Institutional Church Movement." *American Presbyterian* 68 (Fall 1990): 181–192.

Griffin, Clifford S. "The Abolitionists and the Benevolent Societies, 1831–1861." *Journal of Negro History* 44 (July 1959): 195–216.

Grossbart, Stephen R. "Seeking the Divine Favor: Conversion and Church Admission in Eastern Connecticut, 1711–1832." *William and Mary Quarterly* 46 (October 1989): 696–740.

Hamilton, Michael S. "Women, Public Ministry, and American Fundamentalism, 1920–1950." *Religion and American Culture* 3 (Summer 1993): 171–96.

Handy, Robert H. "Trans-Atlantic Evangelicalism in Historical Perspective." *Evangelical Studies Bulletin* 11 (Fall 1994): 1–4.

Hannah, John D. "The Layman's Prayer Revival of 1858." *Bibliotheca Sacra* 134 (January–March 1977): 59–73.

Hardman, Keith J. "Charles G. Finney, the Benevolent Empire, and the Free Church Movement in New York City." *New York History* 67 (October 1986): 411–35.

Henry, James O. "The United States Christian Commission in the Civil War." *Civil War History* 6 (1960): 374–88.

Hill, John B. "A Missouri Missionary Faces Obstacles, More Extracts from the Diary of Timothy Hill 1851–1860." *Journal of the Presbyterian Historical Society* 25 (September 1947): 175–86.

Hoff, Marvin D. "The Fulton Street Prayer Meeting." *Reformed Review* 17 (September 1963): 26–37.

Kerber, Linda K. "Separate Spheres, Female Worlds, Woman's Place: The Rhetoric of Women's History." *Journal of American History* 75 (June 1988): 9–39.

Kolb, Aaron C. "John Fretz Funk, 1835–1930: An Appreciation." *Mennonite Quarterly Review* 6 (July 1932): 144–55; (October 1932): 251–63.

Lambert, Frank. "The Great Awakening as Artifact: George Whitefield and the Construction of Intercolonial Revival, 1739–1745." *Church History* 60 (June 1991): 223–46.

———. " 'Pedlar in Divinity': George Whitefield and the Great Awakening, 1737–1745." *Journal of American History* 77 (December 1990): 812–37.

Long, Kathryn T. "The Power of Interpretation: The Revival of 1857–58 and the

Historiography of Revivalism in America." *Religion and American Culture* 4 (Winter 1994): 77–105.

Loveland, Anne C. "Presbyterians and Revivalism in the Old South." *Journal of Presbyterian History* 57 (Spring 1979): 36–49.

Marsden, George M. "Forum: The Decade Ahead in Scholarship." *Religion and American Culture* 3 (Winter 1993): 9–15.

Mathews, Donald G. "The Second Great Awakening as an Organizing Process, 1780–1830: An Hypothesis." *American Quarterly* 21 (Spring 1969): 23–43.

Mathisen, James A. "From Muscular Christians to Jocks for Jesus." *Christian Century*, January 1–8, 1992, 11–15.

Moore, R. Laurence. "Religion, Secularization, and the Shaping of the Culture Industry in Antebellum America." *American Quarterly* 41 (June 1989): 216–42.

Moorhead, James. " 'As Though Nothing at All Had Happened': Death and Afterlife in Protestant Thought, 1840–1925." *Soundings* 67 (Winter 1984): 453–71.

———. "Social Reform and the Divided Conscience of Antebellum Protestantism." *Church History* 48 (December 1979): 416–30.

Mullin, Robert Bruce. "Biblical Critics and the Battle Over Slavery." *Journal of Presbyterian History* 61 (Summer 1983): 210–26.

Noll, Mark A. "How We Remember Revivals: The Virtues and Vices of Tribal History." Review of Iain H. Murray, *Revival and Revivalism. Christianity Today*, April 24, 1995, 31, 34.

O'Brien, Susan. "A Transatlantic Community of Saints: The Great Awakening and the First Evangelical Network, 1735–1755." *American Historical Review* 91 (October 1986): 811–32.

Penfield, Janet Harbison. "Women in the Presbyterian Church—an Historical Overview." *Journal of Presbyterian History* 55 (Summer, 1977): 107–23.

Shaw, Donald Lewis. "At the Crossroads: Change and Continuity in American Press News 1820–1860." *Journalism History* 8 (Summer 1981): 38–50.

Shelley, Harold P. "Borne of the Current of Revivalism: Origin of the Bible Fellowship Church." *Mennonite Quarterly Review* 63 (July 1989): 265–84.

Shipps, James Fenimore. "The Revival of 1858 in Mid-America." *Methodist History* 16 (April 1978): 139–50.

Sizer [Frankiel], Sandra. "Politics and Apolitical Religion: The Great Urban Revivals of the Late Nineteenth Century." *Church History* 48 (March 1979): 81–98.

Smith, John Abernathy. "How Methodism Became a National Church." *Methodist History* 20 (October 1981): 13–28.

Smith, Timothy L. "My Rejection of a Cyclical View of 'Great Awakenings.' " *Sociological Analysis* 44 (1983): 97–102.

———. "Response of Professor Smith on Cycles of National Awakenings." *Sociological Analysis* 44 (1983): 121–22.

Stout, Harry S. "The Confederate Jeremiad in Defeat." Lecture 3 of "The Life and Death of the Confederate Jeremiad." James A. Gray Lectures, Duke Divinity School, October 1992.

"Symposium on Religious Awakenings." *Sociological Analysis* 44, no. 2 (1983): 81–122.

"The Time for Prayer: The Third Great Awakening." *Christian History* 8; 23 (1989): 32–33.

Weeks, Louis. "The Incorporation of American Religion: The Case of the Presbyterians." *Religion and American Culture* 1 (Winter 1991): 101–18.

Welter, Barbara. "The Cult of True Womanhood: 1820–1860." *American Quarterly* 18 (Summer 1966): 151–74.

Zuckerman, Michael. "Holy Wars, Civil Wars: Religion and Economics in Nineteenth-Century America." *Prospects: An Annual of American Cultural Studies* 16 (1991): 219–24.

Theses and Dissertations

Allen, Milton Robert. "A History of the Young Men's Christian Association at the University of Virginia." Ph.D. diss., University of Virginia, 1946.

Bush, Peter George. "James Caughey, Phoebe and Walter Palmer and the Methodist Revival Experience in Canada West, 1850–1858." Master of Arts thesis, Queen's University, Kingston, Ontario, Canada, 1985.

Caldwell, Thekla Ellen Joiner. "Women, Men, and Revival: The Third Awakening in Chicago." Ph.D. diss., University of Illinois at Chicago, 1991.

Fish, Roy J. "The Awakening of 1858 and Its Effects on Baptists in the United States." D.Th. diss., Southwestern Baptist Theological Seminary, 1963.

Francis, Russell E. "Pentecost: 1858, A Study in Religious Revivalism." Ph.D. diss., University of Pennsylvania, 1948.

Goetzman, Martha M. "Anomalous Features in the Chicago Prayer Meeting Revival of 1858: The Nature of the Revival as Revealed in Contemporary Newspaper Accounts." Master of Arts thesis, Trinity Evangelical Divinity School, Deerfield, Illinois.

Herrmann, Richard E. "Nathan Bangs: Apologist for American Methodism." Ph.D. diss., Emory University, 1973.

Lesick, Lawrence Thomas. "The Lane Rebels: Evangelicalism and Antislavery in Antebellum America. Ph.D. diss., Vanderbilt University, 1979.

Long, Kathryn Teresa. "The Revival of 1857–58: The Power of Interpretation." Ph.D. diss., Duke University, 1993.

Moore, Roberta J. "The Beginning and Development of Protestant Journalism in the United States, 1743–1850." Ph.D. diss., Syracuse University, 1968.

Orr, J. Edwin. "The Millionfold Awakening in America, 1857–58." D.Th. dissertation. Northern Baptist Theological Seminary, Chicago, 1943.

Rogers, Max Gray. "Charles Augustus Briggs, Conservative Heretic." Ph.D. diss., Columbia University, 1964.

Rotundo, Edward Anthony. "Manhood in America: The Northern Middle Class 1770–1920." Ph.D. diss., Brandeis University, 1982.

Senior, Robert Cholerton. "New England Congregationalists and the Anti-Slavery Movement, 1830–1860." Ph.D. diss., Yale University, 1954.

Slocum, Stephen E. "The American Tract Society: 1825–1975: An Evangelical Effort to Influence the Religious and Moral Life of the United States." Ph.D. diss., New York University, 1975.

Spicer, Carl Lloyd. "The Great Awakening of 1857 and 1858." Ph.D. diss., Ohio State University, 1935.

Wilbee, Victor. "The Religious Dimensions of Three Presidencies in a State University." Ph.D. diss., University of Michigan, 1967.

Index

Abbott, Edward, 47, 173n.4

Abbott, Lyman, 47–48, 53, 130, 217n.9

Abolitionists, 31, 96, 108, 203nn.41, 49, 205n.72, 207n.104, 210nn.31, 35, 211n.47, 212n.53
  views of, toward true revival, 93, 110, 112, 117–18, 123
  See also Antislavery; Slavery

Activism, 14, 22, 80, 82, 86–87, 193n.83, 215n.97. *See also* Political activism

Adams, Benjamin M., 52, 122–23, 192n.72, 214n.82

Adams, Nehemiah, 111, 114–15, 208n.8

Adams, William, 116, 207n.101

Advertising, 28, 84, 165n.9, 206n.88

Ahlstrom, Sydney, 20

Albany, N.Y.: prayer meeting in, 76

Alexander, Archibald, 16, 102

Alexander, James W., 11, 13, 102–4, 107, 109, 159n.47, 169n.61, 204n.59, 206n.85

Allen, Moses, 202n.26

Allyn, Robert, 86

American Abolition Society, 93

American Apocalypse (Moorhead), 125

American Bible Society, 104, 111, 212n.52

American Church History Series, 20

American Congregational Union, 116

American Female Guardian Society and Home for the Friendless, 124

American Female Moral Reform Society, 208n.11

American Iron Association, 52

American Peace Society, 208n.11

American Sunday School Union, 54, 82, 104

American Tract Society, 196n.117, 210n.28, 211n.43, 212n.52
  in Boston, 117
  in New York, 65, 81, 104, 110–11, 113–17, 205n.75

Amherst College, 85, 183n.105

Annus mirabilis, 121, 152n.8

"*Annus Mirabilis* 1858" (Wheatley), 4, 22

Anti-Catholicism, 95, 118. *See also* Catholicism

Antichrist, 111

Antiformalists, 6, 12, 153n.16

Antislavery views, 166n.19, 168n.40, 210n.31
  downplaying of, 108
  movement for, in New England and New York, 14, 96, 99, 117, 123–24, 203n.49